W9-BAH-059

Voyages of the Heart

Voyages of the Heart

Living an Emotionally Creative Life

James R. Averill
Elma P. Nunley

THE FREE PRESS
A Division of Macmillan, Inc.
NEW YORK

Maxwell Macmillan Canada
TORONTO

Maxwell Macmillan International
NEW YORK   OXFORD   SINGAPORE   SYDNEY

The Free Press
A Division of Macmillan, Inc.
866 Third Avenue, New York, N.Y. 10022

Maxwell Macmillan Canada, Inc.
1200 Eglinton Avenue East
Suite 200
Don Mills, Ontario M3C 3N1

Macmillan, Inc. is part of the Maxwell
Communication Group of Companies.

Printed in the United States of America

printing number
1   2   3   4   5   6   7   8   9   10

Library of Congress Cataloging-in-Publication Data

Averill, James R.
    Voyages of the heart : living an emotionally creative life / James
R. Averill, Elma P. Nunley.
        p.   cm.
    Includes bibliographical references and index.
    ISBN 0-02-901108-6
    1. Emotions.   2. Creative ability.   3. Self-actualization
(Psychology)   I. Nunley, Elma P.   II. Title.
BF531.A88   1992
152.4—dc20   91-39515
                                                      CIP

Excerpts from Dag Hammarskjold, *Markings,* copyright © 1968,
reprinted with permission of Random House, Inc.

To our parents
Dupree and Rosalie Averill
Howard and Gwendolene Peacock
with love and fond remembrance

The longest journey
Is the journey inwards.
Of him who has chosen his destiny,
Who has started upon his quest
For the source of his being
(Is there a source?).
—Dag Hammarskjold, *Markings*

Contents

———◆———

Preface

The heart is the traditional symbol for emotion. Voyages of the heart are, therefore, explorations in the realm of emotion. But the emotions are not static entities, like islands in an uncharted sea, just waiting to be discovered. The emotions are more like works of art—they must be created. Voyages of the heart are, therefore, explorations in emotional creativity.

Many books discuss ways to live a more adequate emotional life, but most focus on changes in attitudes and beliefs, or on the regulation of behavior. If, for example, you adopt a more positive attitude toward an old antagonist, you will be less likely to experience anger; and if you control the impulse to escape a hazardous situation, you will be less likely to experience fear. Changes in attitudes and the regulation of behavior are clearly important, but they do not require changes in the emotions per se—anger remains anger and fear is still fear, but now redirected into more productive channels. When we speak of emotional creativity, we mean something more fundamental than the redirection of familiar emotional reactions; we mean changes in the underlying structure of the emotions themselves.

Currently, in both scientific and popular literature, two views of emotion are common; neither view is compatible with the idea of emotional creativity. The first is an offshoot of rationalism. It holds that emotions are primitive responses ("brutish," "gut" reactions) over which we must exercise control lest they interfere with reason. Stated most baldly, rationalists view emotions as the animal in human nature; accordingly, mature and civilized behavior becomes almost synonymous with "taming" the emotions.

The second view is an offshoot of romanticism. Advocates of this position regard with suspicion any attempt to constrain, discipline, or even understand the emotions. Emotional inhibition, they believe, is at the root of many ills—literally as well as figuratively. Rational analysis, the romanticist continues, is almost as bad as inhibition, for to dissect an emotion intellectually is to kill it. The problem with this romanticized view is that emotional creativity, like any other kind of creativity, requires a great deal of discipline and understanding. "Letting it all hang out" is more often a sign of crassness than creativity.

In contrast to the rationalist and romanticist conceptions, we present a *Constructionist* view of emotions. An analogy will help illustrate what we mean by this term. Emotions are constructions in much the same sense that language is a construction. Everyone has the capacity for language; that is part of our biological heritage. But any specific language, English or Chinese, say, is a product of social, not biological evolution. And within any particular language there is ample opportunity for individual creativity, as in poetry and literature. Analogously, biology has given us the capacity—actually, a variety of different capacities—for emotion. Exactly how those capacities are realized is a function of social and individual development. In the final analysis, *we are the artificers of our own emotions.*

During the past several decades, considerable research has been devoted to the study of both the emotions and creativity. We have distilled from that research the findings we believe to be the most theoretically interesting and practically useful. This has necessitated some difficult choices. We do not, for example, discuss in any detail the brain mechanisms that mediate emotion, for knowledge of such mechanisms is rapidly advancing and hence quickly outdated. On the other hand, a wide range of issues—in biology, history, anthropology, psychopathology, aesthetics, and even mysticism—is of enduring revelance to emotional creativity. We therefore draw on scholarship in a variety of fields, as well as on clinical experience.

Conversely, emotional creativity has implications for a wide range of issues of contemporary concern. These include, for example, the conflicting needs for solitude and intimacy in human relationships; possible gender differences in emotionality and creativity; the role of pleasure (hedonism) in a meaningful life; the appeal of masochism and asceticism; post-tramatic stress and near-death experiences; the nature of the aesthetic; the role of catharsis in art and therapy; and the limits of freedom. We do not hesitate to comment on these and other issues as they impact on the emotional lives of individuals.

The diversity of subject matter germane to emotional creativity helps explain why we have opted for a large number of short chapters, particularly in Part IV (Conditions for Emotional Creativity), rather than a small number of long chapters. To the extent possible without sacrificing continuity, we have tried to make each chapter a self-contained essay of interest in its own right. This organization allows the reader to focus on those issues that are most relevant to his or her concerns.

There was a time when books of scientific merit were written not just for one's professional colleagues but for the general public as well. We would like to think of this book within that tradition. We have written it with three audiences in mind: First, academic psychologists, sociologists, and others interested in the study of emotion, and their students; second, the practicing therapist (psychiatrist, psychologist, social worker, professional counselor) who wishes to explore in more detail the nature of emotion and creativity; and, third, interested laypersons who want to better understand, improve, and enrich their emotional lives.

It is no easy task to write a book that is both scholarly and enjoyable to read, and also accessible to audiences of diverse backgrounds. We have tried, and may have failed more often than we would like to think. But no book, just as no life, can be continuously interesting. There must be dull moments and difficult moments, as well as exciting moments and moments of inspiration.

Throughout the book, we offer concrete examples of creative emotional responses, and we explore the conditions for their achievement. But this is not a how-to book. Emotional creativity is no easier than creativity in other domains. It cannot be reduced to simplistic formulae and one-minute exercises. Yet, with an understanding of the underlying processes and a willingness to take responsibility for our own lives, emotional creativity is within the reach of all of us. It is an adventure. Indeed, it is an adventure without end, for the heart does not come to port until death.

Part I

◆

Images of Emotional Creativity

When a person has an inborn genius for certain
emotions, his life differs strangely
from that of ordinary people.
—William James,
Varieties of Religious Experience

1

◆

Emotions and Creativity

One should not think slightingly of the paradoxical;
for the paradox is the source of the
thinker's passion, and the thinker
without paradox is like a
lover without feeling:
a paltry mediocrity.
—Kierkegaard, *Philosophical Fragments,* III

The very idea of emotional creativity presents something of a paradox. Imagine for a moment a typical emotional episode—a frightening experience, an outburst of anger, or even a time when you were "crazy in love." Now conjure up an image of a creative episode—an occasion when you were attempting to solve a particularly difficult problem. Are the two images compatible? Probably not. The person who is frightened wants to flee or hide; the person who is angry wants to attack; the person in love wants to be with the loved one. During such emotional states, a person's attention tends to be narrowly focused ("tunnel vision"), and responses tend to be stereotyped or perhaps uncoordinated ("crazy"). By contrast, creativity requires that the individual be open to experience, flexible in response, and effective in outcome.

There are other contrasts that make the notion of emotional creativity seem paradoxical, even self-contradictory. For example,

3

many emotions are regarded as negative—fear, anger, envy, jealousy, and the like are conditions we would just as soon avoid. Creativity, on the other hand, is highly prized, something to be encouraged, not shunned. Also, emotions are often viewed as primitive ("instinctive," "animal-like," "gut") reactions, whereas creativity is among the highest of our "higher" thought processes.

However, emotions and creativity are more closely related than these popular stereotypes might suggest. In fact, it is sometimes difficult to distinguish an emotional from a creative episode, so closely are they intertwined. The experience of Lynn, a 40-year-old professional woman, illustrates this point. Lynn had returned to the university to obtain an advanced degree. She had collected the data for her thesis, but became stymied in the analysis of results. There were too many distractions and demands on her time. In desperation, she moved into a secluded lakeside cabin owned by a friend. Since it was winter (late February), the area was nearly deserted. For days on end, she did not hear or speak to anyone. This is how she later described the course of events:

> I had worked on similar research projects before, but this time the answers just weren't forthcoming. I had a massive amount of data, and I knew something was there. But nothing jelled. I made graph after graph and chart after chart. I scarcely ate or slept. I lost all perspective of time and place. I felt like my whole future somehow hinged on my finding the answer.
>
> One day, after working several frustrating hours with little progress, I decided to go for a walk. Although the terrain was flat, and the day was crisp and clear, I felt like I was climbing a mountain in a fog. I could not see above or below me. Suddenly, the mass of data I had collected began to make sense. Everything fell into place. I knew what I had! I was overcome with tremendous joy. I was now on the top of the mountain, and the clouds had lifted. I started to sing and dance. In retrospect, it strikes me as a bit silly, but that is what I literally did—sing and dance. I'm certain if anyone had been watching they would have thought they had a crazy woman on their hands.
>
> When I had moved into the cabin, it was winter. Now, for the first time, I realized that the grass was turning green, the trees were budding, and flowers were blooming. Spring had arrived. For over a month I had been so preoccupied with work

*that I had not noticed a gradual change in the weather. A season
had passed without my being aware of it.*

*That day, I experienced emotions that I had never before
experienced. It is hard to explain, to put into words. At first, I
was on a real high. It was a mystical kind of thing. I felt filled
with light, illuminated. I know that doesn't make much sense,
but that is how I felt—literally radiant. That feeling lasted for
several hours. I then settled into a more peaceful joy. I was
serene, yet very energetic. When I returned to the cabin, I
worked well into the night with hardly a stop. It was exhilarating. For the first time I knew what the words self-confidence and
self-respect meant, as well as courage, dignity, and integrity. I
felt gentleness and tenderness for myself, and an appreciation
for my strength.*

*Looking back, it is as though I went through a "rite of
passage." American Indians used to go through such rites,
signaling the transition from childhood to maturity. They would
go out to survive on their own and come back transformed, even
bearing a new name. That was the way I felt. I had suffered and
endured, and I had reached a new maturity. I was changed, and
I knew I'd never again be the same.*

Clearly, this was not only an intellectually creative episode, but
also a highly emotional one. For analytical purposes, it will be
helpful to break the episode into three phases. The first phase was
marked by considerable effort and hard work on the project. But a
solution would not come. During this initial phase, Lynn experienced a great deal of frustration, anxiety, and despair. She was
obsessed and unable to eat or sleep. Her future seemed in jeopardy.

The second phase occurred rather suddenly during a walk. A
solution to the problem suddenly crystallized. Lynn was now
overcome with joy, she danced and sang, and acted like a "crazy
woman."

The third phase was the aftermath. The problem on which
Lynn had been working could best be described as intellectual. In a
narrow sense, then, hers was an act of intellectual creativity.
However, because of her life circumstances, it was much more than
that. It was also, as she put it, a "rite of passage." She herself was
changed, and she began to experience emotions that she had never
experienced before, ones that she could not easily describe in

ordinary language. Hers was also (if somewhat inadvertently) an act of emotional creativity.

As the example of Lynn illustrates, (1) emotions may be among the forerunners or antecedents of creativity; (2) emotions may accompany creativity; and (3) emotions may be creative products in their own right. Our primary concern in this book is with emotions as creative products; that is, with the development of new, more adaptive, and more authentic emotional responses. But in order more clearly to delineate this concern, we will first examine some of the ways in which emotions are antecedents and accompaniments of creative endeavors.

Emotional Antecedents of Creativity

As antecedents or forerunners, emotions may both inhibit and facilitate creativity. Positive emotions, in particular, tend to facilitate creativity, provided they do not lead to complacency or distraction. Fear, by contrast, is one of the greatest inhibitors of creativity. But even fear can have facilitating effects, as the following incident illustrates:

> Karla, a woman in her thirties, lived alone. Early one morning a man entered her home, pulled a knife and held it to her throat. He threatened to kill her if she moved. At first she was immobilized with fear; her only thought was to stay alive. The man told her that he didn't want to rape her, that he only wanted money. However, he started dragging her down the hall toward the bedroom. She later described what happened as follows: "I knew I had less than ten dollars. I also knew that if he ever got me in the bedroom I was a goner. Something in me came alive. I knew I had to fight for my life, and fight I did. I used every resource I had. It was like all the things I had ever heard, read, or seen on T.V. came back to me." Although a small woman, Karla fought off the man's advances and escaped with minor knife wounds.

We are not accustomed to thinking of self-defense as a form of creativity. But one of the points we wish to emphasize is that creativity can be manifested in a great variety of different ways.

That night, few professional athletes or ballet dancers could have performed with greater skill and creativity than did Karla. The broader point we wish to illustrate is that fear, anger, love, and other emotions, both positive and negative, can motivate a person to explore new approaches, to consider new options—in a word, to create—in an attempt to change a situation or to achieve a desired goal.

Emotional Accompaniments of Creativity

Creative endeavors are frequently charged with emotion, as we saw in the case of Lynn. Her experience is by no means unique. To take another example, the following is a description by the philosopher Nietzsche of the emotional vicissitudes he experienced during the composition of *Thus Spake Zarathustra*.

> There is an ecstasy whose terrific tension is sometimes re-leased by a flood of tears, during which one's progress varies from voluntary impetuosity to involuntary slowness. There is a feeling that one is utterly out of hand, with the most distinct consciousness of an infinitude of shuddering thrills that pass through one from head to foot;—there is a profound happi-ness in which the most painful and gloomy feelings are not discordant in effect, but are required as necessary colors in this overflow of light. There is an instinct for rhythmic relations which embraces an entire world of forms (length, the need for a widely extended rhythm, is almost a measure of the force of inspiration, a sort of counterpart to its pressure and tension). Everything occurs quite without volition, as if in an eruption of freedom, independence, power and divinity.[1]

The kind of emotion that is experienced often depends on the stage (beginning, middle, or end) of a creative endeavor. Most acts of creativity involve new responses—at least for the individual. Before the new can be established, old and familiar responses may have to be abandoned. Not surprisingly, therefore, the early stages of a creative endeavor are often associated with feelings of loss, anxiety, and sadness. If a solution does not appear feasible, tunnel vision may develop; that is, the person continues to apply old and ineffective methods, failing to notice alternative approaches. Depression and despair may ensue. But if a new solution does appear, often suddenly, anxiety and depression give way to intense joy and a sense of aliveness.

Emotions as Creative Products

An emotion may be a creative product in any of three ways, each involving a progressively greater degree of creativity. We call these three ways the acquisition, refinement, and transformation of emotion—in a word, the ART of emotion.

Acquisition

This is the most common variety of emotional creativity. It refers to the development, cultivation, or mastery of an emotion that is already standard within the culture. We have all been creative in this way during the course of growing up. For example, falling romantically in love for the first time is a highly novel experience for most adolescents, and one that involves considerable creativity if it is to be negotiated effectively. Childhood fairy tales (Cinderella, Beauty and the Beast, Snow White, etc.), popular songs, romance novels, and the like may provide a good deal of information on love, but how do you know that what you feel is *really* love? And how are you supposed to behave when in love? Love is not something that just happens "naturally," it must be learned. And each new learning experience is an act of creativity.

Unfortunately, many of us cease to grow emotionally simply because we are now presumably "mature," and we may even regard emotional displays as "childish." But ask yourself: Of the hundreds of emotions recognized in ordinary language, how many can you actually name, no less experience? How sophisticated are you emotionally? Can you, for example, differentiate romantic love from sexual infatuation, jealousy from envy, or indignation from anger?

Some people can experience only a narrow range of emotions. On account of a sterile emotional environment, or too much pain and too many disappointments early in life, a person may fail to attain a normal emotional repertoire. As a consequence, consider-able effort and creativity may be needed to acquire even common-place emotions during adulthood.

Refinement

Once an emotion is acquired, a person may learn to apply it in novel ways or to new and unusual situations. The emotion is, in a sense, personalized—made unique to the individual. Initially, this may involve little more than making fine discriminations among closely related emotions, for example, among anger, resentment, and animosity, or fear, anxiety, and panic. At more advanced stages, the emotion is refined and used inventively to achieve ends that are not customary, and that may be either admired or condemned (and sometimes both) by society as a whole. The legendary amorist Don Juan is a good example. He so perfected the art of love that he supposedly seduced 1,003 women in Spain alone. There also are Don Juans of anger, fear, grief, jealousy, and other emotions. These are people who charm, cajole, intimidate, and persuade others, not through rational argument but through displays of emotion. When we agree with such persons, we call them charismatic and even sometimes select them as leaders; when we disagree, we call them histrionic and dismiss them as foolish, immature, or even neurotic.

Transformation

Transformation represents the highest kind of emotional creativity, for it requires the development of new and different types of emotion, ones not standard in the culture. The new emotion may involve the metamorphosis of a standard emotion, the amalgama-tion (blending or fusion) of several different and seemingly incom-patible emotions, or it may be made from whole cloth, so to speak, having few identifiable antecedents among standard emotions. The important thing is that the transformed emotion be an innovative break with, or evolutionary departure from, customary practice.

Transformation is the most difficult kind of emotional creativi-ty to illustrate in a short space; much of the rest of the book will be devoted to its explication. Yet emotional transformation is not an unfamiliar phenomenon. Over and over again in clinical practice, clients talk about experiences that have changed and enriched their lives. When asked to explain, their response frequently is: "I can't. I just don't have the words." When pressed for details, it often becomes apparent that the experiences they can't explain consist of new emotions, ones for which there are no words in ordinary language. Clients in psychotherapy are not exceptional in this regard. Poets, artists, musicians, all attempt to express in symbolic form emotional experiences that transcend or go beyond the ordinary.

The simplest way to illustrate emotional transformation is through historical and cross-cultural examples. That is what we do in Chapters 2 and 3. Emotions that we consider standard in our society were at one time new and innovative; and emotions that are considered "basic" in one society may be unknown in another. Emotional transformations are thus "writ large" on the sociocultural level, making them particularly easy to demonstrate. But before getting to relevant examples, we should place our general approach to emotional creativity within its proper historical and cultural context.

Emotions, Self, and Society

The emotions are moored both in a person's sense of self and in society. Love, for example, extends the boundaries of the self to include the happiness and well-being of another; anger defends the self from infringements and slights by another; and fear protects the self from danger. But while the emotions are serving the self, they are also serving society. Love provides the proper rationale for marriage, one of the most fundamental institutions in society; anger preserves group norms by punishing violators; and fear validates one's membership in a group by affirming socially defined dangers, real and symbolic. This last example (of fear) is not so obvious, which makes it all the better for illustrative purposes. We often fear impersonal events, such as heights, snakes, and sounds in the night. Unless they become extreme, as in phobic reactions, such fears are of little personal or social consequence. Many fears, however, are not so trivial. A good Christian not only loves but also fears God; a member of the "Greens" (an environmentalist group) fears nuclear energy; conservatives fear the counterculture; hippies fear the establishment; and so it goes. Such fears need have little to do with actual dangers; their function is to preserve the group, not the self.

In short, emotions help define what we are as individuals and as members of a society. That, at least, is a central assumption behind this book. It is not the only way to view the relation of emotions to the self and society. Potter has painted a very different picture of emotion among villagers in mainland China.[2] There an individual's sense of self is derived from the social context, not from inner feelings. When a villager is asked how he or she feels about a particular event, the question is met with quizzical indifference. "How I feel doesn't matter," is a typical reply. Potter calls this Chinese view the "image of irrelevant affect." Such an image does not imply the suppression or lack of emotion. On the contrary, since the idiosyncrasies of personal feelings are of little consequence, emotions may be expressed in an uninhibited fashion. An exception is "love." Public displays of affection (not only between a man and a woman, but also between a parent and child) are considered inappropriate and potentially disruptive. Socially established relationships require that a respectful distance be kept between the partners. Sincerity of the relationship is thus judged, not against inner feelings, but against civil behavior and the willingness to work unselfishly for the good of the other.

Westerners tend to find the Chinese inscrutable, in part, because of their seeming indifference toward personal feelings. Not surprisingly, the Chinese also find Western attitudes difficult to understand. "The world of people who speak of emotion in order to symbolize and affirm human relationships is an exotic, alien world to the Chinese; it is a world founded on what they regard as a trivial basis."[3]

In this book, when we speak of emotions as central to the self and society, we are proceeding within the Western cultural tradition. That tradition can be traced back at least three thousand years, to the ancient Greeks and Hebrews. By way of introduction, we will touch briefly on a few of the highlights.[4]

The Homeric Greeks (roughly the ninth century B.C.) apparently had no unified concept of self. In works such as the *Iliad* and the *Odyssey*, a variety of different terms was used to refer to psychological and physiological functions. This does not mean that the Greeks had no sense of personal identity. To them, however, the individual was a cacophony of parts and responses, strongly under immediate stimulus control and subject to direct intervention by the gods.

It is difficult to imagine from a contemporary perspective a society in which there is no unitary sense of self. However, there are many ways to achieve a sense of coherence and predictability in life. When the external world or society provides structure, there is little need for an inner "glue"—symbolized as the self—to maintain cohesion.

By the time of classical Greek antiquity (ca. the fifth and fourth centuries B.C.), a unified concept of self or *psyche* became prevalent, especially in the works of Plato and Aristotle. However, neither Plato nor Aristotle was much interested in the *psyche* of the individual person. For them, rationality was the hallmark of humankind, that which distinguishes humans from lower animals —but not one human from another. Given the same information, and the ability to reason logically, all rational beings should reach similar conclusions. It follows that rationality does not individuate the self from others. It is the nonrational, the emotional, that gives individual meaning to experience.

When Greek thought became integrated with the Judeo-Christian tradition, the *psyche* took on theological connotations alien to classical Greek culture. Correspondingly, the focus of attention shifted from epistemology to ethics, from "How do I gain knowledge?" to "How do I save my soul?" Still, for reasons both intellectual and social, there was little emphasis on the individual self. The soul, "made in the image and likeness of God," was no more variable from person to person than the rational self of the Greeks. Medieval hagiographies (idealized biographies of saints) were little concerned with the idiosyncrasies of individual lives. Their purpose was to further Christian ideals, and medieval biographers felt free to borrow anecdotes from one saint's life to embellish the life of another. To the extent that differences among people were accorded significance, such differences were based on preestablished regional, class, and gender expectations. A person was born into a certain social station (a nobleman, say, or a serf), and that station determined the meaning of his or her life.

In addition to religious orthodoxy and a preestablished social order, privacy in the modern sense was practically unknown during most of the middle ages. Medieval halls were open to people from all walks of life, food was served in common bowls with few eating utensils, and strangers in roadside inns shared the same bed. In the absence of privacy, personal feelings and desires counted for little in comparison to social station and public ritual. Emotions were not inhibited, but neither were they accorded great significance, except as they reflected the virtues and vices of Christian ethics. In this respect, the medieval attitude toward emotions and the self bears some similarities to that of contemporary China as discussed by Potter. The similarities should not be overinterpreted, however, for the social structure and ideology, which help give meaning to the emotions and the self, were far different in feudal Europe than they are in modern China.

With industrialization and urbanization in Europe, possibilities for privacy and anonymity expanded greatly. And with the breakup of the feudal system and diminished church authority, an emphasis on the individual self emerged. It was a slow but ever accelerating process. From the twelfth to the sixteenth century, the now familiar distinction between a private and public self gradually gained recognition, and with it emerged a new concern: How could a person be sure what lay behind the masks that other people display in public? It is a short step from doubt about another's sincerity to doubt about one's own: How can I be sure that my conscious experience accurately reflects my true feelings and desires? The idea of a submerged (unconscious) self, hidden even from one's own (conscious) self, has reached its apogee in twentieth century "depth" psychologies. It is sometimes said that Freud discovered the unconscious. His was less a discovery than the culmination of a long developing cultural trend.

"Get in touch with your feelings." "Be authentic." "Stop playing a role." "You can't be intimate with another until you are intimate with yourself." These are catch phrases of contemporary pop psychology. It would be easy to dismiss them as mere hackneyed expressions with little real meaning. But an expression becomes hackneyed only because it is widely used; and it becomes widely used because it reflects real concerns of a great many people. Cut loose from their social moorings, both the emotions and the self may take on unreal dimensions. Richard Rorty has expressed the matter well:

> [O]nce upon a time we felt a need to worship something which lay beyond the visible world. Beginning in the seventeenth century we tried to substitute a love of truth for a love of God,

treating the world described by science as a quasi divinity. Beginning at the end of the eighteenth century we tried to substitute a love of ourselves for a love of scientific truth, a worship of our own deep spiritual or poetic nature, treated as one more quasi divinity.[5]

In a secular, psychologically oriented society, celebration of an "inner" self can easily become a substitute religion, and the emotions may be regarded, like the oracles of ancient Greece, as harbingers of truths that are somehow deeper or more fundamental than the truths revealed by ordinary reason and social custom. We are obviously sympathetic to the potential value of an emotionally rich life. Emotions *can* be a spiritual force for the betterment of humankind. If we did not believe that, we would not have written this book. At the very outset, however, we wish to warn against a certain trend in the contemporary society, namely, an uncritical glorification of the emotions, a let-it-all-hang-out attitude. As sketched earlier, during the long course of Western history emotions have come to form a link between the individual and the moral order. For the long-term betterment of both selves and society, therefore, emotional creativity requires sound judgment and discretion, as well as a willingness to innovate and the courage to risk disapproval. Emotional creativity is not an excuse for the frivolous display of one's emotional bric-a-brac.

An Overview of the Book

The general thesis of this book may now be stated as follows: *To achieve our full potential, to actualize our unique and genuine selves, we must be open to discovery, exploration, and challenge in the emotional as much as in the intellectual domain.* Although the capacity for emotional creativity is a universal, fundamental part of human nature, the way that capacity is actualized will vary from one culture to another. Creativity in any domain must build upon past achievements. In the case of emotional creativity, this means that we must build upon the emotions as they are presently constituted within our own culture. The emotions as we experience them today are, as we described earlier, the products of a cultural heritage that goes back to ancient Israel, Greece and Rome, and to medieval Europe.

There are other roots, to be sure, in Africa, Asia, and native America, but the dominant roots are broadly European. That is not a value judgment, simply a statement of fact.

The book is divided into five parts. Part I consists of this introductory chapter and two additional chapters, each of which illustrates emotional creativity on a broad sociocultural level. Specifically, Chapter 2 traces the evolution of romantic love within Western cultures, and Chapter 3 describes a variety of anger-like responses observed in different cultures around the world.

Love is often considered one of the most fundamental of emotions; it is what "makes the world go 'round." Yet, love today is very different than in times past. The biblical Song of Solomon is often taken as one of the great literary expressions of love. Solomon had a lot to sing about—seven hundred wives and three hundred concubines. Obviously, his ideal of love was very different than the contemporary romantic ideal. How did the change come about? That is the question we explore in Chapter 2. Or, try to imagine the following: While strolling along a river bank you come across a young woman whom you have never met before. You proceed to cut off her head and toss it with great exhilaration to the ground. Returning to your village, you celebrate the feat in song and dance. A new and different kind of emotional experience? For you, perhaps, but not for the Ilongot, a headhunting people of the Philippines, as discussed in Chapter 3.

The above examples illustrate how emotions can—and do—vary across time and place. Such variation on the social level would not be possible if emotions were not also subject to innovation and change on the individual level. Throughout the book we refer back to these and other examples discussed in Chapters 2 and 3, in order to lend substance to issues that might otherwise seem abstract and divorced from everyday reality.

To be creative in a given domain, a person must understand the fundamentals of that domain. For example, to be a creative mathematician, a person must be familiar with the foundations of mathematics; and to be a creative painter, a person must understand principles of design and color. Part II, which consists of six chapters, provides the theoretical foundations necessary for understanding emotional creativity.

Intuitively, we all know what we mean by emotion; but intuition is not enough. In Chapter 4, we offer a working definition of emotion; we relate emotions to feelings and expressions; and we explore the biological, social, and psychological determinants of emotion. Special emphasis is placed on the social and personal "rules" that aid in the construction (and sometimes misconstruction) of emotional reactions. In Chapter 5, we debunk nine common misconceptions ("myths") about emotions. Chief among these myths is the notion that emotions are passions—primitive, animal-like responses over which we have little control. The possibility of emotional creativity begins with the knowledge that our emotions are of our own making and that they are subject to change—not just superficially, but "in essence."

Chapters 6 examines the criteria—novelty, effectiveness, and authenticity—for evaluating creative products, whether the product be a scientific innovation, a work of art, or an emotional response. This chapter also reviews research on the characteristics of creative persons, and on the psychological processes that make creativity possible. Chapter 7 examines some common misconceptions about creativity, including, among others, the belief that creativity proceeds without rules, that it requires little effort, and that it is limited to a few highly gifted individuals.

In Chapter 8 we return to the issue of emotional creativity. Specifically, this chapter explores the ways that emotions can either meet, or fail to meet, the criteria for creativity. Chapter 9 attempts to short-circuit some potential misconceptions about emotional creativity. For example, emotional creativity is not simply emotional reactivity; it has more to do with the quality of a response than with its frequency or intensity.

Part III (Chapters 10–13) explores the relation of emotional creativity to core aspects of a person's being. One reason emotional creativity is so difficult to conceive, no less achieve, is that the emotions are intimately related to a person's sense of self. Do you want to know what a person is like? Find out what makes him or her angry, hopeful, afraid, ashamed, sad, and joyful. Change the emotions and you change the self (Chapter 10). A central aspect of any person's sense of self is his or her gender identity. Stereotypically, women are often depicted as more emotional than men, but as less creative (at least in the arts and sciences). The bases for these stereotypes are examined in Chapter 11, and possible sex differences in emotional creativity are explored. Chapter 12 deals with one of the main vehicles by which both emotions and the self (as a conceptual entity) are created and modified, namely, language. In Chapter 13, we explore the relation between emotional creativity and psychopathology. When emotional innovation and change is adaptive (effective), it is creative; when maladaptive, it is psychopathological. Psychotherapy is, to a large extent, an exercise in emotional creativity.

Part IV (Chapters 14–22) consists of a series of short essays devoted to specific conditions (situational and personal) that demand, invite, or simply facilitate emotional creativity. Although these chapters follow a rough progression, they can be read in almost any order. Among the topics discussed are challenge, pleasure and pain, death and dying, solitude, intimacy, autonomy, freedom, imagination, and the arts.

We conclude the book (Part V) with three chapters devoted to the achievement of emotional creativity. In Chapter 23, we take the ART of emotion not simply as an acronym for the acquisition, refinement, and transformation of emotional responses; rather, we treat the emotions as an art form in their own right. Wordsworth defined poetry as "the spontaneous overflow of powerful feelings . . . recollected in tranquility."[6] Much the same could be said with respect to other art forms—painting, music, and the like. To the extent that is true, we can learn much about the emotions from the study of art, as well as vice versa.

In Chapter 24, we discuss the ways that society can foster, and sometimes inhibit, emotional innovation and change. Particularly in a society like ours, where social relationships of many kinds are reinforced and legitimized by reference to personal feelings, any change in the meaning and structure of our emotions may have far reaching ramifications. In the short run, at least, those consequences may include the disapproval of others who are important in our lives and whom we respect and care for. Emotional creativity requires a genuine concern for the well-being of others as well as a commitment to personal fulfillment.

Finally, in Chapter 25, we outline the concrete steps that can be taken by the individual to achieve a more creative emotional life. Emotional creativity is no easier than creativity in other domains; yet it is within the capacity of each of us, if we are willing to devote the effort and take responsibility for our own emotional lives. Many people are afraid of their emotions, bound and restricted by what their emotions might "do" to them; others feel empty on the inside, devoid of all emotion. In either case, the person is not living life to its fullest potential. Even for most of us who live satisfactory emotional lives, there is still much to be gained from a more complete understanding of our emotions. A rich, full life means an emotionally creative life.

2

◆

Romantic Love

It is with true love as with ghosts;
everyone talks of it, but few
have seen it.
—La Rochefoucauld, *Maxims*

Creativity and love also have long been associated in popular conception. In part, this is due to the obvious fact that love is associated with biological (pro)creation. The highly creative person is often considered a genius. The terms "genius" and "genital" stem from the same Latin root. According to the ancient Romans, everyone had a genius, which was located in the head, or more specifically in the brain. The Romans also believed that the brain is connected to the genitals via the spinal cord and fluid. An orgasm has jokingly been described as similar to a sneeze—but a lot more fun. For the Romans the connection was more than a joke. Some of a man's genius was expelled during a sneeze as well as during an orgasm.

Love is not limited to biological procreativity; it is also the inspiration for much art, music, literature, and even philosophy. But

19

our concern in this chapter is not with sneezes or orgasms, or even with love as an inspiration to creativity. Rather, it is with love as a creative product in its own right. To narrow the discussion even further, we are concerned not with love in general, but with romantic love, and with its early precursor, the courtly love of medieval times.

By tracing the social development of romantic love, we demonstrate how emotions are created. Such a demonstration is more easily performed on a social rather than an individual level of analysis. The two levels are, however, closely related. Creative acts of individuals provide variations in behavior on which social evolution depends. To take a nonemotional example, the Scientific Revolution that began in the sixteenth and seventeenth centuries represented the creative acts of many individual scientists, from Copernicus (1473–1543) to Newton (1642–1727), and it continues today. The same is true of the revolution in sexual relationships that, beginning with the courtly love of the eleventh century, has led to romantic love as we know it.

Romantic love is so interwoven into the fabric of our society that we tend to view it as a basic biological need, on a par almost with hunger and thirst. We find it difficult to imagine that love between sexual partners has not existed in much the same form everywhere and at all times. A belief in the universality of romantic love is reinforced by the tendency to reinterpret love stories from other cultures or other times (e.g., the Biblical stories of David and Bathsheba, or the Hindu story of Siva and Parvati) within the framework of our own romantic ideal. We thus overlook the fact that romantic love is the product of a long history of social innovation and change.

The Social Origins and Functions of
Romantic Love

The story of romantic love has been told many times. Morton Hunt has described its origins as follows:

> Toward the end of the eleventh century A.D., a handful of poets and noblemen in southern France concocted a set of love sentiments most of which had no precedent in Western civilization, and out of them constructed a new and quite

original relationship between man and women known as *l'amour courtios* or courtly love. [It] began as a game and a literary conceit, but unexpectedly grew into a social philosophy that shaped the manners and morals of the West. It started as a playful exercise in flattery, but became a spiritual force guiding the flatterers; it was first a private sport of feudal aristocracy, but became finally the ideal of the middle classes . . . and men and women throughout the Western world still live by and take for granted a number of its principal concepts.[1]

Needless to say, courtly (romantic) love did not spring *ex nihilo* out of the heads and hearts of "a handful of poets and noblemen." Prior to that time love was conceived of largely in terms of sexual desire (*eros*), brotherly love (*philia*), tenderness (*storge*), or, in its purest form, an altruistic, God-like love (*agape*). These forms of love were suited to a feudal age when marriages were prearranged for political and economic reasons, and individual identity was subordinate to preassigned roles in life. By contrast, courtly love shifted the accent to the individual; it stressed the validity of the individual's own experiences as a source of values and as a basis for decisions about interpersonal relationships.

On the shelves of nearly any bookstore today are numerous "how to" books on the art of love. These are not a new phenomenon. The twelfth century cleric, Andreas Capellanus (Andreas the Chaplain), also wrote a "how to" book entitled *The Art of Courtly Love*. In one passage of this manual, a man asks a more experienced woman to "teach me those things that are specially demanded in love, those which make a man most worthy of being loved, because after I have been instructed I shall have no defense for any mistakes I make and no opportunity to excuse myself."[2] The woman thereupon provides a list of behaviors and characteristics that are highly desirable in a lover. Among other things, a man must be generous to others and completely free of avarice; he should never blaspheme against God; he should not speak ill of any man, nor utter false praise; he should never mock the unfortunate; he should not make promises too readily; he ought to be courageous in battle; he should be moderate and wise in all that he does; especially, he should be discreet in his love and love only one woman; and in her name he should be devoted to the service of all women.

Clearly, Andreas Capellanus was not writing a book on the "joy of sex." Indeed, in its purest form, the pleasures of courtly love were to be more of the mind than of the body. Andreas describes courtly love as:

> . . . the pure love which binds together the hearts of two lovers with every feeling of delight. This kind consists in the contemplation of the mind and the affection of the heart; it goes as far as the kiss and the embrace and the modest contact with the nude lover, omitting the final solace, for that is not permitted to those who wish to love purely.[3]

Yet, Andreas Capellanus was not preaching prudery. Next to pure love in worthiness was that "mixed love which gets its effect from every delight of the flesh and culminates in the final act of Venus."[4]

Everyone, according to Andreas, is duty-bound to love someone. Some of the worst tortures in his concept of hell were reserved for women who refused to love, for withholding love was even worse than loving in a profligate manner. Also, and perhaps most surprising to modern readers, love could not occur between husband and wife.

The extramarital aspects of courtly love would seem to pose little problem provided the love remained pure, as ideally it should. But what if one of the partners wished to enjoy the pleasures of mixed love? The other should agree, according to Andreas, "for all lovers are bound, when practicing love's solaces, to be obedient to each other's desires."[5] And what happens, say, if a woman marries the man she loves? The love ceases (but not necessarily the mutual caring and affection), and she may take a new lover.

Let us speculate briefly on the possible social functions of courtly love. Why did it arise when and where it did? According to Hugo Beigel, the ideals of courtly love provided the newly formed ruling classes with moral distinction, helping to consolidate their position.[6] Consistent with this view is the fact that Andreas Capellanus wrote his treatise on love for the nobility and for the rising bourgeoisie; peasants were specifically excluded from "Love's court"—farmers, like horses and mules, "give themselves up to the work of Venus, as nature's urging teaches them to do."[7]

In other words, courtly love helped to rationalize and stabilize the emerging social order in which the married woman of the upper classes had lost her economic function. Gentleness and refinement became her virtues. Nevertheless, social custom, the need for family alliances, and the like prevented free choice of mates. These conditions—idealization of the woman, loss of her economic function, and prearranged marriage—would normally tend to make the marriage relationship unstable. Among other things, courtly love helped to deflect such potentially disruptive factors as sexual covetousness into constructive channels. (Jealousy, it might be noted, was considered unseemly between husband and wife, but not between lovers.)

Dante and Beatrice

Did anyone actually love in accordance to the courtly ideal, outside of fairy tales and treatises on the art of love? There are numerous anecdotal examples of individuals who, in the name of love, performed rather bizarre acts. One of the most renowned troubadours of the time, Peire Vidal, became enamored of Loba de Peinautier, a noblewoman who lived in Carcassonne, a city in the south of France. The name Loba means she-wolf. Peire therefore put on the skin of a wolf and asked some shepherds to hunt him with their dogs. In one respect, the hunt was all too successful. The troubadour was brought to the house of his beloved more dead than alive. Loba was not particularly impressed. As we have seen, the worthy lover was supposed to be wise and prudent in all his actions. Fortunately, Loba's husband took kindly to Peire and hired the best physicians to nurse him back to health.[8]

Perhaps the most famous example of courtly love in practice involved the Italian poet, Dante Alighieri and Beatrice Portinari, the daughter of a prominent Florentine citizen. One commentator, Henry Theophilus Finck, placed the date of origin of romantic love at 1274, the year that Dante fell in love with Beatrice—clearly an exaggeration, for Andreas Capellanus had written his treatise on courtly love nearly a century earlier. Moreover, Italian poetry in Dante's youth was almost exclusively devoted to love, and many of the themes were well established, such as the torment of unrequited love, need to keep secret the name of the beloved, vilification of death as the destroyer of beauty, ecstasy in the presence of the beloved, mortification at her mockery, and so forth. Dante was very much a product of his time. Nevertheless, Finck was correct on one point, namely, that Dante was an emotional as well as an intellectual genius who did much to legitimize and perpetuate the romantic ideal for future generations.[9]

Dante first met Beatrice in 1274 when she was eight years old and he nearly nine. He fell immediately in love, but although he often went where he could see her, no real verbal interaction occurred between them until nine years later. Then one day he met her while walking on a street in Florence. She greeted him, and he was filled with joy. However, their love was not to be consummated. Both became betrothed to others—Dante to Gemma Donati, by whom he had five children, and Beatrice to Simone dei Bardi. Tragically, Beatrice died at age 24, the year following her wedding. But neither marriage nor death quelled Dante's love. Beatrice remained a central figure in his poetry throughout his life; Dante never mentioned his wife or children in any of his poetry—only Beatrice.

Dante's early book of poems, *La Vita Nuova*, includes commentary on his poems to Beatrice. Following one occasion in which Dante swooned in Beatrice's presence, and was subsequently mocked by other women, he resolved that henceforth he would find peace of mind rather than torment in contemplating Beatrice's beauty and goodness. In the opinion of Barbara Reynolds, this event "was a turning point not only for Dante but also for European poetry."[10] A poem that Dante wrote after his resolve to find peace of mind, Reynolds goes on to note, "opened up vistas and depths in which the human experience of love was glimpsed as being ultimately one with the power by which the universe is governed."[11]

Dante is, of course, best known for his epic poem, the *Divine Comedy*. This is one of those works which, in the words of Will Durant "all men praise and few men read."[12] It is an account of Dante's guided tour of hell (*Inferno*), purgatory (*Purgatorio*), and heaven (*Paradiso*). The Latin poet, Virgil (70–19 B.C.), author of the *Aeneid*, is Dante's guide through hell and purgatory. Virgil stands for knowledge, reason, and wisdom—great virtues, to be sure, but not sufficient to allow one to pass through the gates of heaven. Beatrice, who personifies faith and love, takes over as Dante's guide through paradise.

Dante completed the *Paradiso* three years before his death at the age of 57. His love for Beatrice had remained steadfast for nearly five tumultuous decades.

From a contemporary perspective, Dante's devotion to Beatrice might be considered a literary affectation, or even a form of erotomania. From the perspective of his own time, however, it was a creative embodiment of the developing romantic ideal. Dante did not invent romantic love, as Henry Finck insinuated; he did, however, live that ideal in a highly creative way, and he wrote from his experiences in a manner that profoundly influenced subsequent generations.

Further Historical Developments

The story of Dante and Beatrice epitomizes the first or "courtly" stage of the romantic ideal. A second stage in the institutionalization of romantic love began in the fourteenth century and reached its climax with the Romanticist movement approximately four hundred years later.[13] By the fourteenth century the extended, feudal family system was breaking down under the impact of urbanization and industrialization. Romanticism (then as now) was a reaction to materialism and rationalism which tended to accompany this transition, a reaction that sought stability and fulfillment in the wonders of emotion. More specifically, by the seventeenth and eighteenth centuries, many of the original values and premises supporting courtly love were no longer valid. The nobles of this period still adhered to the tenet that love and marriage are irreconcilable, but sex and love became united outside marriage in the relationship between the noble woman and her gallant. A similar integration of love and sex was occurring among the bourgeoisie, but their economic struggles and religious conservatism would not permit illicit, extramarital relationships. The ideal of love was therefore displaced to the marriageable woman who, after betrothal, was to be "courted" with displays of emotional fervor designed to win her affection. Marriages were still largely prearranged, however, and before betrothal, relationships between the sexes tended to be strict and well regulated. This second stage in the development of romantic love culminated with the Romantic writers of the eighteenth century who argued that love is the necessary foundation for marriage, taking as the ideal the feelings of courtly love depicted in medieval romances.

In contemporary society, romantic love has entered yet another stage. This third stage reflects the increasing freedom of young people to choose their own marriage partners. Under the influence of democratic and egalitarian principles, economic and social status have lost their rationale as reasons for marriage (in theory, if not in practice). Love has thus become the favored ground for betrothal, and happiness its goal.

As in the twelfth century, today's ideal of romantic love is proclaimed in song and literature—with many of the same themes apparent. For example, in the refrain from a popular song, the protagonist intones that her love springs from "deep in my soul," that it burns "out of control," and that it is "everlasting."[14] In this one refrain, three of the characteristics of the romantic ideal are emphasized: First, love is a highly personal and authentic experience ("deep in my soul"); second, it is a passion and not an action ("out of control"); and, third, it is timeless ("everlasting"). To what extent do these characteristics accurately reflect the realities of romantic love? We will consider them in reverse order.

Everlasting: At the time of occurrence, romantic love may indeed seem as though it might (should) last forever. Unfortunately, everlasting love is the exception rather than the rule. Oscar Wilde once remarked, "A person should always be in love; that is why he should never marry." Cynical, perhaps, but also insightful. When passions of romantic love subside, many couples find themselves unable to cope with the realities of an intimate relationship. Currently, one out of every three American marriages ends in divorce, and the figure is much higher for couples who marry young, where love is supposedly the primary motivation.[15]

Out of control: According to the romantic ideal, love is a passion—the very antithesis of a rational, calculated act. In popular discourse, the term "passion" has even become largely restricted to romantic relationships. But although love may be the epitome of a passion, there is method to the "madness"; love is not as uncontrollable as the popular conception suggests. The mother's advice to her daughter, "It is as easy to fall in love with a rich man as with a poor man," is not without effect. Most people tend to fall in love with someone of the "appropriate" ethnic, social, and religious background.

Deep in my soul: Love is presumably a highly personal experience, one that not only overcomes restrictive social expectations and pressures, but that is even intensified by such pressures (the so-called Romeo-and-Juliet effect). Yet, as described earlier, the romantic ideal is itself a social creation. This is not as contradictory as it might seem. A culture that emphasizes individuality is also going to attribute the source of behavior to the individual, while downplaying any social origins.

In short, the romantic ideal as depicted in song and literature serves as a kind of model or paradigm, representing a complex blend of characteristics to which few people actually conform in practice. As an abstraction, however, the ideal aids in both the guidance and interpretation of behavior. That is, people may try to emulate the model, and even if they fail, may still interpret their behavior as being more in conformance than it actually is.[16]

What function might romantic love serve in modern society? The sociologist Sidney Greenfield has suggested that the romantic ideal is one way of encouraging couples to marry, even though marriage may be counter to their immediate self-interests.[17] In contemporary American society, according to Greenfield's analysis, an individual is encouraged to be self-reliant, independent, and, in a sense, economically selfish. This is the "rational" way to behave. On the other hand, society also encourages interdependence between the sexes, with both giving up something of themselves for the sake of the other. The husband is supposed to give up part of his wages to support a wife and children; the wife, in turn, is supposed to give up a career in the marketplace for a less prestigious domestic role, devoting herself and her energies untiringly to her family. How can these conflicting demands be resolved? The answer, according to Greenfield, is found in the romantic ideal. One marries because one has fallen in love—an event that cannot be helped.

It is not necessary to agree with the details of Greenfield's analysis in order to recognize its essential point, namely, that romantic love is one inducement to marriage in a society where other inducements (e.g., economic necessity, maintenance of kinship lines) are weak and/or divisive pressures are strong.

Living in the contemporary West, it is easy to assume that romantic love is an inborn trait rather than a socially created one. If the above general point is correct, however, then emotions similar to romantic love should have been "invented" by other societies in similar need of marriage inducement or cement. Cross-cultural research has found this to be the case.[18]

In sum, both historically within Western civilization and across cultures today, patterns of romantic love vary as a function of societal needs. Moreover, there are indications that romantic love is undergoing further change in response to altered conditions in contemporary society. As the divorce rate tells us, it is now acceptable to be in love a number of times, albeit sequentially; among advocates of communal living and open marriage, love may not even be restricted to one partner at a time. How far or in what direction love will continue to change in the future is not ours to predict. But one thing seems certain: Romantic love was not created in heaven; it was created right here on earth by particular societies to meet specific needs. It will change as those societies and those needs change. And what is true on the societal level is also true on the individual level. Probably no other emotion provides a greater opportunity for individual creativity than does love.

3

✦

On Being a Wild Pig and Other Such Things

> We always require an outside point to stand on, in order
> to apply the lever of criticism . . . How, for
> example, can we become conscious of national
> peculiarities if we have never had
> the opportunity to regard
> our own nation from outside?
> —Jung, *Memories, Dreams,*
> *Reflections*

- In the highlands of New Guinea, a man is bitten by a ghost and begins to act *like a wild pig,* shooting arrows at bystanders, looting houses, and the like. No serious harm is done.
- In the Philippines, a tribesman discovers a young woman by a river. Feeling *liget* (vital energy), he cuts off her head. Later, back in his village, his feat is celebrated in song and dance.
- In Micronesia, on the island of Ifaluk, a child is repeatedly disrespectful. An adult dressed as a ghost threatens to kidnap and eat him if he continues to misbehave. In this way, the child learns what it means to become the object of another's *song* (righteous indignation).
- In the United States, a man discovers his wife's infidelity. After several days of seemingly normal behavior, he hunts her down and kills her. At his trial, he attributes his behavior to "repressed anger."

Wishful thinking to the contrary, human beings are an aggressive species. In ordinary English, we tend to label a wide variety of aggressive acts as "anger," and because aggression is universal, we then assume that anger, too, must be universal. In the present chapter we will examine the extent to which that assumption is warranted. For example, do the conditions described in the above scenarios ("being a wild pig," *liget, song,* and anger), each of which involves an aggressive act, represent variations on a single underlying emotion (anger), or do they represent fundamentally different (but overlapping) emotions, each a creation of the culture in which it is observed?[1]

Our purpose in asking this question perhaps bears repeating. To the extent that emotions vary across cultures (as well as across time, as in the case of romantic love), they must be subject to change. And, to the extent that they are subject to change on the social level, they must also be open to innovation on the individual level.

Being a Wild Pig

Our first scenario involves an emotion-like condition which the Gururumba (a people of the highlands of New Guinea) call "being a wild pig."[2] There are no undomesticated pigs in the area where the Gururumba live, and the analogy is to domesticated pigs that have escaped and run wild. The Gururumba do not understand why pigs sometimes run wild, but they believe that through proper procedure and ritual the animals can be redomesticated. So it is with a person who is afflicted by being a wild pig—he has temporarily broken the bonds of society and must be "redomesticated."

The Gururumba believe that being a wild pig is caused by the bite of the ghost of a recently deceased individual, usually a relative. These ghosts are malevolent, destructive entities; they reflect the qualities of men before they had learned to live together in society. The Gururumba take a rather dim view of uncivilized human nature: Primeval man supposedly attacked, stole, and raped on whim. When bitten by a ghost, a person loses the veneer of civilization, and primitive impulses are once again released.

Being a wild pig involves a variety of aggressive acts, including looting, shooting arrows at bystanders, and the like. Significantly, harm is seldom done. The behavior may continue for several days, until the affected individual disappears into the forest where he destroys his ill-gotten goods (usually inconsequential items left for him to steal). He may then return in a normal condition, neither remembering anything about his previous behavior nor being reminded of it by the villagers. Alternatively, he may return still in a wild state, in which case, he is captured and "redomesticated" according to proper ritual.

Although being a wild pig is not a normal emotional response even among the Gururumba, it illustrates in exaggerated form many typical features of more standard emotions: The affected individual presumably has little control over his own behavior; the behavior is regarded as irrational, bizarre, and out of character; and it is accompanied by a good deal of physiological arousal.

As already noted, the Gururumba believe that an episode of being a wild pig is triggered by the bite of a ghost. On a deeper and less well-articulated level, the Gururumba seem to recognize that it is not just a ghost that causes a person to behave like a wild pig; the inability of the individual to cope with frustrations imposed by society is also an important factor. Only males between the ages of approximately 25 and 35 exhibit the syndrome. This is an especially stressful period for the Gururumba male. He must forego the considerable freedom of his youth and accept economic and social obligations prescribed by the group. His success in these endeavors determines not only his personal prestige and power, but also that of his clan. A *voluntary* renunciation of social obligations is thus not allowed. Yet, due to situational or personal factors, not everyone can cope—not all of the time. An involuntary "out" is therefore provided.

In a sense, being a wild pig is a way to declare psychological bankruptcy. Following an episode, members of the society apparently reevaluate the afflicted individual, and expectations are adjusted accordingly. The society can thus maintain pressure on individual members to conform voluntarily to social norms. If being a wild pig is to serve its function, however, it (like bankruptcy in our own society) must be used sparingly and only in extreme cases. Therefore, although in one sense accepted, being a wild pig is not condoned.

The role of ghosts in eliciting wild-pig behavior is also worthy of brief comment. Ghosts are primarily of recently deceased kinsmen, and they may be either benevolent or malevolent, depending on the quality of prior relationships. Elderly persons sometimes threaten younger relatives with ghostly retaliation if they (the elderly) are not treated properly. Thus, in addition to its function in declaring psychological bankruptcy, being a wild pig (or, more accurately, the threat of being bitten by a ghost) provides a form of social security.

Liget (Vital Energy)

The Ilongots, who number about 3,500 people, inhabit a forested area in Northern Luzon, the Philippines. They are an egalitarian people who recognize no difference in class or status. They also have a taste for violence. One of the most important occasions for young men to establish their equality and social identity is the taking of heads. For the Ilongots, cutting off the head of another person is not a sign of vengeance or hatred, but of virtue. Although a headhunter may prefer to kill within a particular kin group or locality, the personal identity of the victim is not of great importance—a man, woman, child, anyone will do.

Through killing, an Ilongot man may realize his *liget*. This is a complex concept that Michelle Rosaldo translates as "anger," but sometimes also as "energy," and "passion," depending on the context.[3]

Liget finds expression in a wide variety of ways—in giving as well as in taking life. For example, although not linked to sexuality per se, male *liget* is implicated in both courtship and childbirth. "Concentrated" in the sperm, it makes babies. In other manifestations, *liget* stimulates work and provides the strength and courage to overcome obstacles.

Like anger, *liget* can be occasioned by insults, slights, and other affronts to the self, or the violation of social norms. One of the main occasions for *liget* is an intimation of superiority on the part of another. The superiority may be deserved (e.g., by superior performance on a hunt), or it may be the result of inadvertent good fortune. The source does not matter. The Ilongots are fiercely egalitarian. By providing the "vital energy" for accomplishment in any of a variety of endeavors, *liget* is a primary means for a person to attain or demonstrate equality.

The taking of heads, then, is only one manifestation of *liget*, but a very important manifestation. It is a form of self-affirmation. It is also a social enterprise in which a whole clan can participate, vicariously if not actually. After a killing, the clan may gather for a night of celebration and song, during which the men boast of present and past exploits as the women provide a choral counterpoint. The following is one man's boast: "Downstream on the great river I came upon a maiden, she kicked, but I am here to tell the tale."[4]

Rosaldo emphasizes that *liget* is not so much an expression of a person's inner volatility as it is an aspect or emergent property of interpersonal relations:

> *Liget*—like all Ilongot emotions—is not associated with any form of spontaneous, physical, or "natural" impulse, be it sexuality, hunger, or thirst; rather, passions are generated through and coordinate with patterns of action, processes of conflict, emulation, and competition in social life.[5]

As we will see shortly, much the same could be said with respect to anger and other emotions in our own culture. From Rosaldo's description, however, it should be evident that anger and *liget* are quite different emotions. Indeed, they are no more similar than the way of life of the Ilongots is similar to that of contemporary Westerners.

Song (Righteous Indignation)

In stark contrast to the Ilongots, the Ifaluk are a gentle people who live on a small atoll in Micronesia. The Ifaluk find even the intimation of physical or verbal aggression intensely disturbing. They value calm, peaceful, and harmonious relationships. Physical aggression is rare outside of childhood. According to Catherine Lutz, who has studied the Ifaluk intensively, they are among the most peaceful people known.[6]

How do the Ifaluk maintain such amicable relationships? Ironically, it is through an emotion, *song*, that itself connotes aggressive acts. Lutz translates *song* as "justifiable anger" or "righteous indignation." The qualifiers, "justifiable" and "righteous," require some explanation.

Whether or not an emotion is considered justified obviously depends on the value system within which it occurs. The Ilongots, discussed above, believe their own "anger" (*liget*) to be justified, even though it sometimes leads to the taking of heads, an act that most "civilized" people would consider abhorrent. By translating *song* as *"justifiable* anger," the implication is that *song* not only connotes aggressive tendencies, but that it is also congruent in many respects with our own value system.

Song bears many similarities to anger. Both emotions are considered unpleasant experiences. Common occasions for *song*, as for anger, are a violation of social taboos or customs, for example, not sharing benefits with others (stinginess), not helping with communal chores (laziness), loud and boisterous behavior, disrespect for authority, and so forth. Also like anger, *song* involves the threat of retaliation if the transgression is not rectified.

There are also subtle but important differences between *song* and anger. Perhaps most important, *song* is a more narrowly circumscribed emotion. At best, it might be considered a subvariety of anger (i.e., "justifiable"). But even here, distinctions exist. For example, *song* is more a communal emotion than an individual passion. It is often expressed in the first person plural (We are *song*) rather than in the first person singular (I am *song*). The "we" in such an instance stands for an appropriate reference group (chiefs, elders, or all mature island residents) who presumably have some moral authority to pass judgment on the offense. When the nature of the offense is ambiguous (e.g., because of changing social norms), considerable negotiations may occur before a pronouncement of *song* is made or accepted.

Unlike the Ilongot, Ifalukian society is hierarchically organized. The chiefs (men or women) of the various clans are the primary guardians of the island's customs and taboos. In general, older adults have authority over younger adults, brothers over sisters, and parents over children. *Song* is most properly displayed along these lines of authority; indeed, it is one of the primary vehicles for maintaining such lines. In fact, "political and moral leadership are [among the Ifaluk], as in many other social systems, closely linked with emotional leadership."[7]

Although the threat of violence is implicit in *song*, actual violence would be a transgression of the very values *song* functions to uphold. Therefore, *song* is expressed as indirectly and as nonviolently as possible. Gossip—letting others know of the transgression—is perhaps the main way of expressing *song*. Other ways of expressing *song* include a refusal to speak with the offender; dropping polite "markers" from speech; facial expressions of disapproval; hitting or throwing inanimate objects; and, in the extreme, threatening to harm oneself.

Persons who are *song* are often advised by those in authority to forget the transgression and not to deal with it on a personal level. They are advised in a soft, gentle manner to "throw out" their thoughts and feelings about the offender, and they are reminded that if they fight they themselves will be laughed at and ostracized by the community. The offender is considered unreasonable and "crazy," not the person who is *song*. At least, that is the way it should be. Appropriately experienced, *song* is taken as a sign of maturity, wisdom, and moral rectitude, not unbridled passion.

Parents are expected to express *song* when their children misbehave, in order to teach the children the difference between right and wrong. If children misbehave the parents are also held accountable, regardless of the age of the child. Transgressions are seen as occurring because the parents did not become sufficiently *song* the first time the inappropriate behavior was exhibited.

The typical response to being the target of *song* is a complementary emotion, *metagu*, which can best be considered a variety of fear. The Ifaluk consider *metagu* to be the primary inhibitor of misbehavior, and it is carefully cultivated in children. For the most part, this is accomplished through words and stories. Children are told over and over about the way people are expected to behave, and the *song* that greets those who do not live up to expectations. One of the stories told to children when they are especially recalcitrant is that a ghost may kidnap and eat them. On occasion, the story may actually be acted out, with an adult dressed as a ghost. This induces *metagu* in an especially dramatic way.

In short, the Ifaluk use words and stories as a kind of scaffolding on which to construct the emotions of their culture. As children learn the proper use of such terms as "*song*" and "*metagu*" they are not simply learning to describe or label a preexisting state; they are also learning the social rules that constitute the experience and expression of the emotion itself.

Anger

Now let us turn to anger in our own culture. Like a Gururumba man who behaves like a wild pig, the angry individual is often portrayed as acting like a wild animal—a roaring lion or a raging bull, if not a wild pig. That, at least, is part of our conception of anger. But is this an accurate conception?

Anger is a more benign emotion than is generally assumed. In this respect it is more like *song* than *liget*. Consider the following facts. In everyday affairs anger is most often directed at loved ones and friends, and only seldom at strangers or people we dislike; the most common instigation to anger is misconduct, for example, negligence or intentional wrongdoing; the typical expression of anger seldom involves aggression, particularly physical aggression; and most episodes of anger are constructively motivated—that is, they are intended to correct or prevent recurrence of the "wrong," not to hurt the instigator.[8]

The constructive uses of anger are quite explicit in traditional moral teachings. Although, anger is counted among the "seven deadly sins," the failure to become angry at injustice has also been condemned as "sinful." According to the Judeo-Christian tradition, a presumably righteous person cannot help but become angry at injustice or wrongdoing. Jehovah of the Old Testament is often depicted as wrathful, vengeful, and punishing. He is spoken of as possessing a "fierce" or "burning" anger. Deuteronomy 29, for example, reads in part: "The Lord will not forgive such a man [one who worships idols]. Instead the Lord's burning anger will flame up against him . . . until the Lord has destroyed him completely."[9] Even Jesus, often considered the epitome of goodness and love, became angry at the moneychangers, overturned their tables, and drove them out of the temple.

In a secular society, the law is the presumed custodian of morals. Therefore, the legal treatment of anger offers additional insight into the social significance and functions of this emotion. Within the legal system, anger serves to mitigate a charge of homicide from murder to manslaughter. This is no trivial matter. Murder (homicide committed "with malice aforethought") can bring a penalty of life imprisonment or even death, whereas manslaughter (homicide committed out of anger—the typical "crime of passion") carries a much lighter sentence. Why should this disparity exist? And how does a jury decide whether a defendant was truly angry at the time of the crime?

Before a jury can attribute anger to a defendant, certain criteria must be met. The primary criterion is adequacy of provocation, as judged by the so-called "reasonable-man test." That is, did the provocation violate socially accepted standards of conduct so flagrantly that a presumably reasonable member of the community might be roused to violent anger. If so, and the behavior of the defendant is also within certain limits (e.g., he did not chop the victim up into little pieces and ship the remains to Florida), then the defendant is guilty of a lesser crime than murder.

Note that the "reasonable-man test" does not refer to the state of mind of the defendant. To kill another without adequate provocation cannot count as anger no matter how "frothing at the mouth" the killer may have been. In a crime of passion, the victim is on trial as much as the defendant. And if the victim was sufficiently guilty (committed a provocation egregious enough to be judged "adequate") then the defendant is given an out—anger. Of course, if anger is to serve as an excuse, the response must be regarded as beyond personal control, perhaps due to the release of some primitive impulse (the "wild pig" in each of us).

Another important criterion for attributing anger in a court of law is "insufficient cooling time." That is, the homicide should follow shortly upon the provocation, before the anger has had time to dissipate. However, if the provocation is sufficiently severe, the notion of "repressed anger" may be used to bridge a considerable time span (days or even weeks), during which interval the defendant may have engaged in relatively normal behavior.[10]

The above considerations suggest that anger, far from being a biologically primitive response, is instead a social construction, the function of which is to uphold accepted standards of conduct, for example, by making the violation of social norms subject to retribution. According to this formulation, anger is, in a sense, a kind of informal judiciary. For most of Western history, it has been up to individuals to see that rights were respected and justice maintained. Where no formal legal system exists, or when the formal system is inappropriate, inadequate, or unwieldy, then the power and threat of anger and retaliation helps to regulate social relations among family, friends, neighbors, and coworkers.[11]

Implications for Emotional Creativity

The ancient Greek philosopher Empedocles (ca. 495–435 B.C.) argued that love and strife are the cosmic forces responsible for the constitution of the universe. Much more recently, and only a bit less grandiosely, Freud argued that sex and aggression are the major forces responsible for human behavior. Both Empedocles and Freud were correct in recognizing the importance of love and strife (sex and aggression). However, as we have shown in this and the previous chapter, love and strife are not unitary phenomena— universal and unchanging. Love takes many forms, depending on the social context. So, too, does strife. Romantic love, "being a wild pig," *liget*, and the other syndromes we have described, attest to emotional innovation and change on the social level. And if emotional creativity exists on the social level, then it must also be possible on the individual level, for social innovation and change is ultimately the cumulative product of many individual creative acts.

But how is emotional creativity possible? How can emotions change, not just superficially, but fundamentally? To answer this question, we must first examine in some detail the nature of emotion and then the nature of creativity.

Part II

Emotions and Creativity in Reality and Myth

*Man is a great deep, Lord. You number his very hairs
and they are not lost in your sight: but the hairs
of his head are easier to number than his
affections and the movements
of his heart.*

—Augustine, *Confessions*

4

◆

The Nature of Emotion

> Knowledge of mankind is a knowledge
> of the passions.
> —Disraeli, *The Young Duke*

I didn't mean to do it; I was overcome by emotion." "My emotions get in my way." "I don't trust him; he's emotionless." "Trust your heart, not your head." "My emotions frighten me; I can't keep them under control." "Get in touch with your feelings."

As these commonplace expressions indicate, emotions are the frequent subject of both praise and blame: On the one hand, persons who are overly emotional are viewed as childish or unstable, or even worse, as animal-like or brutish; on the other hand, persons who are devoid of emotion are viewed with suspicion—as cold, calculating, and perhaps untrustworthy. Mr. Spock of the popular television series *Star Trek* reflects many people's conception of the nonemotional, completely rational being. Although basically good, the emotionless Mr. Spock is not entirely human. His father was a Vulcan, a being from another planet. The emotions are part of what makes us human, for good and bad.

What are the emotions, such that they evoke so much ambivalence? When asked to give a definition of emotion, we are typically at a loss for words. We are left in a position similar to that of Justice Potter Stewart of the Supreme Court, who, when asked to give a definition of pornography, responded: "I can't define it, but I know it when I see it."[1] The Supreme Court could not, of course, leave the matter at that. And neither can we.

The Problem of Definition

Two approaches to definition can be distinguished: One approach we will call *essentialist*, and the other, *connectionist*. The essentialist approach is the more traditional of the two. It is the preferred mode of definition in some branches of science, particularly mathematics. A circle, for example, can be defined as a closed two-dimensional figure, every point of which is equidistant from the center. Equidistance from a center is both a necessary and sufficient condition for a plane figure to be a circle; it is, in a word, the "essence" of a circle.

Connectionist approaches are more difficult to illustrate. They do not rely on necessary and sufficient conditions, but on interconnected features, or what the philosopher Wittgenstein called "family resemblances."[2] Consider a typical family—the Joneses. Some members of the Jones family may be recognizable by their big ears; others may share similarly shaped noses; and still others may have the same short, stocky build. Not every member of the Jones family need have all these features—the big ears, aquiline nose, stocky build, and so forth. In fact, two cousins, Bob and Bill Jones, may not look at all alike. Nevertheless, if we examine closely the aunts and uncles and other cousins, we can detect many intermediate stages between Bob and Bill, so that we can see how they belong to the same family.

Connectionist approaches to definition also have an important place in the history of science. For example, ever since Darwin it has been common to define species in terms of interconnected features (family resemblances), none of which is necessarily common to all members of the species.

Are emotions more like circles (definable in terms of essences), or are they more like species (definable in terms of interconnected features)? Both logic and empirical research suggest the latter.[3] The point is an important one, not only for the definition of emotion, but also for the issue of emotional creativity. Essentialism and change are inhospitable ideas. A circle is a circle, no matter where or when. As long as species were defined in terms of essences, the idea of one species changing into another seemed as implausible as circles evolving into squares. A shift from an essentialist to a connectionist definition of species was central to Darwin's theory of evolution and one of his most important insights.[4] Michael Ghiselin has summarized the essentialist nature of pre-Darwinian theory as follows:

> What was real was the essence and the differentiae, and the peculiarities of individuals were overlooked. An implication, of enormous historical importance, was that it became very difficult to classify things which change, or which grade into one another, and even to conceive of or to discuss them. Indeed, the very attempt to reason in terms of essences forces one to ignore everything dynamic or transitory. One could hardly design a philosophy better suited to predispose one toward dogmatic reasoning and static concepts.[5]

Like pre-Darwinian conceptions of species, essentialist approaches to the definition of emotion have tended to mask the possibilities for—indeed, the widespread occurrence of—emotional innovation and change.

Toward a Definition of Emotion

We must, then, abandon any search for the essence of emotion. Instead, we must examine some of the major resemblances that lend coherence to this broad and diverse family of experiences. Among the many features characteristic of one emotion or another, three stand out as particularly prominent: (1) *passivity*—emotions are passions (things that happen to us) rather than actions (things we do); (2) *subjectivity*—emotions describe a relationship between the subject and the object of the experience; and (3) *nonrationality*—emotions are not considered rational or logical in the usual sense.

Passivity

In colloquial English, we are "gripped," "seized," "torn," and "overcome" by emotion. We cannot "do" an emotion in a deliberate, self-controlled way. I might plan to read a book this evening after supper; however, it would seem odd for me to plan to be angry (in love, afraid, hopeful, etc.) this evening after supper. To use a somewhat archaic terminology, emotions are *passions* rather than *actions.* Literally, a passion is something a person suffers, that is, a response over which a person has little control.

In Chapter 5, on myths of emotion, we argue that the experience of passivity, of being "overcome" by emotion, is largely an illusion. For the most part, it is a benign, even beneficial, illusion fostered by society and reinforced by our ordinary language. To the extent, however, that it leads us to treat our emotions as alien and disruptive forces over which we have little control, the illusion of passivity can be highly restrictive of emotional development, innovation, and change.

Subjectivity

Emotions involve judgments. If I am angry, I have judged that someone has wronged me; if I am in love, I have judged that someone is worthy of my affection; if I am afraid, I have judged that a situation is dangerous; and so forth.

A judgment may be either objective or subjective. Objective judgments refer to matters of fact. To be objective is to be dispassionate, unbiased, uninvolved. Subjective judgments are evaluative. My emotions concern not simply the facts of the matter, but whether the matter is good or bad, beautiful or ugly, just or unjust. Facts exist "out there"; values, it is sometimes said, are "in the eyes of the beholder." That is an overstatement. However, values do imply a relation between the object evaluated and the person doing the evaluating.

Being subjective, the emotions have a privileged place in defining a person as a unique individual. The emotions, to borrow another colloquialism, reflect a person's "true" self, as opposed to a public self where thoughts and actions conform to opinions of others or are dictated by the logic of external events. If you want to know what a person is like, discover her loves and hates, hopes and fears, joys and sorrows, what makes her angry, and so forth.

Nonrationality

"Must you always be so emotional? Try to be rational just this once." As this familiar but exaggerated complaint indicates, emotional behavior is often contrasted with rational behavior. When rational, we try to conform our beliefs and behavior to external reality, following the rules of logic; during emotion, by contrast, we try to make external reality conform to our own desires and aversions. This view of emotion has been expressed most starkly by the philosopher Sartre, who argued that emotions represent a kind of magical thinking by which the world is transformed according to our needs. Sartre uses the following example to illustrate his point: I reach for a bunch of grapes, but they are beyond my grasp; I therefore conclude they are not worth having—they are too green, anyway. I have, in a sense, transformed the grapes to fit my situation.[6]

This is a frivolous example, Sartre admits, "but let the situation be more urgent, let the incantatory behavior be carried out with seriousness; there we have emotion."[7] Thus, when "madly" in love, I make the object of my love the repository of all that I hold dear; when "crazy" with fear and I cannot flee, I may obliterate the threatening object in a swoon or faint; and when sad, I turn the world into an impoverished, neutral place so that I do not have to act nor deal with it.

To say that an emotion is nonrational does not imply that it is without reason. A person can always be asked to justify his or her emotional responses. ("Why do you love Mary?" "Why are you angry with me?") The justification may not be expressed in logical terms; yet it is open to argument and counterargument. ("Mary is not the wonderful woman you think." "You have no right to be angry with me; I didn't do anything wrong.") Needless to say, when emotions and logic clash, it is often the latter that defers judgment: "The heart has its reasons of which reason knows nothing."[8]

To summarize the discussion thus far, we offer the following working definition of emotion:

> Emotions are those states of affairs, such as love, anger, fear, grief, and the like, that are typically experienced as beyond personal control (passivity), that involve evaluative judgments (subjectivity), and/or that are not readily explainable in a strictly logical way (nonrationality).

This definition describes, it does not explain. For the latter, we must consider briefly the origins and functions of emotions.

The Explanation of Emotion

To keep the discussion short, we will again resort to analogy. Colloquially, when a person is angry, frightened, or in love, we might say that someone has "pulled her strings." The implied reference is to another person—the presumed instigator. But with a little stretch of the imagination, we can generalize this colloquialism to the origins and functions of emotions in general. Who is pulling our collective strings when we become angry or fearful, fall in love, and so forth?

Imagine a puppet show. The puppet is enacting a scenario, the meaning and significance of which we do not fully understand. The scenario being enacted is an emotional syndrome—love, say, or being a wild pig. Behind the scenes are three puppeteers, representing the biological, social, and psychological determinants of behavior. As in any good puppet show, we cannot look behind the scenes and observe the puppeteers directly; we can only observe the behavior of the puppet. Our task is to infer the scripts the puppeteers are following, and to determine how those scripts combine to constitute an emotional scenario (syndrome). That is no easy task, for the three puppeteers sometimes pull in different directions. For example, Biology may pull in one direction, while Society tugs on an antagonistic string; or perhaps Psychology pulls in a direction contrary to what either Biology or Society prescribes. When such conflicts occur, the puppet's behavior may represent a compromise, the meaning of which is quite difficult to discern.

To illustrate the workings of each puppeteer, we make a few

observations on the biological, social, and psychological origins and functions of romantic love. Generalizations to other emotions are relatively straightforward.

Biological Strings

In the case of romantic love, it seems that Biology actually pulls two strings—sex and attachment. The sexual string requires little elaboration; it is nature's way of assuring reproduction of the species. But love is more than sex, even from a biological perspective. It also involves strong interpersonal bonds, as illustrated by grief upon separation from the loved one.

Cupid was a young rhesus monkey who lived up to his name. As an adolescent, he was housed with an older female to whom he became very attached. She also provided him with his first sexual experiences. The two monkeys were eventually separated and housed in different pens. At first, Cupid exhibited many of the symptoms characteristic of grief, including depression and hostility toward other monkeys. After a time, however, he established a seemingly satisfactory relationship with a new female partner. One day Cupid happened to be led past the pen of his former mate. The result was traumatic. Cupid became agitated and restless, he bit himself repeatedly and severely, he would not eat, and he withdrew all contact from his new mate and his human attendants.[9]

Was Cupid in love? That is probably not a very meaningful question, if by love we mean the kind of emotion discussed in Chapter 2. Cupid was no Dante. But neither was Dante merely a product of the times. Love has biological as well as social origins.

Reactions similar to those exhibited by Cupid have been observed in a number of different species. What these species have in common is a form of group living that depends on individual recognition and attachment. Some fish live in groups ("schools"), as do sheep and other such mammals. In these species, however, individuals are readily replaceable; attachment is to the group and not to specific members of the group. In contrast, most primate species (including monkeys, apes, and humans) form groups based on attachments among specific individuals. Such attachments are often related to mating, but that is not their only (or even primary) function. Sex obviously occurs in solitary species as well as social species. Attachment among individuals is a separate biological adaptation that helps preserve group cohesion, which in turn facilitates foraging for food, protection against predators, and so forth.

Social Strings

In Chapter 2, we argued that romantic love is more the product of social/historical forces than of biological evolution. The following anecdote may serve to reinforce the point:

> Dr. Audrey Richards, an anthropologist, who lived among the Bemba of Northern Rhodesia in the 1930s, once related to a group of them [the Bemba] an English folk-tale about a young prince who climbed glass mountains, crossed chasms, and fought dragons, all to obtain the hand of a maiden he loved. The Bemba were plainly bewildered, but remained silent. Finally an old chief spoke up, voicing the feelings of all present in the simplest of questions: "Why not take another girl?" he asked.[10]

The Western ideal of romantic love, although it may seem quite natural to us, strikes many people in other cultures as rather bizarre. All societies recognize temporary infatuations between (and sometimes within) the sexes. But most societies attempt to cure the victims, not encourage them in their unfortunate state. Of course, love as we know it is not simply infatuation. It is a complex pattern of behavior, organized and structured according to social rules. In fact, accuracy would be better served if we did not use the same term ("love") to refer to the many ways that sexual attachments can be—and have been—organized in various societies. But simplicity requires that we continue to refer to love in a very broad sense, relying on context to make our meaning clear.

Given the biological strings (sex, attachment) described above, how much freedom does biology allow for society to exert a creative influence on love? In addressing this question, we will limit discussion to a few brief comments on sexuality. Similar considerations apply to the other major component of love (attachment), and indeed to biological determinants of emotion in general.

In humans, sexuality is highly malleable, that is, it can be molded and shaped into a variety of different patterns. One indication of this is found in the various "paraphilias"—disorders of sexual desire. Sadism is a familiar example; the sadist becomes sexually aroused by inflicting pain upon another. A wide variety of other paraphilias are also recognized. For instance, in necrophilia, sexual desire is stimulated by dead bodies; in coprophilia, by the taste or smell of feces; in kleptophilia, by stealing or the fantasy of stealing; in zoophilia, by infrahuman animals; and so forth.

The paraphilias imply some disorder of sexual desire. However, we should not assume that all paraphilias differ fundamentally from socially more acceptable manifestations of love. Whether or not a particular kind of sexual expression is regarded as appropriate depends to a large extent upon culture. Some conditions, such as necrophilia, are probably universally condemned because they are contrary to basic psychological and/or social needs. Most paraphilias, however, cannot be considered pathological in any absolute sense. For example, along the Caribbean coast of Colombia, sex with a donkey is considered a normal part of growing up for young boys.[11] Among other things, it helps preserve the virginity of young girls.

Pursuing the above line of reasoning a step further, it is evident that sexuality may become associated with socially desirable as well as undesirable conditions. Thus, while the sadist may become sexually aroused by inflicting pain on another, an altruist may become aroused by offering kindness to another. If the latter condition were focused on an appropriate member of the opposite sex, we might not consider it a paraphilia, but a normal manifestation of romantic love.

Psychological Strings

One more puppeteer remains to be discussed, namely, Psychology or the Self. As before, we confine our discussion to romantic love. What might be the origins and functions of love on the psychological level? One aspect of romantic love—idealization of the loved one—has proven to be a rich source of speculation relevant to this question.

As the popular saying goes, "love is blind." This has led many theorists to speculate about the content of the idealization. Freud, for example, suggested that a man's repressed oedipal feelings toward his mother, and presumably a woman's toward her father, influenced the perception of later love objects.[12] Carl Jung believed that every man had a dissociated feminine side, his "anima," and every woman had a masculine aspect, her "animus."[13] The person in love projects this dissociated aspect of the personality onto his or her partner, thus achieving self-integration. Theodor Reik, another of Freud's disciples, argued that projections during love are reflections of the ideals and aspirations we have for ourselves, but which we fail to meet.[14] To this list, David Orlinski has added another source of projection commonly found in older persons who have romantic affairs. This is the cleavage between their current selves and the selves—real or fantasized—of their youth.[15]

Other possible sources of projection not so wedded to particular theoretical positions can easily be imagined. The major theme of these arguments is similar, however; namely, that romantic love is an integrative response which helps reconcile dissociated aspects of the Self. By projecting parts of ourselves onto persons we love, we achieve union with ourselves through them.

Related to the above theme, but even more general, is the contention by Viktor Frankl and other existentialist writers that through love we are able to achieve meaning in our lives. That is, love is not simply a matter of self-integration; it is a way of integrating one's self with, or finding meaning in, the world around us.[16]

Relative Contributions

Which puppeteer—Biology, Society, or the Self—makes the greater contribution to the organization of emotional behavior? There is no single answer to this question. For one thing, the relative contribution of each may differ from one emotion to another (e.g., fear versus hope), and even from one situation to another within the same emotional category (e.g., fear of heights versus fear of ghosts). For another thing, each determinant can be said to be more fundamental than the others, but in a different sense. Thus, Biology is most fundamental in the sense that it is first or prior to the others. We are, after all, a biological species, a product of millions of years of evolutionary development. However, biology sets only loose constraints on human behavior. If we are talking about standard emotions (i.e., those recognized and named within a culture, such as love in contemporary America or *liget* among the Ilongot),

Society determines the form or pattern of the response; and in that sense, Society is the most fundamental. And, of course, social and biological influences can only be actualized in and through individuals; and in that sense, Psychology is the most fundamental source of our emotions.

As far as emotional creativity is concerned, primary emphasis is on the social and psychological determinants of emotion. As will be explained in more detail shortly, emotions are constituted according to rules laid down by society and adapted and modified by the individual. Without rules there could be no emotions. Or perhaps it would be more accurate to say that without rules our emotional life would be anarchic, a loose concatenation of biological impulses and urges, with little coordination or meaning.

Feelings and Emotion

In a deservedly popular book entitled *Feelings,* Willard Gaylin takes note of the considerable literature about emotions. He complains, however, that "if you examine this corpus in search of feeling, you generally seek in vain. It is possible to plow through an entire book (let alone an article) without encountering a single feeling."[17] That is a grievous oversight, Gaylin believes, for a society can ignore feelings only at considerable risk. "Feelings are the fine instruments which shape decision-making in an animal cursed and blessed with intelligence, and the freedom which is its corollary. They are signals directing us toward goodness, safety, pleasure, and group survival."[18] Needless to say, not everyone agrees. B. F. Skinner, one of the most influential psychologists of the twentieth century, has the opposite complaint: "The exploration of the emotional and motivational life of the mind has been described as one of the great achievements in the history of human thought, but it is possible that it is one of the great disasters."[19] According to Skinner, feelings are invoked as explanations for behavior primarily when we do not understand the true causes of a response. References to feelings are masks for ignorance.

What are feelings, anyway? And what is the relation of feeling to emotion?

"I am angry." "I feel angry." Under many circumstances, these two expressions can be used interchangeably. Not surprisingly, therefore, the three characteristics described earlier in this chapter (passivity, subjectivity, and nonrationality) can refer either to emotions in general or more specifically to feelings. Since similar considerations apply to each, we will not make any sharp distinction between emotions and feelings throughout most of this book. This does not mean, however, that emotions *are* feelings, or that what is true of feelings is necessarily true of emotions.

For example, a skeptic might argue that emotional creativity applies only to emotional behavior and not to the underlying feeling (the "real" emotion). It is certainly true that a person may learn to express anger, say, in new and more effective ways without altering the experience itself. However, this should not obscure the fact that feelings, too, are subject to innovation and change. *Emotional creativity is as applicable to the way people feel as to the way they behave.*

"But I can't help how I feel," our skeptic might respond. "And aren't emotions like anger experienced the same everywhere, no matter how they are expressed?" To answer objections such as these, we must examine in greater detail the relation between emotions and feelings.

The Domain of Feeling

I may feel a pin prick, the soft touch of velvet against my skin, the cold of a winter day, or the pounding of my heart after strenuous exercise. Feelings in this sense are simple sensory experiences. I may also feel ill, nauseous, or lethargic, all of which imply some general bodily condition (perhaps involving hormonal rather than sensory feedback). On occasion I may feel confused and disoriented, or knowledgeable and enlightened—states that involve cognitive evaluations of events. At times, I feel like going to a movie, at other times I feel like reading a book, and at still other times I feel like doing nothing. Feelings in this sense refer to motivational states or response tendencies.

Within the broad domain of feelings, where do feelings of emotion lie? Are they simple sensations, vague bodily awarenesses, cognitive evaluations, or motivational states? The answer is: All of the above, and more. In order to illustrate how much more, we must introduce a very important distinction, namely, between prereflective and reflective experience.

To gain a "feeling" for this distinction, imagine how a cat might feel at the approach of a snarling dog. The cat, we may assume, is conscious of the dog's approach, its bared teeth, and its menacing growl. We may also assume that the cat intuitively recognizes the potential danger and has a tendency to flee. Finally, we may assume that the cat experiences proprioceptive feedback from its heightened state of physiological arousal. But is the cat experiencing fear? In a sense: But what exactly does the cat fear? It cannot fear death, because a cat has no concept of death. Does it fear being eaten? That also seems unlikely, for the cat has had no experience with being eaten and no concept of a predator-prey relation. We can most reasonably assume that the cat is simply reacting to the immediate situation, and that it is experiencing fear in only the most rudimentary sense. In a word, the cat's experience is prereflective.

In contrast to a cat, human beings are not simply aware of, and responsive to, their immediate environment, they are also aware of their own awareness, conscious of their own consciousness, so to speak. This "higher-order" awareness is what we mean by reflective experience.

Emotional feelings are often regarded as the epitome of prereflective experience. However, if it were not for the capacity for reflective thought, our emotional life would be little richer than that of a cat. Emotional feelings are reflective, not prereflective.

Recall the example of "being a wild pig" discussed in Chapter 3. No actual pig could have such an experience, only a well socialized Gururumba. "Being a wild pig" cannot be understood, and certainly not felt, apart from the culture which gives it meaning.

Similar observations could be made with respect to *liget*, also discussed in Chapter 3. Try to imagine how it would feel to cut off the head of another person (man, woman, or child, it doesn't matter). In particular, try to imagine the exultation that an Ilongot man feels on such an occasion. Michelle Rosaldo variously translates *liget* as "anger," "energy," and "passion," but none of these terms is entirely adequate.[20] This is not simply a problem of translation. The experience of *liget* is in important respects different than any emotion experienced in our own society, for it is a product of a different life style, a different way of being in the world.

But let us take a more familiar emotion, namely, love. Sexual love can take as many forms as there are arrangements for procreating and rearing children, or simply for mating. In many cultures, it is standard for a man to have several wives; and in a few cultures, for a woman to have several husbands. Among the Nyinba, an ethnic group of Tibetan Buddhists, a woman simultaneously marries all the brothers in a family. The feelings of love in such instances undoubtedly conform to the behavior of the individuals and the expectancies of the group; they would not conform to our own conception of romantic love.

Feelings and the Expression of Emotion

Earlier, we noted a potential argument against the possibility of emotional creativity. Specifically, a critic might argue that emotional creativity may apply to the expression of emotion, but not to the underlying feeling. This argument assumes that emotional feelings are somehow simpler, less mutable, and perhaps more authentic than emotional expression. We have seen, however, that such is not the case. Emotional feelings and expression are subject to many of the same considerations. But if that is so, why do we sometimes speak of feelings (e.g., "I feel angry") and sometimes of emotion (e.g., "I am angry")?

To *feel* emotional implies conscious awareness; to *be* emotional carries no such implication. Thus, a person can be angry (in love, etc.) without being aware of the fact; and conversely, a person may feel angry without in fact being angry (in love, etc.). The first of these possibilities is easily illustrated. Assume that Mary is angry with her husband. If she admits her anger, she may have to do something about it, perhaps jeopardizing the relationship. She therefore denies her anger, even to herself. She does not feel angry. Yet, her friends can tell that she is angry from the way she acts. She frequently complains that her husband treats her unfairly; and she retaliates in subtle and indirect ways. It is the reflective nature of emotional experience that makes such self-deception possible.

The second possibility, namely, to feel angry without being angry, can be illustrated by reference to our discussion in Chapter 3 on the attribution of anger in courts of law. As may be recalled, anger serves to mitigate a charge of homicide from murder to manslaughter, which can literally mean the difference between life (a short prison term or even probation) and death (capital punishment). How does a jury decide whether a defendant was *really* angry at the time of the killing? Primarily, by application of the so-called "reasonable-man test." That is, did the provocation violate socially accepted standards of conduct so egregiously that a presumably reasonable member of the community might be roused to violent anger; and, if so, was there insufficient cooling time between the provocation and the homicide. How the defendant actually *felt* at the time of the killing is only tangentially relevant to the verdict.

Feelings can be illusory. In this respect, feeling an emotion can be compared to hearing voices; no matter how vivid and realistic the voice might seem to the individual, it will not be considered real unless there is some adequate stimulus to account for its occurrence. (Parenthetically, the "adequate stimulus" need not be the actual voice of another person. If the individual hearing voices is a saint or shaman, say, the voice might be attributed to some mystical power. In psychological matters, reality is often what the community decides it to be.)

In short, there is an important distinction to be made between feeling emotional and being emotional. Being emotional is, in a sense, anchored in reality (however reality may be defined). Feeling emotional is, by contrast, a product of reflective experience, and hence may be correct or incorrect, veridical or illusory.

We may now answer our skeptic who claims that emotional feelings are simple and immutable, that only the expression of emotion is subject to creative change. In one sense, at least, emotional feelings are more—not less—subject to innovation and change than is emotional behavior. This is because the expression of emotion is open to social approval or disapproval. If we do not conform our behavior to social expectancies, the fact is immediately obvious, and we may suffer the consequences. Our feelings, on the other hand, are less open to scrutiny; and hence they are more free to vary as a function of our own personal needs and desires.

In another sense, however, our skeptic is correct, but for the wrong reasons. The privacy of our feelings—not their simplicity or immutability—shelters them from change. *De gustibus non est disputandum* (matters of taste are not subject to dispute). Social convention may regulate my behavior; but how I feel is my business—as long as I keep it to myself. Thus, in the absence of social pressure, a change in emotional feelings is often more difficult than a change in emotional behavior alone. But it is not impossible, not if we are willing to take responsibility for the way we feel as well as for the way we act.

Rules of Emotion

One more topic remains to be discussed before we conclude this chapter. Earlier, we stated that emotions are constituted according to rules laid down by society and adapted and modified by the individual. *Rules are not peripheral, they are central to the notion of emotional creativity.* We must therefore indicate more precisely what we mean by rules of emotion.

As a first approximation, we may define rules of emotion as socially acquired principles that determine conduct (thoughts, feelings, actions) through reward and punishment. They are the "do's" and "don't's" of emotion. Perhaps the best way to illustrate the nature of emotional rules is with some concrete examples.

Rules of Love

Pop psychology comes in a wide variety of forms—self-help books, fortune cookies, songs, wall hangings, posters, and the like. One poster enumerates the joys and tribulations of love. Among other bits of wisdom, the poster suggests that asking advice on the rules of love is no better than asking advice on the rules of madness. This counsel misrepresents madness, which is not as unruly as is often supposed; but that is trivial in comparison to its misrepresentation of love, which assuredly is not free of rules—nor is anger, fear, jealousy, or any other emotion.

Romantic love, as may be recalled from Chapter 2, had its origins in the courts of eleventh century Europe. The following are the twelve "chief rules of love," as spelled out by Andreas Capellanus in *The Art of Courtly Love:*

    I. Thou shalt avoid avarice like the deadly pestilence and shalt embrace its opposite.

    II. Thou shalt keep thyself chaste for the sake of her whom thou lovest.

    III. Thou shalt not knowingly strive to break up a correct love affair that someone else is engaged in.

    IV. Thou shalt not choose for thy love anyone whom a natural sense of shame forbids thee to marry.

    V. Be mindful completely to avoid falsehood.

    VI. Thou shalt not have many who know of thy love affair.

VII. Being obedient in all things to the commands of ladies, thou shalt ever strive to ally thyself to the service of Love.

VIII. In giving and receiving love's solaces let modesty be ever present.

IX. Thou shalt speak no evil.

X. Thou shalt not be a revealer of love affairs.

XI. Thou shalt be in all things polite and courteous.

XII. In practicing the solaces of love thou shalt not exceed the desires of thy lover.[21]

Most of these twelve rules are repeated in slightly different form in a second list of thirty-one rules, which according to Andreas must be obeyed "in order to avoid punishment by Love."[22] Several rules from this longer list are worth mentioning. For convenience, we will continue to number the rules in sequence.

XIII. Marriage is no real excuse for not loving.

XIV. He who is not jealous cannot love.

XV. When one lover dies, a widowhood of two years is required of the survivor.

XVI. No one should be deprived of love without the very best of reasons.

XVII. Every lover regularly turns pale in the presence of his beloved.

XVIII. A true lover considers nothing good except what he thinks will please his beloved.

XIX. Love can deny nothing to love.

XX. A slight presumption causes a lover to suspect his beloved.

XXI. A true lover is constantly and without intermission possessed by the thought of his beloved.

XXII. Nothing forbids one woman being loved by two men or one man by two women.

Many of these rules may sound familiar to the contemporary reader. However, their familiarity can be misleading, for they must be interpreted within the context of another historical era. Take, for example, Rule II: Thou shalt keep thyself chaste for the sake of her whom thou lovest. Recall that a person could not love his or her own spouse; hence, the need for Rule XIII: Marriage is no real excuse for not loving. Presumably, also, there should be no jealousy of the beloved's marriage partner, although jealousy of other potential rivals was expected, even demanded (see Rules IV and XX).

Is love today less governed by rules than its earlier progenitor? Hardly. Advice on love is generally no further away than the supermarket newsstand. For example, Leo Buscaglia, a modern day Andreas Capellanus, has offered the readers of *Woman's Day* magazine six "golden rules" of love. These may be paraphrased as follows:

    I. Do not place any conditions on love; for example, do not try to change the other person, nor use love as a bargaining chip.

    II. Allow the other person breathing space; outside experiences and interests enhance a secure relationship.

    III. Don't expect perfection; be willing to forgive shortcomings in the other person.

    IV. Don't let love stagnate; change is an ally of love.

    V. There are many obstacles to love, but none that cannot be overcome; do not fear disappointment.

    VI. If love is absent from your life, you are responsible; the challenge of love is yours to meet.[23]

If these rules seem self-evident, even trite, that is the way it should be. Contemporary rules of love should be "second nature" to the well-socialized reader.

Rules of Anger

Legally, anger is defined as a "short madness."[24] More colloquially, an angry person may "blow his stack," "froth at the mouth," "burst a blood vessel," and "see red." In light of expressions such as these, it might seem even more farfetched to speak of rules of anger than of rules of love. But, not to be outdone by Andreas Capellanus and his twelve chief rules of love, we will present twelve chief rules of anger. These rules are based on historical (moral) teachings regarding the appropriate use of anger, on legal precedence regarding the adjudication of crimes of passion (anger, typically), and on regularities in the everyday experience and expression of anger. Details are presented elsewhere.[25]

I. A person has the right (duty) to become angry at intentional wrongdoing or at unintentional misdeeds if those misdeeds are "correctable" (e.g., due to negligence, carelessness, or oversight).

II. A person should not become angry at events that can be corrected in more standard ways.

III. Anger should be directed only at persons and, by extension, other entities (one's self, human institutions) that can be held responsible for their actions.

IV. Anger should begin with an explanation of the harm done, and only if that fails should it escalate to the denial of some benefit, verbal aggression, and—as a last resort —physical aggression.

V. The aim of anger should be to correct the situation, restore equity, and/or prevent recurrence, not to inflict injury or pain on the target nor to achieve selfish ends through intimidation.

VI. The angry response should be proportional to the instigation, and it should conform to community standards of appropriateness (which may vary depending on the setting and target).

VII. The response should not exceed what is necessary to correct the situation, for example, to prevent the instigation from happening again, or to restore equity.

VIII. Anger should involve commitment and resolve; that is, a person should not become angry unless appropriate follow-through is intended.

IX. Anger should terminate whenever the target apologizes, offers restitution, or gives assurances that the instigation will not be repeated.

X. Anger should not be displaced on an innocent third party, nor should it be directed at the target for reasons other than the instigation.

XI. Anger should not last more than a few hours or days, at most.

XII. An angry person should not be held completely responsible for his or her actions.

As in the case of love, most of these rules will appear intuitively obvious to the well socialized individual in this culture. However, from the cross-cultural analyses of "being a wild pig," *liget*, and *song,* discussed in Chapter 3, it should be clear that not all aggressive syndromes conform to the rules of anger. And from the frequent incidence of spouse and child abuse, it should be equally clear that the rules of anger are frequently violated in our own society.

Kinds of Rules

With the rules of love and anger as background, we may now describe more precisely the nature of emotional rules. We begin with a threefold distinction among constitutive, regulative, and procedural rules. Strictly speaking, these do not represent different kinds of rules. It would be more accurate to speak of constitutive, regulative, and procedural aspects of any given rule. But for ease of presentation, we will treat the aspects as though they represented distinct classes or kinds of rules.

The various kinds or aspects of rules can be illustrated most easily by reference to a game, such as chess. Some rules (e.g., pertaining to the layout of the chessboard, the nature of the pieces, and the moves that are permissible) help *constitute* the game as a game of chess (as opposed, say, to backgammon). If the board were different or there were no king, if pawns could move backward, and if rooks could be checkmated, then the game would no longer be chess. Other rules *regulate* how the game is played. For example, in a chess tournament, it might be stipulated that a certain number of moves be made within a given time period. Regulative rules do not determine the kind of game that is being played, but they do influence the way the game is played. The third type of rule, which we call *procedural,* helps determine the strategy of play. It is not possible to specify exhaustively or succinctly the procedural rules for a game like chess. Such rules are the stuff of books and magazine articles (e.g., instructing players how to recognize situations in which one move might be more appropriate than another). Good chess players can be distinguished from poor ones by their (often intuitive) grasp of the procedural rules of the game.

For a somewhat more extended example of the distinction among these three kinds of rules, consider the grammar of a language. Without a grammar, there could be no language. In this sense, the rules of grammar help *constitute* the language. When a constitutive rule of language is broken, the resulting expression is often meaningless, or has a meaning different from that intended. This sometimes happens during translation. A humorous example occurred when Queen Elizabeth of England was visiting the Federal Republic of Germany. The German Chancellor, wishing to initiate the welcoming ceremonies in English, announced to a bewildered audience, "Now goes it loose"—a literal but meaningless translation of the German expression *Jetzt geht es los*. Spoonerisms offer other examples. The Reverend Spooner (1844–1930) was Chaplain at New College, Oxford. His main claim to fame was the tendency (now named after him) to interchange sounds, usually initial syllables, in two or more words. The following is a spoonerism: It is kistomary to cuss the bride.

Other rules (e.g., of etiquette) help *regulate* how we speak on a given occasion—in a library, say, or at a formal banquet. When a regulative rule of language is violated, the result is typically not very humorous. In this case, the meaning of the expression is clear but the manner of expression is inappropriate. Yelling "fire!" in a crowded theater is a familiar example. Being rude or boorish in conversation violates regulative rules of language.

Still other rules (e.g., of rhetoric) establish *procedures* that allow us to speak persuasively. When a procedural rule is broken, the resulting expression may be both grammatically correct and appropriate, yet in poor style. Examples abound in government documents, as anyone knows who has struggled with the perennially "simplified" instructions to income tax forms. Newspapers are also occasionally guilty of violating procedural rules, as in the following bulletin:

> When Lady Caruthers smashed the traditional bottle of champagne against the hull of the giant oil tanker, she slipped down the runway, gained speed, rocketed into the water with a gigantic spray, and continued unchecked toward Prince's Island.[26]

This bulletin is neither grammatically incorrect nor socially inappropriate; but neither is it a model of clear reporting.

Turning now to the emotions, constitutive rules determine the kind of the emotion that is experienced. For example, if a constitutive rule of love is broken, the emotion will not be counted as an instance of "true" love, but of some other emotion or condition (infatuation, say, or erotomania). Regulative rules determine the appropriate display of emotion. If a regulative rule of love is violated, the response will be recognized as a manifestation of love, but it will be regarded as improper. Finally, procedural rules determine how effectively an emotion is experienced and expressed. If a procedural rule of love is broken, the response may be considered appropriate in kind (e.g., a manifestation of love), but amateurish in execution. We are so used to thinking that emotions "come naturally" that we tend to overlook the fact that emotions may be enacted well or poorly, and that many people are emotional klutzes.

To be more specific, let us return for a moment to the rules of courtly love listed earlier in this chapter. Rule XVIII, "A true lover considers nothing good except what he thinks will please his beloved," is primarily constitutive. By contrast, Rule VI, which stipulates that the love affair is to be kept secret from all but a few confidants, is primarily regulative. As an example of a procedural rule, consider number XVII, which states that the lover should turn pale in the presence of the beloved. This, we may presume, was an effective demonstration of one's love. (It might seem odd to speak of a rule with reference to a physiological response, such as turning pale, which presumably is outside of voluntary control. However, there are a variety of indirect ways by which a person can control physiological processes. Good lovers, like good actors, should have little trouble with this procedure.)

Similar observations can be made with respect to the twelve rules of anger listed earlier. Some of these are primarily constitutive, for example, the rule that one has the right (duty) to correct intentional wrongdoings on the part of certain others. This rule helps constitute the response as one of anger as opposed to some other emotion (envy, say). Other rules are primarily regulative, for example, that anger should begin with an explanation of the harm done, and only if that fails should it escalate to actual punishment. Procedural rules are not as evident among those listed. However, we all know people who seem to be masters of anger; at the other end of the continuum, there are people who just cannot seem to get angry without making matters worse. The current popularity of "assertiveness training" is testimony to the need of many to acquire appropriate procedural rules of anger.

Implications for Emotional Creativity

There is a very rough correspondence between the three types of rules (procedural, regulative, and constitutive) and the three stages of emotional creativity outlined in Chapter 1 (acquisition, refinement, and transformation). In childhood, of course, emotional development involves the acquisition of all three kinds of rules, but not necessarily in equal degree. Procedural rules are the most difficult to master. By adulthood, most people have acquired the constitutive and regulative rules for a wide range of emotions; however, they may not know how to experience or express those emotions effectively. In such cases, what is needed is the acquisition of more effective procedural rules.

The second domain of emotional creativity involves the refinement of an existing emotion so that it becomes applicable in new and different contexts. This may require not only the mastery of procedural rules, but also the development of new and different regulative rules. The emotions are, in a sense, personalized, made unique to the individual. If the change in regulative rules is sufficient, the resulting emotion may be labeled "delinquent" or "nonconformist," but it will still be recognized as a standard emotion within the culture.

The third domain of creativity involves a more radical transformation of behavior, so that a new and different emotion, one not commonly recognized by the culture, is brought into being. This type of emotional creativity requires the development of new constitutive rules. If the new emotion is damaging to the well-being of the individual and disruptive of society, it may be regarded as "neurotic." If it proves beneficial to the individual and harmless to others, it may simply be dismissed as "eccentric." On occasion, a new emotion may actually prove beneficial to the larger group and be adopted by others. What begins as a personal eccentricity thus becomes standard for the society.

Earlier, we defined emotions as "those states of affairs, such as love, anger, fear, grief, and the like, that are typically experienced as beyond personal control (passivity), that involve evaluative judgments (subjectivity), and/or that are not readily explainable in a strictly logical way (nonrationality)." This definition is primarily descriptive. For example, to say that emotions are typically experienced as passions rather than actions is silent with respect to the source of that experience—biological impulses, social imperatives, and psychological compulsions are all experienced as beyond personal control. And what exactly do we mean by "experienced"? To add some depth to our definition, we have considered, however briefly, the origins and functions of emotion, the relation between emotions and feelings, and the social rules (procedural, regulative, and constitutive) that lend emotions coherence and meaning. There are some topics traditional to theories of emotions that we have not discussed, such as the role of physiological responses. The idea that emotions are "visceral" or "gut" reactions is one of the major myths of emotion, about which we will have more to say in the next chapter.

5

◆

Myths of Emotion

Myths get thought in man unbeknownst to him.
—Claude Levi-Strauss, *Myth and Meaning*

Science must begin with myths, and with
the criticism of myths.
—Karl Popper, *British Philosophy in the Mid-century*

Myths are stories we tell about the world and of our place within
it. Myths are, however, a special kind of story. The term "myth"
implies a fictional, even incredible account of events. That is why
we almost always use the term to characterize the stories other
people tell themselves, not the stories we tell ourselves. We often
describe, for example, the religious beliefs of another people as
myths, especially if those beliefs are no longer widely held (as the
stories of the ancient Greek gods), or if the beliefs are held by
people with little political power (small tribal groups).

Our own myths seem too close to the truth to be called such.
But truth in what sense? Scientific theories reveal truths about the
world; yet we recognize the difference between myths, even our
own myths, and scientific theories. Science attempts to describe
reality in an *objective* fashion; it depicts the world as it might be in
and of itself, independent of any particular observer or cultural

65

orientation. Myths aspire to a different kind of truth—a *subjective* description of reality. Through myths we find *our* place in the world.

People can live—and for most of human history have lived—without science. But people cannot live without myths. Myths are so interwoven in our lives—through rituals, rites, and custom—that we become to a significant extent what our myths construe us to be. We literally embody the myths of our culture.

Myths can be arranged in hierarchies. At the base of a hierarchy are myths that apply rather directly to the realities of everyday life. We need not be consciously aware of these lower-order myths; indeed, typically we are not. That is one reason their hold on us is so powerful. Not being recognized as myths, the "truths" they reveal appear self-evident.

In order to rationalize and legitimize the basic myths of everyday life, we develop other, more encompassing myths. One (lower-order) myth thus becomes the object of another (higher-order) myth. An example from the political domain may help to illustrate the process. Every nation writes its own history, based partly on fact and partly on myth. Its heros and leaders are made larger than life, and its institutions are perceived as superior to all others. Was George Washington really unable to tell a lie when his father asked who chopped down the cherry tree? The issue is trivial, but this is a favorite myth told to school children to indoctrinate them into the values and ideals of the society.

How are heros to be protected from debunking, and institutions fortified against change? Here is where higher-order myths come into play. In ancient Greece and Rome, heros were made into gods, thus solidifying their position within a more encompassing theological framework. During the middle ages and later, monarchies were made safe by attributing to kings certain "divine rights." The everyday allegiance of subjects to their monarch was thus reinforced, in spite of their often poor treatment. In the case of George Washington, he was only made Father of his Country.

We can now apply some of the above considerations to the domain of emotion. The philosopher Robert Solomon speaks of emotions as "mythologies."[1] The analogy is apropos. Emotions, like myths, pertain to subjective reality. Emotions lend meaning to our private lives much as myths lend meaning to our public lives. Moreover, emotional judgments differ from rational judgments in much the same way as mythology differs from science. If in anger I describe my boss as a horse's ass, I am not making an objective analysis of his digestive system; rather, I am placing his behavior in a meaningful framework in relation to my own needs, values, and ideals.

It is difficult to imagine what life would be like without our emotional mythologies—our loves and hates, joys and sorrows, hopes and fears. These are lower-order myths that make our everyday existence meaningful. We also have higher-order myths of emotion—myths about myths. These higher-order myths of emotion help rationalize and legitimize our everyday emotional experience. We are thus loath to give them up, or even to admit that they are myths. Yet, like any other kind of myth, our myths about emotions conceal as well as reveal.

In this chapter, we examine briefly nine higher-order myths of emotion. In one way or another, we have touched upon each of these myths in previous chapters, although we have not labeled them as such. To a certain extent, then, this chapter is a review and summary. But it is much more than that. We have selected these particular myths for further discussion and elaboration more for what they conceal than what they reveal about emotions. Part of what they conceal is the possibility of emotional creativity.

Emotion Myth #1:
The Myth of the Passions

The idea that we are "gripped," "seized," and "overcome" by emotion (i.e., emotions are beyond our control) constitutes what Robert Solomon has appropriately called the "myth of the passions." It is perhaps the most fundamental myth we have about the emotions.

The way that the experience of passivity may become embedded in a hierarchy of myths is well illustrated by the syndrome of "being a wild pig" among the Gururumba. As may be recalled from Chapter 3, this condition only "strikes" young men within a certain age group, and then only under specific conditions. The person who "becomes a wild pig" loots and shoots arrows at bystanders, seemingly in an uncontrollable fashion. Such lack of control is, however, a (first-order) myth, at the level of lived experience. In reality, the behavior of the afflicted individual is finely tuned to the social situation; "being a wild pig" is something the person does, not something that happens to him.

At a higher mythological level, "being a wild pig" is attributed to the bite of a ghost, which releases primordial impulses. At this level, the myth is consciously recognized—but, of course, not as a myth. At a still higher level, the ghosts that bite are presumably of recently deceased individuals who may have been mistreated before their death, and the primordial impulses that are released represent characteristics of people before they became civilized as Gururumba. Thus, at the very highest level, "being a wild pig" is rationalized and legitimized within the cosmology and history of the society.

At this point, a critic might want to object: "That may well be true of 'being a wild pig'; but surely the same could not be said of the emotions *we* experience—of love, anger, grief, and the like." But imagine a psychologist going among the Gururumba and trying to convince *them* that their own experiences are, in a sense, mythic. Would the psychologist be believed? Not likely. "Being a wild pig" is experienced as too real, and it serves too many valuable functions (e.g., as a declaration of psychological bankruptcy and a form of social security) to be dismissed so lightly. Our own emotions are no less meaningful, and no less functional, within the context of our own society. And we are no less loath to admit their mythic aspects, for to do so would rob them of some of their power and significance.

Emotion Myth #2:
The Myth of Emotional Innocence

People are typically not held fully responsible for events beyond their control. From the myth of the passions discussed above, it follows that we are not fully responsible for our behavior during emotion. Stated somewhat differently, we are presumed to be the innocent victims of our own passions. We will call this presumption "the myth of emotional innocence." This myth can be illustrated most dramatically by the treatment of "crimes of passion," for example, a homicide committed out of anger. If one person kills another in a premeditated fashion, the charge will be murder, which is punishable by a life in prison or even death. By contrast, the typical punishment for a crime of passion is several years in prison, and often not even that. The rationale behind this differential treatment is that, in the case of the crime of passion, the individual was provoked by the victim to react in a way that was beyond control, and hence for which he was not fully responsible.

There are many actions, not just homicide, for which we might like to disclaim responsibility. Consider for a moment a hysterical conversion reaction. The hysterical person may hear voices, or suffer paralysis of a limb, without any organic damage to the nervous system. The voices and paralysis are actions which the hysterical person performs in order to achieve some goal, but for which any responsibility is disclaimed, even to oneself.

According to the psychoanalyst Roy Schafer, ordinary emotional reactions are also disclaimed actions. That is, emotions are modes of acting, the goals of which are not fully recognized at the level of reflective experience. Schafer recommends that, when we speak of emotional experiences, we use only verbs (e.g., to love, to hate, to fear) or adverbs (e.g., lovingly, hatefully, fearfully). The use of nouns (e.g., love, hate, fear) fosters the tendency to think of emotions as things that happen to us, rather than as actions we perform.[2]

The reasons why we might wish to deny responsibility for our emotional actions may differ depending on the emotion. In the case of "negative" emotions the reasons are often obvious (e.g., some harm is done out of anger, some obligation is avoided out of fear or depression). But as we saw in Chapter 2, even a highly positive emotion such as love may alleviate a person of responsibility, thus encouraging behavior that might otherwise be discouraged.

We do not wish to claim that emotions are *only* disclaimed actions. Like all good myths, the myth of emotional innocence has some degree of truth. The passionate element of emotion can be explained from a variety of perspectives—biological and social, as well as psychological. The important point that we wish to emphasize now is this: *Our passions do not make us innocent.* If our emotions are to be a source of benefit rather than harm, we must take responsibility for them.

Emotion Myth #3:
The Myth of the Emotional Artichoke

Another of the major myths of emotion, one with many ramifications, can be introduced with a botanical metaphor. Consider an artichoke. As you peel away the outer petals, you eventually come to the heart of the vegetable. According to "the myth of the emotional artichoke," if you strip away the more overt, superficial aspects of behavior and experience, you will eventually reach the heart, or essence, of the emotion. And what, precisely, is the presumed heart of an emotion? Below, we will discuss three common answers to this question, each sufficiently distinct and important to deserve the title of a myth in its own right (namely, the myth of primary emotions, the myth of true feelings, and the myth of fervid viscera). But before getting to those varieties, we need to say a few words about artichoke myths as a general class.

The myth of the emotional artichoke is actually the essentialist position discussed and rejected in Chapter 4. As an alternative, we have defined emotions in terms of overlapping features or "family resemblances" (e.g., passivity, subjectivity, nonrationality). There is no simple name for this alternative, so we will return to our vegetable garden for an analogy—this time, to the onion patch. As you peel away one layer of onion after another, what is finally left? Nothing. An onion has no heart, but that does not prevent it from being an onion. Emotions, we would argue, are similar—as you peel away the various layers or manifestations of emotion, eventually nothing is left. This does not mean that emotions have no characteristic features, only that no one feature is essential to the whole.

We emphasize the myth of the emotional artichoke because an essentialist position, if it were true, would considerably limit the extent to which emotional creativity is possible. As traditionally conceived, essences do not change. Plato placed them in a separate realm of ideal Forms, independent of the world of corruptible matter. Others have not been so extreme, but the implication is similar: Discovering an essence may require a great deal of ingenuity; the essence itself, however, is not transformed in the process.

Emotion Myth #4:
The Myth of Primary Emotions

This is one of the most common variants of the artichoke myth. It contends that the heart of one emotion is actually another, more elementary emotion, for example, that the heart of depression is really anger. Stated somewhat differently, this myth postulates a few primary emotions that are not further reducible, from which all other emotions are compounded.

The number and kind of primary emotions actually postulated varies from one theorist to another. For example, Robert Plutchik maintains that there are eight primary emotions (fear, anger, joy, sadness, acceptance, disgust, expectancy, surprise), each related to a basic biological adaptation.[3] Jaak Panksepp has argued for four fundamental emotions (fear, anger, sadness, and expectancy), based on neurophysiological evidence.[4] Gerald Jampolsky, working within a clinical context, has gotten the list down to two, love and fear, with fear negating love.[5] None of these authors deny that people experience many more emotions than these primary few. The contention is, rather, that most commonly recognized emotions (love, envy, guilt, etc.) represent combinations of the primary emotions. Plutchik draws an analogy with colors to illustrate this point. All the colors of the spectrum can be obtained by mixing only three primaries; similarly, he suggests, all the colors of the emotional spectrum can be obtained by mixing the eight primary emotions.[6]

Simplicity is commendable. It is one of the major goals of science. Simplicity can also be very helpful in a clinical context, where easy to understand guidelines are often more beneficial than complex analyses. However, the myth of primary emotions, if taken seriously, can also be detrimental to emotional creativity, at least as far as the primary emotions are concerned. The primaries are presumed to be elementary phenomena that can be combined in various ways, but not fundamentally altered. That is not a trivial limitation, for the primaries are also generally considered the most important of the emotions.

Rather than comparing emotions with the colors of the spectrum, we believe a more appropriate analogy would be with works of art—paintings, for example. The *Mona Lisa* by da Vinci is not simply an admixture of colors: It has form and content. At their best, the emotions, too, can be like works of art; and like other artistic productions, human emotions represent endless possibilities. Only a small fraction of these possibilities have ever been actualized in any given culture.

Emotion Myth #5:
The Myth of True Feelings

This is another popular variant of the artichoke myth. It assumes that at the heart of the emotional artichoke lies a "true feeling." We have touched upon this myth in Chapter 4, but its hold on our imagination is sufficiently strong that it deserves additional discussion.

Perhaps the best way to introduce the myth of true feelings is with a hypothetical example. John is in love with Mary and will not admit the fact. He actually swears the opposite is true. John, it seems, is afraid of intimacy and avoids commitment. His friends, however, know that he is in love from the way he acts (e.g., he talks about Mary constantly, goes out of his way to be near her, is miserable when she is away and jealous when she is with others). But when it is suggested that he is in love, John vehemently denies the fact, averring that he has no feelings for Mary, and that in truth he wants to break up and go his separate way. His friends, believing that John and Mary are very good for one another, urge him to "get in touch with his true feelings."

According to advocates of this particular myth, John is not alone in being out of touch with his true feelings. Arlie Hochschild, a sociologist, has argued that whole groups are "alienated" from their true feelings. For example, flight attendants must be jovial and caring even toward passengers who act in a demanding and obnoxious manner. This emotional labor may become so habitual that an attendant ultimately does not know how she really feels.[7]

To help people like John and the hapless flight attendant, groups devoted to "consciousness raising" abound. There is, however, a certain paradox to the myth of true feelings. If people need to get in contact with their feelings, at some point they must have lost contact (or perhaps never have made contact to begin with). But at what point? When do people normally establish contact with their feelings? At six months of age? At ten years? Or is there a continuous process of emotional development, extending into adulthood? The very oddness of these questions suggests the need to examine underlying assumptions.

People often "discover" that they have lost contact with their feelings as they move from one social or personal context to another. Consider the situations of a young man (such as John in the above example) who is faced with the responsibilities of an intimate relationship; of an employee (such as the flight attendant) suffering from "burnout" on the job; of a housewife after the last child has left home; or of a person who retires after forty years on the job. All such transitions involve some emotional readjustment. Sometimes they also require fundamental changes in values and beliefs. It is precisely when old values must be abandoned and new standards acquired that a person may face the need to get in contact with his or her "true" feelings.

Feelings and emotions are determined, in part, by a person's values and standards. Change the one and you change the other. Thus, getting in touch with one's true feelings is not so much a process of discovery as it is an act of emotional creativity.

Emotion Myth #6:
The Myth of Fervid Viscera

This is yet another variant of the artichoke myth. It asserts that bodily changes, particularly of the viscera (heart, stomach, etc.) are necessary, if not sufficient, conditions for emotions. Like most myths, this one contains some truth. There are conditions, such as sudden fright to a loud noise, nausea on smelling a putrid odor, aggression when attacked, depression following loss of a loved one, and so forth, that are accompanied by pronounced physiological changes. In such states, a person may be struck by the autonomy of bodily responses. The body seems to "know" something that the person does not, and it acts "on its own," sometimes against the person's will and desires. Such seemingly autonomous responses may appropriately be regarded as "happenings"—as passions rather than as actions.

Since emotions are also conceived of as passions, an association between emotions and visceral responses is easily made. Colloquially speaking, emotions are "gut" reactions. More specifically, when fearful, a person may get sweaty palms; when angry, she may become hot under the collar; when in love, she may get butterflies in her stomach; and so forth. The myth of fervid viscera elevates such colloquialisms to the status of self-evident truths.

It might be objected that scientific evidence demonstrates the importance of visceral responses during emotion. When fearful, for example, a person's palms may in fact sweat; and during anger, skin temperature may increase "under the collar" due to an increased flow of blood to the skin in that area. But there are many more colloquialisms for which there is no basis in fact. When fearful, for example, a person's belly does not turn yellow, nor does his liver become like a lily; and although a person may turn red with anger, he does not turn green with envy or blue with sadness.

Until relatively recent times, actual knowledge of physiological functioning has been meager. Not surprisingly, therefore, common-sense interpretative schemes (folk anatomies and physiologies) are heavily imbued with meanings that have less to do with the physiological functions of an organ or body part per se, than with its use as food, its involvement in ritual sacrifice, its role in sexual activity, and the like. From a psychological point of view, our body is as much symbol as substance.[8]

Once a symbolic association has been made between psychological and physiological processes, it can be extremely tenacious. We will illustrate this fact with a single example, namely, the ancient identification of hysterical conversion reactions as a female disorder. The term "hysteria" is derived from the Greek word for the womb or uterus (*hystera*), which was presumed capable of wandering through the body inducing fainting spells, paralyzing limbs, and otherwise disrupting normal functions.[9] Hippocrates (ca. 460–370 B.C.) was the first to call certain symptoms hysterical, in metonymic reference to their presumed cause. These early theorists did not seem too concerned about how the womb could wander so widely. The localization of function was apparently based on the vague recognition that some types of symptoms stem from sexual difficulties and that the uterus is an important organ of female sexuality. It is more difficult to determine why such symptoms became associated almost exclusively with female disorders. Probably it had something to do with the status of women and their sex roles. Moreover, downward movement of the uterus has some empirical foundation in uterine prolapse, whereas the male organ is obviously not free to wander. (In some parts of Asia, though— particularly Malaysia and Southern China—men occasionally suffer from a condition, *koro* or *su yang*, which involves a fear that the penis will retract into the abdomen. A variety of physical and behavioral methods have been devised to prevent such a retraction —all of them evidently successful![10])

In any case, once the wandering womb came to symbolize hysterical reactions, the notion that these symptoms are sex-linked proved extremely tenacious, even after the uterus was made immobile through advancing physiological knowledge. Freud described an "old surgeon" who exclaimed to him regarding the possibility of male hysterics: "But, my dear sir, how can you talk such nonsense? *Hysteron* (sic) means the uterus. So how can a man be hysterical?"[11]

In short, any association between emotions and visceral activity must be interpreted with caution, even when (or especially when) that association appears self-evident. And even when the association is correct (as it sometimes is), two other points should be kept in mind. First, changes in visceral activity normally occur to support whatever overt behavior is called for in a situation. This says little about the origin of the behavior, which may be biological, social, or psychological. The involvement of physiological arousal is frequently taken as prima facia evidence that the behavior in question is of biological origin, and hence relatively impervious to change. That is not necessarily the case.

This brings us to the second point. Myths of emotion are not simply fanciful explanations for events that occur "naturally"; they are also veiled instructions about how a person should look and react when emotionally involved. It is not uncommon for people to "stoke the fires" of their passion in order to conform to the myth of fervid viscera. The precise means by which people control their physiological responses are not well understood and are undoubtedly multiple. But that such control can and does occur is beyond dispute. Perhaps the most dramatic example of this is voodoo death. The person who is hexed adopts the role of a dying person—and dies (often with the unwitting and subtle assistance of those around him).[12] As a more mundane example, consider the Victorian lady who would faint "on demand," for instance, upon hearing a sexually suggestive remark. Such behavior has gone out of fashion, but it illustrates well the fine control that can be exerted over physiological responses even by ordinary persons.

Emotion Myth #7:
The Myth of Phylogenesis

The next two myths that we will consider have to do with the origin (genesis) of emotions. The first attributes the origin of emotions to our animal ancestry (phylogenesis); the second, to early childhood experience (paedogenesis).

Recall again our discussion of "being a wild pig." According to the wild-pig myth, the affected person reverts to an animal-like state—the way people were before they acquired the veneer of culture. Western societies have long had a similar myth about the emotions. Plato, for example, postulated a kind of reverse evolution. The man who fails to live a life of reason may be "punished" by being reincarnated as a woman or as an animal—a bird, land mammal (quadruped or polypod), reptile, or fish, in descending order—depending on the passion that dominated his life and the severity of his transgressions (e.g., a lion, perhaps, for the ferocious, a deer for the timid, or a cow for the slothful).[13]

The myth of phylogenesis reverses Plato's evolutionary sequence but retains his emphasis on the animal-like qualities of emotional reactions. Greatly oversimplified, the rationale underlying this myth runs as follows: During emotion we cannot help responding the way we do because we still retain remnants of our phylogenetic past; or, put even more simply, emotions are the animal in human nature.

It should go without saying that emotions, like other forms of behavior, are subject to biological constraints. However, if emotions were biological givens we could assume that all peoples, being biologically similar, would experience the same emotions, and there would be little room for emotional creativity on either the social or psychological levels. But as we saw in our historical and cross-cultural examples (Chapters 2 and 3), there is a lot more to emotions than the myth of phylogenesis would lead us to believe.

Emotional Myth #8:
The Myth of Paedogenesis

In analogy with *phylogenesis,* which refers to the origins of characteristics during earlier stages of biological evolution, we may speak of *paedogenesis* (from the Greek *paedo,* child) to refer to the origins of behavior during infancy and childhood. The myth of paedogenesis is often put forward by those who dispute the myth of phylogenesis. Psychoanalytic theory, for example, assumes that adult emotional reactions are basically determined by events occurring within the first six years of life. Other theories may not be as explicit on this issue, but the tenor of analysis is often similar.

There is a sense, of course, in which all behavior has its roots in childhood experiences. The child is the father of the man. But discussions of emotional development often go beyond this truism and imply that adult emotions, if not innate, are constituted during infancy and early childhood.

We do not question the importance of paedogenesis as a general principle; however, we do question the implication that emotional change during adulthood is correspondingly limited. The myth of paedogenesis is based, in part, on the notion that adult emotions are only elaborate and sophisticated versions of their childhood counterparts. By contrast we assume that emotional syndromes can be acquired at any age; and that even when there is continuity (as between the anger of the child and that of the adult), the transformation may be so great that one can speak of the "same" emotion in only a limited sense.

The problem of identity through time has long been puzzling.[14] The Greeks posed the problem in an allegory about the ship of Theseus. This ship had its boards replaced gradually, one at a time, until not a single plank of the original ship remained. Was the ship still the same ship of Theseus? Most people would answer, Yes. But consider the following possible complications. Suppose that as each board was removed, it was carefully saved. After all the planks had been replaced, a new ship was constructed from the original boards. There are now two ships. Which one is the "real" ship of Theseus— that which showed the greatest continuity in time (with gradual replacement of planks) or that closest to the original in material content (being rebuilt from the original planks)? Now let us add yet another complication. Suppose that as the old planks were removed, they were destroyed so that a second ship like the original one could not be rebuilt from them. But also suppose that as the planks were being replaced, the ship was also being redesigned— its hull enlarged, the interior quarters rearranged, an extra deck added, and so forth. Eventually, the ship not only has completely new parts, but also a new configuration. Is it still the same ship of Theseus? And if not, at what point did the original ship cease to be and a new ship come into being?

Emotional development across the life span presents a puzzle not unlike the ship of Theseus. If we compare anger in the adult with the temper tantrum of an infant, there seems to be little in common. Yet, there is continuity, and it is not possible to say at any given point in time that now the infantile emotion has ceased to be and the adult emotion has come into being. Because of this, we are tempted to conclude that there must be something—the essence or "heart" of the emotion—that remains constant throughout the entire sequence.

We do not deny that the "same" emotion (anger, say) may be observed in adulthood and childhood. But as in the case of the ship of Theseus, what is the same in one sense may be quite different in another sense. Emotional creativity is a lifelong enterprise.

Emotion Myth #9:
The Myth of Emotional Equality

According to this myth, all people are able to respond emotionally in much the same way. In one version, this is an extension of the myth of phylogenesis. That is, people in all cultures experience the same primary emotions, albeit in different combinations and with different cultural accouterments. Here, however, we are concerned with individual differences within a culture. The myth of emotional equality assumes that all people within a culture are able to respond emotionally in much the same way—for example, that all can (or should) aspire to the same kind of love, that all can grieve alike upon the loss of a loved one, that all can be similarly angry when rights are violated, that all can be equally fearful of certain hazards and equally courageous in the face of others; and so forth. The person who does not conform to such cultural expectations is liable to be regarded as eccentric at best, and immoral at worst.

Yet even casual observation makes plain that people differ greatly in their emotional capabilities. Some people are relatively imperturbable, while others show great swings in emotional reactivity, being ecstatic one day and terribly depressed the next. To a certain extent, such variations depend on unique events in each individual's life history; but to a certain extent they also depend on innate difference in reactivity of the nervous system. Even newborn infants show marked differences in temperament.

We may assume that individuals who differ in temperament will also differ in the emotions they develop. For example, the emotionally creative extravert, who relishes the company of others, may develop a different repertoire of emotions than the emotionally creative introvert, who prefers solitude or the quite companionship of a few close friends. We should accept such individual differences and take advantage of them. To be creative is to be different, but each person must be different in his or her own way (authenticity).

Toward Emotional Creativity

Of the nine myths of emotion that we have considered, two stand out as the most fundamental. These are the myth of the passions and the myth of the emotional artichoke. The first assumes that emotions are beyond our control, things that happen to us rather than things we do. The second assumes that each emotion has some essential feature (e.g., pattern of physiological arousal or true feeling) that remains invariant across place and time. The remaining myths can be viewed as elaborations on, or attempted explanations of, these basic assumptions.

The possibility of emotional creativity begins with the knowledge that our emotions are under our control, and that they are subject to change—not just superficially, but "in essence." We are responsible for our emotions. We can choose to develop emotions that support us, or we can, as the myth of the passions suggests, be a pawn of our emotions. The task, then, is to develop emotions that enhance our personal well-being and interpersonal relationships, and to change those that hold us back. Emotional creativity is a lifelong quest for excellence; it begins with the awareness that our emotions are our own doing, a product of our own resourcefulness.

6

♦

The Nature of Creativity

All may be summed up in this formula: that
in the making of a work, an act comes
in contact with the indefinable.
—Valéry, <i>A Course in Poetics:</i>
First Lesson

Creativity. What is it? There are almost as many definitions of creativity as there are persons who write about it. That is not surprising. Creativity strikes many people as so mysterious and complex as to be indefinable. And nobody seems more perplexed than creative individuals themselves, when they attempt to describe the sources and mechanisms of their own inspirations.[1]

But simply because something is mysterious and complex does not mean that it is unfamiliar or out of the ordinary. Nothing is more mysterious than life itself, or more familiar. Creativity is a part of life. To live is to grow and change. Those aspects of life that we single out and call "creative" are distinguishable from the ordinary more in terms of degree than in kind.

To simplify discussion, it is helpful to distinguish between creativity as an aspect of persons, processes, and products. We

80

begin with the last, for there would be little point in talking about creative persons or processes if they did not result in noteworthy products.

Creative Products

Creative products take many different forms. A painting is a creative product; so, too, is a scientific theory or a business enterprise. But not all products are so tangible or enduring. An improvisational dance, for example, does not outlast its performance. In the most general sense, then, what we mean by a creative product is any act or response that meets some variable combination of the following three criteria: First, the response should be novel; second, it should be effective in meeting some challenge, or be of value or benefit to the individual or society; and, third, the response should be authentic, that is, it should reflect its origins within the individual and not simply be a product of outside forces.

Novelty

Undoubtedly the most commonly mentioned criterion for a creative product is that it be in some way unique or distinct. This might seem obvious enough. However, novelty does not exist in an absolute sense; it implies some frame of reference. That is, something can be novel only by comparison to that which is commonplace. The commonplace may refer to what is customary either for the individual or for the society. Thus, a response may be novel in comparison to an individual's own past behavior (as in the case of a student learning to solve calculus problems for the first time), or it may be novel in comparison to the society as a whole (as when Newton and Leibnitz independently developed the calculus as a new mathematical technique).

Too often, novelty is interpreted only in terms of social comparison. We thus overlook the creativity involved in individual development. All learning—indeed, all psychological growth—involves the acquisition of new responses and hence, for the individual at least, meets the criterion of novelty.

But we do not want to overemphasize the importance of

novelty per se. Not every novel or unusual response is creative, whether on the individual or the social level. We must distinguish the creative from the bizarre, the merely eccentric, the random—all of which can be quite novel or unique.

Effectiveness

To be considered creative, a response must be effective in meeting some challenge or problem; that is, it must be of some potential benefit to the individual or society. Three broad classes of benefits can be distinguished—practical, aesthetic, and psychosocial. Practical benefits accrue when the creative response presents a viable solution to a significant problem. When a corporation holds a creativity seminar or "brainstorming" session for its employees, practical benefits are the primary goal. Aesthetic benefits refer to the pleasure (sensory or intellectual) that a response can offer. The arts are the prime domain of aesthetic benefits. By psychosocial benefit, we mean more effective ways of relating to others. The psychosocially creative response should lead to higher and more complex levels of integration, both within the individual (self-actualization) and between the individual and others (social well-being).

The above three kinds of benefits accrue differentially to creative responses in different domains—for example, practical benefits to creativity in science and technology; aesthetic benefits to creativity in the arts; and psychosocial benefits to emotional creativity. Yet, no one kind of benefit is limited to only one domain of creative endeavor. The effectiveness of a scientific theory, for example, may be judged on the basis of its aesthetic appeal (simplicity, elegance, beauty) and its contributions to human dignity (a psychosocial benefit), as well as its practical implications. Similarly, works of art traditionally have been created for practical and psychosocial ends, and not just for their aesthetic appeal. Art for art's sake is a rather recent phenomenon, culturally speaking. And, to anticipate future argument, the truly creative emotional response is an effective means of coping with a real problem (practical benefit), in a manner that is both tasteful and elegant (aesthetic benefit), such that one's self and/or interpersonal relationships are enhanced (psychosocial benefit).

Authenticity

This third criterion might better be labeled "originality" if the latter term were not so often confused with novelty. An original response is often unique, but originality is not just novelty. To illustrate the difference, imagine a very talented (but uncreative) art student who copies a masterwork in every detail, so that now there are two paintings—one original and one copy—identical in every detail except for an identifying mark on the back of the canvas. By definition, both paintings, since they are equal in every relevant detail, are equally novel and equally beautiful. Yet we prize the original for the creativity it manifests and only marvel at the copy for its technical expertise. What makes the difference when there is no difference? The original, it may be said, is authentic, and the copy is only a *re*-production.

Originality, in its root meaning, refers to the origin of something. In the above example, we prize the original painting because its origin is, in a sense, internal—a manifestation of the artist's own "genius." The form of the copy, by contrast, is dictated from without; it is a very sophisticated version of "painting by the numbers," so to speak.

Rudolf Arnheim, for many years Professor of the Psychology of Art at Harvard University, has captured well the difference between originality and mere novelty:

> The creative individual has no desire to get away from what is normal and ordinary for the purpose of being different. He is not striving to relinquish the object but to penetrate it according to his own criterion of what looks true. . . . The desire to be different for the sake of difference is harmful, and the urge to evade the given condition derives from a pathological state of affairs inherent either in the situation . . . or in the person, as in the "escape mechanism" of neurotics, attributed to artists by the Freudians. Faced with the pregnant sight of reality, the truly creative person does not move away from it but toward and into it.[2]

Stated somewhat differently, novelty simply for the sake of being different is often a disguise for an underlying fear of involvement in reality. But what is reality? It is not simply the world "out there," devoid of all human passion and desire. The world in which we live is, to a large extent, a symbolic world, a projection of our own needs, values, and ideals. To the extent that such is the case, "the pregnant sight of reality" is actually a confrontation with oneself.

We are now in a position to say more precisely what we mean by authenticity as a criterion for creativity. An authentic response is one that has its origins in the self; it is a true expression of an individual's own personality. And why should that be important for creativity?

The answer to this question is not simple. To the extent that a response meets the criterion of authenticity, it reveals something about the creator—and about ourselves. Through an appreciation of the creative product we experience, albeit vicariously, some of the inner trials and triumphs of the creator. This fact has often been noted with respect to art appreciation, but it is no less true in the case of scientific discoveries. Students in the sciences often repeat (or are required to repeat) classical experiments and discoveries, just as young artists often copy the works of past masters. If the lessons are well learned, the aspiring scientist or artist acquires a way of looking at the world that is similar to, but that eventually will go beyond, the way of the originator.

This brings us to the most important reason that authenticity is prized as a criterion of creativity. In the words of Arnheim quoted above, authenticity involves the "pregnant sight of reality." The emphasis here should be on *pregnant*. Authenticity allows—indeed, demands—further development. The authentic response is vibrant with new possibilities. A copy is stillborn. Unless or until it becomes incorporated as part of another self (in which case it ceases to be a *mere* copy and acquires an authenticity of its own), the copy admits of no further development, for it is cut off from the source of its vitality.

Creative Persons

"There are two kinds of people in the world: Those who think there are two kinds of people and those who don't." This old saw serves as a warning against oversimplification. It is unrealistic to expect people to fall neatly into two categories, the creative and the uncreative. Everyone is creative to some degree; and a person who is highly creative in one domain may be a complete dolt in another.

Even if we limit consideration to persons who are highly creative within a given domain, tremendous individual differences exist. According to popular stereotype, for example, natural scientists (physicists, chemists, engineers, and the like) tend to be cold, rational, meticulous, abstract, and somewhat conventional in their life-style. By contrast, artists and musicians are presumably volatile, expressive, impulsive, and bohemian in life-style.

Although these stereotypes may contain a grain of truth, they can also be misleading.[3] The differences in personality within groups (scientists, say, as opposed to artists) is far greater than average differences between groups. Peter Medawar, himself a Nobel-prize winning biologist, has stated the matter well:

> Scientists are people of very dissimilar temperaments doing different things in very different ways. Among scientists are collectors, classifiers and compulsive tidiers-up; many are detectives by temperament and many are explorers; some are artists and others artisans. There are poet-scientists and philosopher-scientists and even a few mystics.[4]

With such evident diversity, both between and within fields of creative endeavor, any attempt to characterize the creative person might seem doomed to failure. And yet, there is considerable agreement that creative persons share certain characteristics in common, no matter how much they may differ in other respects. A study by Donald MacKinnon and his colleagues at the Institute for Personality Assessment and Research at the University of California, Berkeley, provides a good introduction to these common characteristics.[5] These investigators studied three groups of architects, matched in terms of education and technical competence, but distinguished in terms of creativity as judged by their peers. Included among the assessment procedures was a list of adjectives describing personality characteristics. The architects used the list to rate both their actual selves (how they perceived themselves to be) and their ideal selves (how they would like themselves to be). The following adjectives best distinguished the highly creative architects from their less creative counterparts:

inventive	individualistic	determined
independent	enthusiastic	industrious

The less creative architects had a very different, but in many respects equally positive, self-image. Specifically, they were more likely to rate themselves as:

clear-thinking   sincere   dependable   understanding
responsible   reliable   tolerant

The differences between these two lists of adjectives are instructive. For the most part, the creative architects saw themselves as more autonomous and dedicated to their work, whereas the less creative architects saw themselves as more socially oriented and considerate of the needs of others.

Since the above descriptions are based on self-ratings, their accuracy might be questioned. Perhaps the highly creative architects were simply trying to make themselves look good. That seems unlikely, however, since both sets of descriptions are about equally positive: It is no more desirable to be "inventive" than to be "clear-thinking," or to be "individualistic" than "tolerant," and so forth. According to MacKinnon, moreover, one of the most impressive things about highly creative architects was the degree to which they conformed to the type of person they would like to be. They were not preoccupied with the impression they made on others or the demands others made on them; rather, they were more concerned with living up to their own standards. This does not mean that the creative architects were socially irresponsible; rather, their behavior was guided by aesthetic and ethical standards which they had set for themselves.

Numerous other studies have sought to describe the personality characteristics of creative people.[6] In the following discussion, we will list (in italics) some of the most frequently noted characteristics. But first we must address an apparent paradox: If creative persons are as diverse and individualistic as Medawar contends (see above quote), how can they be described in terms of common characteristics? The resolution to this paradox is found in the following observations by Carl Jung:

> Every creative person is a duality or a synthesis of contradictory qualities. On the one side he is a human being with a personal life, while on the other he is an impersonal, creative process. As a human being he may be sound or morbid, and

his personal psychology can and should be explained in personal terms. But he can be understood as an artist only in terms of his creative achievement.[7]

In other words, to the extent that creative products share certain "impersonal" features (such as novelty, effectiveness, and authenticity), creative persons must share characteristics conducive to those features.

Characteristics Conducive to Novelty

The creative person must be *talented* in his or her field of endeavor (mathematics requires abstract reasoning, writing requires verbal fluency, architecture requires aesthetic sensibility, dance requires bodily coordination, and so forth). This characteristic is perhaps so obvious that a qualification is worth noting. Beyond the minimum or threshold level of talent required to become competent in a given field, creativity depends more on temperamental variables than on talent per se.

Certain temperamental characteristics are, almost by definition, conducive to the production of novelty. For example, creative persons are *sensitive* to subtleties in the environment: They see differences where others see sameness; and, conversely, they see similarities where others see only differences. Creative persons thus have the ability to *recognize patterns and relationships* among disparate events, to forge new links between seemingly irreconcilable elements, to bring order out of chaos. This synthesizing function may be so immediate that it is sometimes described as a kind of "sixth sense" or "leap of intuition"—hence, the frequent characterization of creative persons as *intuitive*.

Sensitivity and intuition are not sufficient for the production of novelty. Creative persons must also be *open-minded, tolerant of ambiguity,* and *flexible* in their approach to a problem, lest novel ideas be squashed at the outset. Even more important is an active *striving after novelty*. Creative persons deliberately seek new and different ways to approach a problem. They are *adventurous* and *willing to take risks*. They do not wait for lightning to strike; they stalk the lightning.

The importance of striving after new ideas is easily illustrated.

If a person had only three novel ideas per day, in one year he or she would have generated over a thousand new ideas. To strive in such a manner, a person must be highly *dedicated* and *persevering*. Not surprisingly, these (dedication and perseverance) are among the most frequently noted characteristics of creative persons. Anne Roe has summarized her research on a group of eminent physical and biological scientists as follows: "There is only one thing which seems to characterize the total group, and that is absorption in their work, over long years, and frequently to the exclusion of everything else."[8]

E. Paul Torrance, who has developed some of the most widely used tests of creativity, has made the same point in a more picturesque way: "The essence of the creative person is being in love with what one is doing. . . . This characteristic makes possible all the other personality characteristics of the creative person."[9]

Characteristics Conducive to Effectiveness

Many of the same characteristics relevant to the production of novelty—sensitivity, adventurousness, perseverance—are also relevant to the achievement of effectiveness. But not all are. For instance, flexibility, open-mindedness, and tolerance may conflict with a selection process that demands high standards and a willingness to impose those standards on one's self and others. Thus, creative persons are often seen as *demanding* and *self-critical*, and at times even *arrogant* and *intolerant*.

Return for a moment to the example of the person who thinks of three new ideas a day, or over a thousand a year. The majority of the ideas would probably be inconsequential at best, and outright silly or dangerous at worst. Creative persons *take responsibility* for recognizing and eliminating ideas and behaviors that are of little consequence. This requires that they be *thorough* and *rigorous*. They must also be *self-confident*, for it is not always easy to admit, even to oneself, when one is wrong; and sometimes it is even difficult to admit to others when one is right, for nonconforming ideas typically meet with criticism, no matter how valid or effective they ultimately may prove to be.

Characteristics Conducive to Authenticity

The creative product, to the extent that it meets the criterion of authenticity, is an extension of the self—an expression of the person's innermost needs, conflicts, and desires. Not surprisingly, therefore, creative persons are often described as *inner-directed, intrinsically motivated,* and *autonomous.* They work, not to please others or for material gain; but because they want to—indeed, because they have to. Research has shown that if people are offered external rewards, such as money, the creativity of the product often declines.[10]

Here we meet another paradox or contradiction in the personality of creative individuals. Although intrinsically motivated, they nevertheless tend to be highly *ambitious* and, more than most people, they *seek recognition* from their peers.

These seemingly opposite characteristics (autonomy yet need for recognition) are understandable once it is realized that a creative product, to the extent that it is authentic, is an extension—an outward manifestation—of the self. Although creative persons may not work in order to achieve fame and fortune, they do crave the self-validation that public recognition implies.

Also related to authenticity are tendencies on the part of creative persons to be *introspective, reflective,* and *self-aware.* Their inspiration comes from within as well as from without.

The last core characteristics of creative persons that we will mention is a *lack of psychological defensiveness.*[11] To the extent that the creative product is an extension of the person's self, its authentic expression cannot be masked and distorted by layers of defense. This does not mean that creative persons are psychologically more healthy than others. In fact, some psychoanalytically oriented theorists maintain that creative undertakings are themselves a defense against incipient psychopathology: The painter paints and the writer writes in order to resolve internal conflicts or to stave off impending anxiety. However that may be, to the extent that creativity is itself a defense, it is not the product of other, less adaptive defenses. This perhaps accounts for the findings that highly creative individuals tend to be, in the words of Frank Barron, "more troubled psychologically, but they also have far greater resources with which to deal with their troubles."[12]

Creative Processes

We have now looked at the *what* of creativity (the product) and the *who* of creativity (the person); it remains to look at the *how* and the *why* of creativity (the underlying processes). By the *how*, we mean the mechanisms or abilities that make creativity possible; by the *why*, we mean the motives or purposes that give creativity direction.

In the previous section, we noted that no matter how much creative persons differ among themselves, they all must share characteristics that contribute to products that are novel, effective, and authentic. The same logic applies to creative processes. On the basis of the evidence that we will review below, we doubt that there is any single process that distinguishes creative from routine activities. Yet it is possible to characterize processes on the basis of their contribution to the criteria for evaluating creative products.

We will consider first the *how* of creativity; and within the how we will make a further distinction between processes related to novelty and those related to effectiveness. (As will be discussed later, motivational processes—the *why* of creativity—are more closely related to the criterion of authenticity.) The dual criteria of novelty and effectiveness suggest a "variation-and-selection" model of creative change. The logic of this model is familiar from its application to biological evolution. Variations arise within a species due to "random" mutation and recombination of genes. Such genetic variation may be stimulated by environmental conditions (e.g., radiation), or may occur "spontaneously." But whatever the source of variation, natural selection favors the more effective (adaptive) outcomes, resulting in the evolution of new and different species.

William James was among the first to note that "a remarkable parallel . . . obtains between the facts of social evolution on the one hand, and of zoological evolution as expounded by Mr. Darwin on the other."[13] Moreover, it is not just social evolution, James argued, that parallels the biological. In the realm of individual mental activity,

> the new conceptions, emotions, and active tendencies which evolve are originally produced in the shape of random images, fancies, accidental out-births of spontaneous variation in the functional activity of the excessively unstable human brain,

which the outer environment simply confirms or refutes, adopts or rejects, preserves or destroys,—selects, in short, just as it selects morphological and social variations due to molecular accidents of an analogous sort.[14]

A variation-and-selection model of psychological creativity is diagrammed in Figure 1. The left-hand side of the figure represents mechanisms for variation (novelty), and the right-hand side represents mechanisms for selection (effectiveness).

In ordinary language, we distinguish among activities that are largely intuitive (spontaneous, holistic, nonlogical, and unconscious) and those that are largely discursive (deliberate, analytic, logical, and conscious). This distinction, which is represented along the vertical axis in Figure 1, finds its counterpart in several well-known theories of creativity. We will describe briefly three such proposals.

Freud considered one of his greatest discoveries to be the distinction between what he called primary and secondary proc-

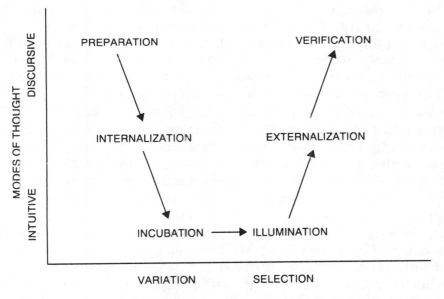

FIGURE 1. Stages in a verification-and-selection model of creative processes. The vertical axis represents the continuum between two modes of thought: intuitive (unconscious and nonlogical) and discursive (inductive and deductive reasoning).

ess.[15] *Primary process* thought is nonrational; time and causality have no meaning; similarities become identities; contradictory ideas can exist in easy compatibility; and remote associations are easily made. Dreaming is a good example of primary process. Secondary process, by contrast, is rational and reality oriented. It is the kind of thought that accompanies deliberate, conscious behavior. Primary process thought, presumably, is related to the generation of novel ideas, while secondary process thought is more closely associated with selection for effectiveness.

J. P. Guilford, coming from an academic rather than a clinical tradition, has also made a twofold distinction among thought processes.[16] Like primary process, *divergent thinking* is marked by flexibility and fluidity; but unlike primary process, it can be conscious, deliberate, and enhanced through learning. "Brainstorming" is a familiar means of facilitating divergent thinking. What Guilford calls *convergent thinking* is similar to Freud's secondary process. It is the kind of thought, logical and focused, that is measured by traditional tests of intelligence (IQ).

As a third example, Arthur Koestler, essayist and social theorist, has distinguished what he calls *bisociative* from *associative* thinking.[17] Routine thought, according to Koestler, typically remains within a given universe of discourse or associative network. For example, when a lawyer approaches a problem, he or she typically draws upon legal precedent and rules of procedure to draw a conclusion. Those precedents and procedures form a matrix within which associations are made and solutions reached. Creativity involves a bisociation of ideas taken from normally independent matrices, as when a lawyer sees a relation between some legal and engineering practice, and thus arrives at a novel solution to a problem. Because bisociation crosses substantive and procedural boundaries, it has many of the same characteristics described above for primary process and divergent thinking.

In relating the above distinctions to creativity, two separate issues must be distinguished. The first issue concerns the existence of distinguishable modes of thought. The second issue concerns whether some modes of thought have a special relation to creativity. On the first issue, there is actually widespread agreement. Biological evolution and social practices assure that a wide variety of mechanisms are involved in the processing of information and the organization of responses. These can be arranged along a dimension that corresponds roughly to the distinction between intuitive and discursive thought depicted in Figure 1.[18]

It is with regard to the second issue that opinions diverge, that is, on whether some modes of thought (such as primary process, divergent thinking, or bisociation) have a special relation to creative as opposed to routine activities. We believe the bulk of the evidence favors those who deny a special process approach. The same thought processes, whether intuitive or discursive, are important in all behavior, albeit perhaps in different combination and degree. There is nothing special about creativity in this regard.[19]

Returning now to Figure 1, creativity does not occur all at once, but unfolds in stages over time. Graham Wallas has distinguished among four stages: preparation, incubation, illumination, and verification.[20] To these four we add two others, namely, internalization on the side of variation and externalization on the side of selection. The relation of these six stages to the intuitive-discursive dimension and to the variation-and-selection dimension is depicted in Figure 1. Each stage is described in more detail below, with illustrative quotations drawn largely from Brewster Ghiselin's excellent anthology of firsthand accounts (by outstanding scientists, artists, and writers) of creative moments and activities.[21]

Processes Related to Novelty (Variation)

The first stage (preparation) is, for the most part, a conscious and deliberate process in which a solution (e.g., to a mathematical problem, or a musical score) is sought. When Isaac Newton was asked how he discovered the law of gravitation, he replied simply, "By thinking on it continually."[22] Unfortunately, thinking on a problem continually sometimes ends not in creative insight, but in frustration. When that occurs, many creative individuals have little tricks or rituals that they deliberately employ to stimulate the flow of ideas. The German poet, Schiller, for example, kept rotten apples under the lid of his desk, so that he could smell the aroma while writing poetry. Others have used more common stimulants— coffee, cigarettes, music, even sexual activity.[23] On a less idiosyncratic level, an artist in search of new ideas may explore different kinds of paint or other media of expression; a writer in need of inspiration may move to a different locale where the scenery, people, and customs are unfamiliar; a scientist working on a new theory may devise experiments to further probe the secrets of nature; a business entrepreneur may conduct brainstorming sessions in an attempt to develop new and useful products; and so forth.

New or unusual situations are not, by themselves, sufficient for the production of novel ideas. The stimuli must be incorporated in such a manner that the person's own cognitive framework or structure of thought is somehow altered. This is the stage of internalization; it is essentially what the developmental psychologist Jean Piaget has termed accommodation.[24] The painter George Rouault has given a more picturesque description of the process:

> In truth, I have painted by opening my eyes day and night on the perceptible world, and also by closing them from time to time that I might better see the vision blossom and submit itself to orderly arrangement.[25]

If in preparation we open our eyes, during internalization we close our eyes so that we may better "see" what we have observed.

The fruit of internalization is not always immediate. Often there follows a period of incubation which may last from a few moments to years. During that time, the person may not be consciously thinking about the issue, and yet problem-solving activity continues outside of awareness and without deliberate effort. The following observations by the French mathematician Henri Poincaré illustrate this stage of the creative process.

Poincaré had been working on a set of problems he called "Fuchsian functions," but to no avail. Then one evening, contrary to habit, he drank some black coffee and was unable to sleep.

> Ideas rose in crowds; I felt them collide until pairs interlocked, so to speak, making a stable combination. By the next morning I had established the existence of a class of Fuchsian functions; I had only to write out the results, which took but a few hours.[26]

Following this incident, Poincaré attempted to relate his discovery to other mathematical functions. However, his work was interrupted by a trip. While on the trip, he set aside all thought of mathematics—or so it seemed to him. Then one day, he entered an omnibus to go somewhere. This is how he described the succeeding events:

At the moment when I put my foot on the step the idea came to me, without anything in my former thoughts seeming to have paved the way for it, that the transformations I had used to define the Fuchsian functions were identical with those of non-Euclidean geometry. I did not verify the idea; I should not have had time, as, upon taking my seat in the omnibus, I went on with a conversation already commenced, but I felt a perfect certainty. On my return to Caen [where he was then living], for conscience's sake I verified the result at my leisure.[27]

There is no reason to doubt the accuracy of Poincaré's description, for many others have described similar events. Moreover, something akin to incubation can be demonstrated in the laboratory.[28] The question is, how is incubation to be explained? And are the cognitive processes that underlie the incubation of creative ideas any different than the processes that underlie the more routine insights of daily life? The first question cannot be answered satisfactorily at the present time, for the relevant cognitive mechanisms are not well understood. Fortunately, an answer to the second question does not depend upon an answer to the first. The same processes that lead to products judged as creative can—and often do—lead to products that are judged pedestrian or mundane. Creativity is not an intrinsic property of any given process, but of the product—which brings us to the mechanisms for selection.

Processes Related to Effectiveness (Selection)

Dean Simonton, Professor of Psychology at the University of California, Davis, has outlined a three-tiered process that corresponds roughly to the illumination, externalization, and verification stages depicted in Figure 1. "The human intellect," Simonton suggests, "is programmed to self-organize its cognition and emotions into hierarchical structures such that experience is most efficaciously organized."[29] That is, when a new thought or feeling contributes to a reorganization of a larger whole, so that the person is able to perceive or think or act more efficiently, the person will be intrinsically rewarded. This constitutes the experience of illumination—the "eureka" or "aha" phenomenon.

We may again turn to the mathematician Poincaré to illustrate this stage of the selection process. Recall Poincaré's earlier description of ideas rising in crowds, colliding and interlocking, until some had formed stable combinations. How did Poincaré recognize which combinations were more stable (i.e., fit) than others? By the degree to which they affected his "emotional sensibility."

> It may be surprising to see emotional sensibility invoked à propos of mathematical demonstrations which, it would seem, can interest only the intellect. This would be to forget the feeling of mathematical beauty, of the harmony of numbers and forms, of geometric elegance. This is a true esthetic feeling that all real mathematicians know, and surely it belongs to emotional sensibility.[30]

Once illumination has been achieved, the creative insight must be externalized—communicated to others. This means that the new combinations of ideas or feelings must be given symbolic form, for example, in words or some other expressive medium (e.g., music, painting, or behavior).

The need to externalize can be an acutely felt and sometimes even painful process. The author Thomas Wolfe describes it in the following manner:

> I actually felt I had a great river thrusting for release inside me and I had to find a channel into which its flood-like power could pour. I knew I had to find it or be destroyed in the flood of my own creation. . . . For the first time I realized another naked fact which every artist must know, and that is that in a man's work there are contained not only the seeds of life, but the seeds of death, and that power of creation which sustains us will also destroy us like a leprosy if we let it rot stillborn in our vitals. I had to get it out of me somehow. I saw that now. And now for the first time a terrible doubt began to creep into my mind that I might not live long enough to get it out of me.[31]

But regardless of the motive or need to externalize, the mere attempt to put the creative insight into symbolic form demands some selection for effectiveness. Insights that cannot be symbolized in some manner can have little effect on the world.

Once given symbolic form, the creative product must meet relevant social criteria of acceptability. A mathematical proof must meet public standards of logic; a work of art must appeal (eventually) to critics and audiences; and so forth. This is the stage of verification. Like the initial preparatory stage, the stage of verification is better understood than the intermediate stages (e.g., of incubation and illumination). To the extent that the distinction between intuitive and discursive thought has any significance, the preparatory and verification stages primarily involve the latter.

Processes Related to Authenticity

We turn now from the *how* of creativity to the *why*, from mechanisms to motives and to the criterion of authenticity. Much speculation has focused on motivational processes related to creativity. For example, most of Freud's writings explicitly related to creativity (e.g., his analysis of Leonardo da Vinci and Michelangelo) focused on the meaning and content of a particular work. Why did da Vinci paint the infant Jesus with two madonnas? Why did Michelangelo sculpt the statue of Moses the way he did? Without going into detail, Freud's answer in both cases lies in unresolved conflicts left over from childhood and unmet needs of the present.

Classical Freudian interpretations have often been criticized for their overreliance on instinctual processes (especially sex and aggression) and their view of creativity as a psychological defense mechanism.[32] However that may be, all motivational explanations suffer from a generic shortcoming, namely, they do not distinguish effective from ineffective products, for example, good art from bad art, or even between art and neurosis. Nevertheless, motivational explanations are crucial to a full understanding of creative activities.

Authenticity, we have said, is one of the main criteria for creativity. For a work to be judged authentic, it must exemplify an individual's values and ideals. In other words, the motive for the work must come from within, and not just from without.

Motives for creativity may vary greatly, from individual to individual, from situation to situation, and from one creative endeavor to another. If it is at all meaningful to speak of a motive for creativity in general, that motive would have to be a drive toward self-realization or self-actualization.[33] This statement may seem too sweeping to have much empirical content. However, it does point to a central truth about creativity that cannot be overemphasized: Creativity is a part of the life process itself. In this respect, perhaps the best answer to the question "Why" has been given by the author Henry Miller.

Writing, like life itself, is a voyage of discovery. The adventure is a metaphysical one: it is a way of approaching life indirectly, of acquiring a total rather than a partial view of the universe. The writer lives between the upper and lower worlds: he takes the path in order eventually to become that path himself.[34]

We cannot, however, leave the topic of motivation at such a general level. People act for specific purposes, to achieve particular goals. Henry Miller did not get out of bed one morning and say to himself, "I think I will write today in order to gain a total view of the universe." At best, this might describe his life activities, not any particular act, no matter how creative. We emphasize this point, for there is a dialectical relation between specific motives and mechanisms involved in any particular creative act. Purposes and processes are not independent.

People are often motivated to do what they are able to do: Mechanisms help determine motives. A person with athletic ability, for example, typically likes to engage in sports; a person with good musical ability enjoys playing an instrument; and so forth. The converse is also true: Motives help determine mechanisms. Within limits, a person who wants to do something can, through hard work and practice, develop the relevant abilities. There are, of course, limits. Not everyone can be an Einstein or a Beethoven, no matter how hard he works. But the limits are less severe than we like to think.

We have argued that no special mechanisms are involved in creativity, beyond those intuitive and discursive processes routinely involved in everyday activities. It follows that everyone has the ability to be creative to some degree. It also follows that motivation is as important as mechanism in determining the final product. In the words of D. N. Perkins: "Purpose shapes process."[35]

To conclude, we have not attempted here to provide a theory or explanation of creativity. That would be impossible, for there is no single or distinctive process that accounts for all creative products. Rather, creativity depends on many routine processes organized to meet goals that reflect a person's own vision of reality (authenticity), that may or may not be out of the ordinary (novelty), and that are of value to the individual or society (effectiveness). A theory of creativity, therefore, would necessarily encompass almost all of psychology.

We started this chapter by asking, What is creativity? We can now provide an answer:

"Creativity" refers to those aspects of a person or process that contribute to a response that is judged to be novel, effective, and authentic.

7

◆

Myths of Creativity

A myth is, of course, not a fairy story. It is the presentation
of facts belonging to one category in the
idioms appropriate to another.
To explode a myth is accordingly
not to deny the facts but
to re-allocate them.
—Gilbert Ryle, *The Concept of Mind*

Creation myths—tales of how the world began—are among the
grandest products of human imagination. How did the world
originate? Did it have a beginning? If so, what existed before the
beginning? Questions such as these have held a special fascination
for humankind. But myths of creation are also myths *about* creativity. We therefore begin this chapter by recounting briefly two
grand myths of creation (Greek and Hebrew); we then describe a
number of more specific myths that surround the creative process
per se.

Early humans drew on two familiar types of creative experience for their myths of creation: biological reproduction and
technological (or artistic) innovation. Correspondingly, many creation myths can be divided into two categories—the universe as a
product of sexual union, and the universe as the work of a master

100

craftsman. Hesiod's *Theogony* is of the first kind; the Biblical story of creation is of the second.

Hesiod's *Theogony* is a long poem written around the eighth century B.C. It tells the story of the Greek gods and the world at the very beginning. First of all, there was Chaos (the unformed primeval substance). From Chaos arose "broad breasted" Gaia (Earth). Erebus (Darkness) and Eros (Love or sexual desire) also arose, evidently, by some form of spontaneous generation. The remainder of creation was largely the product of sexual liaisons among the gods. After making love to Erebus, Gaia gave birth to Ouranus (Sky or Heaven). Ouranus was not only her offspring, but an equal who covered her like a lover might (literally as well as figuratively). Together, they (Gaia and Ouranus, Earth and Sky) begot many children, some of rather remarkable constitution. For example, the three Hecatoncheires each had fifty pairs of shoulders, as many heads, and one hundred arms reaching out in all directions. Not surprisingly, these creatures became formidable foes in subsequent battles among the gods.

Ouranus was a tyrannical father who imprisoned his children within Gaia's ample body. At last, she could tolerate the burden no more. Gaia convinced one of her sons, Cronos, to castrate his oversexed father. The severed genitals, when cast upon the waters, produced even more progeny, including the beautiful goddess, Aphrodite. Ouranus—*sans* genitals—continued to exert a profound influence over the lives of gods and men; he was, after all, the starry sky.

Cronos went on to become a tyrant, only slightly less oppressive than his father. He married his sister, Rhea. Forewarned, however, that he, too, would one day be supplanted by one of his own sons, Cronos devoured the children that Rhea bore him. But, as she was about to give birth to Zeus, Rhea connived with Gaia and Ouranus (who was all too happy to avenge his castration) to hide the child. Cronos was tricked into swallowing a stone instead. Zeus rapidly grew in strength and eventually vanquished his father, who was forced to vomit the offspring that he previously had swallowed. After a long and ferocious battle among the sons of Ouranus and Cronos, Zeus emerged as chief of the Hellenic pantheon, and the one to whom Hesiod dedicated his poem.

The Biblical story of creation is of a far different kind. Devoid of the lust, strife, and chicanery characteristic of the Greek gods, it is much simpler but no less dramatic:

In the beginning God created the heavens and the earth. Now the earth was formless and empty, darkness was over the surface of the deep, and the Spirit of God was hovering over the waters. And God said, "Let there be light," and there was light. God saw that the light was good, and he separated the light from the darkness. God called the light "day" and the darkness he called "night." And there was evening, and there was morning—the first day.[1]

And so on for five more days, followed by a day of rest. Here, God is depicted as a master craftsman, not a cruel and insatiable lover like Ouranus or Cronos. (The Israelites, it might be noted, were no less subject to human foibles than were their Greek counterparts; however, the Israelites did not attribute their own base characteristics to their god.)

What relevance do these myths of creation have for us? Creation myths are prime examples of human creativity—attempts to make meaningful events that seem beyond human comprehension; and the imagery they evoke is as much emotional as intellectual. That is not surprising: Emotions are not simply ways of *re*acting to events taking place in an impersonal world of objective reality. Emotions are subjective; they are ways by which we attempt to understand the world and our place within it. The Greek myths in particular (and later Greek tragedies, which were often based on myths) tend to evoke new and different emotions. It is difficult, for example, to contemplate Cronos castrating his father, marrying his sister, and devouring his children, without some strange mixture of awe and revulsion. The Biblical story of creation, too, has inspired people for millennia with the grandeur of its vision. The same is no less true of the many other myths of creation from around the world that we have not mentioned. They all inspire, fascinate, and provide insight—not so much into the macrocosm that is the world around us, but into the microcosm that is the world within us.

Myths about the creation of the world, it should be evident, are also myths about the creative process itself, and that brings us to the main topic of this chapter—myths of creativity. Our concern is not with grand myths, such as those told by Hesiod or the Bible. Rather, our concern is with myths about the creative acts of ordinary people. Like all good myths, these minor myths of creativity both reveal and obscure some basic truths. An example is the myth that creativity proceeds without rules. We touched on this myth in the previous chapter; however, it is so ingrained in our thinking that it deserves separate treatment. The same is true of the other myths that we will be discussing, namely, that creativity requires little effort (God only had to say, Let there be light, and there was light), that creativity strikes suddenly (like one of Ouranus' cosmic orgasms), that creativity is limited to a few highly gifted individuals (the gods among us), and that creativity is limited to a few domains (the emotions not included).

Creativity Myth #1:
Creativity Proceeds Without Rules

Creative people are often described as a "free spirits," as though they were unfettered by rules. Like many myths, this one contains a grain of truth. Einstein once made the following observation regarding his formal education:

> . . . one had to cram all this stuff into one's mind for the examinations, whether one liked it or not. This coercion had such a deterring effect that, after I had passed the final examination, I found the consideration of any scientific problem distasteful for an entire year.[2]

Many students would heartily endorse the sentiments expressed by Einstein; and even some teachers, afraid that they might inhibit creativity, are loath to impose restrictions and rules on students' work. This is true not only of regulative rules (how a student should learn) but also of constitutive rules (what is learned, e.g., logical or grammatical rules).

However, Einstein's observation is of interest not only for what it says, but also for what it omits. Perhaps no one in this century has been more creative in his own field than was Einstein; and, undoubtedly, this was due, in part, to his formal education. Would Einstein have been even more creative were it not for the "deterring effect" of having to cram "all that stuff" into his head for examinations? It is difficult to imagine how. It is, however, easy to imagine how, with a less rigorous education, Einstein might have been less creative than he was.

There is no contradiction in saying that a condition (in this case, formal education and the rules it entails) can have both an inhibiting and facilitating effect on creativity, although in somewhat different respects.

To take a more specific example of the interaction between rules and creativity, consider the task facing a poet who wishes to write a sonnet. To be counted as a sonnet, the poem must consist of fourteen lines and have a fixed pattern of meter and rhyme. Further stipulations may be imposed, depending on the type of sonnet. In an Italian sonnet (e.g., of the kind written by Dante for Beatrice) the first eight lines, called the *octave,* embody the statement of a theme, and the last six lines (called the *sestet*) provide a resolution. An English sonnet, represented by Shakespeare, follows a somewhat different pattern. It consists of three *quatrains* (four-line stanzas) followed by a *couplet.*

The poet who wishes to be innovative may develop new sets of rules, but while the new rules may differ from custom, they are typically no less constraining in their own way. Again, we take Dante to illustrate the point. As discussed in Chapter 2, Dante divided his Divine Comedy into three parts or "canticles"—*Inferno, Purgatorio,* and *Paradiso.* Each part was further subdivided into 33 cantos, to correspond to Christ's life on earth. (An extra canto was added to the first part to bring the number to an even 100.) Each canto had to be written in groups of three lines, and the second line of each group had to rhyme with the first and third lines of the next group. It is difficult to imagine a more constraining set of rules; and yet those same rules help make the poem the masterpiece that it is.

What is true of poetry is true of other fields of endeavor. Creativity cannot proceed without rules, for rules enable as well as restrict. The rules can, of course, be changed, but they cannot be eliminated completely. That would invite chaos, not creativity.

Creativity Myth #2:
Creativity Requires Little Effort

Creative individuals themselves often perpetuate this myth. Take, for example, the following comment by Willie Nelson: "[T]he air is full of melodies. . . . If I need a melody, I pluck them out of the air. . . . [As soon as I wrote the first words] the rest of the words simply flowed as if someone else was moving my pen."[3] Willie Nelson is a talented musician and song writer; he has also worked hard to develop, foster, and promote his creativity. Creativity, it must be emphasized, does not come easily or naturally. Evidence suggests that about ten years of experience is required to achieve world-class performance in a given field (chess, music, mathematics, etc.), provided one has the ability.[4]

The above generalization would seem to be contradicted by the fact that some people are most creative when they are young, or when they change fields. However, even child prodigies (such as Mozart, who started composing at age four) require many years to "mature." And persons who change fields at an older age seldom make a radical shift. Pavlov, the great Russian physiologist, is a good example. He is best known today for his studies on learning (classical conditioning), which he did not begin until he was in his fifties. However, the switch from gastric physiology (for which Pavlov received a Nobel prize in 1904) to the study of learning was not as radical as might at first appear. Much old knowledge was transferred. Pavlov continued to focus on gastric functions (e.g., salivation) in his learning experiments, and he always considered that he was doing physiology, not psychology.

The case of Pavlov is typical. Often the greatest innovations occur when knowledge and skills acquired over many years are applied to new problems.

Creativity Myth #3:
Creativity Strikes Suddenly

In commenting on his composition of *Thus Spake Zarathustra*, the philosopher Nietzsche made the following observation:

> The notion of revelation describes the condition quite simply; by which I mean that something profoundly convulsive and disturbing suddenly becomes visible and audible with indescribable definiteness and exactness. One hears—one does not seek; one takes—one does not ask who gives; a thought flashes out like lighting, inevitably without hesitation—I have never had any choice about it.[5]

Many similar observations by highly creative individuals could easily be cited. (Recall, for example, the descriptions by Poincaré of his mathematical discoveries, discussed in Chapter 6). There is no reason to doubt the accuracy of most such descriptions. However, they tell only part of the story. In Chapter 6, we divided creativity into six stages: preparation, internalization, incubation, illumination, externalization, and verification. If we focus only on the stage of illumination, then creativity may indeed strike suddenly, like the proverbial bolt of lightning. It must be remembered, however, that lightning is only the culmination of a slow process in which electric charges accumulate until they reach the flash point. The same is true of sudden flashes of insight or illumination. To repeat what we have said before, creativity involves a long and often arduous process from preparation to verification. Moments of illumination are only a small, albeit dramatic, part of the story.

Creativity Myth #4:
Creativity Is Limited to a Few Highly Gifted People

Some of the things that are written about creativity would lead us to believe that it is characteristic of a select few. Again, that is true, but only in a superficial or even trivial sense. Great accomplishments are, by definition, rare. Not everyone has the talent to be a great mathematician, artist, or athlete. Rarity, however, is a relative concept; and so, too, is creativity.

If ordinary people had the talents of an Einstein, then the achievements of Einstein would strike us as average or routine. Conversely, if human evolution had stopped at the level, say, of *Homo habilis*, with a cranial capacity roughly half that of our own species *(Homo sapiens)*, then a modern human of very modest ability might easily be accorded the status of an Einstein.

Everyone has the talent to be creative to some degree; indeed, to a much greater degree than is commonly assumed, especially if the field of endeavor is taken into account. Watch children at play. In some respects, they are among the most creative of all individuals. They are adventuresome, imaginative, energetic, and freely expressive. They are not bound by the restrictions and often rigid expectations that we, as adults, have placed on ourselves. To be creative in everyday affairs, we do not need the talents of an Einstein, only the freshness and enthusiasm of a child.

Creativity Myth #5:
Creativity Is Limited to a Few Domains

According to this myth, there are only a few fields of endeavor in which creativity is possible. It is certainly true that excellence in certain activities, such as art and science, calls for a high degree of creativity. However, there is ample room for creativity in almost any undertaking. Ruth Richards and her colleagues at Harvard Medical School have developed what they call the Lifetime Creativity Scales.[6] Ordinary people are asked to describe their most creative undertakings in both work and leisure activities. These descriptions are then scored for creativity by trained judges. An example of low creativity is the person who washed store windows for several years under a foreman's supervision, then worked on an assembly line in several factories, and, finally, spent a decade doing routine quality-control for a brewery. At the opposite extreme is the person who designed and constructed a complex apparatus to help her handicapped child move about, change posture, and manipulate objects. Subsequently, she worked as a volunteer teacher helping other handicapped children to use her invention.

Richards and her colleagues not only found that creative accomplishments are common in all types of work and leisure activity, but that such accomplishments are only moderately correlated with education, socioeconomic status, or intelligence. This reinforces the point we made in connection with Myth #4, namely, creativity is not limited to a few highly gifted individuals any more than it is limited to a few domains of activity.

Implications for Emotional Creativity

What are we to conclude from this brief discussion of myths of creativity? Namely this: As long as we believe that creativity proceeds without rules, requires little effort, and strikes suddenly, we are unlikely to devote the time and effort to be truly creative; and as long as we believe that creativity is possessed only by a select few, we may believe that creativity is beyond our reach, regardless of effort; and, finally, as long as we believe that creativity is limited to a few domains, we may fail to meet the challenges and realize the opportunities that are everywhere around us. Our lives thus become narrow and restricted. Nowhere is this more true than in the area of emotions, which many consider to lie outside the domain of creativity. That is perhaps the most limiting myth of all.

8

◆

Emotional Creativity

> I go to encounter for the millionth time the reality
> of experience and to forge in the
> smithy of my soul the uncreated
> conscience of my race.
> —Joyce, *Portrait of an*
> *Artist as a Young Man*

The two terms, "emotional" and "creativity" are in many ways incompatible. For example, emotions are often viewed as primitive, stereotyped responses over which we have little control; creativity, by contrast, calls for flexibility, openness, and deliberation. By now, we hope it is evident that things are not so simple as this stark contrast might imply. In fact, emotional and creative responses are in important respects more similar than different. To illustrate, consider the following observation by Dostoyevsky:

> If you wish—he [the author or poet] is not the creator; life is—the powerful essense of life, the living and essential God, putting his strength in many distinct creations at various places, and most of all in the great heart and in the strong poet, so that if the poet himself is not a creator—(and one must agree with this . . . because certainly a creative work comes

109

suddenly, as a complete whole, finished and ready, out of the soul of a poet). . . . [1]

This observation by Dostoyevsky is somewhat mythical, as described in the previous chapter, but it is a myth that applies to emotions as well as to creativity. For many people, emotions are "the powerful essence of life," put in us by nature, if not by God.

In *The Person and Primary Emotions*, Peter Bertocci has gone further than simply comparing emotions and creativity; he argues that creativity *is* an irreducible emotion that is accompanied by the experience of "enlivement." There is an innate striving toward creativity, according to Bertocci, just as there are innate strivings toward self- and species-preservation.[2]

We agree with Bertocci that people are inherently creative, that creativity is an integral part of life, but we disagree that creativity can be considered an emotion in its own right (any more than self-preservation can be considered an emotion in its own right). What we do suggest is that emotions can be—and often are—the *products* of creative endeavors. Observations such as those by Dostoyevsky and Bertocci are of relevance primarily as they help breach the conceptual barriers that have traditionally separated these two domains of human activity.

In Chapter 6, we gave the following general definition of creativity:

> Creativity refers to those aspects of a person or process that contribute to a response that is judged to be novel, effective, and authentic.

This definition can be applied directly to the emotions. Specifically, an emotional response is creative if it is in some way *novel* with respect to the individual or group; if it is *effective* in enhancing the well-being of the individual and/or society; and if it is *authentic,* that is, a reflection of the individual's own self.

Novelty

As described in Chapter 1, an emotional response may be novel in any of three ways; these ways help define what we have called the art (acquisition, refinement, and transformation) of emotion. First, a newly *acquired* response may be novel for the individual, yet quite standard for the group. A familiar example would be first love, which may require a good deal of creativity on the part of the individual (usually an adolescent), the performance of which may nevertheless appear amateurish and even bumbling to others. Second, an already acquired response, one that is standard within the society, may be *refined* and applied in novel ways. For example, in order to maintain discipline in a classroom, a teacher may have to be highly creative in the way he or she experiences and expresses anger. Third, a completely new and different emotional syndrome may be developed, one that is not standard for the culture, and hence that cannot easily be described in ordinary language. A good deal of art and poetry is an attempt to give form to such *transformed* emotional experiences.

Acquiring a Standard Emotional Response

In the broadest sense all learning is to a degree creative, in that it requires the acquisition of new ways of thinking and responding on the part of the individual. We tend to overlook this rather simple fact, since what is learned is often "old hat" from the point of view of more experienced observers. A child learning long division for the first time is being creative, although the response might not be recognized as innovative by parents, teachers, and older school-mates. And developing artists often spend long hours copying the works of past masters, trying to develop their own skills. This, too, is creative activity, although it is not generally recognized as such since the final product is a "mere copy."

Emotional development on the part of children is also a creative endeavor. Children play at being angry, sad, in love, etc., just as they play at being doctors, lawyers, parents, and garbage collectors. And, through example and sometimes explicit instruction, they are taught the emotions appropriate to their culture. Too often, however, emotional instruction is haphazard, incomplete, or even faulty. As a result, a person may grow up emotionally illiterate, unable to experience the depth, warmth, and meaning normally associated with the emotions. For example, the person may not be able to become angry or afraid under appropriate circumstances, or to experience intimacy. On an even broader scale, the person may have difficulty experiencing emotions at all. In such cases, simply to learn to experience emotions in an ordinary way may require a good deal of creativity, even though that creativity may not be noticed or acknowledged by an outside observer.

To illustrate this kind of emotional creativity, we recount the story of Cassie, an emotionally impoverished but highly resourceful middle-aged woman. Cassie had been abandoned by her mother at a very young age. Her father remarried when she was five, but her stepmother was a cold, embittered woman who was extremely harsh with her. Cassie became quiet and withdrawn, trying very hard to please everyone around her by "looking pretty and acting pretty." She worked at not feeling pain, but in the process of not feeling pain, she shut herself off from other emotions as well, and thus she never acquired the normal repertoire of adult emotions. For much of her adult life she felt little except emptiness, depression, and loneliness. Joy, pleasure, and even sexual arousal were foreign to her. Ultimately, she lost the desire to live. Here is how she told her own story during an interview:

> *Because of the pain, I spent a good part of my life not feeling. Even when I did things I really wanted to do, they brought me little pleasure or joy, and I couldn't figure out why. I'd go through all the motions (not emotions, motions), and I'd think, Why don't I feel something?*
>
> *Feelings and emotions are all interconnected. You cannot kill one emotion and nurture another. So, when I refused to feel pain, I just got numb—cut off from the capacity to give or receive love or to know joy. To live without feeling is like being dead, like existing in a body and yet not being there at all—in a body, that is.*

That is how Cassie described her life up to the point that she faced a series of major crises: She graduated from college (as an older, "nontraditional" student); her children, now grown, left home; she stopped attending the church in which she was raised; she went to work outside the home; and she separated from her husband. In learning to cope constructively with these changes, she also learned to experience new emotions.

> *As painful as all this was, and it was extremely painful, I am grateful because I felt, really felt, every bit of it. It's wonderful to feel, to look forward to the next day, just to be alive. I want to tell you something about this being alive. . . . I know what it's*

like to be dead, and I know what it's like to be alive. I chose life, and it shows.

People even respond to me differently. For example, previously in my place of employment, I was a loner. People would speak, but they spent their time with someone else. They didn't ask me to have lunch with them nor would I ask them. I doubt they noticed me. I told myself that was the way I wanted it, that I liked being all alone. The truth is, I didn't like *the isolation; I was* comfortable *with it. I am learning there's a big difference between liking something and being comfortable with it. Anyway, now I'm included in everything; my coworkers want to eat with me, talk to me, be with me. What I've learned is—when I feel better about me, everyone feels better about me.*

At this point, Cassie was experiencing many emotions that other people in our culture take for granted. Yet, they were new and different *for her*. She was, in a very real sense, being emotionally creative, and quite effectively so.

Refining a Standard Emotion to Fit New Contexts

A person may be capable of responding adequately (e.g., with anger, fear, love) under some circumstances but not others. In such a case, creativity may involve using familiar responses in novel ways. That is what we mean by emotional refinement. In Chapter 1, we used the fictional character of Don Juan to illustrate emotional refinement. Don Juan refined love to such a degree that he was able to apply it in many, but not always appropriate, circumstances. At the opposite extreme, demonstrating a lack of refinement, is the movie villain who has no compunction about killing people, but who grieves at the death of a dog. The villain has failed to extend a normal emotion (grief) to all appropriate circumstances.

Unfortunately, not all instances of emotional refinement are as clear-cut as these fictional examples might suggest. But imagine being joyful in a situation where you are degraded in some fashion, for example, by a slap in the face. In Part I of his *Notes from Underground*, Dostoyevsky, who was highly creative emotionally as well as artistically, describes such an emotional experience.

I'm terribly proud. I'm as mistrustful and as sensitive as a hunchback or a dwarf; but in truth, I've experienced some moments when, if someone had slapped my face, I might even have been grateful for it. I'm being serious. I probably would have been able to derive a peculiar sort of pleasure from it—the pleasure of despair, naturally, but the most intense pleasures occur in despair, especially when you're very acutely aware of your own predicament.[3]

From this brief passage, it is difficult to determine whether Dostoyevsky was experiencing a standard emotion in a highly personalized way, or whether he was experiencing a different kind of emotion altogether (a "peculiar sort of pleasure," one born of despair). Perhaps it does not matter, for once a person acquires a standard emotion, the process of refinement and even transformation may begin.

Cassie, whose experiences we described above, also illustrates the progression from acquisition to refinement—indeed, in a manner not too dissimilar to that described by Dostoyevsky. A major conflict developed between Cassie and one of her adult daughters. Cassie had always prided herself on putting her children's wishes before her own. But now circumstances arose that pitted her needs against those of her daughter. They both cared for the same man, and Cassie made a decision to put her own aspirations first—not in a selfish way, but simply by giving due recognition to her own legitimate rights and desires. She knew that she risked the wrath of her daughter and even other members of her family. However, there were also gains to be had.

For the first time, I didn't block out, withdraw emotionally, or dilute my feelings with drugs or alcohol. I stayed in the present and dealt with the situation as it was. I remember well the afternoon Linda [her daughter] came over. She was out of control, screaming accusations and even becoming physically violent. She certainly was not open to reason or discussion. Strangely, throughout all this distress and pain (which was considerable), I experienced an intense, underlying joy and sense of aliveness. For the first time I didn't abandon myself or my needs in deference to someone else. I was alive. I was experiencing life. I'd been working hard on myself and this was tangible evidence that I'd grown emotionally. I had finally become my own best friend.

Cassie had refined or personalized her emotions so that they now worked for her. She no longer felt empty, as though she were playing a role dictated by others.

Transforming Emotional Responses

The highest level of emotional creativity involves the development of new and different emotional responses. As discussed in Chapter 4, emotions are constituted according to rules; if those (constitutive) rules are changed, or new rules developed, a new kind of emotion will ensue. This is the most difficult kind of emotional creativity to describe or illustrate. By definition, if the experience is truly new, words do not exist in ordinary language to describe it. And when the person tries to put the experience into words, it necessarily becomes circumscribed and accrues some of the meaning connoted by those words. Borrowing terminology from Piaget, novel emotional experiences are continually being *assimilated* into preexisting categories of thought, even while the latter are being *accommodated* (transformed) to suit the new experience.[4] This means that the dividing line between the refinement and transformation of emotional responses is necessarily vague and shifting.

Perhaps the best source for descriptions of transformed emotional experiences, at least in incipient form, is the literature on mysticism. The Canadian psychiatrist R. M. Bucke has referred to such experiences as "cosmic consciousness," a term commonly adopted by others. According to Bucke:

> The prime characteristic of cosmic consciousness is, as its name implies, a consciousness of the cosmos, that is, of the life and order of the universe. . . . Along with the consciousness of the cosmos there occurs an intellectual enlightenment or illumination which alone would place the individual on a new plane of existence—would make him almost a member of a new species. To this is added a state of moral exaltation, an indescribable feeling of elevation, elation, and joyousness, and a quickening of the moral sense, which is fully as striking and more important than is the enhanced intellectual power. With these come what may be called a sense of immortality, a consciousness of eternal life, not a conviction that he shall have this, but the consciousness that he has it already.[5]

The kind of experience described by Bucke is not as unusual as is often assumed. In a national survey, the sociologist and novelist Andrew Greeley found that 35 percent of Americans reported having had at least one mystic-like experience, and 5 percent have had such experiences repeatedly.[6] Common triggers for such experiences are natural wonders (sunsets, etc.), music and art, sexual intimacy, intellectual conversations, and meditation.

Cassie, whose experiences we have already discussed with reference to emotional acquisition and refinement, gave the following description of emotional transformation. Shortly after the episode with her daughter described earlier, Cassie was engaged in a conversation with a man whom she found very stimulating.

Stan and I were in the kitchen. Stan was working, and we were talking. I asked when and how he had developed his sensitivity and gentleness. Then he came to where I was sitting and knelt down. He touched me gently and spoke softly—telling me how he felt, making love with words.

It wasn't really physical, but I felt it physically—like an all over experience. It was like I opened myself completely to see and hear what he was saying, and I felt what he was feeling and saw what he saw. When it happened I stood up, sucked my breath in deeply several times, and tears came. It was like an explosion in my head, not a violent explosion, more like an energy burst. I felt it in my head and all around me. Then I felt real weak. This lasted eight to ten seconds. It wasn't a physical orgasm—not connected with a sexual orgasm. It was like an emotional orgasm. A soul orgasm. It was transforming—like crossing over into emotional freedom. I felt emotionally satisfied in and around my body, but my body wasn't involved. After a while there was a gentle energy—our energies mingled and settled around us. It was like we flowed together without saying a word. That's the emotion. There's no words for it—just no words. I just felt it.

I wasn't the same after that. I wasn't as closed emotionally. I became more open to challenge—freer in my thinking and physical response. I reached a point of development that I'd been working toward for a long time. It was like an old door that you have to work on, oil its hinges, etc., until it finally opens; or like a plant that you prune and nurture until it finally blooms. Once you reach that level, you can never go back.

Needless to say, not all transformed emotional experiences are as dramatic or positive as this one by Cassie. In fact, some can be terrifying. Consider the following description by an anonymous surgeon of an anxiety attack:

It is as difficult to describe to others what an acute anxiety state feels like as to convey to the inexperienced the feeling of falling in love. Perhaps the most characteristic impression is the constant state of causeless and apparently meaningless alarm. You feel as if you were on the battlefield or had stumbled against a wild animal in the dark, and all the time you are conversing with your fellows in normal and peaceful sur-roundings and performing duties you have done for years. With this your head feels vague and immense and stuffed with cotton wool; it is difficult, and trying, to concentrate; and, most frightening of all, the quality of your sensory appreciation of the universe undergoes an essential change.[7]

Experiences such as those described by Bucke, Cassie, and the unnamed surgeon represent the early, highly fluid stages of trans-formed emotional responses. If they are to be effective or adaptive, they must be allowed to solidify into meaningful patterns of response. Nor should it be assumed that the vague feelings of anxiety described by the surgeon are independent of the more ecstatic kinds of experiences described by Bucke and Cassie. In Nietzsche's words, "One must still have chaos within oneself to be able to give birth to a dancing star."[8]

Effectiveness

No matter how novel an emotional response might be (in any of the three senses described above—acquisition, refinement, transfor-mation), it must also be of some value to the individual or group before it can be regarded as truly creative. Simply stated, the emotionally creative response should be adaptive, or meet certain standards of excellence.

In what ways can an emotion be effective or adaptive? Most emotions are ways of dealing with problems that tax an individual's usual coping resources. Anger is a good example. The most typical occasion for anger is a wrong committed by another, either deliberately or through negligence. Anger is effective if it corrects the wrong and restores amicable relationships. It is ineffective if it is unwarranted or exceeds the provocation, thus inviting retaliation, or if it remains unexpressed, thus leaving the situation unchanged.

Most emotions are like anger in that they have specific aims or objectives, such as escaping from danger in the case of fear, making retribution in the case of guilt, protecting a relationship in the case of jealousy, and so forth. But not all emotions have an aim in this sense—joy and grief, for example, seem to have no aim beyond themselves. Yet, even these "aimless" emotions can be expressed well or poorly, appropriately or inappropriately. The person who experiences more joy than is called for by the situation, or too little joy, is liable to be considered either superficial or mean-spirited. The same is true with respect to grief. In the novel *The Stranger*, by Albert Camus, the protagonist is convicted of murdering a stranger; one of the main pieces of "evidence" used against him is that he did not grieve appropriately at his mother's funeral.

At a higher level of abstraction, we may enumerate a number of values that emotions should fulfill if they are to be truly effective. Among the most important of these are vitality and a sense of aliveness; fullness and complexity of life; and integration and harmony, both within the self and between the self and others. Stated most generally, an emotionally creative response should help expand personal horizons and enhance interpersonal relationships. Ideally, the emotionally creative person reaches a new level of integration and a new and higher maturity.

The ideal is a goal to be striven after; it is seldom fully achieved in practice. Nor should it be, for that would mean an end to striving—and to creativity.

At this point, a qualification needs to be added. Emotional creativity—perhaps more than creativity in any other domain—is liable to meet with misunderstanding and even censure. Sometimes the censure reflects a realistic assessment of the situation; emotional innovation can be disruptive of social relations, and creativity is no guarantee of wisdom. Too often, however, the censure reflects ignorance, or even worse. Conventional people may perceive deviations from accepted social standards as criticisms of themselves; or, they may be envious of the freedom that the creative individual exhibits, a freedom they are unable or unwilling to exercise. In any event, an emotionally creative response, even when effective from the individual's own perspective, may be accompanied by unavoidable social strain. This is illustrated on a small scale by a young woman named Dawn.

Dawn didn't feel her husband was treating her with courtesy and respect. He expected her to be submissive and obedient, while at the same time he was dependent on her. For example, once when she wanted to attend a week–long conference, he told her to go ahead, but he would get his sexual needs taken care of elsewhere. She had always done as he asked, but no longer. She was tired of being treated as a child. She tried to share her experiences and aspirations with her husband; it was as though they spoke two different languages. He heard the words, but ignored their meanings. He initially agreed to enter therapy with her, but soon did what people often do when threatened: He withdrew from therapy, increased his use of alcohol and marijuana, and became more unyielding and sarcastic. When this didn't work, he resorted to more menacing and violent tactics. This did work for a while, but then Dawn decided she could not stay in the relationship and maintain her integrity. The marriage dissolved.

The criterion of effectiveness or adaptiveness may appear simple at first, but as the case of Dawn illustrates, it is actually quite complicated. From the perspective of her own personal growth, Dawn's openness to new experiences could be judged adaptive, but from the perspective of her marriage (which ended in divorce), it was not. A response is never effective in and of itself; it is only effective with respect to some situation or goal. What is effective when viewed from one perspective may be ineffective, even maladaptive, when viewed from another perspective. In evaluating emotional creativity, we should in general take a broad perspective: *In the long run*, are personal horizons expanded and interpersonal relationships enhanced? Often, it is only in retrospect that an accurate assessment can be made.

Authenticity

Our third criterion for creativity is authenticity or originality. The creative product should reflect in some fashion the individual's own values and beliefs about the world. Authenticity in this sense is often confused with novelty, but as explained in Chapter 6, the two are actually quite distinct. We are sometimes more authentic when we conform rather than diverge from social expectations—provided we have adopted those expectations as our own. Too often, authenticity is sacrificed in a vain attempt to be different.

What makes an emotional response authentic? To answer this question, it is helpful to begin with the unauthentic. In everyday affairs, when we say that an emotion is unauthentic, we typically mean that there is a disjunction between the internal experience and its external manifestation. For example, an employee may present a calm and polite exterior to his boss while seething on the inside. Conversely, a parent may scold a child in mock anger while inwardly laughing at the child's antics. When the disjunction is deliberate, as in these examples, we have an intuitively obvious contrast by which to distinguish the authentic from the unauthentic. But what if we ask about the authenticity of an unfeigned emotion, or about the internal experience of emotion? For such a question to be meaningful, we must also have some contrast in mind. What might that contrast be?

Physical pain is an experience that most people regard as incorrigible. If I feel a pain, the experience is real, immediate, and unquestionable. Its authenticity is beyond dispute. Or is it? Consider the following: Under hypnosis, a person may experience pain when no adequate stimulus is present. In this case, we might say that the pain, although real, is unauthentic.[9]

As the example of pain illustrates, authenticity is not an inherent property of experience; it is a judgment about experience. Like any judgment, authenticity is based on presuppositions. For the most part, these presuppositions have to do with the perceived best interests of the individual or, in a more extended sense, with the best interests ("true values") of the group (which sometimes may be contrary to the welfare of the individual). In the case of pain, the best interests of the individual are seldom in doubt; and hence, only under highly unusual circumstances (such as hypnosis) does the question of authenticity even arise. The emotions are far more complicated in this regard, for they are partly constituted by social norms and expectancies that may vary from one group to another. Thus, one person's anger, no matter how keenly felt, may be denied legitimacy by another person who approaches the issue from a different ideological stance. In terms of the current argot, the former person (from the standpoint of the other) is suffering from "false consciousness."

We have argued that standard emotions are, for the most part, social constructions. The relationship, however, is bi-directional, not one way. That is, emotions are not only socially constituted, they also help to sustain and validate the norms and rules, beliefs and values, that provide the blueprint for their construction. This dialectic between emotions and social norms is perhaps best exemplified during religious or political conversions. How does the convert know that he or she has "arrived"? In part, by experiencing the emotions considered authentic by the new reference group. But there is a catch. If the emotions are recognized as social constructions, they lose some of their air of authenticity. Why should one emotion be considered more authentic than another if both are socially constituted? The way out of this dilemma is to postulate that the new emotions reflect the person's own true self, independent of social influence. They were there all along but had been submerged, repressed, or otherwise denied awareness.

From these considerations, it is apparent that emotional creativity—to the extent that it meets the criterion of authenticity— necessarily involves self-creation. We shall return to this issue in Chapter 10.

We may summarize the observations of this chapter with the following definition:

> Emotional creativity is *expressing oneself* (authenticity) in *new and unique* ways (novelty), such that one's *personal horizons are expanded* and *interpersonal relationships enhanced* (effectiveness).

9

What Emotional Creativity Is Not

For sweetest things turn sourest by their deeds;
Lilies that fester smell far worse than weeds.
—Shakespeare, Sonnet, 94

Folly is wont to have more followers and
comrades than discretion.
—Cervantes, *Don Quixote*

We devoted Chapter 5 to myths of emotion and Chapter 7 to myths of creativity. It might therefore seem appropriate to devote this chapter to myths of emotional creativity. However, the idea of emotional creativity, although not without precedent, is relatively new. Hence, there are few well-established myths surrounding it. In fact, the major myth of emotional creativity is that it does not exist. Nevertheless, the idea of emotional creativity carries considerable potential for misunderstanding and even mischief. We therefore devote this brief chapter to some possible misconceptions about emotional creativity.

Emotional Creativity Is Not Emotional Reactivity

Anybody can throw a bucket of paint on an empty canvas, but a mere splash of paint, no matter how colorful or dramatic, does not constitute a creative work of art. Similarly, anybody is capable of an emotional outburst, but emotional outbursts per se are not a sign of emotional creativity.

People who are otherwise quite critical—for example, with respect to business or politics—may embrace a superficial emotionality with an earnestness and enthusiasm that borders on the ludicrous. They are ready to accept nearly any emotion—whether it be anger, love, grief, or whatever—no matter how excessive or inappropriate to the situation, as long as it is somehow "authentic." This overvaluation of the emotions, this belief that affect and feeling are ends in themselves, is a kind of dilettantism.

Psychotherapists sometimes inadvertently abet this tendency when they advise clients to express their emotions, not to "bottle their feelings up," lest some dire consequences follow. But emotional expression alone will not solve a client's problem; the emotion should be expressed with grace and tact; even more importantly, it should in some way relate to or form part of a more coherent self.

In short, emotional creativity cannot flourish apart from a reasonable and realistic philosophy of life. Emotional creativity has more to do with the quality of experience than with the quantity or intensity of feeling.

Emotional Creativity Is Not Immersion in the Inner Self

In Chapter 4, we discussed a number of "family resemblances" that help characterize emotional responses. Included among these was subjectivity. Emotions are subjective or "inner" experiences. At least, that is part of our conception of emotion. It is also part of our conception of creativity that it should be authentic; that is, the creative response should stem from within and not simply be a reaction to external circumstances. This emphasis on the subjective aspects of both emotions and creativity might lead to the misconception that emotional creativity has little to do with external or objective reality. That is not true, as the following parable by Bertrand Russell suggests:

> Two sausage machines were exquisitely constructed for turning pigs into fine meat. One of the machines turned introspective, fascinated by the intricacies of its own internal workings. It thereupon refused to accept more pig and set to studying its own insides. Without pig, however, its insides ceased to function, and the more it studied itself, the more impoverished it became. All the exquisite machinery that previously had transformed pig into sausage now ran idle, seemingly without purpose and certainly without product. The other machine, by contrast, retained its interest in pig, and continued to create the most wonderful sausage.[1]

It is a silly little parable, but it makes an important point: Persons who ignore the external world and become absorbed in their own inner workings are unlikely to be creative, emotionally or otherwise. The world is full of drama—the tragic, sad, fearsome, comic, heroic, puzzling, and awe-inspiring. Those are necessary ingredients for emotional creativity.

Emotional Creativity Is Not a License to Do Whatever One Pleases

One of the most important misconceptions we want to short-circuit is the notion that emotional creativity is justification to "let it all hang out." Emotional inhibition is sometimes viewed as a deterrent to authentic growth, and possibly even dangerous to one's health. In some cases, that can be true. However, emotional creativity involves knowing how *not* to respond, as well as knowing how to respond. Effectiveness almost always demands some inhibition or regulation of behavior.

This issue can be approached from another direction. Among the myths of creativity discussed in Chapter 7 was the notion that creativity proceeds without rules. That myth is no more applicable to emotional creativity than it is to creativity in other domains. As was discussed in detail in Chapter 4, emotions are constituted and regulated by rules. Rules inhibit, but they also enable. Without rules, a person's emotional life would be a disorganized hodge-podge, dominated by vague feelings of anxiety and depression.

Emotional creativity, then, is not a license to flaunt social standards and decorum. Emotional creativity, if it meets the criterion of novelty, may go against conventional standards of conduct. But most conventional standards are not without reason; they are typically the product of a long history of social evolution. The desire to be different for difference's sake is more often the sign of immaturity than creativity.

Emotional Creativity Is Not Happiness or Adjustment

The requirement that a creative emotional response be effective (enhance a person's self and interpersonal relationships) is subject to misunderstanding. This requirement does not imply that the emotionally creative individual is any happier or better adjusted than less creative individuals. Often, the opposite is true.

In evaluating the effectiveness of a response, two crucial distinctions must be kept in mind. The first distinction is between short- versus long-term effects; the second is between individual versus group or social effects. A response that is adaptive in the short run may be maladaptive in the long run, and vice versa. As will be discussed in Chapter 13, many neurotic responses (e.g., obsessive-compulsive behavior) may provide immediate satisfaction or solution to some problem, but at the cost of long-term effectiveness. Similarly, a response that is adaptive for the individual may be maladaptive from a larger (group) perspective. Thus, abandonment might satisfy the needs of a disaffected spouse, but at considerable cost to other family members and ultimately to society.

Creativity involves change; and change, at least in the short run, generally involves turmoil and disruption. Hence, emotional creativity will more often than not be associated with a good deal of anxiety, depression, and even guilt. Moreover, new forms of emotion are likely to call into question values that are deeply held by the group. The emotionally creative individual is therefore likely to suffer condemnation and even ostracism by others.

In what sense, then, can an emotionally creative response be judged as "effective"? In the final analysis, the judgment must be made from the point of view of the individual's life as a whole—and that judgment can sometimes be made only posthumously. Many emotionally creative individuals (e.g., Nietzsche, van Gogh, Dostoyevsky) have, in fact, paid dearly for their creativity during their lifetime. We, posterity, are the ones who reap the benefits of their endeavors.

Fortunately, most emotionally creative responses need not await the judgment of posterity before their effectiveness can be judged. It remains the case, however, that emotional creativity is a difficult and often painful endeavor, with no guarantee of success or happiness. To undertake such an endeavor a person must have a sense of purpose, a vision of what the future could be, whether or not the goal is achieved by oneself. If a person adopts this outlook, then a kind of adjustment, a deep sense of well-being, is possible regardless of one's immediate or personal fate.

Emotional Creativity Is Not Mere Excitement or Pleasure Seeking

From what has been said thus far, it should be clear that emotional creativity is not simply the pursuit of pleasure and excitement. On the contrary, pleasure seeking is often little more than a form of escape. It is a way to lose oneself in the moment, temporarily camouflaging the dullness or unbearable chaos of one's existence.

Too much stimulation dulls the taste for the more subtle pleasures of life. The person who habituates to very spicy food can no longer enjoy mild or delicate flavors. And in the quest for ever spicier food, the nutritional value of what one eats may become secondary. Poor health, and an ultimate loss of enjoyment, may thus be the price paid for momentary titillations of the palate. What is true of the palate is also true of other forms of pleasure.

On the surface, Judd seemed to epitomize the American success story. Born poor, he had to go to work at 14 to help support the family. But by the time he was 35, he was a millionaire several times over, having amassed a fortune in the oil business. He married a beautiful woman and had two fine children. His closet was full of tailor-made suits and other fine clothes. He had sports cars, his own Lear jet, and a cabin cruiser. And he became bored. He sought the company of other women; he raced cars and horses. They, too, lost their appeal. He tried cocaine, but that only briefly covered the sense of dullness that had come to pervade his life. His wife finally decided that no amount of money was worth what she was going through, and she left him. In short succession, he also suffered a heart attack and lost a fortune in the collapse of the oil boom. He was contemplating suicide when he sought therapy.

In one respect, Judd was more fortunate than many people— he realized before it was too late that there is more to life than pleasure seeking and excitement. As we will discuss in Chapter 15, pleasure presents a surprisingly difficult challenge to emotional creativity.

Emotional Creativity Is Not Found in Drugs

One morning in May, 1953, Aldous Huxley swallowed four-tenths of a gram of mescaline dissolved in a glass of water. It was an "experiment," conducted in collaboration with an experienced observer, designed to gather data on the psychological effects of the drug. Huxley subsequently wrote a small book, *The Doors of Perception*, describing his experiences. In part because he was a noted author, and in part because of the evolving *Zeitgeist*, Huxley's book helped to popularize the notion that mind-altering or "consciousness expanding" drugs are a short-cut to a wide range of new, different, and highly meaningful experiences. For example, on observing a flower arrangement in his study, Huxley reported "seeing what Adam had seen on the morning of his creation—the miracle, moment by moment, of naked existence."[2] Space and time, the frameworks for ordinary perception, seemed to give way, and ordinary values and strictures lost their rationale in light of a "transcendental otherness," "timeless bliss," and the "manifest glory of things." In fairness to Huxley, he was also careful to point out the potential dangers of drug abuse; but he was naively optimistic that neurologists and pharmacologists would discover newer and safer drugs that would open ever wider the doors of perception.

David Crosby was one of the most creative and popular rock musicians of the 1960s. His albums sold in the millions. He was also one of the country's leading drug advocates, progressing from marijuana to heroin and cocaine. But no more. Drugs slowly eroded his talents and ultimately robbed him of his freedom. (In the mid-1980s, Crosby served a year in a Texas penal institution for drug and firearm violations; his conviction was, however, over-turned because evidence was obtained in an improper search.) In an interview promoting his autobiography, *Long Time Gone*, Crosby described how he worked eight years to complete the album, "Oh yes I can." "With all the drugs," he reported, "I couldn't even get my shoes on a lot of the time."[3]

Crosby has by no means become an apologist for the "system." The only part of his former life-style that he admits being wrong about is the use of drugs—and the admission does not come without a certain amount of chagrin: "They [the authorities] also said marijuana would lead to harder stuff. We knew better, didn't we? But they turned out to be right. Isn't that infuriating?"[4]

It would be fatuous to deny that drugs can provide certain pleasures, and even open the doors to new and different kinds of experience. However, it is not puritanical to observe that pleasures, if they are to be self-enhancing, must also be meaningful. The person who seeks gratification without effort, as in drugs, is liable to feel dissatisfied—not because the gratification is wrong, but because it is robbed of meaning. But more than that: Drug-induced emotions are not only shallow, they also can stultify the develop-ment of more authentic emotional experiences. One final example will serve to illustrate the point:

> Steve characterized himself as a product of the sixties. His main love was painting and writing songs, but he drank and drugged too much to do either. He would go from a drinking binge to an amphetamine or cocaine binge, smoking marijuana in between to "ease" himself down. Steve claimed he had never experienced adult feelings and emotions; his emotional development seemed to have stopped at the time he had started using drugs. Many of his verbal expressions were even reminiscent of an adolescent. Drug induced highs and lows had replaced normal emotions.

Not until his health began to deteriorate did Steve admit he had a serious problem. In his own words, he had been living his life as an "emotional idiot."

After a "drying out" period, Steve returned to his painting and did, in his judgment, some of his best work ever. He had always worked with very dark colors; he now experimented with different colors and unusual mediums, textures, shapes, and designs. Within two years he was self-supporting through his paintings.

Steve's emotional life expanded in conjunction with his art work. Referring to the new emotions he was experiencing, he described himself as being like a kid in a candy store, "Give me this one, and this one, and this one, and. . . ." It is wonderful, he maintained, to be able to choose how one feels.

Emotional Creativity Is Not a Mere Change in Mood

Often when people hear the term "emotional creativity" their first statement is something like, "I know what that is. It's like when I get up in a bad mood, and I flip it." That, however, is not what we mean by emotional creativity.

In part, the confusion stems from the fact that the concept of emotion is often used in two different senses. In one sense, "emotion" refers to the transitory, vague feelings or moods that defy description in more analytical terms. It is the subtle and diffuse kind of experience one has when listening to a symphony, observing a sunset, or suffering from the "blues." Emotions in this sense are like a kind of psychological fog, a diffuse and opaque background out of which more delineated thoughts and feelings emerge. In a second and more restricted sense, "emotion" is used as a generic term to refer to such specific states as anger, fear, grief, love, and so forth. Unlike moods, these states have structure and organization; they are public, sharable, and bounded by rules—not the rules of logic, to be sure, but the rules of emotion. When we speak of emotional creativity, we are referring to emotions in this second sense.

However, even though a change in mood is not per se

emotionally creative, moods may in fact play a part in emotional creativity. When we are in a happy or positive mood, we are more open to challenge and new experiences; and we are more willing to explore alternative ways of responding—in short, we tend to be more creative. A depressed mood tends to have the opposite effects. When we are feeling sad or hopeless we are unlikely to undertake new initiatives. What is true of depression, however, is not necessarily true of all negative mood states. When we are in a crisis—in pain, worry, or despair—we may be more willing to experiment with new emotions, because we feel we have nothing to lose or no way to go but up.[5]

Emotional Creativity Is Not a Quick Fix

We are a "one minute" society. We want things done "now": Quickly, easily, and painlessly. If you doubt this, a quick look at the supermarket magazine stand or newspaper advertisements will tell you that it is so. Supposedly, we can change everything from our thighs to our management styles in just one minute a day. Oftentimes people seek hypnotherapy because they believe it has a magical quality or property that will cure whatever ails them (whether it be smoking, overweight, or divorce) quickly and without conscious effort.

Emotional creativity is not something to be achieved in one minute a day or on the weekends. It is an ongoing process of growth and awareness. Emotional creativity requires a willingness and commitment to honest expression and having the courage to take a definite position consistent with one's values. This is no task for the weak or fainthearted. It takes commitment, perseverence, and courage.

Emotional Creativity Is Not Selfishness

Emotional creativity necessarily centers on the self, but it is not narcissistic or selfish. To understand the difference, we must look at what selfishness is and isn't. Putting oneself first in one's own life is not selfishness; demanding to be first in everyone else's life is. All of us have been taught (women especially) that self-sacrifice, giving one's self to others, is a virtue. It is hard to argue with such teaching. We rightfully admire a Mother Teresa who devotes her life to aiding the poor, and we honor the man who risks his life to save another from a burning building. Too often, however, such teachings lead to effects opposite to those intended. In the long run, the most selfish thing a person can do is *not* to take care of herself or himself. In counseling, a man once remarked of a friend, "He takes care of everyone but himself. Therefore, in some way, that leaves others to take care of him. After a while the burden and responsibility become too great, and he's left alone again."

Selfishness is like that astronomical oddity, a black hole, which sucks everything into itself, even light. Emotional creativity, by contrast, is outward directed. Having freedom to reach one's potential, becoming and expressing one's genuine self, provides the best foundation for interacting with others and building healthy, honest relationships. Authenticity, remember, is one of the main criteria for emotional creativity. An authentic emotion is an expression of the self; and moving outward from the self—it gives, it does not absorb, light.

Emotional creativity is not without its dangers and pitfalls. It takes place on the border of the permissible. On one side of the border lies established social values and a comfortable sense of self; on the other side, a rejuvenating freedom from constraint which permits new ways of feeling and acting and relating to others. The cost of crossing the border is possible social rejection and even perhaps a temporary loss of self-identity. No wonder many people shun the anxiety and turmoil of emotional creativity and opt instead for a deadening conformity to established reality. Others, in a misguided attempt to be different for difference's sake, discard all rules and opt instead for an equally shallow nonconformity. Still others, in an attempt to escape the meaninglessness of their lives, retreat into a world of drugs and other cheap pleasures, not recognizing that theirs is only a pop art of the emotions.

Part III

---◆---

Emotional Creativity
and the Self

Do I contradict myself?
Very well then I contradict myself,
(I am large, I contain multitudes).

—Whitman, "Song of Myself"

10

Transformations of the Self

Some souls one will never discover,
unless one invents them first.
—Nietzsche, *Thus Spake Zarathrustra*

Emotions are intimately related to the self. They are, as the saying goes, "mirrors of the soul." In pride, the boundaries of the self are expanded; in grief, they are contracted; in anger, the self's values are reaffirmed; in fear, the self is protected from danger; in guilt, the self is exculpated; in love, the self is united with another. An event that does not touch in some way a person's sense of self is not likely to arouse emotion. This presents a difficulty for emotional creativity.

We like to think of our selves—our "true" selves—as stable and incorruptible. Even though I have undergone many changes, physically and psychologically, over the years, I am essentially the same person now that I was ten years ago; and even should I undergo some radical change in beliefs (adopt some new religious or political creed, say), I will still be tomorrow the same person I am today. Indeed, I might maintain that my new creed has simply, or

135

finally, allowed me to discover my true self—who I *really* was all along. (The notion of an unchanging true self is perhaps best captured by the concept of a soul, a nonmaterial entity that presumably remains unchanged not only throughout this lifetime, but in an afterlife as well.)

If the emotions are a reflection of an immutable self, how could they undergo change, creative or otherwise? The answer is, they could not. Emotional creativity is inextricably linked to self-creativity: Any fundamental change in the emotions necessitates a corresponding change in the self; and, conversely, any fundamental change in the self entails a corresponding change in the emotions.

Aspects of the Self

We often wonder what is "going on inside" another person. We don't know his or her "true" feelings or how we fit in, so we guard against trust and vulnerability. Even when we are told how the other feels, we may still harbor doubts, although we may pretend otherwise. We often become so desperate to trust someone, *anyone*, we unwisely trust those who are not trustworthy. So in the long run we learn to trust no one, becoming more lonely and alienated than before, as we withdraw increasingly into ourselves.

Unfortunately, our own selves, not just the selves of others, cannot always be trusted. Of all living creatures, humans alone are capable of deceit, pretending to be or feel one thing while actually being or feeling another. The self is a great pretender, a charlatan who deceives itself. Which is the true self: The one who deceives or the one who is deceived? What exactly is the self, anyway?

In the widest possible sense, the self is everything embraced by the pronouns "I," "me," and "mine." It is what *I* do and think, that which is under my immediate control; it is what happens to *me*, the joys and sorrows, ill and good fortunes that befall me; and it is what I call *mine*, my heritage, my family, my profession, and my intimate possessions. Because the self encompasses so much and is so multifaceted, we must distinguish among aspects or parts of the self if we are to talk coherently. The first distinction to be made is between the self as a biological organism and the self as a concept (or a network of concepts) of who we are. The conceptual self can be further subdivided into two parts: a core or nuclear self and a peripheral self.

The organismic self is what we are as members of a biological species (*Homo sapiens*). It comprises all those aspects of experience and behavior that are "instinctive": pleasures of the senses, comfort in the company of others, ebullient energy, as well as avoidance of harm, attacking the source of pain, and so forth. Ascetics of all kinds have disparaged the organismic self as the animal in human nature. Saint Simeon Stylites (ca. 390–459) provides an extreme example. He purportedly tied a rope around his waist so tightly that it ate into his flesh, creating a maggot-infested wound. As worms fell from the putrefied flesh, he would replace them with the admonition, "Eat what God has given you."[1] Romanticists, in contrast to ascetics, have tended toward the opposite extreme, elevating the organismic self to almost mythical proportions—the "noble savage," more clever than other animals but without the conceits and self-deprecations that so often distort the conceptual self.

The conceptual self is the way a person conceives of one's being and place in the world. Like any other complex concept, or set of interrelated concepts, the conceptual self is built up during the course of interaction with others. It is a kind of autobiography that we write and constantly rewrite in order to make sense of our experiences. Infrahuman animals do not need, nor do they have the capacity for, a conceptual self. Human beings are different. Our instincts—our biological selves—are not so tightly knit and pre-adapted to the environment as those of other animals. In order to survive we must construct models of the world and of our place within it.

A newborn infant has no conceptual self, only an organismic self. As the infant matures and gains experience with the world, a conceptual self is gradually constructed. Those early experiences form a core set of beliefs, values, goals, and aspirations that together constitute the nuclear self. Since the foundations for this aspect of the self are laid during the child's preverbal years, the nuclear self is largely unconscious. Moreover, it is heavily influenced by the important people in the child's world, especially the mother. This does not mean that the nuclear self is entirely and irrevocably laid down during infancy and early childhood. It is not. People do grow and change, sometimes radically. Nevertheless, the nuclear self is relatively stable and enduring.

"I don't feel like I really know her; she doesn't share herself with me." "He is charming on the outside, but you don't know his real self." "I am afraid to be myself with him." Commonplace expressions such as these illustrate the need to distinguish between nuclear and peripheral selves. The peripheral self is the self we present to others. It is a later and more superficial accretion on the nuclear self, and more subject to change depending on the circumstances.

No one aspect of the self is more important than the others— not the organismic self, the nuclear self, or the peripheral self. Each is vital and necessary in its own way. It is not uncommon, however, to find one aspect of the self elevated above the others in status and importance. Romanticists disparage the conceptual self in favor of the presumed naturalness of the organismic self; martyrs and ascetics, on the other hand, willingly sacrifice their organismic selves to preserve the integrity of their conceptual selves. Among the two aspects of the conceptual self (the nuclear and the peripheral), the nuclear self is often considered the more fundamental. In some respects that is true, but not in every respect. An adaptable peripheral self is essential to amicable social relations.

The quality of emotional experience (and even the kinds of emotions experienced) may differ depending on the aspect of the self that is primarily implicated. This is perhaps most easily illustrated with respect to fear, which is actually a complex set of overlapping emotions. A simple (biologically based) fear, such as falling from a height, has its origins in the organismic self; fear of making an embarrassing *faux pas* in public may focus on the peripheral self; and the fear of meaninglessness (*angst*) so emphasized by existentialist writers, or the terrible anxiety experienced during a psychotic breakdown, involves a threat to the nuclear self. To take another example, consider romantic love. At the level of the organismic self, love may take the form of sheer sexual infatuation (lust). What many people experience as love, with its self-centered vanities and jealousies, proceeds at the level of the peripheral self. The almost mystical love of Dante for Beatrice would be an emotion primarily of the nuclear self.

The following two examples illustrate the often Byzantine connections among aspects of the self. A client we call Ann, a well-adjusted professional woman, came for counseling during a transient crisis in her life. During therapy, she related the following events that had occurred ten years previously.

At the time, Ann had difficulty seeing her own face when she closed her eyes; she would see instead someone else such as her sister, mother, or daughter. One day she caught a glimpse of herself in the mirror and was startled to realize that her little granddaughter had eyes like her own. She stood looking in the mirror for a moment and gently touched her face. She had never touched herself quite that way before. Much to her surprise, tears started to stream down her cheeks. She was equally surprised to hear herself say, "I forgive you for not being the perfect Jan," her twin sister. Somehow, she had always felt that she was supposed to be an idealized version of her sister. The next words she heard herself saying were, "I forgive you [speaking to her daughter] for not being the perfect me." Ann had not been able to conceive of herself as an individual in her own right; either she had to be someone else (her sister), or someone else (her daughter) had to be her. But as she stood in front of the mirror, she now recalls, "somehow within my deepest being I knew there had been healing. I then thought of myself and could clearly see myself in my mind's eye for the first time in memory. It was at that time I really started accepting and appreciating my own uniqueness, my looks and my personality."

Ann's childhood had been unproblematic, but early marriage and a rapid succession of children had cut short the development of an independent sense of identity. At the time of the events described, her nuclear self, which had a firm foundation in her early upbringing, finally "broke through" the facade of her peripheral self.

How can such a "sudden" transformation be explained? Like most everyone else, Ann had seen herself in a mirror literally thousands of times since childhood. Yet, something was different this time. She was ready for change. Ann's relationship with her husband had been troubled for some years. She had been thinking a great deal about her situation, but without clear direction or resolution. Seeing herself in the mirror served as a trigger for a rapid transfiguration of the self.

Many events can serve as triggers for creative changes in the self, given sufficient desire and preparation on the part of the individual. The situation here is not unlike that for other kinds of creative endeavors, as discussed in Chapter 6, where sudden illumination often follows a long period of preparation and incubation.

Mirrors seem to have special potency in matters related to the self, a fact that deserves brief comment. Laboratory research has shown that the unobtrusive presence of a mirror makes more salient a subject's fundamental beliefs and attitudes. One common result is an increased resistance to coercion; the person becomes more willing to stand up for herself. The presence of a mirror also intensifies any affective reactions that might otherwise be elicited in a situation, including angry aggression, feelings of elation and depression, and phobic reactions.[2] In a clinical context, too, the presence of a mirror has been found to be a useful adjunct to therapy.[3] A mirror brings two images of the self into direct confrontation—the inner self of thought and feeling and the outer self of appearance. The result can be dramatic, as it was in the case of Ann.

According to Ann, she looks as young today as she did ten years ago, and she feels even better. Her relationships with her sister, daughter, and mother are also on a firmer foundation. "I realize now" she asserts, "that it takes so much less energy to be genuine, to be authentic, to be me, than to put on a front—and it's a lot more fun."

For Ann, healing involved recognition and acceptance of her nuclear self and, less directly, of her organismic self. Unfortunately, the nuclear self is not always superior in a valuative sense to the peripheral self. Sometimes the opposite is true, as the following case illustrates:

> Connie was a middle-aged woman who sought therapy because she wanted more self-confidence on the job. As is often the case, her problems were much deeper than that. She had been sexually and physically abused as a child by her father; her mother, although aware of the situation, had done nothing. Connie had managed to "repress" much of this information. She had constructed a story in which she came from a loving, supportive family. And that is how she viewed herself—as loving and supportive. Yet, she could not mask an underlying hostility toward, and suspiciousness of, others. Without realizing why or how, she alienated those close to her. Feeling alone, she would then become depressed and even suicidal.

Due to her early abuse and betrayal, Connie's nuclear self was vindictive and distrustful. Therapy was directed at making her nuclear self congruent with her more favorable peripheral self. However, where change in the nuclear self is concerned, therapy is not always successful, at least initially. Connie was quick to recognize the discrepancies in her behavior, but insight alone did little good. In spite of professed good intentions, Connie would sabotage her own desire for change. She would skip appointments, or call for appointments at inappropriate times; then, if a therapist was not available, she would threaten suicide. With a male therapist she became seductive, possessive, and jealous. With a female therapist she used different tactics (such as calling at night, "borrowing" books from the office without asking) that were no less destructive.

During Connie's lengthy therapy, many different therapeutic techniques were tried. Establishing trust, however, was a key to her eventual recovery, for it is primarily in an atmosphere of trust that changes in the nuclear self can proceed. Through relaxation, imagery, and hypnosis, Connie finally allowed herself to recall a number of events surrounding her early abuse. Only then could she begin to deal with the pain and betrayal she felt not only toward her father, but also toward her mother. It was like growing up anew, at least as far as emotional development was concerned.

We have said that emotions may differ in quality as well as in kind, depending on the nature of self-involvement. The difference is not always easy to portray in words, but it can be dramatic. In the case of Connie, her day-to-day emotions seldom extended beyond her peripheral self. As her nuclear and peripheral selves became more integrated, the quality of her emotional experiences also changed; and, conversely, as the quality of her emotions changed, so did her sense of self. This is the way she related it: "I didn't know that all this allowing myself to be angry, when I am angry, laughing when I'm happy, feeling afraid when I am afraid, could bring a person together so. It has really brought and tied me all together."

Tyrannies of the Self

One or another aspect of the self is sometimes allowed to become dominant and to exert almost tyrannical control over the others. Tyranny of the organismic self results in a person who is preoccupied with hedonistic pleasures, who is unable to delay gratification, and who shows little appreciation for others or social custom. Such a person is, to put it bluntly, uncouth and uncultured. Tyranny of the nuclear self results in a person who is egocentric (literally "self-centered") and individualistic. Such a person may forego bodily pleasures and disdain social graces, subordinating all to his or her own inner directives. Some saints and revolutionaries, and despots of all kinds, are of this type. Tyranny of the peripheral self results in a psychological chameleon, that is, a person who changes his or her "colors" to fit the situation. Such people may be outwardly charming and ingratiating, but they are shallow and lack inner convictions. The "organization man" and the politician who follows rather than leads are good examples.

Since the time of Plato's *Republic*, analogies have been drawn between the self and political systems. Pursuing this analogy, we should reject all tyranny, whether as a form of self-governance or as a form of social governance. The self, in its broadest sense, should be a democracy, where each aspect has its rightful place and none dominates the others.

Going even further, we might ask: What would happen if the self were eliminated entirely? On the political level, the elimination of governing structures is called anarchy. The term "anarchy" is, however, ambiguous; it has two almost diametrically opposed meanings. Political anarchists often maintain that once government is eliminated, people will live together in peace and harmony, without the need for external rules or coercion. But more often than not, attempts at such an idyllic state have resulted in anarchy in a different sense—tumult and chaos. Political anarchy has its psychological analogue in transcendence of self-governance, the goal of which is *nirvana* (mystical bliss), but the result of which is, more often than not, anxiety and despair.

Transcendence of the Self

In the *Chandogya Upanishad*, one of the oldest and most revered texts of Hinduism, a story is told of the god Indra and the demon Virochana. The two went to a famous sage to learn about *atman*, the true self that is beyond fear and sorrow, hunger and thirst, suffering and death. After they remained 32 years, the sage told Indra and Virochana to adorn themselves in beautiful clothes and then to look in a bowl of water; there, they would see themselves as they are. Virochana, being just a demon, understood the sage's advice to mean that the Self is one's physical attributes. He therefore returned to his people and advised them to glory in their own bodies (organismic selves). Indra, being a god, soon discovered the inadequacies of the sage's advice. If the Self is the body, then the Self must become blind when the body becomes blind, lame when the body becomes lame, and sick when the body becomes sick. Indra therefore returned to the sage for further instruction. After another 32 years he was informed that the Self is the spirit that wanders in joy in the land of dreams. Soon, Indra also saw the inadequacies in this explanation, for dreams can be filled with terror and suffering as well as joy. Returning yet a third time, and waiting another 32 years, Indra was told that the self is found in the quietness of sleep without dreams. That explanation, too, proved unsatisfactory, for in such a deep sleep the Self would know nothing and would fall into darkness. On a fourth return, Indra needed to wait only five years before being told that the Self transcends all seeing, all dreaming, even the abyss of the deepest sleep. The Self is like a "bridge between time and eternity." What can be seen, or heard, or known, other than the self, is always finite— bound in space and time. The Self is infinite; and where there is infinity, there is joy; and where there is joy, there is creation.

The story of Indra and Virochana is typical of mystical literature the world over. In order to discover the "true" self, one must transcend the empirical self in all its customary aspects—the organismic self, the peripheral self, even the nuclear self. The empirical self is not, however, easily transcended. The person who tries is more likely to be met by anxiety and despair than by bliss, at least initially. Nowhere has this been better described than by the sixteenth century Spanish mystic, St. John of the Cross. In order to reach perfection, John wrote, the soul must pass through two dark nights, each passage leading to a higher stage of love. The first night involves a purgation of the senses and ordinary intellectual thought. The person is thus led "from love of pleasure and self . . . to a higher degree of divine love."[4] In our own terminology, passage through the first night begins with a transcendence of the organismic and peripheral selves. This part of the passage is not particularly difficult, according to John, and the rewards and satisfactions are great. However, as in the development of any skill, an impasse is soon reached, where further progress seems blocked.

Frustrations develop, satisfactions pale, and the night becomes dark.

> God now leaves them in such darkness that they do not know which way to turn in their discursive imaginings. They cannot advance a step in meditation, as they used to, now that the interior sense faculties are engulfed in this night. . . . As I said, when God sees that they have grown a little, He weans them from the sweet breast so that they might be strengthened, lays aside their swaddling bands, and puts them down from His arms that they may grow accustomed to walking by themselves. This change is a surprise to them because everything seems to be functioning in reverse.[5]

For the person who successfully passes through this first night, and few do, far greater tribulations await. The soul has not been completely purged. There remain "ignorances and imperfections, natural and spiritual"; that is, remnants of the nuclear self. How are these to be eliminated? Since the person has supposedly abandoned (during the first night) all active modes of thought and meditation, further enlightenment must be a purely passive process in which God illumines the soul, which does nothing on its own. But if that is the case, why is this second night even darker than the first? Because the more one looks at the sun, the more the brightness overwhelms and darkens the sight. The darkness, however, is not simply blindness. The divine light brings into sharp relief the soul's remaining imperfections, thus causing great misery and suffering.

The Transcendental Self

What remains once the self is transcended in all its aspects (the organismic, nuclear, and peripheral selves)? In Hindu philosophy, what remains is *atman*, which in the final analysis is identical with *Brahman*, the indestructible and infinite ground of all being. The Christian answer to this question is somewhat different, for the soul is created, personal, and distinct from God; but in spite of these differences, there are obvious similarities between the concepts of *atman* and soul.

As St. John of the Cross vividly portrayed, the self is not easily transcended, if it can be transcended at all. Anxiety and despair, rather than mystical bliss, await the initiate. That is one reason why most mystics attempt to ground their experience in some broader frame of reference, such as religious faith. Indeed, we would go so far as to say that a complete transcendence of the self is impossible, or can occur only under conditions of severe psychological break-down (e.g., during an acute schizophrenic episode). For the Hindu, the concept of *atman* forms part of the nuclear self; without it the person would not be Hindu. Similarly, for the Christian, the concept of soul is inextricably interwoven with the individual's own self-concept. (Whether *atman* or the soul actually exist is a separate issue that need not concern us here; the concepts clearly exist, and that suffices for our analysis.) In mysticism, it might be said, the self is stripped to its barest essentials, not transcended.

The above considerations can be stated somewhat differently. The first step in nearly all mystical traditions is self-mortification, that is, breaking the ties of the organismic self. The organismic self cannot, of course, be completely overcome, for that would mean death, but its relative influence can be considerably diminished, and the influence of the conceptual self correspondingly increased. But as we have explained, the conceptual self (the nuclear as well as peripheral aspects) is a construction, built up during the course of socialization. What is constructed can also be torn down. When the conceptual self is demolished, two kinds of response can occur. The first is a catastrophic reaction, as in an acute anxiety attack.[6] With sufficient preparation and training, however, the breakdown need not be complete or catastrophic. Rather, the individual enters a state in some respects like an unborn infant still in its mother's womb. There is a lack of differentiation between self and other, a sense of union and passive fulfillment. Of course, the individual does not in actuality return to an infantile state; yet the metaphor is appropriate. Few mystics would object to the assertion that they have returned to the womb of the world, to the center and origin of their being.

We have discussed mysticism for two reasons. First, it is among the most creative of emotional experiences; and, second, it illustrates well the need to distinguish among various aspects of the self. However, mysticism is also an imbalanced state, one in which the nuclear self (and a very stripped down version of the nuclear self, at that) has achieved clear dominance. There is another way to emotional and self-creativity, one that we believe is preferable to the way of the mystic, but no less difficult. Enhancement of the nuclear self need not be purchased at the price of the organismic and peripheral selves. Each aspect of the self can and should be valued and enhanced, for each has an important role to play in our lives. Self-integration, not self-transcendence, is the path to emotional creativity.

We will approach the issue of self-integration by a short detour. We began this section with the question: What (if anything) remains once the self is transcended? The traditional answer is some form of spirit (*atman*, soul). This answer points to a vital dimension of human experience—the spiritual. Below, we will argue that spirituality is an attribute (a way of relating to the world); whether or not there is a corresponding thing in itself (a spirit) is an issue we will leave for philosophers and theologians to debate.

Spirituality

The 1971 White House Conference on Aging defined "spiritual" as that which pertains to "man's inner resources especially his ultimate concern, the basic value around which all other values are focused, the central philosophy of life—whether religious, anti-religious, or nonreligious—which guides a person's conduct, the supernatural and nonmaterial dimensions of human nature."[7] This is a good definition. However, in its attempt to be inclusive it risks the appearance of inconsistency. On the one hand, by emphasizing the "supernatural and nonmaterial dimensions of human nature," the definition acknowledges the close relation between spirituality and religion. On the other hand, the definition explicitly recognizes that a nonreligious (and even anti-religious) person can be spiritual. How can the "central philosophy" of a nonreligious person embrace the "supernatural and nonmaterial dimensions of human nature"?

If by "natural" we mean only those things that can be explained by natural science, then there is much that is "supernatural" about human nature and about the world in general. This, however, is only an admission of our own ignorance. It does not imply the existence of forces that are somehow "beyond" nature—that are, to use a somewhat different term, "preternatural."

But the spiritual is not simply a reflection of ignorance—a sense of wonder at the unknown. It is a way of knowing in its own right. "All men by nature desire to know." That is the first sentence of Aristotle's *Metaphysics*. It could also be the first sentence of almost any work on spirituality.

Two kinds of knowledge can be distinguished. The first kind is objective or scientific; it informs us about the world in and of itself. The second kind is subjective or spiritual; it informs us about our place in the world. No matter how complete our scientific knowledge, we still desire to know what events *mean* for us. This hunger for meaning cannot be satisfied by any purely scientific system of knowledge. It is the stuff that myths are made of.

Scientific and spiritual knowledge are complementary, although they are sometimes placed in false opposition. The philosopher of religion Mircea Eliade has described this opposition in the following way:

> For modern [i.e., scientific] consciousness, a physiological act—eating, sex, and so on—is in sum only an organic phenomenon. . . . But for the primitive, such an act is never simply physiological; it is, or can become, a sacrament, that is, a communion with the sacred.[8]

In many so-called "primitive" religions—religions that today are often dismissed as superstitious and mythical—the physical world is not mere inanimate matter, like a giant machine devoid of purpose or meaning. On the contrary, the world is inherently meaningful; gods and goddesses eat, make love, and so on, much as humans do—only more creatively; and on the human level, the body and its "physiological acts" are regarded as sacred.

By contrast, modern religions—even more than modern science—seem to rob the body of much of its naturalness and meaning. By postulating a preternatural realm that is the repository of all that is good or "higher," the material world is, to a large extent, despiritualized. Divorced from its meaning and significance (the spiritual), the body becomes debased; and, conversely, divorced from that which gives it substance (the organismic self), the spiritual becomes empty.

The observation by Eliade, quoted above, is reminiscent of Nietzsche's call for a spiritualization of the instincts. For Nietzsche, God is dead, which means that we, as human beings, must become more—not less—spiritual. We must accord to the body and its functions the respect, honor, and even awe that they deserve.

To survive as individuals and as a species, human beings must eat, have sex, and engage in many other physiological acts that are pleasurable "by nature." For many religious people, unfortunately, such pleasures of the organismic self are viewed, not as natural, but as sinful. The activities are therefore suppressed; or if not suppressed, then viewed with disdain—as a duty or necessity that must be performed, but only reluctantly. Such asceticism diminishes the self. Prudery, intolerance toward others, and self-reproach for inevitable relapses—these are some of the signs of spiritual impoverishment.

A despiritualization of the body also comes in secular form. The preoccupation of many people with drugs, one-night stands, and cheap thrills of all kinds; the crime and senseless violence that plague our streets; and the rapacious despoilment of our environment: these, too, are signs of spiritual impoverishment—a lack of appreciation of and respect for our own selves, for the selves of others, and for the world in which we live.

Spirituality requires a harmony within, a congruence of one's thoughts and actions with one's biological needs; it also requires a harmony without, a congruence of one's self with the best values of one's culture and with the natural environment. Spirituality is an affirmation of wholeness, a celebration of life in all its aspects.

Harmonies of the Self

Harmony is never absolute, for not all aspects of the self can be maximized at once. It is therefore better to speak in the plural rather than the singular—of harmonies rather than harmony. The optimal balance among the organismic, nuclear, and peripheral selves is an ever varying function of a person's age, abilities, temperament, and immediate circumstances. During early childhood, the organismic self may predominate, even as the basis for a nuclear self is being laid; during adolescence, the peripheral self comes to the fore as the maturing individual tries on various identities, striving to find one that "fits"; during maturity, the nuclear self may take precedence as the person becomes more self-sufficient and autonomous.

With regard to temperamental differences, the balance proper for a person with an introverted disposition may be discordant for a more outgoing, extraverted individual, and vice versa. And, since harmony is not simply internal to the individual, external circum-

stances also must be taken into account; thus, the balance appropriate in a business relationship may be inappropriate in an intimate
relationship.

One of the most frequently asked questions in psychotherapy
is, "How can I raise or enhance my self-esteem"? Self-esteem is a
value we place upon ourselves, the conviction that we are worthy
and competent. In an attempt to achieve self-esteem, people often
protect and nurture the aspect of the self that is dominant at the
moment, thus further pushing themselves out of balance. The
libertine intensifies his hedonistic pursuits; the socialite adroitly
fashions a different mask for every occasion; and the ascetic draws
further into his inner world. And all feel increasingly dissatisfied.
Self-esteem presumes balance and harmony; it cannot be built on
denial of any aspect of the self.

When an imbalance exists, a conscious attempt may be necessary to enhance the subordinate aspects of the self. For some
people, it is the organismic self that requires attention; for others,
the conceptual self. As already described, during the course of
development, the conceptual self is added to a maturing organismic
self. Correspondingly, emotions become more systematic in form
and cognitive in content, and their practical value is greatly
increased. Such cognitive transformation is important for emotional creativity as well as maturity. But not all is gain. Maturity also
brings a certain blunting of immediate experience. In order to
counteract that blunting, a deliberate effort may be required to
reinforce the functions of the organismic self, to become more open
to touch, smell, and taste, to experience more fully the life of the
body as well as the mind.

How do we know if we are living a balanced life? We are in
harmony and communion with ourselves and with our surroundings; we have a sense of freedom that enables us to be spontaneous
and yet responsible; and we are open to the possibility of truly
intimate, healthy relationships with others, not forcing or manipu-
lating the results, but rather allowing a harmonious ebb and flow
that provides texture and sparkle to our days and enrichment and
joy to our lives.

11

◆

Emotional Creativity in Men and Women

Man and Woman may only enter Paradise hand
in hand. Together, the myth tells us,
they left it and together
must they return.

—Richard Garnett, *De Flagello Myrteo*, Preface

Inherent within and permeating throughout the organismic, nuclear, and peripheral selves is our sexual identity. Our self-concept—how we think, feel, and present ourselves to the world—is closely tied to our biological selves as male or female. In this chapter, we examine possible differences between men and women, first in emotionality, then in creativity, and finally in emotional creativity.

Prologue

Unfortunately, whenever differences are observed between men and women (or between any two groups, for that matter) there is a tendency to make value judgments. Traditionally, these value judgments have worked to the disadvantage of women. Biblical scriptures, for example, are full of admonitions and warnings about

150

women and how they are to be subservient to men. In fact, the downfall of *man*kind, represented by Adam, is blamed on *woman*kind, represented by Eve. The punishment is laid out for her in Genesis 3:16: "I will greatly increase your pains in childbearing; with pain you will give birth to children. Your desire will be for your husband, and he will rule over you."[1]

To bring Egypt to its knees, Isaiah prophesied that the Egyptians "will be like women. They will shudder with fear" (Isaiah 19:16). The Greeks believed women to be a case of arrested development, that is, stunted or inferior human beings. As may be recalled, Plato suggested that men would be reincarnated, first as women, and then as animals, depending on the extent to which emotions rather than reason dominated their lives.

There have, of course, always been countervailing views. In spite of Plato, who reflected widespread misogynous attitudes of his time, Athena (goddess of war, wisdom personified, and guardian of the Athenian state) was one of the most revered of the Greek deities. And during the middle ages the cult of the Virgin Mary afforded women considerable veneration and status—but not enough to keep untold thousands from being burned at the stake as witches.

The historical legacy of misogyny (prejudice against women) is evident today even in the language we speak. Jessie Bernard, in her 1981 book *The Female World*, highlights the fact that the English language is not designed for females; it is "user unfriendly" to women. For example, there are more derogatory terms for women than for men; obscenities (until recently used almost exclusively by men) consistently malign women; "dirty" jokes are originated by men with women being the brunt of them; and there are ten times as many terms in the English language for sexually promiscuous women as men (220 vs. 22).

In contemporary society, the feminist movement has done much to challenge traditional attitudes, ideas, and values regarding women. Some feminists have argued that there are no biologically based differences between the sexes except for the "plumbing"— men can impregnate and women can bear children. All other differences of psychological importance can, according to this view, be accounted for largely in terms of socialization. That is, children are socialized into different roles and ways of life depending on the primary and secondary sex characteristics evident at birth (the "plumbing").

The more traditional view in psychology (until recently, a largely male discipline) is well represented by the following quotation from Lewis Terman and Catherine Miles:

> Masculinity and femininity are important aspects of human personality. They are not to be thought of as lending to it merely a superficial coloring and flavor; rather they are one of a small number of cores around which the structure of personality gradually takes shape. . . . The M–F dichotomy, in various patterns, has existed throughout history, and is still firmly established in our mores. In a considerable fraction of the population it is the source of many acute difficulties in the individual's social and sexual adjustment.[2]

Before proceeding further, a terminological distinction needs to be made. No one doubts that differences exist between men and women in many areas of psychological interest, including emotional reactivity and creativity. However, the origin of those differences —society or biology—is subject to considerable dispute. In order not to prejudge the issue, we will use the term "gender differences" in a generic sense to refer to socially recognized distinctions between men and women, whether or not those differences are intrinsically linked to a person's biological sex. We will use "sex differences" when we wish to emphasize distinctions that are biologically (genetically) determined.

Gender Differences in Emotionality

If we were to summarize a large body of data in a single phrase, it would be that women are more emotional than men. When Stephanie Shields, Professor of Psychology at the University of California, Davis, asked a group of 164 students to describe the most emotional person they knew, over 80 percent (both male and female) described a woman.[3] Such results might simply reflect cultural stereotypes. However, on most psychological tests designed to measure emotional reactivity, women also rate themselves higher than men. It may be, of course, that women have internalized and apply to themselves the culturally available stereotypes; or perhaps women are simply more willing to *report* their emotions than are men. Such explanations, however, cannot be the entire story. Women are also nonverbally more expressive than men, and they are better able to recognize nonverbal emotional cues in others.[4]

To summarize a large body of data, of which the above is only a small sample, women are *on the average* more emotional than men. We should hasten to add, however, that the differences *within* sexes is larger than the differences *between* the sexes. That is, many men are more emotional than the average woman, and many women are less emotional than the average man.

The major point of controversy is not whether women are (on average) more emotional than men, but why. Two major possibilities exist: Biology and society. After an extensive review of the relevant research, Anthony Manstead concludes that the small but consistent gender differences that have been observed in emotional reactivity are better explained in terms of social-psychological processes than biological processes.[5] What might some of those social psychological processes be?

In a study by John and Sandra Condry of Cornell University, subjects were shown a videotape of a nine-month-old infant responding to a series of stimuli, including a teddy bear, a jack-in-the-box, a doll, and a buzzer. For one group of subjects, the infant was described as a boy; for another group, the same infant was described as a girl. The responses of the "boy" were more likely to be seen as "active" and "potent" than were the responses of the "girl." The jack-in-the-box elicited especially strong reactions in the infant, and these reactions were more likely to be perceived as anger if infant was a "boy" and as fear if the infant was a "girl."[6] It is not just the *perception* of behavior that differs depending on the presumed sex of an infant. Other research has found that mothers tend to *respond* differently to male and female infants.[7] Differences in the way adults perceive and respond to an infant on the basis of its presumed sex cannot help but influence the infant's subsequent emotional development.

Sex stereotyping does not end with infancy. In ordinary language, we often have two terms to describe the same behavior, one complimentary and the other derogatory. For example, a person who is reluctant to part with money might be described as either frugal or stingy, depending on whether we agree or disagree with the behavior. Such dual descriptions are particularly common with reference to emotional behavior, and they typically work to the disadvantage of women. Thus, men are aggressive, women are bitchy; men discuss, women nag; men get angry, women fret; men are calm, women subdued; men yell, women scream; men growl, women squeal; men are dissatisfied, women whine.[8]

Lest one think that such descriptions are overdrawn for effect and have little relevance to the real world, consider the case of Ann Hopkins, a wife, mother, and employee of one of the nation's leading accounting firms (Price Waterhouse). In 1982 she was the only woman out of 88 candidates proposed for full partnership in the firm. Her credentials seemed impeccable. She had more billable hours than any of the other candidates proposed that year; she had brought in business worth $25 million; her clients praised her; and she was turned down. Her supporters described her as "driven," "hardworking," and "exacting"; her detractors described her as "macho," "overcompensating for being a woman," and needing a "course at charm school." Ms. Hopkins sued Price Waterhouse for sex discrimination. After eight years of litigation that ultimately reached the Supreme Court, she won her case.[9]

In short, early in life young girls learn that feminine behaviors are largely passive in nature; caretaking and nurturing are presumably a woman's forte. Young boys, by contrast, are taught to be independent and action-oriented. As the psychologist Eileen Nickerson emphasizes:

> Learning these stereotyped traits tends to foster in women a lack of assertiveness, a felt need to be controlled, and an internal rather than external focus, e.g., home, etc. Hence, women in our society are taught to behave in a manner in which they feel dependent upon others for directions since they tend not to feel in control of their environment.[10]

To gain a little different perspective on the issue of gender differences, we might consider briefly the !Kung, a people indigenous to southern Africa.[11] The !Kung may be divided roughly into two groups, depending on their life-style. One group consists of nomadic hunters and gatherers who continue to live in the Kalahari Desert much as they have done since the Stone Age. (Artifacts have been found that date back to the Pleistocene—11,000 years ago.) The women of these nomadic communities enjoy equal status with the men. On a given day the men and women who do not leave the camp to seek food share in the caretaking of the children.

In recent decades many of the !Kung have forsaken lives of hunting and gathering and have begun to farm and keep herds of domestic animals, thus adopting a more sedentary life-style. Women in sedentary !Kung communities have far less mobility than men, and they contribute less to the food supply. The men leave the villages to clear fields and raise crops; the women remain behind to prepare the food, maintain the shelters, and care for the children. With these and other changes, the women have lost their egalitarian status. In comparison to the nomadic !Kung, women in the sedentary communities have less independence and less influence on group decisions.

Until a few thousand years ago, most peoples of the world were hunters and gatherers. It is not too farfetched to believe their existence was similar to that of the nomadic !Kung today. In other words, the loss of women's equality and status is not attributable solely to biological givens but rather to the changes in roles and social structure.

We do not mean to imply that differences in emotionality between men and women are *merely* social creations. We disagree with the notion that sex differences are limited to "plumbing." Mother Nature would have been rather foolish if she had not provided people with psychological propensities that correspond with important biological functions. Women do bear and nurture children, and men are on average physically stronger and more aggressive. These biological differences should have reverberations in the emotional lives of men and women. Having said this, however, we must also recognize that popular stereotypes and socialization practices greatly exaggerate whatever biological influences might exist.

Gender Differences in Creativity

Throughout history, women have failed to match the recognized achievements of men in the arts and sciences, either in quantity or quality. In 1895 G. T. W. Patrick counted the number of patents issued to men (480,059) compared to women (3,458). This vast differential, he argued, demonstrates that women are less capable than men of abstract thought. Woman's tendency, according to Patrick, "is toward reproduction, while man's is toward production."[12]

Patrick's data may be old and his argument biased, but even the most ardent feminists today agree that women have not equaled men in creative pursuits.[13] As in the case of emotionality, disagreement centers on the explanation. Among some feminists, men are viewed as the main culprits in preventing women from realizing their full creative potential. There is probably more truth to this accusation than most men would like to admit—and less truth than most feminists are wont to claim. Men have been only too willing to keep women "in their place," which as the German expression goes, is *Kinder, Kirche, und Küche* (children, church, and kitchen). However, the pressure on women to conform to stereotypic feminine roles stems as much from other women as from men; there is considerable truth to the contention that women dress and behave more to please (or to outclass) other women than to please men.

With somewhat more justification, society in general (the "system") may be taken as the culprit for the failure of women to achieve in traditional domains of creative endeavor (e.g., the arts and sciences). Societies consist of institutions which, in turn, consist of interlocking social roles. Historically and across cultures, women have been limited to roles within the institution of the family (wife, mother), and they have been afforded limited educational opportunities. Men have been more free to go wherever their interests and abilities might lead them, whether it be fighting wars, conducting business, painting pictures, writing poetry, or simply sitting in the town square discussing philosophy.

It might be objected that at least some women, for example, members of the nobility in earlier times, or the wives and daughters of the well-to-do of today, have ample opportunity to pursue creative endeavors. And, indeed, many such women have excelled as writers and poets. However, simply being a member of the "leisure class" does not mean that one has the time and space to be creative—what Virginia Woolf called *A Room of One's Own*.[14] Regardless of social status or position, women in "advanced" cultures traditionally have had primary responsibility for maintaining the home and raising the children. Competing obligations of family and children have thus robbed many women of the opportunities to engage in creative activity. Princess Elizabeth of Sweden poignantly expressed this situation in a letter to the seventeenth century philosopher Descartes:

. . . the life I am constrained to lead does not allow me enough free time to acquire a habit of meditation in accordance with your rules. Sometimes the interests of my household, which I must not neglect, sometimes conversations and civilities I cannot eschew, so thoroughly deject this weak mind with annoyances or boredom that it remains for a long time afterward, useless for anything else.[15]

What was true for Princess Elizabeth is no less true for women today, in spite of labor-saving devices and other accommodations to ease the burden of being a wife and mother. B. W. Hayes compared 174 men and 174 women listed in *Who's Who*.[16] Over 90 percent of the men were married, which is consistent with the rate of marriage for men in the general population. Only 62 percent of the women were married, a much lower rate than for women in general. Moreover, the women who were married had fewer children (mean = 1.5) than their male counterparts (mean = 2.5). Evidently it is still more difficult for women than for men to achieve eminence in a career while meeting the interests of a household.

The problem, however, goes deeper than unfavorable circumstances or insufficient free time. Men, too, have duties to perform and obligations to meet. But there is a difference. The roles traditionally open to women have not been conducive to creative endeavors. In order to see how this is so, we must digress briefly.

The requirements for satisfactory performance of a role are fourfold: ability, knowledge, motivation, and social legitimation. For example, to perform the role of a judge within the legal system, a person must have the ability to follow complex arguments, knowledge of legal procedures and precedents, motivation to do the work, and, perhaps most important of all, he or she must be duly appointed and recognized by the appropriate authorities (legitimation).

With regard to ability, there is no evidence that women are less capable of creative achievement than are men. However, with regard to the other three factors necessary for the successful performance of a social role (knowledge, motivation, and legitimation), women have traditionally been at a severe disadvantage. Educational opportunities for women have been limited; women have been socialized to nurture rather than achieve; and the roles women have occupied have often been afforded low status or legitimation. These last two points deserve special emphasis.

Some roles allow for, even demand, greater innovation than do other roles. For example, scientists and business entrepreneurs are expected to come up with new ideas or products. Innovation and change are requirements of the role. Elementary school teachers, by contrast, are not expected to be innovative, except perhaps in methodology; their task is to pass on to the next generation the stock of knowledge and values inherent in society.

As the primary agents of socialization of the young, women are the transmitters of convention. Therefore, traditional female roles (mother, teacher) have emphasized conventionality over innovation. And to the extent that women have themselves been socialized to be compatible with their expected roles, some of the very characteristics that help promote and foster creativity—inventiveness, independence, unconventionality—have been discouraged, and even condemned, in women. The "double standard" extends far beyond the realm of sexual conduct.

But the difficulty is more than simply a lack of opportunity and encouragement. Not only have the roles traditionally open to women discouraged creativity, but when women have achieved, their accomplishments have often gone unrecognized. This is only part of a larger problem. Women's work—regardless of what it is—is not considered as important as men's work. Ira Reiss has stated the issue well:

> It is not just a question of different roles—anyone looking fairly at the division of roles will see that women's roles are given low status as compared to men's roles. The particular role does not matter; whatever a woman does is valued less and whatever a man does is valued more, e.g., if men herd then herding is highly valued—if women herd it is not.[16]

Times are changing. Modern technology has made obsolete many divisions of labor that previously had some rationale, for example, machinery negates the significance of sex differences in upper body strength. Similarly, technology has freed women from many of the burdens of childbearing and nurturance that previously was their assigned lot. Biology may predispose, but society disposes. What is now needed is an attitude change. Society can no longer afford to waste the creative talents of its female members. As Silvano Arieti says in his book on creativity, given free rein it is fair to believe that women can be equally as creative as men. Arieti goes on:

> We cannot avoid experiencing a sense of utter dismay when we think of the waste of so much talent among women, oppressed

minorities, and people kept from having access to cultural enrichment by the undeveloped state of their society. Who could predict how much more advanced civilization would be today were all the denizens of the earth given the possibility of participating in the growth of culture?[17]

To summarize the discussion thus far, we have noted the "superiority" of women in the emotional domain. This does not necessarily mean that men are "by nature" less emotional than women, but with few exceptions (e.g., anger), emotionality in men has been devalued and discouraged. We have also noted the "superiority" of men in creative achievement. This does not necessarily mean that women are "by nature" less creative than men, but like emotionality in men, creativity in women has been devalued and discouraged. Given these conflicting states of affairs, what gender differences might we expect in the overlapping domain of emotional creativity?

Gender Differences in Emotional Creativity

Men are expected to be stoical and to "keep a stiff upper lip," pretending that all is well no matter how they feel; by contrast, women are allowed, even expected, to express verbally and nonverbally what and how they feel. On this basis alone, we might expect women to be emotionally more creative than men, even if their creativity in this domain would largely go unrecognized.

Some support for this expectation was obtained in a study by Carol Thomas-Knowles. Five tests, three of emotional creativity and two of intellectual creativity, were administered to 100 university students (48 men and 52 women). Comparisons among the tests suggest that women may be emotionally more creative than men, with no corresponding difference in the intellectual domain.[18]

Needless to say, one study can hardly be considered conclusive, especially one that relies on paper-and-pencil measures of emotional creativity. Therefore, to gain further insight on possible gender differences in emotional creativity, one of the authors (EPN) reviewed the records of the clients in her practice who met the following three criteria: (a) they were over 21 years of age at the start of therapy (the median age was 36); (b) they were seen for at least 10 sessions (the median was 24 sessions); and (c) they had been seen at least once within the past two years. Two hundred and sixty three clients (110 men and 153 women) met these criteria.[19]

The clients were first divided into two groups depending on their creative potential as suggested by their progress and attainment during therapy. One group consisted of clients who were judged to be moderately or very creative emotionally; the other group consisted of those who indicated little capacity for change, who actually resisted change, or who used their potential in destructive ways. Men outnumbered the women in the creative group (60 percent to 53 percent), but the difference was relatively small and not statistically reliable.

At first, these results might appear to contradict the findings of Thomas-Knowles mentioned above (where the women demonstrated greater emotional creativity than the men). The contradiction, however, may be more apparent than real, for the women clients also were superior to the men in an important respect, if not in overall creative potential. In order to explicate the difference, we need to return to the three stages of emotional creativity outlined in Chapters 1 and 8. These stages are:

Stage 1: *Acquisition*   Development, cultivation, or mastery of an emotional standard for the culture.

Stage 2: *Refinement*   Fine tuning or personalization of a standard emotion.

Stage 3: *Transformation*   Development of a new and different type of emotion, unrecognized and unnamed within the culture.

When clients were divided into groups roughly corresponding to the above three stages, a marked difference between the sexes became apparent. Stage 1 clients (acquisition) consisted of those who, at the beginning of therapy, experienced few emotions or who, even if they were in considerable pain, were unable to express their needs in standard emotional reactions. Stage 2 clients (refinement) had a normal repertoire of emotions, but were ineffective or deviant in their expression. Stage 3 clients (transformation) also had a normal repertoire of emotions but, due largely to changes in life-circumstances, were experiencing new and different emotional reactions.

The results of this classification are as follows:

	MEN(%) ($n = 110$)	WOMEN(%) ($n = 153$)
Stage 1: Acquisition	89	18
Stage 2: Refinement	7	78
Stage 3: Transformation	4	4

As can be seen, the majority of men (89 percent) were at the acquisition stage, whereas the majority of women (78 percent) were at the refinement stage.[20] That is, the men tended to be more limited in their range of emotions and less able than the women to identify the emotions they did experience. Often, the men acted as though they simply did not know what they were experiencing. Thus, their first step toward emotional creativity was the cultivation and recognition of emotions that not only are standard within the culture, but that are common among most women.

For the most part, the women were emotionally more skillful than the men, and they enjoyed a wider range of emotional experience and expression. Being more accomplished in the emotional domain to begin with, the women tended to work on other aspects of their lives; and, when they did work on their emotions, it was toward the further refinement and expression of already achieved emotions. This state of affairs could easily be mistaken for a lack of emotional creativity on the part of the women. It is, perhaps, what Freud was alluding to when he commented:

> We also regard women as weaker in their social interests and as having less capacity for sublimating their instincts than men. . . . A man of about thirty strikes us as a youthful, somewhat unformed individual. . . . A woman of the same

age, however, often frightens us by her psychical rigidity and unchangeability. Her libido has taken up final positions and seems incapable of exchanging them for others. There are no paths open for further development.[21]

Freud may have interpreted as a shortcoming ("an inability to sublimate instincts") the greater range of emotions that his women patients were able to experience and display, however ineffectively. We clearly disagree. Freud's observation may simply be another instance of the disparagement of women's accomplishments. We also disagree that women are more rigid and unchangeable than men, although already having acquired a wide range of emotional responses, further advancement may indeed prove to be difficult. Innovation and change are sometimes easier when a person starts at a less differentiated stage of development.

This brings us to the question: Why did the women clients have a larger emotional repertoire than the men? As we discussed earlier in this chapter, even in infancy the behavior of boys and girls is interpreted and reacted to differently, and such differential treatment continues throughout the lifespan. It is not too much of an exaggeration to say that men and women in contemporary American society live in different emotional worlds. Women are socialized to nurture and maintain interpersonal relationships, a task that requires emotional acuity. Conversely, men are socialized to be independent and assertive, to be rational problem solvers, and thus to view emotionality as hazardous and unmanly. As a burly young man said to his wife during a counseling session,

> What you said hurt me. It hurt me real, real, real bad. It's hard for me to say to you I'm hurt, and I can never say I'm afraid, so when I'm hurt I always act like I'm angry. Because all of my life, if I said I was hurt somebody would have thought next thing they knew, I'd be wearing a pink tutu and hair ribbons. And in my job I'd be a goner if anybody knew that I was hurt or afraid. So what I learned early on was, to let it out in anger. That's a man's way.

Language plays a major role in the socialization of the emotions (a topic about which we will have much more to say in Chapter 12). It is therefore not surprising to learn that women and men also speak different emotional languages. The words are the same, of course, but the meanings differ in subtle ways. To paraphrase what Winston Churchill said about the United States and Great Britain, men and women are like two great nations separated by a common language.

"Genderlect" is the term coined by the linguist Deborah Tannen to highlight subtle differences in meaning between the language of men and women. In her book, *You Just Don't Understand: Women and Men in Conversation,* Tannen provides numerous examples of how "genderlect" makes communication between the sexes a continual source of potential conflict: Men want "the facts," women speak of feelings; men isolate and analyze, women combine and synthesize; men dispose, women disclose.[22]

Sad and in tears, a male client remarked, "I needed you to tell me it was okay to feel like this." Men no less than women are capable of experiencing a wide range of emotions, but they often need permission. The psychologist Murray Scher has accurately presented the plight of many men: "They have been raised to deny themselves permission to feel, to be weak, to be in need, to be dependent, to demand, or to fail. They enter counseling so that the counselor will grant them permission for one or more of these."[23]

Once a man acquires the emotional language and is given permission to speak of his emotions, he often becomes a very adroit, eager student. The following observation, made by a man to his teenage sons during a family counseling session, is typical:

> *What I've learned about my emotions is, I can laugh, and I can cry. I can cry because I am happy, and I can cry because I am sad. I've also learned to express what I feel, and I've learned how to do it. I don't have to let things build up inside me, pretending they are not there. Not doing that [expressing emotional feelings] got me into a lot of trouble and nearly cost me my family. Yeah, real men do cry.*

Real men don't *just* cry. Like real women, they are open to the full range of emotional experience.

Epilogue

Diversity fosters creativity. Women have strengths and weaknesses that are uniquely their own; the same is true for men. It is typical of human nature to want to find scapegoats, to blame others for our weaknesses. In finding a scapegoat, it is helpful if the other is somehow different from ourselves—women in the case of men and men in the case of women. To fight such prejudices, many people understandably wish to deny that any differences—strengths as well as weaknesses—exist between the sexes. A far better (and more difficult) tack would be for each person to accept responsibility for his or her own self, regardless of gender.

Gender differences are to be valued, not lamented. Homogenization of the sexes should not be our goal. The differences we have in mind are not, however, those that traditionally have been imposed on men and women. It is time for new types of women *and* men to emerge—ones that are willing to be supportive of themselves and each other in growth and creativity in all domains. One gender cannot win at the expense of the other. Either both win, or both lose.

12

◆

Language, Self, and Emotion

Language!—the blood of the soul, Sir!
into which our thoughts run, and
out of which they grow.
—Oliver Wendell Holmes, *The Professor at
Breakfast-Table*

–

Consider how young children want to know the name of almost everything they see. Naming an object brings satisfaction—a sense of power or control. The name need have no real conceptual content or meaning for the child. The fact that one animal is called a "cow" and another is called a "horse" does not by itself add greatly to a child's understanding of either cows or horses. As far as the child is concerned, the two names could just as easily have been reversed. It is the act of naming, not the name itself, that is important. Giving something a name has a kind of magical quality, like an incantation.

The magic of words does not end with childhood. At one time or another, most of us have had the experience of walking through a meadow in springtime. As we walk, we wonder about the name of each wildflower. Is this a black-eyed Susan? Is that a goldenrod? We seem embarrassed to see nature in her nakedness; we must adorn her in a garment of words.

If the mere act of naming can have such a powerful influence, how much greater the influence must be when the word represents a meaningful concept, not simply an arbitrary label. For the botanist, a black-eyed Susan is not just another pretty flower, it is a *Rudbeckia hirta*. Words have greater influence still when the object named is an aspect of ourselves. A rose is a rose by any other name, and so, too, is a black-eyed Susan—but human beings are different. The way we think, feel, and act is determined in large part by the way we conceive of ourselves.

The conceptual self (both nuclear and peripheral) is closely related to the words we use to name and describe ourselves. Surnames are often used to identify with a particular ethnic or national background, or even to make a political or social statement (as when women retain or hyphenate their birth names following marriage). First names, too, often reflect and help form individual identities. It has been found, for example, that children's popularity among their peers is affected by the social desirability of their names, a fact that cannot help but influence their developing self-concepts.[1] Bertha and Hugo are less likely to be elected class officers than are Jennifer and Michael, at least on early acquaintance.

More important than proper names in shaping a person's sense of self are the personal pronouns. *I* am Jennifer—that is *my* name; your name may also be Jennifer, but you will never be *me*. It is through such linguistic markers as "I," "me," "my," and "mine" that the contours of the self are demarcated.[2] To say, "I did it," locates the origin of a response in space and time; that is, in the location of my body at a particular moment. More important, "I did it," locates the response within a moral order. I am responsible for what *I* do; conversely, I am not responsible for what happens to *me*. Thus are the boundaries of the self established; and within those boundaries lie all that is *mine*—my name, my family, my home, my profession, and so on.

We normally do not pay close attention to the way a person uses personal pronouns. That is mistake, for such use can be very revealing.

Randy was admired for his generosity; he was always willing to help others. But what appeared to be his greatest strength actually stemmed from weakness. He had no firm sense of identity; he could only see himself in connection with others.

This was reflected in the language he used. In speaking of what he did, or planned to do, he seldom used the pronoun "I". Rather, he typically referred to himself as "we" (as in, "We are going to work").

Randy was the only child of a middle-aged couple. His father died when he was young, and he identified closely with his mother, who had considerable prestige in the community. He grew up referring to himself and his mother as though they were one, and never ceased the practice. He did not establish close relationships with others of his own age, even as an adult. When his mother died, he fell apart. He undertook one project after another, but without any real focus or success. He had lost his center. Without a "we," there was no "I."

The distinction between actions and passions is also reflected in the way we speak. Consider the difference between the active and passive voice. In the active voice, the self is the initiator of a response (e.g., "I did it"); in the passive voice, the self is acted upon by some (presumably) outside agent (e.g., "I was forced to do it"). The meaning of the passive voice can also be conveyed indirectly, by circumlocution (e.g., "I did it, but I couldn't help myself"). Emotional concepts take the passive voice, either directly ("I was overcome by anger") or implicitly ("I loved her, I couldn't help myself"). That is why emotions have traditionally been grouped among the passions, as things we suffer, and not among the actions, as things we do.

Language can mislead as well as reveal. As explained in Chapter 5, the idea that emotions are passions is largely a myth. "The sun rises in the East" is also a myth, one overthrown during the Copernican revolution. Emotional creativity requires its own Copernican revolution in the way we think about the emotions. At the risk of repeating what we have said before, emotions are actions that we dissociate from the self-as-agent; they are not just "happenings" over which we have no control. To recognize this fact does not lessen the importance of the emotions; it simply places them where they belong—within the domain of the *I* as an autonomous agent.

Thus far, we have been speaking in very general terms. In the remainder of the chapter, we focus more specifically on the words we use to describe and express emotions, and on the relation of language to emotional creativity.

Language, we maintain, is one of the primary means by which we acquire the emotions of our culture. It is also a major vehicle for emotional creativity.

Emotional Vocabularies

"Some people would never have fallen in love if they had never heard of love." The French aphorist La Rochefoucauld was not prone to understatement, but in this case his observation seems unnecessarily conservative.[3] Would *anyone* fall in love if they had not heard of it, if there were no word for love? We doubt it. As discussed in Chapter 2, love—at least the romantic variety to which La Rochefoucauld was referring—is the product of particular social-historical developments that had their beginning in the courts of eleventh-century Europe. These developments have culminated in our current concept of love; and without a concept of love, we would not experience love the way we do.

Human emotions represent endless possibilities. Only a small fraction of these possibilities have ever been actualized in any given culture. The emotions that have been actualized are typically reflected in the concepts of ordinary language. And how many emotions are recognized in ordinary language?

The answer to this question varies from one culture to another. We confine our observations to the English language; and even here, some complications arise. No sharp dividing line exists between emotional and nonemotional concepts. Almost everyone would agree that "anger" and "grief" refer to emotions. But how about "humility" and "fatigue"? Do they refer to emotions or to some other kind of psychological state? To complicate matters even further, some terms that clearly do not refer to emotions nevertheless have emotional connotations. "Home," for example, has a feeling tone that "house" lacks, even though both may refer to the same physical structure. Some linguists have argued that all concepts have an emotional connotation, at least to the extent that they involve some value judgment or preference.

If we restrict consideration to terms that have a rather unequivocal emotional connotation, then there are roughly five hundred words in the English language that describe emotional states.[4] This figure could be easily doubled or even quadrupled if variations on the same root were counted—e.g., vengeful, revengeful—and if "emotional connotation" were interpreted very broadly. In fact, Lynn Bush compiled a list of 2,186 adjectives that, very broadly speaking, might be judged to denote feelings.[5]

Roughly two-thirds of emotional terms have negative connotations. Simply put, there are many more ways to be unhappy than to be happy. The reasons for this negative bias are not entirely clear. It could be that negative emotional states present social and personal problems requiring solution, and hence they demand finer discrimination. It could also be that the connotation of passivity makes emotional concepts less applicable to positive than to negative states. We are all too willing to disclaim responsibility for acts with potentially negative consequences. One way to do this is to interpret the response as a passion (anger, fear, envy, or the like) rather than as an action (a deliberate response). Crimes of passion are legion; good deeds of passion are few. But whatever the explanation, the fact that we have more concepts for negative than positive emotions is of interest in its own right.[6]

There is no reason to believe that human beings are more predisposed toward negative than positive experiences. On the contrary, people generally report being more satisfied than dissatisfied with their lives. That is true in most societies, regardless (almost) of socioeconomic conditions.[7] Nevertheless, the paucity of concepts for positive emotions may have an impoverishing effect on our affective life. As Samuel Johnson observed: "A peasant and a philosopher may be equally *satisfied*, but not equally *happy*. Happiness consists in the multiplicity of agreeable consciousness. A peasant has not capacity of having equal happiness with a philosopher."[8]

There is no evidence that philosophers are any happier than peasants or anyone else. Still, Johnson has a point. Consider the following list of terms, each of which represents a way of being happy.

amused	exhilarated	happy	mirthful
blissful	exuberant	idyllic	rapturous
cheerful	exultant	jovial	serene
content	frolicsome	joyful	tranquil
ecstatic	gay	jubilant	vivacious
elated	gleeful	merry	zestful

There are connoisseurs of happiness, just as there are connoisseurs of wine. To be a connoisseur of wine, one must be able to distinguish among various kinds of grapes, vintages, and so forth. That requires not only a keen sense of taste and smell; it also requires a good deal of background knowledge. Even greater skills are required to *produce* (not just savor) a particularly good wine. Wines do not grow naturally on the vine; they are as much a product of human ingenuity as they are of the grape. The same can be said with respect to happiness: it must be cultivated, nurtured, pressed, fermented, etc., before it can be savored.

This point can be made even more dramatically with respect to the negative emotions, for which we have many more concepts. The following is a partial list of the ways a person can experience and/or express hostility—the "grapes of wrath," so to speak:

acrimonious	detesting	incensed	piqued
aggrieved	disdainful	indignant	provoked
aggravated	disgruntled	inflamed	quarrelsome
affronted	enraged	irate	rancorous
angry	envious	irked	reproachful
annoyed	fed-up	irritated	resentful
antagonistic	fierce	jealous	revengeful
arrogant	fractious	loathing	revolted
berserk	fretful	mad	riled
bilious	fuming	malevolent	ruffled
bitter	furious	malicious	sarcastic
brooding	galled	obstinate	scornful
chagrined	grim	offended	spiteful
choleric	grouchy	outraged	vexed
contemptuous	grudging	peevish	vindictive
crabby	hateful	perturbed	vicious
cross	hostile	petulant	wrathful
defiant			

It requires some skill and talent to be angry without being malevolent, to be arrogant without being scornful, to be chagrined without being petulant, to be fractious without being peevish, to be envious without being vicious, to be jealous without being vindictive, to be outraged without being revengeful, and so forth. Even more difficult is to be angry while joyful, arrogant while humble, chagrined while elated, fractious while gleeful, envious while tranquil, jealous while exhilarated, outraged while mirthful. It is difficult not simply because anger and joy, say, imply seemingly incompatible states. After all, we have little difficulty with such incompatibles as "sweet sorrow." In large part, the difficulty stems from the fact that we have no concepts to describe such conditions. We can, however, form what Silvano Arieti has called endocepts—embryonic concepts, so to speak.[9] With imagination these endocepts can lead to new kinds of emotional experiences. We will have more to say about endocepts shortly. But first, we need to examine more closely what lies behind (gives meaning to) emotional concepts.

The Meaning of Emotional Concepts

The meaning of "meaning" has been much debated among philosophers and psychologists. One very useful, if oversimplified, way of looking at the issues was introduced by Wittgenstein. He asks us to imagine a construction project consisting of a foreman and an assistant. Whenever the foreman says "Slab," the assistant picks up a flat stone and sets it in place. The assistant's response is based on an agreement with the foreman that the word "slab" will have a certain use (meaning) in connection with the work they are doing. Put differently, "slab" has meaning as part of a *language game*, which in turn is part of a larger endeavor, in this example, the construction project.[10]

The notion of a language game focuses attention on the fact that words acquire meaning as part of a larger activity in which a person is engaged. Of course, language games are not games in the ordinary sense; but in common with other kinds of games, they presume a background set of rules or propositions which help guide the activity in question.

In Wittgenstein's example of a foreman and his assistant, the command "Slab!" is given meaning in the context of the construction project on which they are working. Should the assistant quit the project, another might be hired in his stead, and likewise for the foreman. These two individuals occupy social roles, of which the command "Slab!" is one manifestation. The social roles of foreman and assistant are, in turn, only aspects of a larger social structure which helps determine the division of labor, the kinds of material used in construction, and so forth.

Applying the above considerations to the meaning of emotional concepts, consider the expression, "I love you." Like the term "slab" in the scenario of the foreman and his assistant, the term "love" only has meaning as part of a social interaction. Lover and beloved have, in a sense, entered into social roles vis-à-vis one another. They are enacting a culturally determined scenario, and that scenario—not any particular responses or experiences on the part of the individuals—is what gives meaning to the concept of love.

At this point the objection might be raised that we are only talking about words and not about emotions per se. After all, a stone slab does not change in any important way simply because it is labeled and becomes part of a language game. A slab remains a slab no matter what it is called. Perhaps the same is true of emotions.

We have already touched upon this objection earlier in the chapter, but it represents such an ingrained way of thinking that it bears further comment. "My word, is it not like fire, like the hammer that shatters the rock?"[11] On some accounts, one might think that emotions are like rocks or some other hard and immutable object to which a word might be attached but which is not altered in any fundamental way by the process. That is not the case. When it comes to the emotions, words can indeed be like the hammer that shatters the rock. Consider the following examples:

> Ruth (along with one to two million other Americans, mostly adolescent girls and women) suffered from a condition known as trichotillomania. She was literally tearing her hair out—only a stubble of growth remained on her head. In describing a problem she was having with her adolescent, runaway daughter, Ruth made statements like: "It tore me up"; "It pulled me apart"; "I just felt like I could pull my hair out"; and "I'll be bald before this is all over." The statements were prophetic as well as descriptive.

Once one becomes sensitive to the subtle interplay between language and behavior, instances such as Ruth's are not difficult to find.

> Kate was anorectic. She mostly ate salads; to keep trim, she also jogged and worked out with weights. If she gained a pound she was terribly concerned. She weighed herself morning and night. Kate had been abused as a child. When discussing the problems that this presented, she used terms that also symbolized her difficulties with food. For example, during one fifteen-minute

interval she used expressions like "It's eating me up" eleven times.

We do not wish to imply that Ruth tore her hair out because of the language she used, or that words were the source of Kate's anorexia. Both conditions are too prevalent for such a simple explanation, and both can be alleviated to a certain extent through the use of drugs, suggesting some organic as well as psychological involvement. However, the way we talk to ourselves, often without fully appreciating the significance of our words, can have a profound influence on the way we act. There is a dialectical relation between the way we speak and the way we behave. We seldom simply act. Rather, having acted (for whatever reason), we imbue the response with meaning. We name it, we describe it, we express it in words. The language we use—the language game in which we participate—then feeds back upon, to reinforce or redirect, the original behavior. This fact is often used to advantage during therapy; having clients adopt new patterns of speech, new ways of talking to themselves, often facilitates new patterns of behavior.

The above considerations apply to emotional behavior as well as to other kinds of response—indeed, perhaps more so, since most emotional concepts imply a veiled commitment to action. For example, I cannot honestly say "I love you" unless I am committed to your well-being; and I cannot say "That makes me angry" unless I am willing to act to correct the situation, if action is reasonably possible. Words not only shatter the rock; they construct the building.[12]

Words and Creativity

The art historian Germain Bazin contends that naming things is the first creative act.[13] Lest this seem an overstatement, consider the experiences of Helen Keller. At the age of two, Helen was stricken with a disease that left her both blind and deaf. Although she had already begun to learn language, and could name a variety of objects, in her dark and silent world, she soon forgot how to speak. Five years later, when Helen was 7, her parents hired a tutor, Ann Mansfield Sullivan. Miss Sullivan used her fingers to "write" words in the palm of Helen's hand whenever the little girl would touch an appropriate object. For a long time, Helen did not know what to make of this activity. Not only had she forgotten what little language she once knew, she had never known how to spell. Then one day she and Miss Sullivan walked to the well-house. Miss Sullivan placed Helen's hand under the flowing water. In the palm of the other hand, she wrote the letters, "w-a-t-e-r," first slowly, then rapidly. In her autobiography, Helen describes her reactions as follows:

> I stood still, my whole attention fixed upon the motions of her [Miss Sullivan's] fingers. Suddenly I felt a misty consciousness as of something forgotten—a thrill of returning thought; and somehow the mystery of language was revealed to me. I knew then that "w-a-t-e-r" meant the wonderful cool something that was flowing over my hand. That living word awakened my soul, gave it light, hope, joy, set it free!
>
> I left the well-house eager to learn. Everything had a name, and each name gave birth to a new thought. As we returned to the house every object which I touched seemed to quiver with life. That was because I saw everything with the strange, new sight that had come to me.[14]

If naming is the first act of creation for many people, it is by no means the only or the last. Language is not the only vehicle for creative thought. This is obviously true in the case of art and music, which is almost exclusively nonverbal. But it is also true in mathematics and science. In trying to explain his own creativity, for example, Einstein maintained that:

> Words do not seem to play any role in my mechanism of thought. The psychical entities which seem to serve as elements in thought are certain signs and more or less clear images which can be "voluntarily" reproduced and combined. . . . In a stage when words intervene at all, they are, in my case, purely auditive, but they intervene only in a secondary stage.[15]

Arieti has called such amorphous cognitions "endocepts," to distinguish them from the well-formed concepts that typically find expression in ordinary language. When you say, "I know what I feel, but I cannot put it into words," you are trying to express an endocept.[16]

Endocepts are common when a combination of more traditional concepts seem inappropriate to a situation. For example, how would you describe an experience that combines many of the elements of anger and fear? We have no concept in English for such an experience, but the Kaingang Indians of Brazil do. It is called *to nu*.[17]

Endocepts are particularly important during the early stages of creativity. Eventually, however, the creative product—whether a new emotion or a new idea—must be put into words (or perhaps some other symbolic medium—a painting, say) that others may understand. During that process, the endocept may be further refined, given additional meaning through its linkage to broader systems of behavior, and, perhaps most importantly, tested for its value and effectiveness.

If we had to name one feature that sets human beings apart from other animals, that feature is the capacity for language. Infrahuman animals are caught in the web of prereflective experience, an ever flowing *now*. The capacity for language makes possible a characteristically human form of experience, which we have called reflective (see Chapter 4). Selves and emotions are products of reflective experience.

Language can arrest the development of new emotions by prematurely forcing experience into preestablished categories (concepts) or ways of thinking. In this chapter, however, we have chosen to emphasize the liberating influence of language. Ample opportunity exists for emotional creativity simply by making finer discriminations within standard emotional categories, and by combining categories in unusual ways. At least initially, the result may be an endocept—a vague, preconceptual feeling—as described by Arieti. With further elaboration and testing, the intuitive feeling may coalesce into a new emotion—at least for the individual; and, if the individual happens to be sufficiently articulate and influential, perhaps for the society as a whole.

Language, we wish to emphasize, is not an isolated phenomenon, divorced from the remainder of a person's behavior. Nor is language divorced from the remainder of society. Words have meaning only as part of a larger "language game"; a game that, in the broadest sense, *is* society. Each society develops its own unique way of realizing the human potential—a realization made possible by, and manifested through, language.

13

◆

Emotional Creativity and Psychopathology

Human salvation lies in the hands of the
creatively maladjusted.
—Martin Luther King, Jr., *Strength to Love*

The concepts of emotion, creativity, and psychopathology are locked in an uneasy alliance. The connection between emotions and psychopathology finds expression in many colloquialisms. For example, a person is "mad" with anger, "crazy" with fear, "sick" with love, "insane" with jealousy, and so forth. Such colloquialisms have a long pedigree. For most of Western history (until about the middle of the eighteenth century) what we now call emotions were commonly referred to as passions. A passion was anything a person "suffered," which included both emotions and diseases. Hence, from the same root (the Greek *pathe*, and the Latin *pati, passiones*) we get such disease-related terms as "patient," "pathogen," and "pathology" and also such emotion-related terms as "passion," "pathos" and "sympathy." In view of this close conceptual connection, it is not surprising that the emotions have frequently been

176

viewed as diseases of the mind (e.g., by the ancient Stoics and, more recently, the philosopher Kant[1]).

The connection between creativity and psychopathology is also ancient. Referring to the prophetess at Delphi and the priestesses at Dodona, Plato suggested that "the greatest blessings come by way of madness, indeed of madness that is heaven-sent."[2] And, citing Aristotle as his source, the Roman philosopher Seneca maintained that "no great genius has ever existed without some touch of madness."[3]

The idea that creativity is allied to mental illness was given a veneer of scientific respectability in the nineteenth century by the Italian psychiatrist Cesare Lombroso.[4] Lombroso compiled a veritable *Who's Who* of artists, writers, and scientists who supposedly suffered from "attacks of insanity." Included among his list of notables were Aristotle, Virgil, Michelangelo, Shakespeare, Kant, Florence Nightingale, Haydn, Julius Caesar, Voltaire, Newton, Walter Scott, and Dante, to name but a few.

Among the "signs of degeneration" that Lombroso found associated with both genius and madness (in one person or another) were stammering, lefthandedness, sterility, celibacy, unlikeness to parents or "national type," precocity, delayed development, misoneism (unreasonable rejection of the discoveries of others), vagabondage, somnambulism, double personality, epileptic-like agitation, and lapses into stupidity (as when Victor Hugo remarked of a certain lady, "She did not know Latin, but she understood it very well"). Obviously, Lombroso cast a broad net from which few could escape.

Lombroso wrote with charm, and the numerous anecdotes he offered make for fascinating and often humorous reading. As an analysis of the possible link between creativity and mental illness, however, his work is practically worthless. Nevertheless, his general conclusion is well worth remembering:

> In short, by these analogies, and coincidences between the phenomena of genius and mental aberration, it seems as though nature had intended to teach us respect for the supreme misfortunes of insanity; and also to preserve us from being dazzled by the brilliancy of those men of genius who might well be compared, not to the planets which keep their appointed orbits, but to falling stars, lost and dispersed over the crust of the earth.[5]

Although Lombroso grossly exaggerated the connection between genius and madness, recent research has lent support to at
least an indirect connection between creativity and one form of
mental illness, namely, manic-depressive psychosis. A person
suffering from this affective disorder experiences extreme mood
swings, with severe depression alternating with normal states
(unipolar depression) or with mania (bipolar depression).

Over a fifteen-year period, Nancy Andreasen evaluated 30
faculty members (27 men and 3 women) at the University of Iowa
Writers' Workshop.[6] This is one of the most prestigious creative
writing programs in the United States. Andreasen compared her
sample of creative writers with a group of other professionals, such
as attorneys and administrators, who were similar in age, sex,
status, and I.Q. She found that 80 percent of the writers had, at one
period or another during their lifetimes, suffered from severe
affective disorder (unipolar or bipolar depression); two-thirds of
these writers had required psychiatric treatment, and two eventually committed suicide. By comparison, only 30 percent of the control
subjects had suffered from severe depression. In addition, Andreasen found a much higher incidence of both affective disorders and
creativity in the first-degree relatives (parents, siblings) of the
creative writers than in the relatives of the control subjects. Other
investigators have demonstrated a link between depression and
creativity in a variety of fields, not just literature.[7]

The above findings should not be taken to mean that mental
illness in general, or depression in particular, facilitates creativity. *It
does not.* In persons prone to depression, their creative successes
appear to be limited primarily to periods of relatively normal affect
or even hypomania (a mild elevation in mood). What the findings
do indicate is that the same neurological and psychological conditions that underlie this kind of mental illness may, in mild form or
under other circumstances, facilitate creativity.

Considerable speculation has also focused on a possible link
between creativity and the other major psychosis, schizophrenia. In
this case, however, there is little direct evidence that creativity is
associated with schizophrenia per se. Rather, both schizophrenics
and creative individuals demonstrate certain similarities in temperament and thought processes—such as aloofness, a disregard for
conventionality, and a tendency to make remote associations. The
similarities are, however, only superficial. The thought processes of

the schizophrenic tend to be bizarre, not just novel, and they have little relation to reality.[8]

The possible associations between creativity and severe psychopathology, such as manic-depressive psychosis and schizophrenia, are of considerable interest in their own right. They are not, however, the major concern of this chapter. We mention them primarily to help combat a certain stigma that is often associated with psychopathology. Mental illness in one's self or one's family is not a cause for shame. Under favorable circumstances it may even be associated with creativity. In the words of Lombroso quoted earlier, "it seems as though nature had intended to teach us respect for the supreme misfortunes of insanity."

What is true of the psychoses is even more true of those everyday problems of living grouped under the heading of neurosis.

Neurosis: An Impairment of Emotional Creativity

The term "neurosis" is somewhat of a misnomer since, taken literally, it implies neurological dysfunction. The neuroses, however, are shortcomings in psychological adjustment, typically caused by stresses that exceed a person's ability to cope. They may or may not be associated with underlying neuropathology.

Our current conception of neurosis owes much to Freud, who pioneered the exploration of the psychological origins of certain kinds of mental illness. Freud also saw a close connection between neurotic symptoms and creative acts:

> The deeper you penetrate into the pathogenesis of nervous illness, the more you will find revealed the connection between the neuroses and other productions of the human mind, including the most valuable. . . . If a person who is at loggerheads with reality possesses an *artistic gift* (a thing that is still a mystery to us), he can transform his phantasies into artistic creations instead of into symptoms.[9]

For Freud, both neurotic symptoms and artistic creations presumably stem from the same source, namely, unfulfilled wishes or impulses (primarily sexual and aggressive). We discussed some of the shortcoming of this motivational approach to creativity in

Chapter 6. From our perspective, Otto Rank, one of Freud's early disciples, came closer to the truth.[10] Whereas Freud saw the origins of creativity in the sublimation of primitive urges, Rank believed the creative impulse to be inherent in the striving of all living organisms toward growth, self-preservation, and the desire to become complete and separate beings, in short, the will to live. In humans the creative impulse takes special form, according to Rank. Humans have the capacity for self-reflection and hence the ability to influence the course that their lives will take. Neuroses arise when the creative impulse is, for psychological reasons, inhibited or diverted into nonconstructive channels.

More specifically, Rank recognized three levels or modes of functioning: the first, duty-conscious (normal); the second, guilt-conscious (neurotic); and the third self-conscious (creative). The first or normal mode involves adaptation to the external world, including social norms. Normal persons feel at one with reality and generally act in a socially acceptable manner. They do, however, pay a price, particularly in the loss of individuality. The second or neurotic mode represents a failure in going from the first (normal) to the third (creative) stage. Neurotic persons perceive external demands and social norms as compulsions to be opposed; yet they cannot affirm ideals consistent with their own will to live. The neurotic accepts the Dionysian injunction "Be thyself." But in the absence of a well-formed and integrated nuclear self, the injunction leads to behavior that is personally ineffective at best, and antisocial or unethical at worst. As a result, the neurotic suffers from vague feelings of inadequacy and/or guilt. In the third or creative mode, external demands or norms are made subsidiary to the person's own ideals. These ideals, which help constitute the nuclear self as discussed in Chapter 10, are not created out of nothing; they necessarily reflect social norms and values. Creative persons, however, are not afraid to go beyond what is socially accepted and expedient; they pursue a course dictated by their own "will to live," but within a framework of individual responsibility.

Expanding on Rank's basic insights, we might define neurosis as an impairment of creativity in an otherwise healthy individual. This means that the criteria for neurosis are just the opposite of those for creativity. Specifically, "neurotic" describes behavior that lacks novelty (e.g., is inflexible), or that is ineffective (maladaptive) and/or inauthentic (alienated from the self). We will discuss in detail each of these criteria shortly.

Creativity may be limited to a narrow range of activities (a creative artist need not be an accomplished mathematician or a good business person); so, too, a neurosis may be a partial disturbance limited to just one province of a person's life. This runs counter to a common conception that neurosis is a sweeping condition, almost a way of life.[11] An analogy with physical illness may help make our meaning clear. An otherwise healthy person may have a disease or disability in one organ (a stomach ulcer, say) but not another. Similarly, a person may be highly creative (and hence healthy) in one domain, and yet quite neurotic in another. The chemist Sir Henry Cavendish (1731–1810) offers an extreme example. As a chemist, he had few peers. Yet he was deathly afraid of meeting strangers, especially women. He had his house constructed so that he would not have to meet any of his women servants; and if by chance one should cross his path, she would be dismissed immediately. Men, too, posed a threat. On one occasion at a scientific meeting, Cavendish was introduced with considerable fanfare to a visiting scientist. Embarrassed and confounded, he stood with his head down throughout the introduction. Then, spying an opening in the crowd, he fled with great speed, not stopping until he reached his carriage.[12] Psychological health, no more than physical health, is all of a piece.

We must also recognize, however, that even a focal neurosis may sometimes have profound effects on many areas of a person's life. The effects are often negative; the person may spend so much time and effort trying to control the neurotic behavior that life becomes impoverished. But the ramifications of a neurosis need not be all negative. Again, an analogy with physical illness may clarify the issue. A person who suffers a disability in one area may try to compensate and thus excel in some other domain. Teddy Roosevelt, who was a frail youth, provides a good example. Seeking to overcome his frailty, he became an avid sportsman, author, military leader, and ultimately president of the United States. Similarly, some people suffering from a neurosis in one domain of living may come to excel in another domain, in part as compensation for their disability.

Now let us examine in more detail the ways in which neurosis may be considered an impairment of emotional creativity within a given domain of activity. As already stated, these ways involve a lack of novelty (inflexibility), ineffectiveness, and/or inauthenticity. We begin with a case example:

Zack was a highly self-controlled professional man. It was a source of pride that he did not allow himself to be angry, afraid, jealous, or even joyous or excited. Of course, everyone experiences such emotions sometimes. But when Zack was younger, he had practiced not showing or feeling his emotions. Occasionally, he would grin slightly. Other than that, he maintained a pleasant, neutral expression, what he termed a "professional look." Although self-controlled and successful in his professional life, Zack suffered from multiple sexual deviancies. He was an exhibitionist and voyeurist; he made obscene telephone calls; and he masturbated in public parking lots. He disclaimed responsibility for these episodes, maintaining that they did not represent his true desires or intentions.

Zack's case is extreme. However, a point is often easier to see in the extreme than in the commonplace. Therefore, let us examine how Zack's behavior fails to meet the criteria for creativity or, stated conversely, how it does meet the criteria for neurosis.

Lack of Novelty (Inflexibility)

Neurotic behavior is often highly unusual ("deviant"), and in this sense might be considered novel. For example, masturbating in a parking lot, as Zack did, is highly unusual. However, it is novel only in the sense of being statistically rare—most people find other means of sexual release. As a criterion for creativity, novelty implies more than statistical deviance. It also implies flexibility. That is, a creatively novel response is not just infrequent among members of a group; it is also variable and subject to change, depending on the circumstances. When evaluated from Zack's own perspective, his behavior had an inflexible and arthritic quality that seemingly placed it beyond personal and social control. Such rigidity, which is one of the primary characteristics of neurotic behavior, is antithetical to the production of novelty.

There are times in each of our lives when our emotional responses are less than desirable. The emotionally creative person finds ways to change; the person suffering from a neurosis finds change extremely difficult, no matter how much he or she may want to respond differently. If the neurotic behavior is sufficiently circumscribed and benign (as it usually is), it need not impair innovation in other areas, and it may even serve as an impetus toward creativity, as discussed above. In extreme cases, however, people suffering from neuroses may be so busy trying to change, adapt to, or protect themselves from their undesirable or noxious behavior that they have no time or energy left for growth and expanding their lives.

The epitome of rigid, inflexible behavior is obsessive compulsive disorder (OCD). Josh spent a minimum of four hours a day with his compulsions—straightening pillows on his bed, placing the telephone cord just right, counting the number of strokes when he brushed his teeth, and so on. He lived in fear that someone would learn of his compulsions; yet he could not change. Frank was terrified something would happen to his wife and felt compelled to call her numerous times each day. If she was not where he could reach her, he panicked. Lucy was so concerned about what the neighbors might think of her house, she spent hours cleaning each day. Millie talked incessantly to anyone and everyone, and she seemed incapable of doing otherwise.[13]

Fortunately, most of us do not have to spend hours every day compulsively engaging in one form of behavior or another. But in other, less obvious ways we may do things that are inflexible and limiting. We may tell ourselves over and over again that we are dull, dumb, ugly, stupid, unlovable, clumsy, inept, unworthy, worthless, and on and on and on. We may have become so accustomed to saying and hearing these things that we are no longer consciously aware of them. Flexibility, the ability to initiate new and novel responses, or to cease unwanted behavior, is a prime condition for mental health as well as creativity.

Ineffectiveness

That neurotic behavior is ineffective is perhaps so obvious as to require little comment. Zack's sexual deviancies (exhibitionism, voyeurism, obscene telephone calls, masturbating in public parking lots) provided him with little real satisfaction, and they threatened both his marriage and his career. However, things are seldom as simple or as obvious as in the case of Zack. When evaluating the effectiveness of a response, it is important to keep in mind that behavior is not effective in and of itself, but only with respect to some situation or goal. A response that is ineffective in one situation may be effective in another; and a response that is ineffective in the short run may be effective in the long run. Thus, a person may be greatly troubled by his or her responses; yet the fault may lie with the situation and not the person. One of the most difficult decisions when faced with trying circumstances is what to change—oneself or the situation.

The question to ask in regard to effectiveness is this: Does the behavior enhance one's self and interpersonal relationships? This is not an easy question to answer. Few of us are so wise or so objective that we can foresee all the consequences of our actions. Behavior that may seem very effective at the moment may have devastating consequences for our lives and/or the lives of others. Carol liked to shop and buy nice things. She did this, in part, to correct what she saw as gross defects in her appearance. Wherever she went she received compliments on the way she looked and her impeccable taste in clothing. It was all very rewarding. However, she eventually drove herself into bankruptcy and to the brink of suicide. Fred wanted to be the center of attention, and he did whatever it took to get people to notice him—laugh, joke, flirt, spend money, pout, get sick. It worked very well, initially. But after a while he and his shenanigans became too much for people, they wearied of the routine, and he was alone again.

Immediate pleasure and/or relief from pain are not the only rewards that help sustain neurotic behavior. Mack hit his wife if she didn't do what he said or if she "got out of line." It wasn't pleasant (he claimed), but it did get him what he wanted. Spouse abuse can take many forms and is not limited to either sex. Maria was extremely jealous of her husband. If she saw him talking to another woman in uncertain circumstances, she would have a temper tantrum—screaming, yelling, hitting, and throwing things. Abusive behavior of this type, while unpleasant, may be very effective in winning compliance. It is, however, almost always destructive of a relationship in the long term.

Inauthenticity

An authentic response is one that stems from the self, that reflects the true ideals and values of the person. Zack did not conceive of himself as a voyeur or exhibitionist. Quite the contrary. He wanted to disown his own behavior, as though someone else was doing those things, not he himself.

Even when a response is novel and effective, it can still be inauthentic. Inauthenticity results from a dominance of the peripheral self. The con artist is a good example. Such a person may be quite resourceful and efficient in pursuit of his goals, and he may be relatively satisfied with his life. Hence, he is unlikely to be seen in psychotherapy. But we would still classify his behavior as neurotic. (A person does not have to feel miserable in order to be neurotic, any more than a person has to feel ill in order to be sick.)

More often than not, however, the "satisfaction" that accompanies inauthenticity is a masquerade; and once the party is over, difficulties begin to emerge. Common repercussions of inauthenticity are alienation, emptiness, and a profound sense of loneliness—a loneliness that no amount of busyness or company can cure, for it involves a separation from one's own self. Some people try to overcome such alienation by adopting a kind of pseudo-authenticity, a "let-it-all-hang-out" or "tell-it-all" attitude. However, genuine authenticity is never an excuse for an undisciplined expression of emotion.

Carl Jung observed that "neurosis is always a substitute for legitimate suffering."[14] That is only partly true. Often, and especially in the case of inauthenticity, neurosis is a substitute for legitimate pleasure.

Personal Rules of Emotion

Both emotional creativity and emotional disorders arise as new rules of emotion are acquired, refined, and transformed. In Chapter 4, we distinguished among three overlapping types of emotional rules: procedural, regulative, and constitutive. To recapitulate briefly, procedural rules determines the tactics of a response; regulative rules, the appropriateness of a response; and constitutive rules, the nature of a response. These three types of rules (or, more accurately, aspects of any given rule) may be related to three kinds of emotional disorders. The person who has failed to acquire an adequate set of procedural rules is emotionally *inept*; when regulative rules are broken, the person may be considered *delinquent*; and if ineffective or maladaptive constitutive rules are developed, the resulting emotion can best be described as *neurotic* in the strictest sense. Our concern in this chapter is primarily with the last.[15]

We also saw in Chapter 4 how love must conform to certain rules if it is to be considered "true," and similarly for anger. Indeed, all standard emotions (i.e., those widely recognized as normal within a society) are constituted, at least in part, by social rules. It might be assumed that neurotic syndromes are, by contrast, "unruly." But that is true in only a metaphorical sense.

Within any society there are subcultural and sub-subcultural variations in the rules of emotion. This process of differentiation can be carried to ever smaller units. In the extreme, it might be said that each individual develops a unique set of personal rules that may or may not conform to the rules of the larger society. The following is an immoderate case that illustrates the application (or misapplication) of personal rules of love:

> *Carrie had a presumed "sex problem." The problem, according to Rod, her husband, was that she had an abnormally low sex drive; she didn't want sex very often. As for himself, Rod wanted sex at least once a day; and although Carrie agreed to this, he was not satisfied unless she reached a climax each time. In his mind, an orgasm validated her love for him. If Carrie didn't climax, Rod became either angry and belligerent or sullen and withdrawn. At times Rod would keep Carrie up nearly all night because she couldn't have an orgasm (and didn't really want one).*
>
> *In addition to her presumed sexual shortcomings, Carrie also had a "problem" with privacy. Rod wanted to be with her constantly, even in the bathroom. If she wanted time for herself, just to read or listen to music, Rod became agitated. He wanted to share everything, the things she did, the food she ate, even her innermost thoughts and feelings. She couldn't leave the house without him wanting to know all the details of where she went, whom she saw, what was said, etc.*
>
> *When asked what would happen if she refused some of Rod's requests, Carrie replied that she didn't know. She had never tried saying "No," even though she resented the constant invasion of her privacy and personal space. She kept thinking that someday Rod would realize she really loved him and that everything would be all right. But things did not get better;*

*instead, Rod threatened to divorce her and find a "real" woman
who would really love and appreciate him.*

What rules of love were Rod and Carrie following? Rod's
centered around sex and togetherness. To him love was never
wanting to be apart; it was sharing everything; and it was daily sex.
No, it was more than daily sex; if Carrie didn't have a daily orgasm
then she didn't love him. Surprisingly, Carrie had also internalized
some of these same rules. She also believed she had a sex problem,
and that *that* was what was making her miserable. Neither she nor
Rod recognized the rules that governed their relationship.

Not all neurotic behavior or symptoms are so clear-cut as the
example of Rod and Carrie might suggest.

*June came to counseling because of numbness of the left side and
paralysis of her left leg, which were initially attributed to a
stroke. However, medical specialists could find nothing physically wrong and hence recommended her for psychotherapy. Six
months prior to June's "stroke" her three-year old daughter had
died of a malignant brain tumor. The tumor had severely
affected the girl's left side, the same side as June's paralysis. At
the time of and even after the funeral, June felt she was coping
fairly well. Her disabilities began to manifest themselves shortly
after what would have been her daughter's next birthday (i.e.,
the first birthday following the daughter's death).*

It is impossible to say for sure that June's paralysis was not due
to an actual stroke or other neurological condition. Subtle neurological damage is often difficult to detect; it may only become
apparent with additional deterioration over a period of years.
However, the nature and timing of June's behavioral symptoms
make it reasonable to assume that she was suffering, at least in part,
from a conversion reaction, that is, the conversion of normal grief
into a somatic complaint. Supporting this interpretation is the fact
that June's symptoms gained for her certain advantages. She was
afraid of many things, for example, being alone, being in crowds,
driving, sleeping in her own bed; she suffered from both panic and
anxiety attacks; and she experienced extreme guilt over her daughter's death (she had initially not wanted the pregnancy). June's
condition tied others to her, and hence kept her from being alone; it

alleviated social and other obligations; and the pain she suffered helped assuage the guilt she felt.

Therapy with June was a slow, arduous, and often frustrating process. Early on, she made the statement, "I want help, but I will fight you every step of the way." She was true to her word. Personal rules of emotion are not developed without reason, nor are they abandoned lightly. It is often said of a scientific theory that it will not be abandoned, no matter the countervailing evidence, until a better theory is available. The same can be said for personal rules of emotion. Indeed, for practical purposes, the rules that help constitute a given emotion can be regarded as a kind of mini-theory for coping with relevant life events. The implications for therapy are obvious—discover the person's idiosyncratic rules of emotion and provide more adaptive alternatives. Some specific guidelines for doing this will be offered in Chapter 25.

In spite of numerous setbacks, June's condition improved slowly but consistently during the course of therapy. She now walks without a cane, drives everywhere she wants to go, has steady employment, and has established new interpersonal relationships. We cannot say that June has recovered completely, for she still walks with a limp and has some visual difficulties. This leaves open the possibility that some neurological damage was actually sustained, in addition to whatever psychological factors may have been involved. But be that as it may, June had developed a set of idiosyncratic rules for grief and repentance. Because her rules were personal (not shared by others), they were not subject to customary social feedback and correction. Indeed, they were not even recognized as such until she entered therapy.

Repression Reconsidered

Neurotic behavior, such as June's conversion reaction, is often attributed to the "overflow" of repressed emotion. The notion of repression as a psychological defense originated with Freud and psychoanalysis. The original idea was that certain impulses, primarily of a sexual or aggressive nature, are too threatening for the individual to express directly, or even to admit experiencing. The impulse is therefore repressed. However, a repressed impulse does not simply disappear. It still seeks outlet, but now in a disguised fashion.

Although largely associated with psychoanalysis, the notion of repression has become so widespread that it is no longer tied to any one theory. On a purely descriptive level, people often engage in a variety of subterfuges to exclude from awareness ("repress") undesirable or painful experiences. It is at the level of theory that disagreements arise. We offer here an account of repression that is consistent with our own theory of neurosis as an impairment of emotional creativity.

Perhaps the first thing to note is that repression is not an all-or-none phenomenon:

Sylvia had often been depressed and had attempted suicide on several occasions. When writing a chronological history of her life she suddenly remembered she had been raped twice; once as a teenager and again after she was grown. At the time, according to her, she had "thrown it over her shoulder" (put it behind her) and did not remember either episode unti. she was in therapy, writing her history.

How could Sylvia forget being raped twice? Simply by following a variation of the familiar child's rule: "Don't look and it will go away." While growing up, Sylvia had ample opportunity to acquire this rule. Her mother died when she was young, and she had been sexually abused by both her father and brother-in-law. She learned early "not to look."

Sylvia's was not yet a case of repression, for she could recall the troubling incidents of her past, albeit with some effort. But apply the rule ("Don't look . . .") in a more inflexible manner, and recollection may become impossible.

As noted, Sylvia was severely depressed and had contemplated suicide. Depression is often attributed to repressed anger that is turned against the self. Sylvia certainly had reason to be angry, but we do not believe that was the cause of her depression. Before getting to that, however, let us extend the issue beyond this single case.

In discussing the plight of depressed women generally, the psychotherapist Sonya Friedman observed: "The more I talk to a woman the more anger I uncover. All the depression, the going to sleep early, not having energy, the fact that it's three in the afternoon and she is still sitting around in her housecoat—all these are various forms of anger."[16]

There are times when going to sleep early, a lack of energy, or sitting around in a housecoat until three in the afternoon can be a form of passive aggression (e.g., if it causes inconvenience to others). And if the woman is not consciously aware of the meaning of her response, then we might even speak of repressed anger. However, the term "anger" is used metaphorically in this context, for clearly the woman's behavior does not follow the standard rules for anger. A more parsimonious explanation is that the woman has learned, in this situation, at least, a set of personal rules that helps constitute an emotion that bears some resemblance to both anger (resistance to a perceived wrong) and depression (sitting around in a housecoat until three in the afternoon).

In Chapter 3, it may be recalled, we offered several examples of aggressive syndromes from other cultures ("being a wild pig" among the Gururumba, *liget* among the Ilongot, and *song* among the Ifaluk). Such syndromes bear some semblance to anger within our own culture, but they are constituted by different rules and hence represent different emotions. Similarly, when people *within* this culture develop personal rules, the resulting emotion may bear some semblance to anger, and because we have no better term to describe the behavior, we are tempted to say that the anger is really there, only repressed.

Now let us return to Sylvia. Early child abuse and later rape gave her ample grounds for anger, but repressed anger directed against the self was not a primary cause of her depression. Sylvia had also suffered severe losses in her life, beginning with the early death of her mother. One of her daughters was seriously—and potentially fatally—ill; and in a recent divorce settlement she had lost her home and many possessions. Sylvia was experiencing an amalgam of diverse emotions, including aspects of grief, shame, anger, and fear.

Another example may serve to illustrate further how a standard emotion within the culture (in this case, anger) may be transformed into a neurotic syndrome through the adoption of personal rules.

> *Nellie literally ate herself into obesity, in part, to punish her husband. She had married young, and had four children who were now grown and away from home. Several years before starting therapy, she and her husband had joined a spouse-swapping group, and they started to "swing." She had not wanted to join, but continued in the group for quite some time at*

her husband's insistence. She finally decided that if she were fat
no man would swap his wife for her. She began to eat everything
she could get her hands on. She also knew that her husband
didn't like fat women. She could thus kill two birds with the
same stone—stop swinging and punish her husband.

Nellie's "anger" was not unconscious (repressed). For the most
part, she recognized what she was doing. However, eating oneself
into obesity is hardly a customary way of experiencing or expressing anger. Moreover, Nellie maintained quite sincerely that she did
not want to hurt her husband. She was devoted to her family, and
evidently they to her. (Her children, although now adults, called
her nearly every day.) But she also wanted greater independence;
she felt her family leaned too much on her for support. Yet her
obesity filled her with self-loathing, thus hindering the independence she sought.

In other words, Nellie's behavior represented a mixture of
conflicting desires and tendencies, only some of which conform to
anger in the ordinary sense. To say that Nellie ate because of anger
makes about as much sense as to say that the Ilongot cut off heads
in order to express anger (rather than a distinct emotion, *liget*).
Nellie's was a unique emotional syndrome in its own right, albeit
neurotic in the sense of being inflexible, ineffective, and inauthentic.

A person with less insight than Nellie might well have been
unaware of the reasons why she ate so much. Even standard
emotions are complex and easily misinterpreted. (For example, the
person in love is sometimes the last to recognize it.) When the
emotion is the product of personal rather than widely shared social
rules, it may be particularly subject to misinterpretation. But
nothing is gained by way of clarity, and much may be lost, if we
label the response by some common name ("anger," say, or
"depression") and then attribute its lack of recognition to repression. The repression, if one wants to call it that, is simply one more
rule by which the emotion is constituted.

One final point before leaving this topic: Idiosyncratic rules of
emotion may develop for a variety of reasons. For example, due to
inadequate or inappropriate socialization, a child may never acquire
the standard rules for a particular emotion. Or the rules, once
acquired, may be "bent," so to speak, for personal gain. The
individual who habitually intimidates others through anger is a

case in point. In some instances, physiological dysfunction (resulting in depression or hyperactivity) may help account for the development of inappropriate personal rules. Our concern here has not been so much with the reasons why personal rules are developed, but with how those rules, once developed, may help constitute neurotic syndromes.

The Riddle of Anxiety

Most neuroses are associated with high levels of anxiety. In fact, it is often claimed that most neurotic symptoms are defenses against anxiety. But what is anxiety? Perhaps more words have been written in answer to this question than to any other question in psychopathology. There is even an international journal (*Anxiety Research*) devoted exclusively to the topic. Clearly, we cannot hope in this short chapter to solve the riddle of anxiety. But neither can we avoid the issue entirely. Anxiety is not only a common accompaniment of neurotic syndromes, it is also a frequent experience during the early stages of creativity when familiar ways of thinking and responding must be abandoned. In fact, we would maintain that *the potential for creativity as well as neurosis is proportional to the potential for anxiety.*

We all know what it feels like to be mildly anxious. Luckily, few of us have had the misfortune to experience full-blown anxiety attacks. That was not the case with Nancy:

> *Sometimes, in the middle of the night while secure in bed, or during the day while safe at home, Nancy would experience an inexplicable dread or foreboding. At other times, her anxiety was focused on small and innocuous events. If someone she wasn't expecting approached her, or for whom she hadn't prepared, she would stand speechless for a few moments, "dying on the inside," turn blood red, and start crying. She wouldn't step outside her home alone for fear of being pounced on by a bird or small animal. She would not drive in unfamiliar territory; nor would she go out to eat (she was afraid someone would look at her). Nancy believed she was "helpless" and had no control over her life. She had very low self-esteem and felt that her life was meaningless.*

Nancy illustrates many of the features of an anxiety neurosis. Among the major symptoms are a nameless dread coupled with a sense of meaninglessness and helplessness, smothering sensations, tachycardia (rapid heart rate), dizziness, nausea, difficulty concentrating, and irritability.[17] So painful is the experience, that many people focus their anxiety on some trivial or benign object (a bird, say, or driving alone). That, at least, provides some structure and meaning to the experience.

To understand anxiety, we must return for a moment to our discussion of the nuclear self. As discussed in Chapter 10, the nuclear self is a set of ideas and propositions about what we are and our place in the world. It is built up over the course of a lifetime but has its primary origins in early experience with significant persons, particularly parents or others in a position of trust. As a cognitive structure acquired through experience, the nuclear self is never entirely secure. Anxiety is an accompaniment of any fundamental change in the self, whether or not that change is desired or desirable. In its most extreme form, a catastrophic reaction, anxiety reflects the actual or impending collapse of the nuclear self.

It follows from the above considerations that anxiety involves an inability to impose meaning on events. The inability may be complete, or it may be (and usually is) only partial; and it may be temporary, or it may be a longstanding personality characteristic. Its origins may be traced to many different factors—for example, early childhood trauma, neurological injury, extreme stress, intrapsychic or interpersonal conflict, and even creative endeavors.

The point we want to emphasize is that anxiety is the antithesis of a rule-governed response. Hence it is fundamentally different from other emotions, and even from most other neurotic syndromes. Emotions are constituted by rules; without rules our emotional life would be unpredictable and chaotic. Anxiety is a condition of emotional chaos.[18]

As human beings we are naturally innovative. We are especially innovative at defending against anxiety. When the defense leads to behavior that is inflexible, ineffective, or inauthentic, the result is neurosis.

Ordinary Heroes

We do not want to leave the impression that everyone who comes to psychotherapy is suffering from a neurotic disorder. That is certainly not the case. In fact, most clients are simply in a situation that

momentarily exceeds their ability to cope. They need some assistance in meeting the crisis. Take Alice:

> *Alice is a woman in her early sixties who suffers from diabetes.*
> *Because of her illness, she has widespread physical problems:*
> *obesity, a bad heart, and progressively deteriorating eyesight.*
> *She has been a housewife most of her adult life and has no*
> *marketable job skills consistent with the limitations imposed by*
> *her health. She started therapy when her husband divorced her,*
> *leaving her alone and in poor financial condition.*

The strength and courage that many clients show in the face of
adversity is nothing short of inspirational. That may sound hackneyed, but it is nevertheless true. Even when the crisis is of the
person's own making, as in some neurotic disorders, a solution may
be achieved only after a great deal of struggle and pain. In the short
run, at least, it is far easier to give up in self-pity or retreat behind a
wall of self-deception than to accept responsibility for one's own
behavior.

Earlier, we described the case of Zack, who suffered from
multiple sexual deviancies—exhibitionism, voyeurism, masturbating in public parking lots. These behaviors did not just happen.
Zack grew up in a series of foster homes. He never knew love as
most children do, and to protect himself from hurt, he learned to
inhibit his emotions. It is difficult to say exactly what initiated
Zack's sexual deviancies. Perhaps it was simply happenstance—
hearing or reading about similar incidents when he was in a
particularly vulnerable state. Perhaps it was the result of normal
adolescent experimentation, which then became solidified into a
compulsive behavior pattern. The exact cause is less important than
the fact that Zack ultimately accepted responsibility for his own
behavior. He actively worked on acquiring and refining the emotions that he would not allow himself to experience as a child. He
became as creative in his personal as in his professional life. His
sexual deviancies have all but disappeared; his relationship with his
wife has greatly improved; and there is a new vitality to his life.
Zack, no less than Alice, has shown the kind of courage that in
other circumstances could easily be described as heroic.

Part IV

Conditions for Emotional Creativity

*No occurrences are so unfortunate that the shrewd cannot
turn them to some advantage, nor so fortunate
that the imprudent cannot turn them
to their own disadvantage.*
—La Rochefoucauld, *Maxims*

14

✦

Challenges and Facilitators:
An Overview

We should be careful to get out of an experience only the
wisdom that is in it—and stop there; lest we
be like the cat that sits down on a hot
stove-lid. She will never sit down on
the stove-lid again—and that is well;
but also she will never sit down
on a cold one any more.
—Twain, *Pudd'nhead Wilson's New Calendar*

The conditions for emotional creativity can be divided into two
overlapping categories. The first category consists of events that call
for, even necessitate, a creative emotional response. We call such
events *challenges*. The present chapter provides a brief discussion of
challenge in general. In subsequent chapters we will deal with more
specific challenges, including pleasure and pain, death, solitude,
and intimacy. The second category consists of personal and environmental conditions that make possible, even if they do not call
for, innovative emotional responses. We call such conditions *facilitators*. Among the facilitators of emotional creativity are autonomy,
freedom, imagination, art, and drama. Needless to say, these
challenges and facilitators are not the only conditions for emotional
creativity, but they are among the most important.

Challenge

As discussed in Chapter 6, for a response to be creative in the fullest sense, it should not only be novel and authentic, it should also be effective. But a response cannot be effective in and of itself, it can be effective only in relation to some challenge or problem. The challenge may be practical (as in science and technology), aesthetic (as in art), or psychosocial (as in the emotional realm). Whatever the domain, the old adage holds true—"necessity is the mother of invention."

If conditions are sufficiently extreme or demanding, creativity is to an extent forced upon us. We either change and adapt, or we succumb. Of course, some do succumb—by withdrawing into a protective shell of apathy and depression, pretending that nothing is of any use or value, or by taking that last desperate step in self-negation—suicide. But the will to survive is strong, and the potential for a creative response is inherent in all of us if we have the courage to accept the challenge.

Imagine for a moment being in a situation where, day after day, you are confronted with hunger, disease, humiliation, degradation —and the ever-present threat of extermination on any sign of weakness or rebellion. That was the challenge faced by the Viennese psychiatrist Viktor Frankl when he was sent to the Nazi concentration camp at Auschwitz. Through his own creative spirit that would not be subdued, and a good deal of sheer luck, he survived to tell the story.[1]

After an initial period of shock, new arrivals at Auschwitz tended to sink into deep apathy as they became entrenched in the camp routine. Common human sensitivities were blunted as a protective shell against an unremitting hostile environment. Yet below the surface apathy emotional life continued to flicker. Seemingly trivial pleasures—for example, a humorous remark, a sunset, a piece of stale bread—might be turned into a source of immense joy. The greatest task was to maintain some self-respect— the feeling of being an individual and not just a nameless member of a herd of draft animals, whose end is slaughter when too weak or too rebellious for useful work.

In an environment devoid of any privacy, an almost irresistible yearning for solitude may develop, a yearning to be alone with oneself and one's thoughts. In Auschwitz physical privacy was impossible; nevertheless, some people "were able to retreat from their terrible surroundings to a life of inner riches and spiritual freedom."[2] There, they found—or created—new forms of emotional experience that helped them to survive. To illustrate, Frankl tells of an experience of his own. One early winter morning, as the men were being marched to work in the bitter cold, Frankl saw his wife's image "more luminous than the sun which was beginning to rise." He spoke to her, and she answered him, encouragingly. It was then, for the first time in his life, that he "grasped the meaning of the greatest secret that human poetry and human thought and belief have to impart: The salvation of man is through love and in love."[3] The love which Frankl experienced at that moment, and toward which he thereafter aspired, was not the love typically portrayed in romance literature. It was a love that goes beyond the physical person of the beloved and that finds its meaning in the spiritual self. The actual presence of the beloved somehow even ceases to be of importance. Let there be no misunderstanding, the kind of love of which Frankl speaks is not a mere intellectual appreciation of the other. It is highly emotional, even blissful. Dante would have understood.

Another highly creative emotional response (or set of responses) may be found in Frankl's struggle to find meaning in his suffering—a purpose for a life—and probable death—seemingly bereft of all reason. He found that purpose, not by minimizing or denying the horrors he faced, but by striving to be worthy of his suffering. "The way in which a man accepts his fate and all the suffering it entails, the way in which he takes up his cross, gives him ample opportunity—even under the most difficult circumstances—to add a deeper meaning to his life."[4]

Suffering ceases to be *mere* suffering, depending on the attitude one adopts toward it. For example, the martyr may view suffering as an honor; the masochist, as a form of pleasure; the hero, as an opportunity to display courage; and so forth. The important point is that we are free to choose which attitude we adopt and hence the meaning of our suffering. That is the ultimate freedom of which we cannot be deprived, no matter the circumstances.

Fortunately, few of us will ever confront the kind of extreme challenge faced by Frankl. However, at some time or another we all must deal with misfortunes that necessitate change in our customary ways of responding. When we do not use suffering to grow, when all we feel is pain, we may get mired in self-pity and other nonproductive modes of response. When we use suffering to grow, crises can become turning points for the better. This fact is well illustrated by a young man whom we will call Ben.

Ben lost most of his belongings in a house fire. He and his wife were struggling to make ends meet and had postponed buying house insurance. Within a week after his house burned his car caught fire and the electrical system was destroyed. His reaction to these setbacks was anger and fighting back. As a consequence, he started a fight at work and lost his job. So within a week he had no house, no car, no job, and he had a wife and two small children to support. In discussing this later he said:

That was the most difficult, but in the long run the most beneficial time of my life. Initially I was angry and felt like giving up. I had wanted to go into business for myself but was afraid to. I finally realized I had nothing more to lose. Some of the worst things I feared might someday happen had happened at once, and I was still making it. So with that knowledge, coupled with the encouragement of my wife and mother, I decided to start my own plumbing business. I had a friend that let me and my family stay with him, so with nothing but a few tools and my skills, I started approaching people. Within three weeks I had saved enough money to repair my car and rent a house. I realized I had the courage to face almost anything. In fact, I found a combined sense of courage and pride in myself. A new feeling for me. So when I say that was the most difficult and the most beneficial time of my life, that is what I am talking about.

In recent years, there has been a tendency to view the conditions for positive change (growth or "self-actualization") in a rather simplistic light. If all necessary provisions are met (food, shelter, love, etc.) then people will supposedly grow and mature in a healthy fashion and meet their full potential. Stress and adversity are to be avoided as unnecessary, at best, and as detrimental to self-actualization, at worst. This is not only a gross oversimplification; it is a harmful one as well, for it ill prepares us to meet in creative ways the inevitable misfortunes that we all must occasionally face. Just as important, it ill prepares us to accept the good fortunes that opportunity provides. Fear of success and fear of failure spring from the same source.

Try to recall the events that have contributed most to your own growth and maturity. At the time they were occurring, did you regard them as positive or negative, benign or stressful? Most people, when they conduct this little thought experiment, recall negative, stressful life-events. We do not advocate seeking adversity as a means for growth. If improperly managed, stressful life-events can have detrimental effects on later development. It must be recognized, however, that growth does not come easily. Suffering is inevitable. We pay a high price for it; we might as well learn and grow from it.

Needless to say, adversity is not the only occasion for change. Falling in love, getting married, having a baby, achieving a long-awaited promotion, all may require major readjustments. Good fortune can be as challenging as bad, and as difficult to handle.

Most of us are content to remain as we are until faced with some difficulty, or some stroke of exceptional good fortune. We go by the old adage, "If it ain't broken, don't fix it." That is often good advice. It is also well to remember, however, that few things are working so well that improvement cannot be made. Excellence, not sufficiency, should be our goal.

We need not wait for calamity or good fortune to strike before we discover that many aspects of our life may be far from optimum, far from productive. One day we realize that life has become a standard, uniform pattern of stagnation, a routine of smiling at people we don't see, answering people we don't hear. We get up in the morning, go to work, but feel little accomplishment; we come home in the evening, go to bed, tired but not satisfied; we get up the next morning, and the cycle begins again, day after day. Life is comfortable but lacks meaning, or beauty, or challenge.

Being open and fresh to experience is one of the characteristics of self-actualizing people as described by Abraham Maslow. These highly creative individuals have:

> . . . the wonderful capacity to appreciate again and again, freshly and naively, the basic goods of life, with awe, pleasure, wonder, and even ecstasy, however stale these experiences may have become to others. Thus, for such a person, any sunset may be as beautiful as the first one, any flower may be of breathtaking loveliness, even after he has seen a million flowers. . . . For such people, even the casual workaday, moment-to-moment business of living can be thrilling, exciting,

and ecstatic. These intense feelings do not come all the time; they come occasionally rather than usually, but at the most unexpected moment.[5]

Some challenges are more like invitations than demands. These are what we have called facilitators, along with such personal characteristics as an active imagination. To see the extraordinary in the ordinary, to experience afresh the wonders of life as a child might, but now with the knowledge and wisdom of an adult: The invitation is there for everyone to accept or reject. For many different reasons—ignorance, timidity, and laziness being prominent among them—rejections far outnumber acceptances.

An Overview of Subsequent Chapters

The next eight chapters are devoted to specific challenges to, and facilitators of, emotional creativity. These chapters form a rough progression. However, we have tried to make them sufficiently self-contained so that they can be read as independent essays. To provide an overview of the topics covered, we offer here a brief précis of each chapter.

Pleasure and Pain (Chapter 15). Nothing would seem less of a challenge than the enjoyment of pleasure. History and everyday experience prove otherwise. The people we honor most as cultural heroes are typically those who have suffered greatly. The hedonist, the person who enjoys a life of ease and pleasure, is generally looked upon with suspicion as a kind of anti-hero. The "happy ending," when it does occur, seems meaningless without prior suffering. Suffering not only makes pleasure meaningful, it actually heightens immediate experience. Recall Frankl's experiences in a concentration camp: In the presence of great suffering even minor events became a source of great joy. To take a more mundane example, a person with a severe toothache can envision no greater pleasure than simple relief. In view of facts such as these, it is not surprising that many hedonistic philosophies, both ancient and modern, define pleasure as the absence of pain. This view is also common among psychologists, although the terminology may differ. For example, Freud's "pleasure principle" postulates the release of tension as the source of pleasure. We do not agree that pleasure is the absence of pain; it cannot be denied, however, that pleasure and pain are closely associated. A person cannot be more aware of pleasure without being more aware of pain; conversely, a person cannot blunt the experience of pain without also blunting the experience of pleasure. That is the paradox—and the challenge —of pleasure.

Death and Dying (Chapter 16). In his Pulitzer Prize winning book, *The Denial of Death,* Ernest Becker argues that fear of death is the wellspring of human creativity.[6] Frankl expresses a similar view when he states that any suffering can be endured, if only we can give it meaning. Death seems to rob life of meaning, and hence we want to deny its finality. One way to deny death is by creating a legacy that will outlive ourselves, be it the birth of a child, an endowment, a work of art, a business enterprise, or simply a good name and reputation. But fear is not the only way that death fosters creativity. In bereavement, what is feared has happened, and we grieve our loss. The death of a loved one is one of the most shattering events any of us will experience, and the source of some of our most emotionally creative responses. Ultimately, of course, each of us must die. What is it like to experience one's own death? That is not an idle question. The "miracles" of modern medicine have produced many a contemporary Lazarus—people on the brink of death (e.g., following an accident or heart attack) who have been resuscitated. Their "near-death experiences" have much to teach us about the possibilities of emotional creativity.

Solitude (Chapter 17). Creativity requires solitude. To many people, solitude implies loneliness. Human beings are by nature social creatures. Loneliness can be a painful, dreary, and depressing experience—the closest we come to a foretaste of death. The pain of loneliness can therefore be a spur to creativity, but only if we do not flee from it too rapidly. A person who cannot tolerate aloneness will never fulfill his or her creative potential. But solitude is more than loneliness. Too much, or forced sociality can also be distressing, as Frankl noted with respect to the inmates at Auschwitz. Solitude is the opportunity to be *with,* not just *by* oneself. In solitude, we can mine the depths of our inner experience without distraction or interference. In a society of doing, such as ours, we are urged to be continually active, outgoing, and social. The "loner" is looked upon with ambivalence, a source of both envy and suspicion. No wonder few people develop a capacity for solitude, and with it an important condition for emotional creativity.

Intimacy (Chapter 18). Love, wrote the German poet, Rainer

Maria Rilke, "consists in this—that two solitudes protect and touch and greet each other."[7] The person who lacks the capacity for solitude also lacks the capacity for the kind of intimacy that love implies—an intimacy in which the other is accepted as an individual, separate and equal, and not simply as an appendage of one's own self. Intimacy demands emotional creativity, in that two independent lives must intermesh, without either being diminished. In addition to the demands it places on the individuals, intimacy also facilitates emotional creativity by providing an atmosphere of warmth and acceptance, where new responses can be explored, tested, and either rejected or further refined, as conditions warrant. Such intimacy is much more than the infatuation of two people in love. As we saw in the case of Frankl, it does not necessarily require the physical presence of the other person, nor need it be limited to a single individual. The mystic knows what intimacy means, as does a true friend, as well as lovers.

Autonomy (Chapter 19). Autonomy is often contrasted with intimacy, as when men are said to prefer autonomy and women intimacy. It is a false contrast. Autonomy, which literally means "self-rule," is a higher-order construct. It implies the ability to make choices on the basis of self-chosen principle, rather than on whim or expediency. Stated differently, the autonomous person is able to reconcile competing but legitimate desires, without necessarily forsaking one for the other. Faced with conflicting desires for solitude and intimacy, for example, the autonomous person is able to accommodate both in a principled and emotionally creative way. The conflict between solitude and intimacy is only one of many conflicts that mark a person's life. Above, we cited Becker to the effect that fear of death is the wellspring of creative activity. But fear of death is important only because of the conflict it generates, as Becker himself makes clear. No other animal fears death because no other animal can conceive of death. Death symbolizes our creatureliness: We are both repelled and enticed by it. Of course, not all conflicts are so grandiose; and even the most minor conflicts can call for creative solutions. Thus, if anything deserves to be called the wellspring of creativity, it is conflict. That is why autonomy—the ability to manage conflict in a principled way—is so important.

Freedom (Chapter 20). Everyone agrees that without freedom there can be no creativity. But there agreement ends. What one person considers freedom another regards as bondage. What is freedom? One common mistake is to equate freedom with autonomy. There is a relation, of course, in that the autonomous person is self-ruled. However, the autonomous person need not be, and often is not, free in two important senses. First, an autonomous person may be ostracized or even imprisoned for standing on principle—as was Andrei Sakharov in the Soviet Union, and Martin Luther King, Jr., in the United States. Second, an autonomous person may lack the resources (material, intellectual, spiritual) to act in accordance with principle. We may thus distinguish two kinds of freedom, each distinct from autonomy: One kind presumes the *right* to respond; the other kind presumes the *ability* to respond. As in the case of solitude and intimacy, these two kinds of freedom, each important in its own right, sometimes come into conflict. People who have unlimited rights may nevertheless feel oppressed; without restrictions or guidelines they do not know how to act or which way to turn. The result is what Erich Fromm called an "escape from freedom."[8] Similarly, people who have great ability may also feel oppressed, but for a very different reason: Responsibilities accumulate with resources. This is the moral behind Mark Twain's classic novel, *The Prince and the Pauper*. Needless to say, the resources need not be material, as in the case of a prince: People of extraordinary ability often experience great pressure to "produce"—so much so that many attempt to escape from their own kind of freedom, for example, by finding refuge in drugs or even suicide.

Imagination (Chapter 21). The difference between the two kinds of freedom noted above is perhaps most evident with respect to the imagination. No matter how constrained we might be by external circumstances, we are nevertheless free (in the first sense) to imagine a reality different than the one in which we find ourselves. But before we can exercise that freedom, we must cultivate the ability to use our imagination. That is, we must have the relevant resources (freedom in the second sense). Recall again the plight of Frankl: In a Nazi concentration camp, a prisoner had no rights. Life was highly regimented and the prospect of death ever imminent. Yet Frankl was able to overcome the hardships of his environment, in part through the creative use of his imagination. He, and no one else, determined the attitude he would take toward his own suffering, and in the process his suffering was transformed. Frankl was exceptional in his ability to use his imagination, but we all can learn to be more imaginative than we are. The emotions, no less than other kinds of behavior, involve the imagination. During an emergency we have little choice in the kind of emotion we experience. Rather, we fall back on previously acquired habits. However, with the help of imagination we can develop and test new forms of emotion. Happiness, sadness, anger, envy, hope, and the like can all be aroused, honed, and refined through imagery. But more than that, through imagination we integrate our emotions with the totality of ourselves, so that they become part of us, not alien forces that we must somehow control lest they control us.

Art, Drama, and the Cathartic Method (Chapter 22). No discussion of the imagination would be complete without some reference to works of art, including literature. These are among the most effective and available conditions for emotional creativity. Through art, we can re-create in the convenience of the theater or our own home the emotions that have captured the imagination of great artists and writers from around the world and during all periods of history. Art transcends the limitations of time and place. But how does it exert its effects? We can divide (somewhat arbitrarily, to be sure) a work of art into two aspects: its form and its content. The form has to do with aesthetic values; the content is what the work is about, for example, the wandering of Odysseus, the tribulations of Hamlet, the romances of Don Juan. We explore briefly the nature of aesthetic values and the emotions they induce (wonder, awe, fascination). Our primary concern, however, is with content. Tragedy, in particular, raises a question that has stirred controversy for centuries: Why should we enjoy a work that arouses in us primarily feelings of sorrow and pity? Aristotle provided the most debated answer to this question, namely, tragedy allows a catharsis (purging) of the emotions. Freud offered a similar explanation for the beneficial effects of psychoanalysis, which he initially called the "cathartic method." We offer an interpretation of catharsis not as a purgation, but as a perfection of the emotions. Art, drama, and psychotherapy all stretch and educate the emotions.

The Challenge of Emotional Creativity

To conclude this overview of the conditions for emotional creativity, we should mention what is perhaps the greatest challenge of all—emotional creativity itself. Nietzsche claimed that he desired nothing more than to lose some soothing belief each day.[9] To him, that would be happiness. Today, under psychology's program of "stress management," the goal seems to be to gain some soothing belief each day—happiness is contentment, quietude, satisfaction. These are all desirable states, to be sure, but they are not conditions for emotional creativity. Emotional creativity challenges us to shed soothing beliefs, to explore and develop new way of perceiving, thinking, and responding. "There is in all change something at once sordid and agreeable, smacking of infidelity and household removals," Baudelaire remarked.[10] Emotional creativity cannot occur without some infidelity to one's prior self, some removals from one's inner household. The promise is for a more full, vital, and productive life, but also one punctuated by pain, grief, loneliness, conflict, and anxiety.

15

◆

Pain and Pleasure

I do not know how I can conceive the good, if I withdraw
the pleasures of taste, and withdraw the pleasures of love,
and withdraw the pleasures of hearing, and withdraw the
pleasurable emotions caused to
sight by beautiful form.
—Epicurus, *Fragments: On The End of Life*

When, therefore, we maintain that pleasure is the end,
we do not mean the pleasures of profligates
and those that consist in sensuality, . . .
but freedom from pain in the body
and from trouble in the mind.
—Epicurus, *Letter to Menoeceus*

Pleasure presents a paradox, and that paradox is nowhere more
evident than in the teachings of Epicurus, the ancient Greek
philosopher (341–270 B.C.) who taught that pleasure is the highest,
indeed, the only unconditional good.

In contemporary English, the term "epicure" (with a small "e")
refers to a person with refined taste in food and wine; more
generally, "epicurean" refers to a person devoted to the pursuit of
pleasure. Epicurus was no epicurean in the contemporary sense. He
subsisted on simple foods (mostly plain bread and water); he
shunned fame ("live unknown," he advised[1]); he even abstained

from sexual intercourse ("for the pleasures of love never profited a man and he is lucky if they do him no harm"[2]). Epicurus found his greatest pleasure in conversation with friends. All in all, he was more an ascetic than a hedonist. The reasons are instructive, for they illustrate the challenges that pleasure presents.

Epicurus was a thoroughgoing materialist; he did not believe in a future existence in which any suffering incurred during this lifetime might be redeemed. Some people find such a philosophy depressing; Epicurus thought it essential to happiness. Disbelief in an afterlife, he argued, frees us from fear of Hades, the Greek equivalent of hell. More to the point of this chapter, it also means that we should maximize pleasure in this life, for what we have is all we are going to get.

But what, precisely, is pleasure? It is the absence of pain, according to Epicurus. It would seem to follow from this definition that the good life, the truly happy life, is a life without pain. There is, however, a problem with this conception, as the satirist H. L. Mencken aptly noted:

> Happiness, like health, is a passing accident. For a moment or two the organism is irritated so little that it is not conscious of it; for the duration of that moment it is happy. Thus a hog is always happier than a man, and a bacillus is happier than a hog.[3]

With this *reductio ad absurdum* we are led to conclude that pleasure is not simply the absence of pain or the satisfaction of desires. At best, that is only part of the story. There also are pleasures that, for want of a better term, we will call "carefree." Examples include such simple sensory pleasures as the sweet taste of chocolate, the smell of a rose, the sound of a child's laughter, the feel of a good massage, the sight of a beautiful sunset. Pleasures of this sort are carefree in the sense that their enjoyment does not depend on any prior privation or distress. There are also carefree pleasures of the mind: a good joke, conversations with friends, a match of wits—the list is endless.

To be fair to Epicurus, he was a strong advocate of carefree pleasures, although consistent with his general philosophy, he did not consider them entirely carefree. The goal, he maintained, should be to maximize the total amount of pleasure over an entire lifetime. Pleasures of the moment that go beyond what is natural and necessary for a person's well-being may, in the long run, result in a net increase in pain, and hence should be avoided. This is especially true of simple sensory pleasures. To take an obvious but nontrivial example, the person who consistently eats too much because the food tastes good is liable to suffer unpleasant consequences in the future.

The greatest pleasures, according to Epicurus, are those of the mind, not of the body, for the latter are only temporary. The body lives in the present, the mind—through memory and expectation —comprehends both the past and the future. The wise person stores up memories of past pleasures and expectations of future pleasures. These memories and expectations provide the resources to overcome present pains or suffering.

Epicurus rightly saw that sensory pleasures present a challenge. We disagree, however, with his apparent retreat from the challenge. Pleasure can and should be found in each moment of each day; but to accomplish this, we must actively seek enjoyment in simple things. Far too often we are so embroiled in the pain of yesterday and the fear of tomorrow that we lose sight of today. The ideal—and here we agree with Epicurus—is to learn from the past, dream for the future, but live in the present.

That is easy enough to say, but Epicurus's own austere life, in spite of his explicitly hedonistic philosophy, suggests that there might be difficulties even in the wise pursuit of carefree pleasures. We need to examine more closely the link between pleasure and pain. Is it really as close as Epicurus presumed?

Epicurus, it might be noted, was in poor health for most of his life and that perhaps colored his outlook. A person who is in pain can often conceive of no greater pleasure than to be rid of his suffering. That would not explain, however, the appeal of Epicurus to his followers, who revered him almost as a demigod. Nor would it apply to the Cyrenaics—followers of another ancient Greek philosopher, Aristippus of Cyrene.

Like the Epicureans, the Cyrenaics were materialists. They had no qualms about an afterlife to inhibit their search for pleasure in this world. Unlike the Epicureans, the Cyrenaics viewed pleasure as an independently existing phenomenon and not simply as the absence of pain. Pleasure was to be sought for its own sake, as Aristippus advised:

The man who controls pleasure is not he who stays away from it, but he who uses it without being carried away by it; just as

the master of a ship or horse is not one who does not use them,
but he who guides them wherever he wishes.[4]

Aristippus took his own advice. According to Zeller, he was an
adroit man of the world who was never at a loss when it came to
discovering new means of enjoyment, whether by fair means or
foul.[5] Not all of his followers were equally successful. It takes skill
and wisdom, and on occasion a good deal of courage, to be master
of a ship or horse. To be master of one's own pleasures appears to
be no easier. As the Cyrenaics developed their philosophy, the
widespread incidence of pain became of increasing concern; and
hence the more mild but enduring pleasures of contentment,
friendship, gratitude, love of country, came to be emphasized, as
they were by the Epicureans. Hegesius, a follower of Aristippus,
had so vivid a sense for misery that he was dubbed the "counselor
of death." His lectures in Alexandria led to so many suicides that
they were ultimately banned.

Evidently, the pursuit of pleasure is not a task for the faint of
heart. In fact, if history be our guide, a life of asceticism—the
acceptance of pain, suffering, and self-mortification—is easier to
sustain than is a life of hedonism. It is certainly more highly
honored. Why?

This is an issue that puzzled William James, and his answer is
worth recounting briefly. According to James, asceticism symbolizes the belief that there is real wrongness in the world. Pain,
suffering, and tragic deaths of all manner and kind must be squarely
met and neutralized. But how? Not by the worship of luxury or
indulgence in hedonistic pursuits. At best, these grant only temporary respite. At worst, they make for effeminacy and unmanliness, a
"trashiness of fibre." "In these remarks," James asserts, "I am
leaning only upon mankind's common instinct for reality, which in
point of fact has always held the world to be essentially a theater for
heroism. In heroism, we feel, life's supreme mystery is hidden."[6]

Asceticism is part of our "common instinct for reality." It is not
entirely clear what James intended by this rather enigmatic assertion. To speak of instinct implies a biological origin. We will pursue
that implication, whether or not that is what James intended.

We may assume that, during the course of evolution, organisms—including human beings—that were most able to endure
pain and suffering were the ones most likely to survive and leave
progeny. But how might endurance be achieved? Only, in a sense,

by fighting fire with fire. It is through suffering that we learn to overcome suffering. The person who could not endure pain, who avoided hardship and the dangers of the hunt, who would not forego the pleasure of sex, food, and restful relaxation, such a person would evoke little admiration in followers, and would leave few progeny to extol his or her hedonistic virtues. From a biological point of view, then, we might expect people to seek danger, to find vitality in suffering—in short, to have "some common instinct for reality." And here we are presented with a paradox.

Conditions that are beneficial in the struggle for survival tend to have a pleasurable quality—ripe fruit tastes sweet, mating is pleasurable, and so forth. It would seem to follow that mild forms of pain might also be associated with a kind of perverse pleasure. And such does indeed seem to be the case. If we have a loose tooth or sore muscle, we cannot help but probe the tooth with our tongue or exercise the muscle, in spite of (or perhaps because of) the mild pain that it causes. At a somewhat more complex level, we enjoy a good cry or are enlivened by the thrill of danger.

What most people pursue in mild degree because of its benefits, others may pursue to a maladaptive extreme, either due to faulty biological makeup or to inappropriate early experience. The glutton, for example, eats until he is obese. Are there gluttons for pain? Without doubt.

> Her love of pain and suffering was insatiable. . . . She said that she could cheerfully live till the day of judgment, provided she might always have matter for suffering for God; but that to live a single day without suffering would be intolerable. She said again that she was devoured with two unassuageable fevers, one for the holy communion, the other for suffering, humiliation, and annihilation. "Nothing but pain," she continually said in her letters, "makes my life supportable."

That is the way one biographer has described Marguerite-Marie Alacoque (1647–1690) of the Visitation order of nuns.[7]

One doesn't have to be a religious zealot to find pleasure in pain. Take masochism—the willing embrace of pain and humiliation in the pursuit of sexual pleasure. It is estimated that 1 or 2 percent of the American population (between 2 and 3 million people) engage in masochistic sexual practices on a regular basis; and that between 5 and 10 percent have done so occasionally.[8] We do not believe, as its advocates would have it, that masochism is an emotionally creative response. However, the prevalence of the practice does illustrate the sometimes synergistic effects of pain and pleasure.

Many people do not even alloy their pain with sexual or other forms of pleasure; the pain itself seems enticement enough. Barent Walsh and Paul Rosen define self-mutilative behavior as "deliberate, non-life-threatening, self-effected bodily harm or disfigurement of a socially unacceptable nature," and they estimate its yearly incidence to range from 14 to 600 persons per 100,000.[9] This broad range reflects ambiguities in the definition of self-mutilation and the unwillingness of people to report such behavior. But however the count is made, the numbers are large. In the United States (with a population of approximately 240 million people), somewhere between 33,600 and 1,440,000 people mutilate themselves each year. The reasons for such behavior are not at all understood. Attempted suicide is ruled out by definition. Self-mutilators want to live and, for whatever reason, pain seems to afford them a sense of aliveness.

In short, asceticism—even when it takes an extreme form of self-inflicted pain and injury—holds a strange fascination for many people. When their suffering can be rationalized in terms of a cause with which we agree, we treat ascetics as saints or heroes; if they have no cause, or if we disagree with their cause, we treat them as neurotic. In either case, we sense with James that in their suffering "life's supreme mystery is hidden."

Now let us return to pleasure, for it, too, has its mysteries. A life of pleasure may not excite our wonder and admiration in the same way as a life of pain and suffering. Yet, there is something about the hedonist that fascinates and draws our attention. The great lover, the master gourmet, the virtuoso of song and dance—we envy their capacity for sensual enjoyment. Don Juan is also a hero of sorts.

In his book, *Life Against Death*, Norman Brown resurrects Freud's emphasis on the conflict between life and death instincts, Eros and Thanatos. For Brown, these symbolize two ways of acting on the world. Eros is the impulse to preserve and enrich life; Thanatos, the urge to return to the peace of death.[10] We agree that there is some such opposition, and that it is played out on the simplest level in the tendencies toward pleasure and pain. But we disagree with Brown on a fundamental point. Thanatos is not an urge to return to the peace of death. On the contrary, it, like Eros, represents a way of preserving and enriching life. These are two routes to the same end. The one, Eros, informs us of the good through pleasure; the other, Thanatos, allows us to overcome the bad through mastery of pain.

In support of the above analysis, it might be noted that cultural heroes, whether in myth or reality, are most often individuals who have the capacity for *both* great pleasure and pain. Perhaps nowhere is this dual capacity better illustrated than in the Hindu myth of Siva. In Chapter 10 (on the self), we recounted how the god Indra and the demon Virochana went to a sage for counsel. Indra, heeding the sage's advice, was able to surmount the pleasures of the body (as well as all discursive thought), and in so doing came to recognize the identity of his transcendental self (*atman*) with the indestructible ground of all being (*Brahman*). Virochana, by contrast, being only a demon, mistook the sage's initial advice and became mired in material luxury and sensual pleasures. Thus far, the story seems just another paean to asceticism. There is, however, more to Indra than this one episode suggests. Indra once commanded the god of love, Kama, to break the timeless meditation of the solitary Siva, the archetypal ascetic and master yogi of Hindu philosophy. Kama was supposed to instill in Siva an ardent desire for the beautiful goddess Parvati. Without going into detail, things did not work out entirely as planned. Greatly angered, Siva literally cremated Kama—turned him to ashes. Kama's spirit was, however, preserved, and he now hovers about lovers, intangibly forcing them into each other's arms.

As for Siva, he did, in fact, fall in love with Parvati—and with many other women besides. Not only was he the archetypal ascetic, he was also a voluptuary *par excellence.* He is typically described as ithyphallic (having a constantly erect penis). In Siva, asceticism and eroticism, two seemingly incompatible life-styles, are combined in an emotionally creative way. Like love and hate, eroticism and asceticism can alternate, or even coexist in ambivalent but creative tension.[11]

The creative tension between eroticism and asceticism can also be seen in the *Kamasutra,* a book of aphorisms on the art of lovemaking dedicated to the god Kama. Although exquisite in erotic detail, it does not disparage asceticism; the ascetic who can control the senses and appetites is presented as a desirable and effective lover. Indrana, the consort of Indra, even has a coital position named after her.

The noted Indologist Heinrich Zimmer has speculated that the *Kamasutra* served to counterbalance the ascetic trend in Hinduism, as well as to offset the frustrations of marriages that were arranged more for convenience than love. "It was for a society of frozen emotions, not libertine, that this compendium of the techniques of adjustment and stimulation was compiled."[12] "Frozen emotions" may be an overstatement. Nevertheless, the point should be well taken: The goal of the *Kamasutra* is balance, not licentiousness.

It is not just in myth and cultural heroes that we find a tension between pain and pleasure. In longitudinal studies of day-to-day variations in emotional reactions, Ed Diener and his colleagues have found that people who report strong positive emotions when good things happen also report strong negative emotions when bad things happen.[13] In other words, there is a general tendency among people to respond intensely in both positive and negative directions. We may wish to maximize the positive and minimize the negative, but that may not be a realistic goal, as the Epicureans and Cyrenaics discovered long ago.

To conclude, both pain and pleasure must be acknowledged and given their due. Each person must find a tension and balance proper to his or her own temperament and situation. There is no set prescription that fits everyone and every context. But clearly the challenge of pleasure is not simply to avoid pain. That only leads to the kind of hedonic neutralism satirized by Mencken, in which a bacillus is happier than a hog, and a hog is happier than a human.

16

◆

Death and Dying

First our pleasures die—and then
Our hopes, and then our fears—and when
These are dead, the debt is due,
Dust claims dust—and we die too.
—Shelley, "Death"

We must all face death at least once—our own. Most of us must also face death on other occasions as well—when a parent, sibling, child, or other loved one dies. Death is among the severest challenges that any of us will ever meet, and among the greatest spurs to creativity.

To begin, consider the following facts: On the average, about 8 percent of the population lose a parent before the age of 16. Among criminals (male and female prisoners and delinquents) the rate of childhood bereavement ranges from 20 to 40 percent, much above that for the general population. However, roughly the same high percentages of childhood bereavement have been found among individuals who have achieved eminence in diverse fields, including artists, scientists, and political leaders.[1]

Bereavement during adulthood (e.g., through the death of a spouse) may also inspire—indeed, require—a new burst of creativ-

216

ity on the part of the survivor. The loss of a loved one cannot help but shatter the fragile structure of our world. And from the shards that remain, we must assemble a new world, one that once again provides meaning to our lives. Either we create, or we succumb. What we create depends, of course, on our talents and resources.

But our concern is with emotional creativity, not creativity in general. Can bereavement occasion new and different kinds of emotion? Without doubt. Some of the reactions typically experienced during grief (e.g., depression, sleep disturbances, apathy) have their origin in our biological heritage; not only are such reactions relatively universal among human beings, but similar reactions can be also observed in other social primates (e.g., chimpanzees). But that is only part of the story. As a coherent emotional syndrome, grief is also a cultural creation. The bereaved must learn to grieve in the manner dictated by his or her culture. In some societies, death is viewed as a cause for celebration, a farewell to the deceased as he or she departs for a better place; in other societies, the bereaved are expected to join the deceased on the journey, as in the custom of *suttee* (the immolation of a wife on her husband's funeral pyre); in still other societies, bereavement is a time to wreak vengeance for wrongs, real and imagined, committed against the deceased. The variations are almost endless. At one extreme, contact with the dead is regarded as pollution and the bereaved are "treated" through purification rites; at the opposite extreme, the bereaved are expected to eat the flesh of the deceased in order to incorporate his or her special powers and gifts.

The way grief is experienced and expressed *within* cultures is also highly variable. Unfortunately, we typically attend only to those variations that prove maladaptive, and hence in need of "treatment." Take the famous case of Anna O. (Bertha Pappenheim), originally treated by Josef Breuer (in the years 1880–1882) and later, at the urging of Freud, described in their joint publication, *Studies on Hysteria*.[2] Anna's symptoms first appeared as she was caring for her terminally ill father, to whom she was very devoted. Her condition worsened considerably following his death. Her symptoms were very wide ranging and included at one time or another paralysis over various parts of her body, speech disorders (including an inability to speak in her native German), positive and negative hallucinations, anorexia, and even an hysterical pregnancy (upon which Breuer withdrew as her treating physician).

Anna's reactions to her father's illness and death were highly unusual (and multiply determined); if they were not so ineffective within her personal and cultural context, they might even be regarded as creative.[3] Anna was clearly capable of high levels of creativity. She went on to become an author, a leader of the Jewish feminist movement in Germany, and a pioneer social worker. In 1954, the German government issued a stamp commemorating her accomplishments.

In many Western societies today, traditional mourning practices have been abandoned as superstitious or cost ineffective, and hence the bereaved—whether young or old—often do not know how to behave or feel. In a situation such as this, grieving itself may require a good deal of emotional creativity. Many do not succeed without professional assistance.[4]

In recent years a further complication has been added. The advancement of medical technology has tended to erode the dividing line between the living and the dead. In the United States today, there are roughly 10,000 comatose patients, mostly severely injured accident or stroke victims, who cannot see nor hear nor laugh nor cry. Yet, they are not quite dead. As long as they receive nutrients delivered through tubes inserted into their stomachs or veins, they can continue to "live," sometimes for decades. For the survivors, this creates a kind of bereavement without end. The living cannot get on with their lives because the dying are not allowed to get on with their deaths.

As individuals and as a society, we have just begun to deal with the grim dilemma posed by advancing medical technology. As we win more battles in the "war" against disease, we seem to have ever greater difficulty coming to terms with inevitable death. Pursuing the war metaphor, an instructive parallel can be drawn between the weapons against disease provided by the medical establishment and the weapons of human destruction provided by the military establishment. In each case, technological innovation has outstripped our ability to handle the potential consequences. Our motto seems to be, "If it can be built, build it," whether it is a bomb of unforeseen destructiveness or an artificial heart wheeled about in a cart. That attitude will no longer suffice. The potential costs, both financial and spiritual, are far too high.

There is something noble about battling to save a life, whether one's own or another's. We do not want to give up and, in the words of Dylan Thomas, "go gentle into that good night." On the other hand, there is something demeaning about the notion that life should be preserved at all cost, regardless of quality. Death, after all, is a natural part of life, and if we cannot face death with courage and dignity, neither will we be able to live in a full and creative fashion.

The death of a loved one is fortunately an infrequent experience for most of us. However, bereavement is a relative experience. Being left alone with a stranger during childhood, developing new roles during adolescence, leaving home for work or college, breaking off a relationship, changing jobs, moving to a new neighborhood—these and many other common experiences may involve some degree of loss, separation, or disruption of social relationships, and they may all require a reorganization of behavior that, in important respects, is similar to that occasioned by bereavement.

The way we respond to such necessary losses during our lifetime foreshadows the way we will respond to our own death. We may retreat in fear, give up in depression, rage in frustration—or we may approach death as a challenge to be met, if not overcome. For most of us most of the time, our own death is unthinkable—at least, we do not allow ourselves to think about it. That is healthy enough. And yet, we cannot avoid the issue entirely. In the words of William James, "Let sanguine healthy-mindedness do its best with its strange power of living in the moment and ignoring and forgetting, still the evil background is really there to be thought of, and the skull will grin in at the banquet."[5]

What is it like to come face to face with death? Can we grin back at the skull at the banquet? Albert Heim, professor of geology in Zurich, Switzerland, lost his footing while mountain climbing. He survived the fall, although at the time he believed he faced certain death. As he fell, scenes from his past life flashed before him, and even the future was presaged, as he pictured his family receiving news of his death. He did not panic, however. There was nothing he could do but accept his fate. "It all had to happen that way; it seemed eminently correct." Above him, he saw a beautiful blue heaven filled with small violet and roseate clouds, and he heard solemn music, as from an organ. "I felt myself go softly backwards into this magnificent heaven—without anxiety, without grief. It was a great and glorious moment!"[6]

Fascinated by the experience, Heim collected numerous examples from others who had survived similar mishaps. In 95 percent of the cases, he claimed, the experiences were similar. This is his composite description of a "typical" fall:

> No grief was felt, nor was there paralyzing fright of the sort that can happen in instances of lesser danger (i.e., the outbreak of fire). There was no anxiety, no trace of despair, no pain; but rather calm seriousness, profound acceptance, and a dominant mental quickness and sense of surety. Mental activity became enormous, rising to a hundred-fold velocity or intensity. The relationships of events and their probable outcomes were overviewed with objective clarity. No confusion entered at all. Time became greatly expanded. The individual acted with lightning-quickness in accord with accurate assessment of his situation. In many cases there followed a sudden review of the individual's entire past; and finally the person falling often heard beautiful music and fell in a superbly blue heaven containing roseate cloudlets. Then consciousness was painlessly extinguished, usually at the moment of impact.[7]

"Near-death experience" is the term now commonly applied to the kind of blissful reaction described by Heim.[8] It is somewhat of a misnomer for two reasons. First, imminent death is not a necessary condition for such experiences; the mere belief that one is about to die is often sufficient to trigger the reaction. In fact, not even the belief may be necessary. Many of the manifestations of near-death experiences can be observed in drug-induced states, and during yogic or other meditative practices. Second, as will be discussed shortly, not everyone approaches his or her demise in a state of mystical bliss.

In spite of the above anomalies, the term "near-death experience" has become customary, especially in its abbreviated form (NDE). We will follow that custom here. An NDE comprises a set of overlapping symptoms and manifestations, most prominently a feeling of peace and well-being. Other characteristic features of NDEs are out-of-body experiences (viewing events as though from a distance); vivid sensory impressions (e.g, brilliant colors, unusual sounds and bodily sensations); visions of passing through a dark tunnel or of floating through a void; a panoramic flashback of one's own life; emergence into a light; and mystic-like feelings of joy and great knowledge.

How common are such experiences? As noted above, Heim

claimed that 95 percent of the people he surveyed had NDEs similar to his own. His sample was undoubtedly biased, but his findings do suggest that NDEs are more common than might be assumed. In a Gallup poll, 15 percent of the American population reported having been near death at some time in their lives, and of these, 34 percent reported an NDE in some degree or other. That means roughly eight million Americans have had NDEs.[9]

In studies of unselected victims (patients suffering cardiac arrest, persons involved in potentially fatal accidents, etc.), several investigators have found that roughly 25 percent have had relatively full-blown, mystic-like NDEs, and perhaps another 20 percent have had moderate experiences. Victims of illness are most likely to have NDEs, accident victims next, and suicide victims the least. Few if any gender differences have been observed.[10]

NDEs do not extinguish without aftereffects. Memories of the incident remain vivid and flashbacks are not infrequent. Initially, the person may be reluctant to talk about the experience with others, even doubting his or her own sanity. However, if this sense of estrangement is overcome, the consequences are overwhelmingly positive. Most common are a reduced fear of death; a heightened appreciation and renewed sense of purpose; a greater sense of aliveness; a devaluation of material things; an attraction to solitary and contemplative pursuits; and a broadening and deepening of spiritual values, especially love, acceptance, and compassion for others.

Before commenting further on NDEs, we need to balance the scales, so to speak. The prevalence of NDEs is surprising to many people. Intuitively, one would think that the immediate reaction to the threat of death would be extreme stress. Intuition is correct. The initial response to a life threatening situation is fear. It is primarily after the individual has given up the struggle to survive that the more positive manifestations of NDE seem to appear. And for many, they never appear. In the Diagnostic and Statistical Manual of the American Psychiatric Association (DSM-III-R), two syndromes are specifically identified among the sequelae of extreme stress. They are *brief reactive psychosis* and *post-traumatic stress disorder*. The former has a sudden onset and lasts but a few hours or, at most, weeks; the latter often has a delayed onset and may last for years. We will focus here on post-traumatic stress disorder, usually abbreviated PTSD. In most instances (but not always), PTSD reflects the severity of the original stress reaction, and hence we can use it as a counterpoint to the more positive near-death experience described above.

PTSD can be occasioned by any overwhelming threat to a person's sense of self or well-being, which would include, but is not limited to, the threat of imminent death. Common occasions include military combat, rape or assault, natural disaster, a potentially fatal accident, or the death of a loved one. Thus, PTSD is a more general phenomenon than NDE, but there is sufficient overlap in eliciting conditions to warrant some comparisons.

PTSD is characterized by recurrent nightmares and intrusive flashbacks during which the original trauma may be relived, often in vivid detail. Other common symptoms include hyperarousal, an exaggerated startle response, irritability and hostility, anxiety, depression, and an inability to concentrate. Waves of heightened responsivity may be interspersed with a kind of psychological numbness or constriction of affect, including detachment and alienation from others.

Estimates of the incidence of PTSD vary greatly, depending on the inclusiveness of the diagnostic criteria and the nature of the precipitating event (e.g., rape, physical assault, near fatal injury, or witnessing someone else killed or injured). But our concern here is not with incidence. It suffices to note that some people react to the threat of death with an almost mystical experience (NDE), whereas others react with extreme stress (horror, followed by PTSD). What accounts for the difference in reaction? Indeed, are these two kinds of reaction completely distinct? Unfortunately, we can only speculate on an answer to these questions. Investigators who study NDEs seldom reference research on PTSD, and vice versa.

Research suggests that some of the symptoms of PTSD may have a physiological basis. Under severe stress, brain mechanisms release hormones that prepare the body for fight or flight; other brain structures release naturally occurring opioids (e.g., endorphins) that blunt the feeling of pain. If the initial threat is sufficiently severe, evidence suggests that these brain mechanisms become hypersensitive (reset, like a thermostat, to respond at a lower threshold), thus increasing the likelihood of repeated stress reactions to previously innocuous circumstances.[11]

Some of the same physiological mechanisms that mediate stress might also help account for near-death experiences. A rush of adrenaline and other ergotrophic responses could result in heightened mental activity (e.g., vivid sensory experiences, a rapid review of one's past life), while the release of opioids in the brain would numb any pain and anxiety, resulting in a peaceful and calm feeling.

Physiological speculation aside, psychological and social factors play an important role in determining the nature of both NDE and PTSD. It is not unusual for similar physiological responses to result in quite different emotional experiences, depending on the circumstances. For example, drug-induced "trips" can result in either terror or euphoria, depending on the situation and expectations of the user. The same might also be true with respect to the naturally occurring physiological responses to life-threatening situations. The hypothesis we would like to propose is that both syndromes, NDE and PTSD, are emotionally creative responses to situations of extreme danger.

Carol Zaleski has compared the motifs found in near-death experiences during the Middle Ages with contemporary writings on the topic.[12] The most noticeable difference between medieval and modern NDEs, according to Zaleski, is the inclusion in the former of obstacles to be overcome and purifications to be endured (as in purgatory), as well as outright damnation. Medieval NDEs were not always as pleasant as their contemporary counterparts. Among the numerous examples that Zaleski cites is that of a hermit, whose story is told in the *Dialogues* of the sixth century pope Gregory the Great. When revived from presumed death, the hermit testified that he had been to hell, where he saw figures dangling in fire. He was rescued by an angel just as he, too, was about to be dragged into the flames, and he was advised to "consider carefully how you will live from now on." That he evidently did.

PTSD is also quite sensitive to social and personal expectations. Among veterans of the Vietnam war, for example, the incidence of PTSD rose considerably for soldiers experiencing combat after 1968. Prior to 1968 the rate of psychiatric casualties (soldiers excused from duty for psychiatric reasons) was less than in either Korea or World War II and did not exceed the rate for soldiers stationed in other overseas posts.[13] Following 1968, attitudes in the United States turned increasingly against the war, and PTSD became a major issue.

We are not suggesting that a change in domestic attitudes toward the Vietnam war was the sole cause of the increase in PTSD after 1968. However, we know of no evidence that the intensity or nature of the combat changed dramatically during that period, or that a different type of soldier (e.g., seasoned veteran vs. young recruit) was involved. Of course, any change in domestic attitudes would also be reflected in the attitudes of the soldiers engaged in combat, which could influence the degree of stress they experienced. But be that as it may, no one doubts that the negative publicity and sometimes outright rejection that soldiers met on their return to the United States had an important influence on their subsequent reactions.

Catherine Lutz has described the case of one young veteran who was quite proud of his exploits during the war, and who generally found them exhilarating.[14] On returning home, however, he found himself confronted with another set of values, ones that made him question the legitimacy of his original emotions. What was once a source of pride now became a source of stress. We have seen how, during medieval times, near-death experiences might involve a descent into purgatory. For this young soldier, who was particularly troubled by scenes of mutilation and unnecessary violence, PTSD had similar characteristics—atonement on the way to redemption.

More extreme is the case of a veteran described by the psychiatrists Harry Holloway and Robert Ursano.[15] The man suffered from flashbacks in which he acted the role of a sniper, "just as I had in Vietnam." In actuality, he had been assigned to a supply depot in Vietnam where he was never exposed to intense combat. His PTSD represented not atonement and redemption for acts committed, but rather the fulfillment in fantasy of deeds undone— to be a hero like his highly decorated father.

In short, neither NDE nor PTSD represents "raw" emotional responses to life-threatening events. If an analogy were to be drawn, these emotional syndromes are like small morality plays in which people try to make sense out of their lives, and perhaps impending deaths, drawing on their past history, present circumstances, and future aspirations (not necessarily conscious).

Emotions, it must be remembered, are not simply reactions to events; they are also meanings imposed on events. The meanings, and hence the emotions, may change over time as individual and social circumstances change. Freud made frequent reference to this fact with respect to the effects of childhood trauma on later life. In discussing Leonardo da Vinci, for example, he commented that "Childhood memories are not fixed at the moment of being experienced and afterwards repeated, but are only elicited at a later age when childhood is already past; in the process they are altered and falsified, and are put into the service of later trends."[16]

We would only add that what is true of events occurring in childhood is also true of events occurring later in life; and what is true of memories is also true of anticipations. That is, we impose meanings on events *as they occur*, not simply in retrospect, and those meanings help determine—indeed, are a part of—our emotional experience.

We have now discussed reactions to the death of another (bereavement), and reactions to the threat of one's own death (as reflected in NDE and PTSD). We have yet to consider the act of dying itself and the impact of modern technology on the way we die.

Throughout most of Western history, death at a young age through disease or injury was relatively common. At the height of the Roman Empire, the average life expectancy was only about 25 to 30 years, and the situation did not improve dramatically until the late nineteenth century. During the Middle Ages the dying person, on his deathbed, orchestrated his own death, with family, friends, and children present. Death was a public, collective rite. An "art of dying" was taught, both explicitly in manuals and implicitly through example (as in the *chansons de geste*, epic tales of knights and heroes).[17]

Today, our attitudes toward death are marked by conflict and ambivalence. On the one hand, the graphic depiction of violence in movies constitutes a kind of pornography of death, analogous to the pornography of sex, with which it is sometimes allied. On the other hand, we treat death as something alien and foreign, as though it were unnatural for anyone to die. When the time does comes, as it invariably must, the dying are bundled off to a hospital, there to die among strangers, sedated beyond consciousness.

Signs of a reaction are setting in. Anyone who wishes to avoid being kept "alive" in a comatose state following an accident or illness, is well advised to complete a "living will," stipulating the kinds of medical care that are acceptable. For the terminally ill and their families, the hospice movement provides a humane alternative to traditional hospital care. For the more adventuresome, manuals exist on how to die a "good" death. An example is Anya Foos-Graber's short book, *Deathing: An Intelligent Alternative for the Final*

Moments of Life.[18] Drawing on traditional yogic practices and stress management techniques (e.g, breathing exercises), Foos-Graber outlines procedures that, she maintains, can transform the moment of death from a bleak to a peak experience. But all these measures are modest in comparison with the expanding need.

In most developed countries, the fastest growing segment of the population comprises people over 75 years of age.[19] Such longevity is something new in the history of humankind. For the most part, our emotions have been fashioned for the young. What emotions can we, and should we, fashion as we grow older, in order to maintain a rich and satisfying life? Or must we, like Epicurus, settle for pleasures that are little more than the absence of pain?

Consider for a moment the challenges of solitude and intimacy, about which we will have more to say in subsequent chapters. At each age level men die at a higher rate than women. The ratio of women to men thus increases with advancing age. Should most women plan to forego the pleasures of sexual intimacy during their later years? Should they look to younger lovers? Should several women form a triadic relationship with a man? Or a lesbian relationship with each other? And what about men? While they may have greater opportunities for establishing heterosexual relationships than women, they do not necessarily have the capabilities, either physical or psychological. Many men do not know how to be intimate with a woman without being sexual.

Even more pressing issues are raised by the imminence of death among the elderly. How should we respond to approaching death, either that of friends and loved ones, or our own? When the process of dying is prolonged over many months and even years, how should we grieve? Is euthanasia (mercy killing) ever justified? And should a person be allowed, even assisted, in committing suicide, if the decision is based on rational choice? We ask such questions, not because we have any answers to suggest, but to illustrate the nature of the challenges that confront us. The greatest obstacles to meeting these challenges are emotional, not technological. Emotional creativity will be needed if technology is to prolong meaningful life, not just postpone death.[20]

17

◆

Solitude

Solitude encircles and embraces him, ever more threatening,
suffocating, heart-tightening, that terrible
goddess and *mater saeva cupidinum*
—but who today knows what
solitude is?
—Nietzsche, *Human, All Too Human*

To dare to live alone is the rarest courage; since there
are many who had rather meet their
bitterest enemy in the field,
than their own hearts
in their closet.
—Charles Caleb Colton, *Lacon*

In contemporary American society, we have an ambivalent attitude toward solitude. The solitary individual is, on the one hand, a folk hero—the stranger who rides into town on horseback, almost single-handedly rids the place of assorted crooks and bad guys, only to ride off again, alone and unencumbered. The lone scientist or artist, fighting against an encrusted establishment, is a more sophisticated version of the same romantic myth. On the other hand, solitude is often associated in the popular mind with an inability to make or maintain friends. The solitary individual is, according to this conception, a social misfit ("loner") and not a hero. To the extent that this negative attitude has been internalized, a person who faces the prospect of even a solitary evening at home may respond with anxiety, shame, and feelings of loneliness.

The ambivalence toward solitude is not unique to contemporary society. Aristotle remarked that the person who lives alone is either an animal or a god. Many centuries later, Nietzsche responded that there is a third possibility—the person who lives alone may be an animal *and* a god. Solitude is, in the words of Nietzsche quoted at the outset, a terrible goddess and wild mother of the passions (*mater saeva cupidinum*). We long for her embrace and yet flee in terror as we are drawn to her bosom.

What is it about solitude that makes it so alluring and yet so frightening? Human beings are social by nature. Social living provides many advantages—shared resources, protection from enemies, and the development of culture. An isolated human, with few means of natural defense, would not survive for long "in the wild." Not surprisingly, then, we seek and enjoy the company of others; contrariwise, enforced isolation or loneliness is one of the most painful of human experiences.

But involuntary or prolonged social involvement can also be debilitating. In order to grow and be creative, it is necessary that we separate from others, become individuals in our own right. We must allow ourselves time to be alone—to think, to imagine, to let the mind wander uninhibitedly over new possibilities. We must plumb the depths of our own inner selves—our feelings, thoughts, ideas, dreams, and responses to life. That may sound easy, even enjoyable. In reality, few things are more difficult.

People sometimes go to great lengths to avoid being alone. One common route of escape is to immerse oneself in a maelstrom of activities—social or perhaps work. This route often leads to feelings of even greater loneliness, for if the activities have little meaning or personal significance, then one's own isolation is only accentuated by the presence of others. At the extreme, a person may choose to remain in an unsatisfactory and even abusive relationship —anything seems preferable to the loneliness of solitude.

Ethel had been married for over thirty years to a man who abused her, both physically and psychologically, almost daily. She left the relationship (got a divorce) only after her husband told her he intended to kill her if she stayed. When asked why she had remained in the relationship for so long, she replied that she could not stand the thought of being alone. Financial security was a concern, but not the primary one. Ethel had worked outside the home before, and she knew she was capable of supporting herself.

Shortly after the divorce, she sought counseling due to depression. One of her worst fears was that if her former spouse asked, she would return to the relationship. She had no reason to believe that a renewed relationship with him would be any less abusive, but almost anything seemed more tolerable than the loneliness she was now experiencing.

Stories similar to Ethel's are distressingly familiar. Each year in the United States, roughly 1.8 million women are beaten by their husbands, and nearly 1,700 die from abuse. Nearly 30 percent of all couples report at least one episode of abuse during their marriages. Although exact statistics are difficult to come by, a substantial proportion of women caught in an abusive relationship choose to remain. Even among those admitted to shelters for battered women, the majority eventually return to their spouse or lover.[1] Men, too, often choose to remain in abusive relationships, although for them the consequences are seldom so serious, at least in terms of physical injury.

We are not suggesting that the only reason people—men or women—remain in abusive relationships is fear of loneliness, but that is clearly an important contributing factor in many instances.

Not only have we as a society lost the capacity for solitude, but we have ceased to see the need or value of it. The psychiatrist Anthony Storr believes this loss of capacity is one of the major problems of our time.[2] The Protestant work ethic places emphasis on *doing* rather than on *being;* we feel guilty or ashamed if we are not producing in an immediate and measurable way. But just as a field must occasionally lie fallow if it is to remain productive, so, too, an individual must have solitude.

We can make of solitude what we will—an occasion for loneliness or an opportunity for renewal and creativity. Storr offers numerous examples of famous individuals (Newton, Kant, Beethoven, Admiral Byrd, Edward Gibbon, among others) who cultivated a capacity for solitude, and who derived great benefit from it. We will take a lesser known example to illustrate the point. The poet Robert Francis lived alone for most of his life. From 1931 to 1954 he kept a journal of his thoughts and activities. The journal was published in 1986, shortly before his death. In one of the first entries (July 22, 1931), when Francis was 30 years old, he asked himself: "Why do I enjoy plentiful solitude?" And he answered: "Because it brings me greater harmony with myself and my environment than does any sort of social life, and because in solitude my mind is more active on a contemplative and creative plane than I am with people."[3] This is a theme to which he returned repeatedly. For example, over twenty years later, during a period when he had a difficult time writing and getting published, he had his telephone disconnected and "night after night, made myself incommunicado and invisible in my bedroom, where, luxuriating in complete spiritual and physical solitude, I read and wrote and thought."[4] Solitude, of course, does not necessarily mean isolation, especially forced isolation. Again, to quote Francis: "If my solitude is the warp of my life, people are the woof. I have no desire to make them less, and I couldn't even if I had the desire. When alone I have the freedom of my friends, and am not captured by those who happen to be here."[5]

Clearly, solitude can be a positive as well as a negative experience, and herein lies a danger of a different kind, at least as far as creativity is concerned. Consistent with other authors we have cited, Rollo May also asserts that, in order to be creative, "we must be able to retire from a world that is 'too much with us.' "[6] But May also notes that not any kind of retirement from the world will suffice. For example, transcendental meditation requires uninterrupted quiet, and it has many benefits, but enhanced creativity does not seem to be one of them. According to studies cited by May, teachers of transcendental meditation score no better on tests of creativity than do control subjects. [In] his own experience, May finds that if he meditates for twenty minutes before writing, he has nothing to write: "My 'problems' are all solved. I feel bliss, to be sure, but I cannot write."[7] The solitude that facilitates creativity is not one that affords comfort, but one that allows perplexity and a certain amount of inner chaos to develop.

Solitude, it might be granted, is important for creativity in the intellectual and artistic domains, for these are to a large extent solitary activities. But what about emotional creativity? With few exceptions (e.g., sudden fright at a potential physical danger, disgust at a putrid odor), emotions are interpersonal: They are engendered in us by the actions of other people (real or imagined); and we, in turn, evoke reactions in others through our own emotional expression. Even the mere presence of others, without any direct interaction, can be a potent moderator of emotional behavior. We seldom laugh as heartily when alone as with others, nor do we weep as copiously when there is no one to observe our tears. There is thus reason to believe that social involvement may be more important for emotional creativity than it is for creativity in other domains.

That is not necessarily so. Socializing can be, and often is, a way to avoid constructive confrontation with one's own emotions. Immersed in social activity, people can lose contact with themselves, with who they are and what they feel. Again, the best way to illustrate the point is by way of example. Edgar Allen Poe was highly creative, emotionally as well as intellectually. His stories of mystery and horror, and his poems of love and death, stretch our emotions beyond customary bounds. In a poem called *Alone*, Poe described the origins of his own uncommon emotions:

> *From childhood's hour I have not been*
> *As others were—I have not seen*
> *As others saw—I could not bring*
> *My passions from a common spring—*
> *From the same source I have not taken*
> *My sorrow—I could not awaken*
> *My heart to joy at the same tone—*
> *And all I lov'd—I lov'd alone—*
> *Then—in my childhood—in the dawn*
> *of a most stormy life—was drawn*
> *From ev'ry depth of good and ill*
> *The mystery which binds me still*
> *From the torrent, or the fountain—*
> *From the red cliff of the mountain—*
> *From the sun that round me roll'd*
> *In its autumn tint of gold—*
> *From the lightning in the sky*
> *As it pass'd me flying by—*
> *From the thunder, and the storm—*
> *And the cloud that took the form*
> *(When the rest of Heaven was blue)*
> *Of a demon in my view—*[8]

For most of us, the "common spring" of our emotions origi-
nates in social relationships. Not for Poe. The torrent, the mountain,
the sun, the lightning and thunder, especially the lightning and
thunder, these were the inspiration for a stormy and often lonely
life.

The biography of Poe deserves brief retelling, for it illustrates
well the observation by Nietzsche that solitude can be not only a
"wild mother of the passions" but also a "terrible goddess."
Abandoned by his father shortly after birth, orphaned when his
mother died three years later, Poe was raised in a foster family that
provided some degree of material comfort but little close affection
and warmth. His adulthood was marked by poverty, bitterness, and
rancor.

Ironically, although often alone, Poe never developed a capacity for solitude. His aloneness was to a large extent enforced, even
though the enforcement was often brought about by his own
hostile behavior. His emotional development, no matter how
creative and perceptive in some areas, was markedly deficient in
others. At the age of 26 he wrote to his aunt: "Pity me, my dear
Aunty, pity me. I have no one now to fly to—I am among strangers,
and my wretchedness is more than I can bear. . . . What have I to
live for? Among strangers with not one soul to love me."[9] Shortly
thereafter, he married his aunt's daughter, his own cousin, who was
then only 13 years old. His wife developed into a beautiful woman,
but like his mother, she died young of consumption (tuberculosis),
and he was again alone.

Poe idealized feminine beauty, yet he was sexually inhibited.
Beauty for him was closely associated with images of death. His was
a cerebral kind of love, reminiscent in some respects of the love of
Dante for Beatrice. It was a love that found expression more in
poetry and imagination than in carnal knowledge. Poe died during
an alcoholic binge, while making arrangements to marry a former
sweetheart—a widow whose income could finally provide him
with some security. His lifelong romance with death was thus
consummated.

Clearly, in emphasizing the importance of solitude for emotional creativity, we do not wish to downplay the importance of
sound social relationships. These may take many forms—from the
close bonds between good friends and mates to the mutual recognition of acquaintances at work, and even to the anonymity of a

crowd at a sporting event. All these forms of social interaction contribute to our sense of well-being, but none is more important for emotional creativity than intimate friendship and love. These are among the primary contributors to our happiness, and the sources of our greatest despair. The raw materials for new emotions may be found in the icy waters of solitude, but it is in the fires of an intimate relationship that the final products are often forged.

18

◆

Intimacy

The person who tries to live alone will not succeed as
a human being. His heart withers if it
does not answer another heart.
—Pearl S. Buck, *To my daughters,*
with love

Every deed and every relationship is surrounded by an
atmosphere of silence. Friendship needs no
words—it is solitude delivered from
the anguish of loneliness.
—Dag Hammarskjold, *Markings*

Many people may seek intimacy, in fact, they may desire it above
all else, but when asked to specify exactly what it is they are
seeking, few can respond precisely. Most popular definitions of
intimacy have to do with sexual and/or physical closeness. When
asked the question, "Are you in an intimate relationship?" the
implicit connotation is, "Are you in a sexual relationship?" There is
a great deal to be said for sexual intimacy. However, we limit
ourselves (and our potential for emotional creativity) if we conceive
of intimacy only in sexual terms.

Throughout most of Western history, intimacy was sought—
and found—in friendships rather than in sexual relationships.

Today, the term "friend" is used in a rather superficial fashion, as in, "I made three new friends at a party last night." That is not the traditional view of friendship. During the Middle Ages, for example, a person could expect to have only a few friends. But whereas the number was small, the commitment was large, often lasting a lifetime. Friends were thus not simply "met"; they were sought out and deliberately cultivated. The following exchange of letters is illustrative. In the late 1120s Hildebert of Levardin, Archbishop of Tours, wrote to Bernard of Clairvaux: "From all that I have heard of you I have come to love you, and to desire with a great desire to be admitted to the sanctuary of your friendship."[1]
Bernard responded:

> For my part, I am determined to love you whatever you do, even if you do not return my love . . . I shall cling to you, even against your will; I shall cling to you, even against my own will. Once I bound myself to you with a strong bond, with charity unfeigned, that charity never fails.[2]

Read out of context, one could easily imagine that these letters were exchanged between lovers. We cite them to emphasize the fact that intimacy is not limited to lovers, although that is the most common context today. In fact, sexual intimacy too often seems to conflict with the intimacy of friendship. For example, many couples find that when sexual passion cools, it is almost impossible to regain the intellectual or emotional closeness they once had. But at its creative best, an intimate relationship can combine intellectual, emotional, and physical closeness, without any one element coming to dominate or supplant the others.

The term "intimate" is derived from the Latin *intimus*, meaning "inmost," "within." If we combine this meaning with the Latin concept of *caritas*, which connotes affection or charity, we arrive at the following definition:

> Intimacy is a mutual sharing—both giving and receiving
> —by two people of their innermost thoughts and feelings,
> with affection and respect, for the benefit of each.

In an intimate relationship each person has the freedom to share (or not share) that which is most private, without fear of ridicule or rejection. The key word here is *freedom*. Intimacy does not necessitate indiscriminate disclosure. The person who gives away too much of the self in a desperate attempt to achieve intimacy is as badly off as the person who gives away too little out of fear of rejection. Many details of a person's life are irrelevant (and potentially harmful) to a relationship. The goal is to *know* the other, not *know about* them. Affection (charity) and respect, more than disclosure, are the hallmarks of intimacy. When this fact is ignored, the relationship is placed in jeopardy. Robert Nisbet has expressed the issue well:

> Once entered into with another person, intimacy poses the terrible danger of entrapment. There is a tyranny in intimacy, once one of the individuals has wearied of or become estranged from it. Some individuals, both male and female, possess a kind of lust for intellectual intimacy with another. Typically, they work patiently and subtly, waiting for the day when the other person realizes he has divulged so much of himself, lost so many of his carapaces, that he is trapped. There is only one solution for this entrapment, one form of liberation from the tyranny of intimacy: *Ecrasez l'infame.*[3]

Intimate relationships do not necessarily last forever. This is particularly true when sexual passion is part of the impetus behind the relationship. Due to changing circumstances, the partners may drift apart. How is the relationship to end? Once two people have laid themselves bare to each other, physically or psychologically, it is impossible to return to the status quo ante. Confidences once disclosed cannot be withdrawn; frailties once revealed cannot again be hidden. Embarrassment is thus inevitable at the end of an intimate relationship, as at the beginning. The embarrassment may turn to shame and then to hate. The other person knows too much. What is to be done? Crush the infamous thing! *Ecrasez l'infame,* indeed.

That is not the way it has to be—not if the two individuals have affection and respect for each other. The nature of an intimate relationship may, and often does, change with time. What was lost through disclosure may never be regained; but by the same token, what was gained during the relationship need never be lost. True intimacy does not tear down carapaces of the mind, it honors the other's right to them.

The quest for intimacy begins in early childhood and continues through adulthood. When we were in elementary school, we wanted that one special friend with whom we could laugh and cry and share our innermost thoughts and secrets. It is through such early attempts that we begin to form our attitudes towards intimacy. Although in some respects legitimate, these attitudes often lead to a superficial conception of intimacy, and they may be counterproductive in adult relationships.

True intimacy may be distinguished from several varieties of pseudo-intimacy. One variety is a seamless cleavage of two individuals welded together by the intense fear of aloneness. Each partner attempts to achieve wholeness or fill an inner void through the other. That is not an intimate relationship, it is a parasitic one. Parasitic relationships can be intense while they last, but they seldom last for long. They leave us feeling sucked dry and burned out. To illustrate, take the plight of a client we will call Sol, a professional man in his forties:

> Sol came to therapy because, as he explained it, "Emotionally I feel like a piano that is only playing one note." At the time, he was in his second marriage. His wife was a beautiful, controlling, yet fearful and dependent woman whom he professed to love but not like. In the last year he had felt more and more alone, empty, and without purpose. When describing his wife and their relationship he said, "At times I feel like she is a sponge, just getting into my mind and soaking up my thoughts, my feelings, my emotions. So I shut down and don't show her anything, how I feel or anything." Then he paused and added in a quiet voice, "I think that [what she does] is a terrible thing to do to anyone."

Another kind of pseudo-intimacy is more symbiotic than parasitic. In a symbiotic relationship (as defined by biologists), each individual gives to the other needed resources, but the contact between them remains superficial. In many societies, marriage often begins as a symbiotic relationship, prearranged for social or economic purposes. Only later, if at all, do the partners become truly intimate. Conversely, in our own society, after initial passions have cooled, intimate relationships often become symbiotic ("companionate"). At their best such relationships, like a business partnership, can be quite stable and mutually rewarding. As the interests or needs of the partners change, however, symbiotic relationships frequently deteriorate. The two partners, although in close physical and even psychological contact with one another, become almost anonymous in terms of inner thoughts and feelings. This state of affairs is well illustrated by the following couple:

Fred and Nell had been married for over twenty years. Fred sought therapy because his life was painful and barren, and he didn't know why. He didn't care if he lived or died, and often contemplated suicide. Shortly after he came to therapy his wife came also. She came because she basically did whatever he did. If he wasn't on the job, they were together. But their togetherness consisted primarily of physical proximity. There was little emotional closeness in the relationship, only shared outside interests.

Relationships of this type provide little impetus for growth or change. To outsiders the partners may look like the perfect couple, but within the relationship itself, it is "business as usual." The eighteenth century poet, Matthew Prior, wrote a fitting epitaph for many such couples:

Without Love, Hatred, Joy or Fear,
They led—a kind of—as it were:
Nor Wish'd nor Car'd nor Laugh'd nor Cry'd:
And so they liv'd: and so they dy'd.[4]

Contrast this with a truly intimate couple described by Henry Murray. Only half in jest, Murray dubbed the couple Adam and Eve. Both had experienced unsuccessful marriages, and out of the wreckage of their previous lives, they determined to build a new kind of relationship. Its outstanding feature, according to Murray, was a "dyadic creativity" in which feelings and emotions were freely expressed, circulated, and ultimately integrated into new combinations. This is how Murray recounted the process as related to him by Adam:

By unappreciable transitions—Adam cannot remember any originating incident—he and Eve found themselves engaged now and again in unpremeditated, serious yet playful, dramatic outbursts of feeling, wild imagination, and vehement interactions, in which one of them—sometimes Adam, sometimes Eve—gave vent to whatever was pressing for expression. Walpurgis was the name they gave to episodes of this insurgent nature. Usually it was Eros that supplied the energy, with

some sort of intoxicant—which they called Soma after the
Hindu Dionysius—liquidating the boundary of consciousness.
But besides Eros, there were compelling needs for dominance,
clamoring egotisms and assertions of omniscience, anger and
resentment, not to speak of feelings of helplessness and
inferiority, complemented by nurturance and encouragement.
And so—layer after layer, one might say—each of these two
psyches, through numberless repetitions, discharged its resid-
ual as well as its emergent and beneficient dispositions, until
nearly every form of sexuality and nearly every possible
complementation of dyadic roles had been dramatically enacted. All this within the frame of their conception of the
necessary digressions and progressive spiralings of the creative
process, and all within the compass of an ever-mounting trust
in the solidarity of their love, evidenced in the Walpurgis
episodes by an apparently limitless mutual tolerance of novelty and emotional extravagance.[5]

Why is true intimacy, as opposed to the parasitic and symbiotic
relationships described earlier, an important condition for emotional creativity? There are at least four main reasons:

First, intimacy allows us to expose and express our innermost
thoughts and feelings without constraint or inhibition. We can also
do that in solitude, but in solitude we do not get the feedback that
an intimate partner provides. The intimate partner serves as a kind
of psychological mirror, or even magnifying glass, that allows us to
see ourselves in new and different ways.

Second, intimacy is not just self-exposure; it is a harmonious
synthesizing. Two separate and independent lives combine in such
a way that new properties emerge. Just as new properties may
originate when chemical elements combine, so, too, new kinds of
emotional experiences may originate when two individuals enter
into a truly intimate relationship.

Third, in a truly intimate relationship each partner maintains
and zealously guards his or her own individuality. Conflicts of
interests and needs are therefore inevitable. The resolution of such
conflicts requires not only commitment and effort, but also creativity. If complacency is the enemy of creativity, then conflict is the
enemy of complacency.

Fourth, the intense emotions involved in an intimate relationship are themselves an impetus to further emotional innovation.

True intimacy is a pathway to those spiritual realities, whether real or apparent, to which mystics often refer, and which give ultimate significance to our relationships and to our existence.

> But let there be spaces in your togetherness, and let the winds of heaven dance between you. . . . And stand together yet not too near together: For the pillars of the temple stand apart, and the oak tree and the cypress grow not in each others shadow.[6]

19

Autonomy

Here I stand. I cannot do otherwise.
God help me. Amen!
—Luther, *Speech at Diet of Worms*

One must know oneself. Even if that does not help in
finding truth, at least it helps in
running one's life, and nothing
is more proper.
—Pascal, *Pensées*

Which is more important for emotional creativity: solitude or intimacy? This is not a simple question to answer, for both are important. But more important than either one alone is the potential conflict—both within and without—between the two. Some people find solace in solitude; others (the majority) prefer the advantages of an intimate relationship. But whichever we most prefer, the other never ceases to entice. When alone, we yearn for the companionship of another; and when in an intimate relationship, we long for the comforts of solitude.

The individual who has the capacity for both solitude and intimacy, who is able to resolve the conflict between these two basic human needs, might best be described as *autonomous* (from the Greek *autos*, self, and *nomos*, law). The autonomous person is self-ruled; but the converse is not necessarily true: Not every

241

self-ruled person is autonomous. In addition to self-rule, autonomy implies the ability to make choices, to pursue divergent goals, and to remain flexible in the face of uncertainty. The bases for these characteristics in self-rule will be examined below.

Autonomy is also related to two of the three main criteria for evaluating a creative response, namely, novelty and authenticity. With respect to authenticity, the relation is straightforward and requires little elaboration. Autonomy presumes a well-developed sense of self. Without autonomy, we are hollow, empty beings, our only self being a reflection of others as we live in and through them. To be autonomous—to be our authentic and genuine selves—we must avoid playing roles and wearing masks; we must be aware of our own values and concerns; and we must be willing to take a definite stand consistent with what and who we are.

> Every distortion, every phony, artificial act creates a false self, pulling the person in a direction that is less than whole and forcing upon the self fragments of life; the eyes of another, the heart of another, the soul of another.[1]

The relation of autonomy to novelty is less obvious, and hence is the main focus of this chapter. The production of novelty makes creativity seem mysterious—and sometimes even frightening. The novel response seems to have no antecedent, no cause. It is the muse that speaks through the poet, or the demon that possesses the madman. But muses and demons do not simply occur; they must be coaxed. As discussed in Chapter 6, creative individuals may use a variety of techniques in order to stimulate novelty; for example, a painter may move to a new locale, a musician may experiment with new instruments or scales, a mathematician may explore the consequences of a new axiom, and so forth.

Of all the sources of novelty, perhaps none is more important than conflict. When confronted with competing desires or goals, novel responses are almost sure to be generated. Freud, for one, built much of his psychology around this fact. He attributed not only neurotic syndromes, but artistic products as well, to the conflict between instinctual desires (mainly sexual) and internalized moral codes. According to Freud, for example, a painter may sublimate repressed sexual desires in a work of art. To take another example, Otto Rank argued that the conflict between the competing needs for independence, on the one hand, and dependence, on the other, is the major source of creativity.

The types of conflicts emphasized by Freud and Rank are clearly important, but they hardly exhaust the possibilities. In Chapter 15 we discussed the conflict between pain and pleasure (asceticism and hedonism). Once we begin to make a list, it is difficult to know when to stop. Life is full of conflict: We desire adventure, to be responsible to no one but ourselves, but we cannot shirk our duties; we yearn for the approval of others while we claim to disdain their ways as petty; we give, but not without expecting something in return; we trust, and are suspicious that our trust is misplaced.

Needless to say, conflict does not always lead to novel responses. When faced with conflict, the most common reaction is to embrace one alternative and reject the other; or, if choice seems impossible, to retreat in impotency, disclaiming any desire for either option. Here is where autonomy becomes important. Autonomy entails the ability to face seemingly unresolvable conflict without recourse to a close-minded embrace of either alternative. Without autonomy, we are like flies lured to the sweetness of honey: We may adopt a particular way of life—and then become stuck. Worse, because of the sweetness, we may not even notice our entrapment. Autonomy allows us to incorporate conflicting goals into a larger structure, a more encompassing aspect of the self, and thus to keep our options open. When autonomy is achieved, conflict becomes a source for creativity, not an occasion for retreat.

Not everyone agrees that autonomy is important, or even that such a thing exists. B. F. Skinner, for example, argues that "Autonomous man is a device used to explain what we cannot explain in any other way. He has been constructed from our ignorance, and as our understanding increases, the very stuff of which he is composed vanishes."[2] The autonomous man that Skinner excoriates is "the inner man, the homunculus, the possessing demon, the man defended by the literatures of freedom and dignity."[3] We, too, are all in favor of abolishing homunculi and demons from scientific discourse. They are explanatory fictions that lead nowhere. But autonomy as we mean it does not refer to an "inner person" who somehow guides and directs the "outer person," whatever that would mean. Autonomy refers to a characteristic of the whole and unified person. Like any other psychological characteristic (e.g., intelligence, energy, friendliness), autonomy admits of degree. Some people are more autonomous than others, just as some people are more intelligent or energetic or friendly than others.

Moreover, contrary to Skinner, we believe that autonomy is the type of personal characteristic that "the literatures of freedom and dignity" rightly defend.

But we need to be more precise. What exactly is autonomy? We have already said that autonomy means self-rule or self-governance. In order to expand on this definition, a brief historical excursion might be helpful.

Most contemporary discussions of autonomy owe some allegiance to the philosopher Kant. "Autonomy of the will," Kant wrote, "is the property the will has of being a law to itself."[4] Thus far, there is nothing new here. But then the question becomes: What is the law by which the will governs itself? According to Kant: "The principle of autonomy is, 'Never to choose except in such a way that in the same volition the maxims of your choice are also present as universal law.'"[5] Stated somewhat differently, we should always act in such a way that we would want the rules that guide our behavior to be applied universally—to the behavior of others similarly situated, as well as to ourselves.

Kant's principle of autonomy sounds very much like the Golden Rule—"Do unto others as you would have them do unto you." The major difference is that Kant believed that his principle could be defended on strictly rational grounds, that it need not be accepted on faith or scripture.

From our perspective, the autonomous person may or may not be moral in the sense of having adopted the Golden Rule, however derived, as a guiding principle. Stripped of its moral connotations, autonomy simply refers to the fact that the person is guided by general principles, and that these principles form part of the person's own nuclear self. Autonomous persons cannot violate principles without sacrificing their sense of self. In the words of Martin Luther, quoted at outset: "Here I stand. I cannot do otherwise."

In some respects, autonomy on the psychological level can be compared with homeostasis on the physiological level. Homeostasis refers to the ability of an organism to maintain its own "internal environment" (body temperature, electrolyte balance, etc.) so that it can remain relatively independent of external conditions. Physiological homeostasis is possible because the body is structured in a hierarchical fashion. Cells form tissues; tissues form organs; organs are grouped into larger systems, such as the cardiovascular and gastrointestinal systems; and, finally, the activities of these systems are organized and coordinated in such a way as to maintain a stable internal environment.

Behavior, too, is hierarchically organized. At the most elementary level are well-practiced, relatively automatic responses, such as putting on our shoes or shaving in the morning. At a somewhat more general level are behaviors that require some conscious choice but little deliberation, such as what to eat for lunch. Higher, still, are actions that are important but that do not impact greatly on a person's self-concept. Deciding on which car to buy, or where to go on vacation, would be examples. Next in the hierarchy are important decisions that involve long-range plans and goals, such as choosing a career, getting married, having children, and the like. Finally, at the top of the hierarchy are the broad principles—values, ambitions, basic likes and dislikes—that constitute the nuclear self.

Conflicts occur at all levels of the psychological hierarchy, and they are resolved, if they are resolved at all, by recourse to principles at successively higher levels. For example, a person cannot go to work and stay in bed, no matter how much she might like to do both. Most such low-level conflicts are easily resolved. But as we ascend the hierarchy, the conflicts become increasingly difficult and the consequences more serious and perhaps life-changing. For example, to the extent that it involves a long-term commitment to a particular life-style or to another person, the conflict between solitude and intimacy proceeds at a very high level.

Autonomy, we have said, implies self-rule. That is, it begins at the top of the psychological hierarchy, with the self, and exerts its influence downward. More precisely, autonomy is the ability of the self to integrate in a meaningful way the conflicts that inevitably exist at successively lower levels in the hierarchy. The autonomous person does not eliminate conflict, but is a master at integration.

We all strive to be autonomous, to be masters of our own lives. The process begins early. In Erik Erikson's well-known "eight stages of man," autonomy is designated as the major achievement of the second stage.[6] During the first stage, which lasts approximately the first year of life, the infant is dependent on others to meet its needs. If all goes well, the child develops a sense of basic trust during this initial period. The second stage occupies roughly the second year of life. It is known colloquially as the "terrible twos." During this period children begin to exert their independence and make their wishes known. They often refuse help, insist on doing things their own way, and disobey even the simplest and most reasonable requests of parents. Paradoxically, children at the same time also become very ritualistic. The way something is done the first time automatically becomes the proper way, and any deviation in order or sequence may occasion severe protest. Such willfulness is appropriate *and* necessary for a two-year-old as this is when they are developing balance between independence and recognition of limitations. However, it represents autonomy in only the most rudimentary sense. The achievement of full autonomy must await the development of a coherent sense of self and a coherent set of rules or principles by which to govern behavior.

The autonomous person, we have said, acts on principle. For full autonomy, the relevant principles must meet three conditions. First, they must constitute part of the person's own self and not be imposed from without. Of course, all principles, to the extent that they are a product of learning and socialization, are acquired from without. The autonomous individual, however, has internalized and accepted as his or her own the principles that guide behavior. Second, the principles must be general, so that they encompass a broad spectrum of behavior. Kant's principle of autonomy, cited earlier, is a good example. Third, the principles must be sufficiently flexible and open-ended to allow for innovation and change.

If any of the above three conditions is not met, or is met only inadequately, there is an impairment of autonomy. David Shapiro maintains that "some impairment of autonomy . . . is intrinsic to all psychopathology."[7] We do not go so far; psychopathology can have many sources. However, an impairment of autonomy is almost invariably an impediment to optimal psychological functioning, including creativity. Three kinds of impairment can be recognized: hyperautonomy, hypoautonomy, and arrested autonomy.

Hyperautonomous individuals act on general principles, but apply those principles in a rigid and domineering fashion. The religious or political zealot who will sacrifice everything, even life itself, for a cause, is a good example of hyperautonomy. These individuals are continually competing, trying to assure themselves of their superiority and mastery. If nothing else, the hyperautonomous individual is consistent. However, as Ralph Waldo Emerson wrote, "A foolish consistency is the hobgoblin of little minds."[8] The hyperautonomous individual is foolishly consistent. Conflicts are resolved, not by recognizing the legitimate claims of each side, but by denying one side or the other. The self thus becomes a "little mind" beset by hobgoblins.

Hypoautonomous individuals may also act on general principles, but in their case the principles are drawn from the immediate environment; they have not been internalized as part of the self. For example, a hypoautonomous individual might adopt the Golden Rule as a guide, but only because it is the socially acceptable thing to do. The "organization man" who adjusts his views to fit the prevailing corporate climate also illustrates hypoautonomy. Such individuals are followers, not leaders. They seldom cause problems for others, at least not overtly. Hence, they are less likely to be seen in therapy. Hypoautonomy, however, is a matter of degree. All of us are less autonomous than we might be, just as all of us are physically less healthy than we might be.

Individuals suffering from arrested autonomy show many of the same characteristics as the hyperautonomous person discussed earlier. Both are deliberate and purposeful to a fault; they abhor weakness; and they are suspicious of the motives of others. The difference between the two lies in this: Whereas the hyperautonomous individual acts from general principles, the person suffering from arrested autonomy is stuck at lower levels of the psychological hierarchy. He or she is like a chief executive who cannot delegate any authority, even on the most trivial matters. Such a pervasive need for control is a carryover into adulthood of the kinds of behavior characteristic of the "terrible twos." The following example illustrates the extremes to which arrested autonomy can sometimes go:

> On the surface, Gerald was the epitome of a "nice guy." He was a middle-aged professional man who had been remarried less than a year. His first marriage had ended in divorce after fifteen years. He agreed to counseling after his second wife threatened to leave him. At first, it was hard to see why his wife was unhappy. Gerald was a good provider, amicable and accommodating, and always willing to help others.
>
> Shortly after his second marriage, he asked his wife to quit her job so that they could spend quality time together without additional job pressures. It soon became obvious, however, that that was not the only reason. Gerald had an exaggerated need for control, not only over his own life but over his wife's life as

well. He had a set routine that seldom varied from day to day. He made all the decisions about how the household was to be maintained and how money was to be spent. He even decided which television shows and radio stations he and his wife would listen to. He demanded that his wife follow his instructions to the letter, and that she keep a daily log of her activities. He expected everything to have a place and to be kept there when not in use. He "white gloved" the furniture when he came home, to check that it was dust free. He expected the clocks to be kept accurate—to the minute. When his wife rebelled, as she frequently did, he would become cold and angry, refusing to touch her or speak to her; and if she pressed him to talk, he would become physically threatening. There was no room for spontaneity, flexibility, or ambiguity in Gerald's life.

Like a snake that bites its tail and then proceeds to devour itself, the exaggerated need for control that characterizes both arrested and hyperautonomy can become self-consuming. A person must be able to give up control under appropriate circumstances. Paradoxically, the truly autonomous person can choose—and often does choose—to be nonautonomous. Most of us give up our autonomy in many matters every day—we allow custom or habit to dictate our behavior, not conscious choice. If it were otherwise, we would never be able to accomplish anything important, for even the most minor events—what clothes to wear, what food to eat, what movie to see—would become the occasion for needless reflection and debate.

Impairments of autonomy are particularly damaging to emotional creativity. People suffering from either arrested or hyperautonomy tend to be cold and detached. They attempt to control their emotions in much the same way that they attempt to control the external circumstances of their lives. They leave nothing to chance. They cannot experience the warmth of an intimate relationship, for that would require some forfeiture of control. There is no room for the whimsical, the playful, the novel and unexpected.

Hypoautonomy is also inimical to emotional creativity, but for a somewhat different reason. People suffering from hypoautonomy lack authenticity. They are like reeds that bend in the wind. Their lives seem to be controlled by external events and hence their behavior invites manipulation and abuse. They have neither the fortitude or perseverance to be creative, nor the courage to withstand the opposition from others that creativity often engenders. The old saying that "power corrupts" is only partially true. A lack of power can also corrupt.

Autonomy, we would like to emphasize once again, is not a thing in itself, some inner force or mysterious entity (homunculus) that somehow directs and guides a person's actions. Like homeostasis on the physiological level, autonomy on the psychological level is a process inherent in life itself. It is a vehicle toward ever greater integration within and ever greater independence without.

Needless to say, autonomy is not all of a piece. A person may be autonomous in one domain and yet be considerably impaired in another. The point we wish to emphasize is that autonomy within a particular domain is vital for creativity in that domain. Emotional creativity thus presumes the achievement of autonomy in the domain of the emotions. Conversely, an impairment of autonomy in the emotional domain is a frequent component of psychopathology, no matter how competent and successful the individual might be in other respects.

20

Freedom

The creative individual is a "free spirit"; creative activities "break free" from the bonds of tradition; creativity can thrive only in an "atmosphere of freedom." Clichés such as these are echoed in the results of formal psychological research. Factors that inhibit the freedom of the individual, such as externally imposed goals, competition, a rigid time schedule, preestablished rules, and the like, also tend to inhibit creativity.[1] But what, more precisely, is freedom? And how does freedom relate to the emotions? We begin with the latter question.

The great seventeenth-century Dutch philosopher Spinoza spoke of "human bondage" in reference to the emotions.

The impotence of many to govern or restrain the emotions I call "bondage," for a man who is under their control is not his own master, but is mastered by fortune, in whose power he is, so that he is often forced to follow the worse, although he sees the better before him.[2]

If freedom is indispensable to creativity, and emotions are a form of bondage, what meaning or significance can there be to emotional creativity? Following Spinoza's reasoning, emotional creativity would involve giving up one kind of bondage (an old emotion) for a different kind of bondage (a new emotion). That is not freedom.

According to Spinoza, emotions (passions) indicate imperfect knowledge; freedom is attained only by living according to reason. But reason and knowledge deliver an odd kind of freedom, as Spinoza also recognized. You are free to conclude that $2 + 2 = 5$, but only at the risk of being labeled a fool. As this simple example illustrates, nothing is more coercive than the rational. We often make use of this fact when we need an excuse ("rationalization") for foolish behavior: "I had no choice; it was the only logical thing to do." (Compare this with: "I couldn't help it; I was overcome with emotion.")

Rationality as well as emotionality can be considered a kind of bondage. Is any behavior, then, truly free? One possible answer is that the creative act is free. That, at least, would explain why freedom is so important for creativity. But that answer will not suffice either. Speaking of his musical inspirations, Mozart re-marked: "*Whence* and *how* they come, I know not; nor can I force them."[3] That is hardly the mark of a free act. In the end, perhaps we are led to conclude with the poet Shelley that freedom itself is "sweet bondage."[4]

We do not wish to pursue the issue of freedom versus determinism in human behavior. The point of these introductory remarks has been to break the hoary notion that the emotions, more than other kinds of behavior, lack freedom. That belief is simply another variation on the myth of the passions discussed in Chapter 5. Freedom is as important for creativity in the emotional as in any other domain.

To say that creativity requires freedom remains nothing but a platitude or slogan unless we can specify more precisely what we mean by "freedom." To lend substance to our analysis, consider the case of Andrei Tarkovsky, a film director who died in 1986.

Tarkovsky received many international awards for the artistic creativity of his work. The majority of his career was spent with the state-controlled Soviet film industry. Although he was given large production budgets, little of his work got past the censors. The authorities, he maintained, "spat on my soul." Lacking the artistic freedom he desired, Tarkovsky defected to the West in 1984, living variously in Italy, France, and Sweden. But whereas he gained the freedom he lacked in the Soviet Union, he also felt diminished. "The longer I stay in the West, the more I find that man has lost his inner freedom," he is quoted as saying: "In the West, everybody has their rights, but in an internal, spiritual sense, there is no doubt more freedom in the Soviet Union."[5]

Freedom, evidently, is not all of a kind. Tarkovsky gained one kind of freedom when he defected to the West, but he lost another kind that he enjoyed in the Soviet Union. In order to understand the difference between these two kinds of freedom, we draw on the British essayist and social theorist, Sir Isaiah Berlin.[6]

Berlin distinguishes between two varieties of freedom, which he calls "negative" and "positive." These terms are not to be interpreted in an valuative sense; rather, they refer to the source of freedom. Negative freedom emphasizes the *absence* of coercion or restraint; positive freedom emphasizes the *presence* of resources that enable a person to achieve some desired (or desirable) goal. When Tarkovsky fled to the West, he gained negative freedom; the censors could no longer "spit on his soul." However, he lost the positive freedom, the intellectual or spiritual resources, that he experienced in his homeland.

In more colloquial terms, the difference between negative and positive freedom corresponds roughly to the difference in connotation between the words "may" and "can." A poor person *may* fly to the Bahamas for the winter, but he *can* not, for he lacks the financial resources. He has the negative but not the positive freedom to spend the winter where he wants.

Both negative and positive freedom can apply to internal as well as external conditions. For example, the person who suffers from irresistible impulses lacks negative freedom; he is a prisoner of his own desires. That, evidently, is what Spinoza meant when he spoke of "human bondage" in reference to the emotions. Similarly, the person who is cut off from cultural resources lacks positive freedom; he is spiritually impoverished. That, evidently, is what Tarkovsky meant when he said, "In the West, everybody has their rights, but in an internal, spiritual sense, there is no doubt more freedom in the Soviet Union."[7]

As the experiences of Tarkovsky indicate, negative and positive freedom are not entirely compatible or mutually reinforcing. The inner resources on which positive freedom depends do not automatically flourish in the vacuum created by unlimited negative freedom. Some limitations on negative freedom may be necessary if a person is to gain the inner resources that are necessary for positive freedom. Nietzsche saw this clearly:

> How is [positive] freedom measured in individuals as well as in nations? According to the resistance which has to be overcome, according to the pains which it costs to remain *uppermost*. The highest type of free man would have to be sought where the greatest resistance has continually to be overcome: five paces away from tyranny, on the very threshold of the danger of thraldom.[8]

Highly creative people are able to flourish in an atmosphere of negative freedom only because they erect their own barriers in the form of standards of excellence. Their danger of thralldom is ever constant because it comes from within, not just from without.

Perhaps the epitome of negative freedom, at least so far as intellectual endeavors are concerned, is the Institute for Advanced Study at Princeton University. Opened in 1933, the Institute was intended as a haven where creative thinkers in the sciences and humanities could work in an atmosphere free of financial cares and unencumbered by the immediate concerns of teaching, deadlines, and the other daily nuisances of academic life. Its first resident scholar was Albert Einstein. Others joined him over the years, and some of the most important scientific breakthroughs of this century germinated in the Institute's rarified atmosphere. But all was not serene, as Edward Regis makes clear in his history of the Institute, *Who Got Einstein's Office?* To paraphrase the anthropologist, Clifford Geertz, a resident at the Institute: When ideas don't come and there are no excuses, the anxiety can be extraordinarily high.[9]

Geertz's observation applies in many ordinary situations as well. When external constraints are removed, people at first feel exhilarated, but the exhilaration typically gives way to anxiety, as people must choose among alternatives with few guidelines. This state of affairs is particularly common among adolescents. Away from home for the first time, they may experience a heady sense of liberation. However, as they are forced to take responsibility for their own actions and to make choices for which they have few guidelines, they are often at a loss for what to do. Not wanting to take responsibility for themselves, they blame the "system" for somehow oppressing and preventing them from taking action. Occasionally, some will join a cult or other tightly organized group and exclaim with a paradoxical sigh of relief that now they are free.

What is a common and generally harmless state of affairs among adolescents can sometime assume dangerous proportions as it affects wide segments of the population. Erich Fromm has described how citizens of Germany during the 1930s sought to "escape from freedom" by adopting the totalitarian philosophy of the Nazi regime.[10] The freedom they were escaping from was the negative freedom offered by the Weimar Republic (the German government following World War I). But they were not simply escaping *from* a negative freedom that bordered on anarchy; they also were escaping *to* something. And that something was also a kind of freedom—a positive freedom that promised release and fulfillment through identification with a mythical past and unreal future.

The psychological principle underlying positive freedom was enunciated by the ancient Stoic philosopher Epictetus:

> Of things some are in our power, and others are not. . . . And the things in our power are by nature free, not subject to restraint or hindrance; but the things not in our power are weak, slavish, subject to restraint, in the power of others. Remember then . . . if you think that only which is your own to be your own, and if you think that what is another's, as it really is, belongs to another, no man will ever compel you, no man will hinder you, you will never blame any man, you will accuse no man, you will do nothing involuntarily (against your will).[11]

There are two main ways to achieve positive freedom. One way is to increase our power, so that it encompasses a broader and broader range of activities. There are limits to such a strategy, however, for many things will always remain beyond our reach. We cannot all become concert pianists or professional football players, no matter how hard we try. The second way to achieve positive freedom is to give up pretensions that are beyond our means and focus instead on what we can do, on what is in our power to accomplish. That is the advice offered by Epictetus. When our ambitions and desires match our capacities, we will be free. The two strategies (expanding our power and limiting our ambitions) are not completely independent.

One of the easiest ways to extend one's own power is to identify with others who have power, or to act as part of a group that can exert power collectively. However, identification with a group often involves renunciation of one's independent aspirations. Thus, as we align our own interests with those of the group, we not only achieve greater power, we also renounce what is not within our power to achieve.

Group identification can occur on many levels. At the level of the dyad, we have intimacy in one or another of its various forms, as discussed in Chapter 18. That true intimacy can enhance as well as constrain our freedom, no one would deny. But our concern at the moment is with identification with larger collectives—ethnic or religious groups, a nation state—often personified by a charismatic leader or (in the case of religious groups) a deity. "Follow me, and I shall set you free" is the clarion call of demagogues the world over.

Somewhat surprisingly, creative individuals often show unusual identification with groups or powerful others, to whom they attribute almost supernatural powers. The psychiatrist Heinz Kohut calls this phenomenon "transference creativity."[12] Identification provides not only inspiration but also the courage to overcome the doubts and anxieties that often accompany creative endeavors, particularly during the early stages. This is the "spiritual freedom" which Tarkovsky found in the Soviet Union (a collectivist society). Unfortunately, the group often extracts a price for the spiritual freedom it confers. That price is conformity. As Tarkovsky expressed it, the censors "spat on my soul."

In sum, when we speak of freedom as a condition for creativity, we usually mean some combination of positive and negative freedom. Positive freedom provides the resources to create; negative freedom allows creativity its full and unfettered expression. But each kind of freedom also has its downside. An overemphasis on positive freedom can result in a lowering of aspirations ("Do only what you think you can do"), or to a stifling conformity ("Do only what others say you can do"). Unrestricted negative freedom, in which every individual, and even every desire on the part of an individual, is granted unfettered expression, can be equally debilitating, for it removes all challenge and responsibility. To be truly free, we must continually work to stretch and expand our abilities, and we must challenge ourselves even if others do not challenge us. And to meet the challenge, there must be coordination among individuals within a society, and among desires within an individual. It is from such disciplined freedom that creativity, as opposed to anarchy, springs.

21

✦

Imagination

> The imagination (as a productive faculty of cognition)
> is a powerful agent for creating, as it
> were, a second nature out of the
> material supplied to it by
> actual nature.
> —Kant, *Critique of Aesthetic Judgment*

> To see a world in a grain of sand,
> And heaven in a wild flower:
> Hold infinity in the palm of your hand,
> And eternity in an hour.
> —Blake, "Auguries of Innocence"

Of all the spheres of human activity, the imagination is the most free; no matter how constrained we might be by circumstances, we are nevertheless free to imagine a reality different than the one in which we find ourselves. Through the imagination, we can create a "second" nature out of material provided by "actual" nature (Kant); or, stated more poetically, we can see a world in a grain of sand, and heaven in a wild flower (Blake). In the process, of course, all nature becomes transformed.[1]

The epigram by Blake also highlights one of most important functions of the imagination, namely, to bridge the gap between abstract thought (the world, infinity) and concrete sensory experience (a flower, a grain of sand). Blake's poetic imagery accrues literal meaning in the experiences of Gustav Fechner, one of the pioneers of modern psychology. Fechner was professor of physics at the University of Göttingen during the mid-nineteenth century. At one point during his career, suffering from financial worries and an exceptionally heavy workload, Fechner developed a severe eye disorder. He became so hypersensitive to light that he could not leave the house without bandages on his eyes; he lived in near darkness. The exact causes of the disorder are not known, but psychological factors apparently played a major role. When Fechner eventually recovered sufficiently to venture outside into his garden, this is how he described his initial reactions:

> I still remember well what an impression it made upon me when, after suffering for some years from an ailment which affected my sight, I stepped out for the first time from my darkened chamber and into the garden with no bandage upon my eyes. It seemed to me like a glimpse beyond the boundary of human experience. Every flower beamed upon me with a peculiar clarity, as though into the outer light it was casting a light of its own. To me the whole garden seemed transfigured, as though it were not I but nature that had just arisen. And I thought: So nothing is needed but to open the eyes afresh, and with that old nature is made young again.[2]

This experience so impressed Fechner that he came to believe that plants—and the earth and planets, too—have a spiritual as well as a physical dimension. To prove this vision Fechner developed psychophysics, in which a physical quantity (the intensity of a light, say) is related to a psychological quantity (the sensation of brightness) in precise mathematical terms. Today, few people take seriously, or even know about, Fechner's speculations on the soul-life of plants and planets. But psychophysics, the discipline which he founded to verify his inspiration, remains one of the most advanced and scientifically rigorous subdivisions of psychology. The decibel scale for loudness is a familiar application of psychophysical principles.

We recount the story of Fechner because it illustrates well the nature and function of the creative imagination. As human beings, we live in two worlds—the world of abstract thought and the world of sense perception. The world of abstract thought is a symbolic world. It can be, like Fechner's mathematical formulations, seemingly cold and lifeless; the world of sense perception, by contrast, is marked by warmth and vitality.

Throughout the ages and across cultures, the differences between these two worlds have been described in different ways: the life of the soul versus the life of the body, the mental versus the physical, the sacred versus the profane. This dualistic way of talking, it might be objected, has no place in a modern, scientific worldview, Fechner notwithstanding. The objection is well taken. Strictly speaking, we should not speak of two worlds, but of two ways of relating to the one world in which we live. But a change in terminology does not lessen the psychological reality of the gulf between these two aspects of human existence. The way of sense perception is shared by all animals in one form or another. The way of abstract thought is a later evolutionary development that has reached its epitome in human beings. Many animals have senses more acute than humans, but none has the same capacity for abstract thought.

No matter our philosophical position, monistic or dualistic, we all experience the gap between abstract thought and sense perception. They seem so different, and at times so painfully irreconcilable. It need not be so. Through the imagination we can bridge the gap, substituting for neither, but allowing each to be enriched by elements of the other. That is the lesson we can learn from Fechner, whether or not we follow him in any other particular.

As a bridge between the abstract and the sensory, the imagination must be firmly anchored on both sides. This does not mean, however, that all uses of the imagination engage both sides equally. The arts (painting, music) are closer to the sensory side; the sciences (mathematics, physics) are closer to the abstract side; literature, particularly poetry, falls somewhere in between. So, too, do the emotions. But regardless of where one stands on the bridge, the imagination brings the abstract into contact with the sensory, and vice versa.

As already noted in the case of lower animals, sense perception can lack imagination. Consider the difference between seeing sunflowers and a painting of sunflowers such as that by van Gogh. The latter is not simply a representation of sunflowers; a photograph could do that better. Rather, van Gogh's painting shows imagination: It has an element of abstract thought, as well as sensuous form; it makes one think as well as see; it points beyond itself. A bee would not be fooled by van Gogh's painting, but neither would a bee understand.

In the case of humans, too, sense experience can be devoid of imagination. There may be occasions when we take a moment in time to just feel the sun on our skin or watch the snow fall, with no thought or purpose other than the sensory. That is legitimate. There are other circumstances that are not so legitimate, as the following examples illustrate. Carl would eat an entire chocolate cake at a sitting, just for the taste; Esther used prescription drugs to obtain stimulation; Wesley frequently had sex four times a day, each time with a different woman. One might say they were enjoying the "brute feelings," but that would be unfair to brutes. Carl, Esther, and Wesley were not acting like complete animals; they were acting like incomplete humans. They were using sensory stimulation as a means of escape. But sensory experience divorced from abstract thought is meaningless; at most, it can bring only fleeting pleasure —and then a renewed sense of alienation and vacuity.

Abstract thought can also lack imagination. This is more difficult to illustrate, for too often we assume that thinking automatically implies imagination. Not so: A computer can, in a sense, "think"; it can solve complex mathematical problems, play chess, and even make medical diagnoses. A computer, however, is devoid of imagination.

Like computers, humans can excel at abstract thought and yet show little imagination. Hal had decided long ago how his life should be; and he never allowed any intrusions that did not fit the pattern he had set out for himself or his belief system. Lloyd was very precise about everything he did; he worked almost by rote and repetition. Both Hal and Lloyd were intelligent, but they lacked imagination. In a misguided search for order and unity they squeezed the vitality out of their lives; their thought simulated that of a computer. Such a deficit in imagination is not uncommon among people suffering from hyperautonomy, as discussed in the last chapter.

Through the imagination abstract thought is brought into contact with the sensuous and made "alive." In Chapter 12, we quoted Einstein to the effect that language played little role in his thought processes, at least during the initial stages of discovery. Rather, the elements of his thought were primarily "visual and some of muscular type." Recall also Poincaré's observation (quoted in Chapter 6) that every real mathematician possesses a "true esthetic feeling" and "emotional sensibility." Without imagination and its contact with the sensuous, abstract thought is dead, lifeless, mechanical.

Emotional creativity, even more than creativity in the arts and sciences, requires an integration of the sensory with the abstract. There are many reasons why such integration fails to occur. One particularly poignant example is childhood abuse. In order to survive psychologically, abused children often learn to separate themselves mentally from what they are experiencing. The result is arrested emotional development. Whereas abstract thought may continue to advance, emotional reactions tend to remain at a childhood level. When threatened, the "child" is then called upon to do the work of an adult. For these persons it is especially important to "bridge the gap" between the sensory and abstract. One particularly helpful technique is, in imagination, to go back into the original abusive situation and, as an adult, to rescue, protect, and nurture the child so that it may grow emotionally.

To bridge the gap between abstract thought and sensory experience is only one function of the imagination. A second function, one that sometimes is in opposition to the first, is to liberate us from the limitations imposed by circumstances, to break the bonds of immediate experience and conventional thought.

When we wish to emphasize this second, liberating function of the imagination, we speak of fantasy. Some people have fantasies so vivid that their imaginings are like waking dreams. Sheryl Wilson and Theodore Barber interviewed 19 such women, whom they discovered during an intensive study of highly hypnotic subjects. For these women, fantasy was one of the most important and rewarding aspects of their lives. One woman put it as follows:

> Fantasy is being anything you can be, could be, or are. It's possibilities made possible. It's soaring, thrilling, living. Who is to say what's happening right now is reality? Fantasy is your own private reality, your own private world. You set the stage. You make it. It's being God-like. Anything you believe, if you believe it, it's true.[3]

The fantasies of the women studied by Wilson and Barber were often accompanied by appropriate physiological reactions. For example, one woman described watching the movie *Dr. Zhivago* on television. Even though her living room was comfortably warm, she had to bundle up in a blanket while viewing the cold Siberian scenes. All 19 of the women reported having sexual fantasies that often were more satisfying and enjoyable than actual sexual relations. The majority could reach orgasm solely through fantasy.

Only a small proportion of people (probably less than 5 percent) are free (able) to fantasize in the manner described by Wilson and Barber's subjects. What about the other 95 percent of us? We are all much more capable of vivid imagery than we realize. Each night when we fall asleep we all engage in a dramatic form of imagery—dreaming. J. Allen Hobson uses the term *autocreative* to describe the quality of dreams, in which mutually incompatible, bizarre elements are effortlessly combined and experienced as real. The imaginative yet realistic quality of dreams inspired a school of writers and painters who called themselves *surrealists*. In our dreams, according to Hobson, we are all surrealists, differing only in the extent to which we can give aesthetic expression to our inner experiences:

> Since dreaming is universal, it stands as testimony to the universality of the artistic experience. In our dreams, we all become writers, painters, and film makers, combining extraordinary sets of characters, actions, and locations into strangely coherent experiences.[4]

Needless to say, dreams are seldom creative in the sense of providing effective solutions to problems. And this brings us back to the first function of the imagination discussed earlier: The *creative* imagination must be anchored in reality, as experienced in sense perception and conceived in abstract thought. Imagination, to the extent that it is creative, is more than bringing images into consciousness, or telling stories to ourselves. It is a way of transcending gaps in our knowledge so that we are better able to respond to circumstances.

And here we encounter a paradox: We have said that the imagination is among the most free of human activities; yet the world we create in imagination is sometimes the antithesis of freedom. It is, in fact, like a nightmare from which we cannot awaken. For example, Gladys worried constantly about herself and her family; in her imagination, she contrived and lived every negative event that could happen (injury, sickness, death, economic disaster, and on and on). She lived her life in misery and fear; she engendered resentment in those she tried to "protect"; and yet she seemed powerless to change.

William Lynch has attributed such negative imaginings to what he calls the "absolutizing" tendency.[5] This tendency is particularly evident in children, who can be wonderfully imaginative and yet frustratingly egocentric. Imaginary companions occupy their world; a menagerie of stuffed animals turns bedrooms into jungles; elves, leprechauns, and a rogues gallery of ghosts and goblins protect and haunt them. Yet, being only children, they do not have the capacity to subject their fantasies to critical analysis. They automatically assume that their own perspective is the only valid one, and that their own thoughts and images somehow reflect absolute reality.

As adults, we never completely outgrow the absolutizing tendency of childhood. This is particularly obvious in neurotic syndromes. The depressed person elevates minor shortcomings into major failures that make him unworthy of love or affection; the anxious person imagines that minor or remote dangers are about to overtake her; and the paranoid person takes an inadvertent slight as proof that others are conspiring against him. Needless to say, all of us have shortcomings that we occasionally find depressing; and the world is a full of dangers (most of which never materialize). The neurotic focuses on such inadequacies and improbable dangers, and through the absolutizing tendency the imagination creates a whole out of the part.

It is not, however, simply the child and the neurotic who show an absolutizing tendency. Highly creative people also seem particularly susceptible to a blind loyalty to their own ideas, and an almost paranoid suspicion of the ideas of others. Cesare Lombroso cites many instances of fanaticism and intolerance among otherwise creative individuals.

> The men who create new worlds are as much enemies of novelty as ordinary persons and children. They display extraordinary energy in rejecting the discoveries of others. . . . Anyone who has had the rare fortune to live with men of genius is soon struck by the facility with which they misinterpret the acts of others, believe themselves persecuted, and find everywhere profound and infinite reasons for grief and melancholy.[6]

There is no need to list the names of famous persons whom Lombroso classified as suffering from misoneism (hatred of innovation). Even discounting Lombroso's penchant for hyperbole, anyone remotely familiar with the history of science and art will recognize the unfortunate truth in what he says.

It is not particularly surprising that highly creative individuals should tend to absolutize the products of their own imaginations. Creative endeavors require great effort, typically to the exclusion of other concerns. The individual's own sense of self becomes identified with the creative product. More than that: To the extent that the creative product meets the criterion of authenticity, it is an extension of the self. The situation is not unlike the identification of a parent with a child. Any criticism or questioning of the creative product becomes a criticism of the self, a questioning of one's own worth.

How can we counterbalance the absolutizing tendency that is so characteristic of children, neurotics, and creative geniuses? By capitalizing on another tendency that is also very characteristic of children, namely, play. Through play, we can test the products of our imagination, discarding those aspects that prove ineffective or inappropriate, and retaining those that prove adaptive. Play is imagination put into action.

The young of all mammals play, as do some birds and even reptiles (e.g., alligators). However, the play of animals has a different quality than the play of humans, for animals lack the imagination of humans.

In his classic study *Homo Ludens* (in which "playfulness" is substituted for "intelligence" as the defining characteristic of the human species *Homo sapiens*) the Dutch cultural historian Johan Huizinga outlined a number of characteristics of human play. Among the most important of these for our purposes are the following: (1) Play is a free, voluntary activity, as opposed to a duty or task. (2) During play the "real" world is transcended and new realities are created. (3) The creation of new realities does not mean that play lacks order or rules; on the contrary, play creates its own order, and establishes its own rules. (4) The order that characterizes play has an aesthetic quality; for example, play is marked by tension, poise, balance, contrast, variation, solution, and resolution. (5) Play is intense and involving, an affectively moving experience.[7]

In short, human play goes beyond animal play both in the use of imagination to create new worlds and in the establishment of rules that determine what is permissible and effective in those worlds. In these respects, art and science can be considered among the highest manifestations of human play. Some would even place religion within this category. "There is a sacral secret at the root and in the flowering of all play," writes the theologian Hugo Rahner, who goes on to remark:

> To play is to yield oneself to a kind of magic, to enact to oneself the absolutely other, to pre-empt the future, to give the lie to the inconvenient world of fact. In play earthly realities become, of a sudden, things of the transient moment, presently left behind, then disposed of and buried in the past; the mind is prepared to accept the unimagined and incredible, to enter a world where different laws apply, to be relieved of all the weights that bear it down, to be free, kingly, unfettered and divine.[8]

This description could be applied with hardly a change of wording to the emotions. By means of emotions we can magically transform the "inconvenient world of fact" into one more compatible with our needs and desires.[9] Of course, during an emergency we have little choice in the kind of emotion we experience. Rather, we fall back on previously acquired habits. But with the help of imagination and play we can change, develop and test new forms of emotion, we can become emotionally creative. Young children play at being emotional, for example, at being angry, frightened, and sad, just as they play at being doctors, nurses, mechanics, and parents. As adults, we tend to regard both the emotions and play as "childish," and hence we lose our ability to respond in a free and uninhibited manner. That is as unnecessary as it is unfortunate.

Imagine for a moment how would you might feel and react if on the same day you won the lottery for ten million dollars and you also received word that you were suffering from a fatal illness. Or, to take some more realistic examples, how might you feel if your son "came out of the closet" and took a homosexual lover? Or if your spouse informed you that he or she had contracted genital herpes but doesn't know how? Would you respond in ways that are novel for you or your social group, fitting to the circumstance, and reflective of your own long-term goals and values? Or would you revert to more familiar but perhaps ineffective emotional reactions?

By imagining unusual situations, we are often better able to come to grips with the commonplace. But we need not—and should not—confine our imagination to the unusual or improbable. Everyday emotional experiences, for example, of love, anger, hope, and fear, provide ample opportunity for improvement, if we will use our imagination.

Once an emotion is imagined, it can be refined and even transformed. This provides the basis for a therapeutic method, called "active imagination" by Jungian psychologists, although it is not tied to any one theoretical orientation:

> The method consists essentially in a confrontation with the mood or emotion in an open, contemplative frame of mind, allowing it to take full expression in words, visual images, plastic forms, etc. Once this material is presented, the ego's role is to react to it as if it were real, and not "just an emotion" or "just a fantasy." Through conscious questioning, interpretation and elaboration, a dialectical relation is established between the emotional fantasy product and the attentive ego. The aim is to get the meaning (the representational content or instinctual image) of the mood or emotion and to effect a joint transformation of it and of the ego's attitude through the dialectical interchange.[10]

Like the instructions for riding a bicycle, the instructions for active imagination are deceptively simple. It is easy to say what to do; it is much more difficult to do it—at least without an occasional spill. This is an issue to which we will return in Chapter 25. Fortunately, we do not have to rely entirely on our own imagination for guidance. Works of art and literature provide access to the visions and musings of highly talented and imaginative people from diverse times and different cultures.

22

—✦—

Art, Drama, and the Cathartic Method

Art is the creation of forms symbolic
of human feeling.
—Susanne Langer, *Feeling and Form*

A work of art can arouse emotion in two ways; or perhaps it would be more accurate to say that two relatively different kinds of emotion can be aroused by a work of art. Aesthetic emotions are evoked by the form as distinct from the content of a work. We do not have specific names for the variety of possible aesthetic emotions, but a sense of beauty, wonder and fascination are among their primary qualities. Aesthetic emotions can be distinguished from other emotions, such as anger, fear, grief, sexual arousal, and the like, that are more likely to be aroused by the content than the form of a work. For example, the depiction of injustice may evoke anger; the depiction of danger, fear; and the depiction of loss, grief.

Aesthetic emotions are perhaps best illustrated by music. Most musical scores do not tell a story or depict an event. The sound and rhythm are pleasing in and of themselves. Similarly, the visual arts (painting, sculpture) can be appreciated for their aesthetic value, independent of what they depict. Literature, such as drama, also has aesthetic value, but its primary emotional appeal is typically in its content.

And what, more precisely, is "aesthetic value"? As a first approximation, we might say, "beauty." But that only raises another question: What is beauty? "Measure and proportion," Plato asserted.[1] Like many of Plato's assertions, this one has its modern counterpart in the notion that, for an object to be beautiful, diverse elements must be integrated into a harmonious whole; or stated more simply, "diversity and harmony."

Even good things can be overdone. Plato notwithstanding, a work can have so much "measure and proportion" that its beauty is diminished rather than enhanced. For example, an artificial flower may be better proportioned than a real flower, yet not be as beautiful. A real flower, whose principle of growth comes from within, must necessarily show some "distortions," for example, due to sun and soil conditions. Similarly, human handicrafts (pottery, for example) are often considered more beautiful when they show some flaw, some indication of their human origin. Plotinus, a Neoplatonist who lived in the third century A.D. (204–270), was perhaps the first to clearly articulate this principle. The face of a dead person, Plotinus noted, has the same configuration as the face of a live person, yet the two are not equally beautiful. Beauty stems from a vital principle within.[2]

In sum, we have three main criteria for beauty, namely, diversity, harmony, and vitality. Other criteria could be mentioned, including the hoary notion that beauty is simply in the eyes of the beholder. "Ask a toad what beauty is, the *to kalon*? He will answer you that it is his toad wife with two great round eyes issuing from her little head, a wide, flat mouth, a yellow belly, a brown back."[3] Which simply goes to show that for a toad, diversity, harmony, and vitality are to be found in another toad.

However beauty is conceived, it alone is not sufficient to define the aesthetic. A tragedy, for example, is not usually considered beautiful, and yet it can have aesthetic value. Going even further, some works of art are downright abhorrent. The history of painting is replete with images of human suffering—martyrdoms, massacres, and the tortures of hell. The grotesque can be as fascinating as the beautiful. We might therefore define "aesthetic" as the ability to capture and hold one's attention, whether in agreeable or morbid fascination.

This does not mean that both the beautiful and the grotesque contribute equally to the aesthetic value of art. A work of art cannot be too beautiful, but it can be too grotesque. In the absence of beauty, the grotesque remains simply that—grotesque. The tension between the beautiful and the grotesque may enhance the aesthetic value of a work, just as the tension between pleasure and pain may enhance the enjoyment of an experience (cf. Chapter 15), but not if the latter (the grotesque) overpowers the former.

What is the relation of aesthetic values to emotional creativity? The answer to this question is twofold. First, aesthetic emotions (a sense of beauty, wonder, and engrossment) can be enriching in their own right; and, since they are relatively nebulous or unformed, they allow us to explore the meaning of experience in a free and unfettered fashion. Second, to the extent that aesthetic values capture our attention and increase our enjoyment of a work, they serve to amplify whatever emotions the content of a work might evoke. For example, the tragedy of Hamlet affects us all the more because of the aesthetic qualities of Shakespeare's verse.

To the extent that a work of art has aesthetic value, its appeal is not difficult to understand. Some works of art, however, especially in literature, are valued less for their aesthetic appeal than for the message they convey. Tragedy is a good example. Why do we enjoy a dramatic work in which scenes of pain and suffering predominate? This is a question that puzzled Aristotle. His answer was that "with incidents arousing pity and fear," tragedy accomplishes "its catharsis [expurgation or relief] of such emotions."[4] This explanation is ambiguous, at best. In the history of ideas, however, ambiguity can be a source of longevity, if not enlightenment.

> The immense controversy, carried on in books, pamphlets, sheets and flying articles, mostly German, as to what it was that Aristotle really meant by [catharsis] is one of the disgraces of the human intelligence, a grotesque monument to sterility.[5]

We have no intention of adding another stone to this monument, but we would like to make a modest suggestion with respect to the emotional benefits of tragedy, indeed, of art in general. We take as a point of departure an observation by one of the most prominent philosophers of the twentieth century, Alfred North Whitehead, who was no less struck than was Aristotle by the ability of the ancient Greek playwrights to influence our emotions.

Aeschylus, Sophocles, Euripides were adventurers in the world of thought. To read their plays without any sense of new ways of understanding the world and of savoring its emotions is to miss the vividness which constitutes their whole value.[6]

In other words, the value of tragedy is not to expurgate already formed emotions, as Aristotle suggested, but to stimulate new ways of understanding and new kinds of emotions. Catharsis is less a matter of emotional relief than it is a matter of emotional creativity.

To illustrate this last observation with concrete examples, we recount the story of the house of Pelops, after whom the southern portion of the Greek peninsula is named (Peloponnesus—literally, isle of Pelops). This story, which extends over many generations, has provided material for numerous dramatic works, both ancient (e.g., *Agamemnon, The Choëphoroe, The Eumenides* by Aeschylus, and *Electra, Orestes, Iphigenia in Tauris* by Euripides) and modern (e.g., *Mourning Becomes Electra* by Eugene O'Neill and *The Family Reunion* by T. S. Eliot). The events described, when placed in dramatic form by an accomplished playwright, can not help but stretch the emotions of an audience.

The story begins with Tantalus, the father of Pelops and legendary king of Sipylus in Lydia, Asia Minor. Tantalus was a direct descendent of Zeus by the nymph Pluto. It is from his fate that we get the word "tantalize." According to one myth, Tantalus murdered his son, Pelops, and served his flesh to the gods as a feast. The gods, however, discovered the crime and restored Pelops to life before he was devoured. According to another myth, Tantalus betrayed secrets of the gods to humans. Whichever the case, his punishment was severe and never ending: Tantalus was made to stand in water up to his neck, but whenever he would bend to drink, the water would recede from him; and fruit hung over his head, but whenever he tried to grasp it, a wind blew it out of reach.

Grown to manhood, Pelops became one of many suitors for the hand of Hippodamia, daughter of the king of Pisa (a city near Olympia in ancient Greece). In order to choose among the suitors, a contest was arranged. Whoever could beat the king, Hippodamia's father, in a chariot race would win Hippodamia as his bride. If, however, the challenger lost, his prize was death. Pelops beat the father, but only by treachery. For this, his whole house, future generations included, was placed under a curse. One result was the Trojan war.

In spite of his treachery, Pelops experienced considerable worldly success. The curse, however, was visited upon his two sons, Atreus and Thyestes. In a quarrel over power and a woman, Atreus killed the sons of Thyestes and served them to their father as food. A more horrible fate for both father and sons is difficult to imagine.

Atreus's own sons fared better, at least initially. One, Menelaus, became king of Sparta; the other, Agamemnon, became king of Mycenae (Argos). As if that were not good fortune enough, Menelaus married Helen, supposedly the most beautiful woman alive, and Agamemnon married her sister, Clytemnestra. The good fortune, however, was not to last.

With the aid and blessing of the goddess Aphrodite, Paris, the son of the king of Troy, seduced Helen and took her back with him to his native city. Menelaus called on his fellow Greeks to aid him in the capture of Troy and the return of Helen. A mighty armada was assembled, and Agamemnon was chosen commander-in-chief. However, while on a hunt Agamemnon killed a stag sacred to the goddess Artemis; she thereupon stilled the winds so that the Greek ships could not sail for Troy. To appease the goddess, Agamemnon was informed that he must sacrifice his daughter, Iphigenia. She was brought to him under the pretext of marrying the hero Achilles. As Agamemnon was about to plunge a knife into her, Artemis relented and substituted a hind for Iphigenia. Agamemnon and others believed the sacrifice had been accomplished and that Iphigenia was dead. Unbeknownst to them, she was whisked away in a cloud to the island of Tauris, where she became a priestess in the temple of Artemis. The winds changed, and the Greeks sailed for Troy.

The Trojan war lasted ten years. During his absence, Agamemnon's wife, Clytemnestra, took as a lover his cousin, Aegisthus. Agamemnon also took a consort, Cassandra. When Agamemnon returned, Clytemnestra slew him and Cassandra, in part as revenge for the presumed killing of their daughter, Iphigenia.

Agamemnon and Clytemnestra had two other children besides Iphigenia, namely, Electra and Orestes. Electra was forced by Clytemnestra's paramour, Aegisthus, to marry a peasant, so that any offspring of hers would have no pretense to the throne. Orestes, the youngest of Agamemnon's three children, was to be killed. However, Orestes escaped this fate and some years later, with help from Elektra, he returned and slew his mother and her lover, thus avenging his father's death.

To kill one's own mother is a terrible deed, itself in need of expiation. Orestes was therefore pursued from land to land by the Furies, spirits of vengeance. At last, he was directed to go to Tauris to retrieve a statue of Artemis. Tauris is, it will be recalled, the island to which Iphigenia had been sent. Her duty there was to sacrifice all strangers who landed on the island. Orestes is captured, and Iphigenia is faced with a terrible choice: to remain faithful to her duties as a priestess or to kill her brother. She spares her brother and both escape the island.

We need not continue with the story. Imagine being in a situation where your most basic needs, such as hunger and thirst, are forever frustrated (Tantalus), where you eat your own children at dinner (Thyestes), slay your daughter at her wedding (Agamemnon), kill your husband (Clytemnestra), murder your mother (Electra, Orestes), or have to choose between duty and brotherly love (Iphigenia). Situations such as these are close enough to everyday experience that they can be imagined, yet they are sufficiently unusual that they stretch us emotionally, just as unexpected empirical discoveries may stretch us intellectually.

Lest we leave the impression that the ancient Greeks were somehow unique in their fascination with the grotesque, it is well to remember that one traditional function of art has been to confront complacency—to prod, goad, and affront the sensibilities. Today, that tradition is carried to its extreme in what is known as "shock art." In the process, the line between the aesthetic and the merely grotesque is sometimes transgressed, particularly by "artists" whose pretensions exceed their talents. In a performance before the Boston Film and Video Foundation (October 29, 1989), Joe Coleman bit off the head and front legs of a white mouse, hugged a spectator after he had poured a bucket of blood over himself, and ignited fireworks on his chest. That went too far even for patrons who are wont to excuse almost any excess in the name of art. (The head of the Boston Film and Video Foundation disavowed any connection with Coleman, saying that the performance was an independent project of a foundation member.)

Now let us return to the idea of catharsis. As noted, Aristotle suggested that drama allows a release or purgation of emotion. A more likely explanation for the appeal of tragedy—an explanation that also applies to romance and comedy, as well as to painting and other forms of art—follows from our analysis of emotional creativity. Great art presents us with situations that arouse new and different emotions; it challenges us to think and feel in novel ways. Art does not allow the release of repressed or pent-up emotions; at least that is not its primary appeal. Rather, it creates new emotions that we have not experienced before, or have experienced only imperfectly. The result can be exhilarating.

Outside of art, the idea of catharsis finds its most frequent application in psychotherapy. "I have often in my own mind compared cathartic psychotherapy with surgical intervention," Freud wrote. "I have described my treatments as psychotherapeutic operations; and I have brought out their analogy with the opening up of a cavity filled with pus, the scraping out of a carious region, etc."[7] It is a vivid analogy, but Freud soon abandoned the cathartic method (recalling and reliving traumatic emotional experiences during a psychotherapeutic session), for he believed the results to be too transitory or impermanent. Others, however, continue to advocate catharsis as a therapeutic technique, often without a clear understanding of the underlying processes.[8]

A good deal of psychological research has been devoted to the possible cathartic effects of emotional expression, especially as it relates to anger and aggression. On the whole, the results have not been supportive of the notion that anger can be drained away like pus from a wound (to use Freud's graphic analogy). More often than not, the expression of anger on one occasion facilitates and encourages its expression on subsequent occasions. This is true whether the expression is direct (e.g., actually acting out one's anger) or vicarious (e.g., watching aggressive films or sporting events). Practice makes perfect, so to speak, except that if the original expression was inappropriate, then subsequent expressions are liable to be even more inappropriate. To illustrate, spouse abuse typically starts slowly, with the "venting" of pent-up anger on one occasion. A while later (typically weeks or months) another episode may follow, and then another and another, with increasing frequency and intensity, until the abuse becomes an established way of interacting.[9]

In spite of the above reservation, it must also be admitted that the mere expression of emotion during psychotherapy can sometimes have beneficial and long-lasting effects. Why? The answer is simple in theory, although complex in practice. *Under appropriate circumstances,* an emotional outpouring can change a person's interpretation of a situation, and hence the need for subsequent expression. Take, for example, the person who has been unable to express grief over the death of a loved one. To "break down" and cry signifies admission of the loss and one's own need for support. With such admission, healing can begin. Or take the person who vehemently beats a cushion in anger. Such a seemingly senseless act, if it occurs in the therapist's office, can not change anything. Or can it? Even if no one else were to notice, the act dramatizes to the person his or her own frustrated needs, which may previously have been denied, and it encourages further action in order to correct the offending situation.

If the expression of emotion is to achieve lasting benefits, and not simply provide a temporary release of tension, it must be associated with a suitable reinterpretation of events and a realistic course of action. The role of the therapist, in cooperation with the client, is to provide—or, more accurately, to construct—an account in which the response achieves significance. That is, a skillful therapist helps the client not only to express new emotions, but to make those emotions a meaningful and effective part of life.

We can now see a relation between "catharsis" as it occurs in psychotherapy and in art. Psychotherapy, like art, not only stretches the emotions, it educates them.

Part V

Achieving Emotional Creativity

'Tis to create, and in creating live
A being more intense, that we endow
with form our fancy, gaining as we give
The life we image.

—Byron, "Childe Harold's Pilgrimage"

23

◆

Emotions as an Art Form

The human body is an instrument for the production
of art in the life of the human soul.
—Alfred North Whitehead,
Adventures of Ideas

Throughout this book we have spoken of the art of emotion, using the term "art" as an acronym for the acquisition, refinement, and transformation of emotional experience. But we intend the "art of emotion" be taken more seriously than simply as a catchy, if somewhat trite, mnemonic device. As we saw in the last chapter, one of the most common themes in writings on aesthetics is that art is an expression of emotion. If that is the case, and we believe it is, then perhaps we can use art to help us understand and even enhance the emotions. More than that, There is a sense in which the emotions, at their creative best, can be considered an art form in their own right.

At the outset, we must specify precisely what we mean by "art." In its broadest sense, "art" refers to anything made by human beings, as opposed to a work of nature. A blacksmith, for example, may ply his art, as might a plumber. On the other hand, a cloud formation or a sunset is not a work of art, no matter how beautiful. Applying this definition to the emotions, if emotions are completely natural phenomena, things that happen to us as part of our biological nature, then it would make little sense to speak of an art of emotion. But if emotions are, as we have argued, social and personal constructions, then they are, broadly speaking, works of art (human artifacts).

Needless to say, not every human artifact can be regarded as a work of art—a heap of garbage, for example. To be counted as art, a work should have some value. The art of a blacksmith has *practical* value. The practical arts can be contrasted with *fine* art, that is, art whose value is primarily *aesthetic.* ("Fine art" does not necessarily mean "good art." To say that fine art is made for aesthetic value does not imply that all works of art are equally successful in this regard.)

In earlier times, all art was, to an extent, practical. Images of gods, emperors, etc., were placed in the marketplace and temples not simply to please the senses, but to educate and inspire. The idea of fine art—art for art's sake—is relatively recent, dating from the eighteenth century. Even today most art is created for practical as well as aesthetic reasons.

The emotions have practical value; they are ways of solving problems and meeting challenges. The art of emotion is therefore a practical art. Is it also possible to have a fine art of the emotions? The fine arts can be distinguished along a variety of dimensions, for example, visual arts (painting, sculpture), acoustic arts (music), and symbolic arts (literature). A more relevant distinction for our purposes is between art that exists independent of the creative act (a painting, say) and art that exists only in its performance (a dance, say). The emotions can be counted among the performing arts— provided they are capable of achieving aesthetic value.

To recapitulate briefly what was said in the last chapter, the aesthetic value of a work is attributable to its form as distinct from its content. More specifically, to have aesthetic value, a work should possess the three main qualities that help define beauty, namely, diversity (complexity), harmony (unity), and vitality; and it should be engrossing, even if this entails elements of the grotesque as well as the beautiful.

Nothing that we have said thus far, it will be noted, precludes an emotional episode from being artistic. Emotions are human constructions; they can have harmony in diversity as well as vitality; and they are engrossing, whether in agreeable or disagreeable ways. But before we can use art as a guide for understanding and enhancing the emotions, a potential objection must be met. Art, it is sometimes said, requires "aesthetic distance." The person who is caught up in the exigencies of the moment, who is "gripped" by anger, or "seized" by fear, cannot be artistically creative. At a later time, perhaps, the exiting events may be recalled in safety and, by the person of talent, recreated in art. That, at least, was the view of Whitehead:

> The origin of art lies in the craving for re-enaction. In some mode of repetition we need by our personal actions, or perceptions to dramatize the past and the future, so as to re-live the emotional life of ourselves, and of our ancestors. . . . If Odysseus among the shades could hear Homer chanting his Odyssey, he then re-enacted with free enjoyment the perils of his wanderings.[1]

The requirement for aesthetic distance would seem to remove the emotions from the domain of art, except to the extent that they are sublimated or vicarious copies of the original. This objection may be met in two ways.

First, we grant that an untutored emotional outburst, born in a moment of necessity, is unlikely to be very artistic. Neither is a hastily painted picture, assembled in a moment of duress. However, throughout this book we have emphasized that people have more control over their emotions than they typically realize, and that emotional creativity does not occur spontaneously, without prior preparation and incubation. Good emotions, like good art, often require some aesthetic distance.

Second, it is not the case that art is always created or appreciated in a dispassionate manner. A dancer who becomes thoroughly engrossed in the performance is likely to be more, not less artistic than a more disinterested performer. Given adequate preparation and skill, complete engrossment in an emotional episode does not automatically exclude the enactment from the realm of art.

Form and Medium

The making of any work of art can be decomposed into two aspects—form and medium: The form consists in the arrangement of parts into a meaningful (aesthetic) whole; the medium is that out of which the work is constructed. Each kind of art has its own medium: Solids for sculpturing; oils, watercolors, and acrylics for painting; acoustical instruments for music; language for literature; and so forth. In performing arts such as dance, the human body is the primary medium.

The medium both enables and constrains a work of art. An especially fine piece of marble may enable a sculptor to create a beautiful statue, but it also limits the size and shape that the statue may take. Artistic expression varies in the extent to which it is constrained by its medium. Sculpture is more constrained than painting, and painting more than music. Literature is perhaps the least constrained of all the arts, for its medium is primarily symbolic.

In contemporary art, two trends can be observed, depending upon whether the artist emphasizes form or medium. In abstract expressionism, form is sacrificed to the medium. In an expressionist painting, for example, the viewer is greeted by a seemingly formless swirl of color and texture. Jackson Pollock, one of the originators of this school, developed the technique of "drip painting." Paint was literally allowed to drip from the brush onto a large canvas. The result was a very intricate lacework of color. Of course, it is impossible to eliminate form entirely. A completely random juxtaposition of events would lack harmony and hence have little aesthetic value. Jackson Pollock was an accomplished representational painter before he turned to abstract expressionism. His sense for form is apparent even in his "drippings."

At the opposite extreme is "minimal art," which attempts to overcome the limits of a medium by focusing on "pure form." Minimalism uses rationally derived (even mathematical) procedures to guide composition. A painting, for example, might consist of geometric figures arranged to stimulate the imagination more than the senses. Minimalism is not limited to the visual arts. Some musicians, too, would like to overcome the constraints imposed by acoustical instruments by silently "reading" their music from a written score. In this respect, a minimalist musician might be compared to a poet reading silently from a text. For a person with sufficient prior experience and talent, the sensory aspects of any medium can, to a surprising extent, be eliminated without destroying the form.[2] In music, a well-known example of this is Beethoven, who composed his ninth symphony while deaf. He never heard his masterwork except in his imagination.

In the art of emotion, the body is the medium and the meaning of the response is the form. Traditional approaches to the study of emotion have tended to emphasize bodily changes (cf. the Myth of Fervid Viscera discussed in Chapter 5). It is, of course, important to understand the medium if we are to produce good art. However, such understanding alone is clearly insufficient. For example, the science of acoustics may aid the design of musical instruments and concert halls. However, the tones that become a symphony cease to be just sounds when they are incorporated into a musical score; the piece of marble that becomes a statue ceases to be just a stone; and the paint that colors a portrait ceases to be just pigmented oil when given appropriate form. Similarly, physiological responses cease to be just bodily changes when they become incorporated into an emotion.

Is there anything similar to abstract expressionism in the case of the emotions (where the medium is emphasized over form) and to minimal art (where form is emphasized over the medium)? Yes—we will call the former "emotional expressionism" and the latter "emotional minimalism." An example of emotional expressionism is the hedonist who strives after sensory stimulation for its own sake, sometimes with grace and dramatic flair, but without regard to form or meaning. The ascetic and masochist, too, may glory in mere "works of the flesh"—in their case, for the suffering rather than the pleasure afforded. Thus, emotional expressionism, like abstract expressionism in painting, may satisfy for the moment. But one must continually engage in the activity, for the behavior has little meaning beyond the immediate sensory gratification.

At the other extreme, "emotional minimalism" implies a subjugation of the body to the mind during emotion. Perhaps the best example of emotional minimalism is mysticism. The mystic attempts to overcome the limitations of the body in order to experience "pure emotion." The Greek philosopher Plotinus provides an excellent example of emotional minimalism.

Plotinus was a mystic as well as the last of the ancient Greek philosophers of note. He postulated a scale of being which starts with the One, a transcendent power, emanations of which create a succession of types of existence whose reality and value decrease as their distance from the One increases. It is the One, through its emanation, the World Soul, that is the source of beauty. Matter is the third and last emanation of the One, the point at which its creative powers come to a halt.

According to Plotinus, all nature strives to effect a return from lower to higher forms of being. For humans, mystical reunion can be achieved, but only if all that pertains to the senses and to the material body is left behind.

> Purified, the soul is wholly Idea and reason. It becomes wholly free of the body, intellective, entirely of that intelligible realm whence comes beauty and all things beautiful.[3]

Plotinus's conception of soul, it should be noted, is Platonic, not Christian. The important point, however, is that the soul, although "wholly Idea and reason," is not devoid of passion.

> Such emotion all beauty must induce—an astonishment, a delicious wonderment, a longing, a love, a trembling that is all delight. . . . What is this intoxication, this exultation, this longing to break away from the body and live sunken within yourselves? All true lovers experience it. But what awakens so much passion? It is not shape, or color, or size. It is the soul, itself "colorless," and the soul's temperance and the hueless "luster" of its virtues. . . . [A]nd throughout them all you see the radiance of The Intelligence diffusing itself through them all.[4]

The mystical experience is both a way of knowing and a way of feeling. It is a minimalist emotion par excellence.

Emotional expressionism and minimalism represent the extremes on a continuum. Like their counterparts in the other arts, they are for the most part "experimental"; and like many experiments, the results are not always positive. Emotional expressionism can easily degenerate into debauchery, and minimalism into priggishness. At their experimental best, however, they can clear the way toward new visions, new kinds of emotional experiences. But as those new possibilities are realized, expressionism and minimalism must ultimately give way to a more balanced blend of form and medium.

Where that balance lies depends on the type of emotion. Sudden fright, for example, is largely expressive; hope is largely minimalist. But depending on the person and the situation, any emotion can be given an expressionist or minimalist cast. Consider sexual love. Unrestrained sex is a form of emotional expressionism. By breaking the bonds of conventional morality, sexual expressionism allows a more full and free exploration of sexuality. At the other extreme, sexual minimalism is perhaps best illustrated by the almost mystical love of Dante for Beatrice. In its own way, that, too, was a highly creative and liberating experience.

At its best, sexual love must combine form and medium into an aesthetic whole. Just as an artist must overcome limitations of the material with which she works, while exploiting its advantages, the artistic lover must learn to exploit the advantages of sex while minimizing its limitations. The same could be said *mutatis mutandis* for the other emotions.

Some people habitually prefer to give their emotions an expressive cast, while other prefer a minimalist style. Nietzsche referred to the former as Dionysian, after the Greek god of wine and fertility, Dionysus (Bacchus). The latter he called Apollonian, after the Greek god of the sun, Apollo, who stood for all that is civilized. Dionysus represents the sensuous and disorderly in human nature; Apollo, the rational and orderly.[5] A related distinction from modern psychology is between extraverted and introverted personality types. Extraverts seek excitement and stimulation, especially in social interaction; introverts seek tranquility and composure, especially in the company of their own thoughts.

Life-span Development

A rough progression can be seen in the life of an individual from an early Dionysian period to a later Apollonian period. The psychiatrist Anthony Storr sees a similar progression in the professional work of many artists. In the early period, when an artist is still learning and discovering, his or her work may be marked by exuberance and novelty, but lack originality. In a second or mature period, which may occupy the greater part of an artist's productive life, the artist develops an independent style. There is also during this period a strong need to transmit one's art to as wide an audience as possible, and to convince others of the validity of one's vision. Should an artist live sufficiently long, a third period can often be detected: "the artist is looking into the depths of his own psyche and is not very much concerned as to whether anyone else will follow him or understand him."[6] Works from this last period tend to be unconventional, but (as Plato might phrase it) "measured and proportioned."

Storr illustrates this progression with an analysis of Beethoven's string quartets, along with works by other composers. He also examines the novels of Henry James. The latter are particularly interesting from the standpoint of emotional creativity, for they combine elements from both early and late stages. The following account is based on Storr's analysis.

At the age of 57, James wrote *The Ambassadors.* The thesis of the book, as James himself noted, is contained in the advice given to one of the main characters, Lambert Strether: "Live all you can; it's a mistake not to. It doesn't so much matter what you do in particular, so long as you have your life. If you don't have that, what *have* you had?"[7]

Storr comments that James had singularly failed to heed this advice in his own life. He had been sexually inhibited, preferring intellectual to physical intimacy. He was, in our terms, an emotional minimalist. At an advanced age, however, he came to discover the value of emotional expressionism, without, however, abandoning his Apollonian style. Storr describes this last period as follows:

> His elaborate style makes no concessions, so that it is fair to say that he is less directly concerned with communication or with trying to woo or convince the reader. Pattern and order, although evident throughout his work, are even more insistently present in *The Ambassadors* and *The Golden Bowl.* However, James is not so concerned as some of the artists mentioned in this chapter with exploring remote areas of experience beyond the personal. His late acceptance of the physical element in love actually enriches his work at a time in life when those artists who, like Bach, had fully experienced this aspect of life, seem to be reaching beyond it. In this sense, he is also achieving a new unity between disparate elements.[8]

Storr concludes by noting that James came to see at last that art can not be art without love. We might add the converse: Love cannot be love without art.

Historical Progress

The hope is sometimes expressed that at some future time humans will have evolved psychologically, not physically, to overcome distrust, fear, and hostility, and to become more caring and empathic beings. Is emotional progress possible? Has it occurred in the past? Are we emotionally better today than we were, say, one thousand years ago? Here, again, we may turn to the world of art for instruction.

By certain criteria, progress in art can be observed. For example, starting with Florentine artists of the fifteenth century (Brunelleschi, in particular), advances have been made in the realistic depiction of perspective, that is, the representation of three-dimensional space on a two-dimensional surface. Some contemporary artists may reject the use of perspective, preferring instead the metaphorical extremes of "primitivism" or "postmodernism" (the terminology is instructive). But the techniques for achieving perspective are now readily available; their use is a matter of choice.

From an aesthetic standpoint, however, the notion of progress in art is more problematic. A painting by Picasso is not necessarily better than a painting by Rembrandt simply because it is more recent. Nor is a symphony by Stravinsky superior to one by Beethoven. In art, "new" does not necessarily mean "improved."

Similar considerations apply to cross-cultural variations in art. Is the art of the West superior to that of the East, or to that of Third World (developing) countries? The answer is clearly No. In spite of marked historical and cultural difference, art has a certain timeless quality. We are richer for the diversity of art that has accrued over the ages and across cultures.

Emotions, too, have changed with time, and they show marked differences across cultures. We saw examples of this in Chapters 2 and 3, where we discussed the evolution of romantic love in the West, and variations in anger-like emotions across cultures.

As a rough generalization, it might be said that Western

civilization has "progressed" from a more Dionysian to a more Apollonian style of emotional expression, particularly in the area of aggression. Nietzsche might call this a retrogression, not progression, but be that as it may. Norbert Elias has traced the change in eloquent detail. He notes that in medieval Europe "the pleasure in killing and torturing others was great, and it was a socially permitted pleasure."[9] A martial song attributed to the late twelfth century troubadour, Bertran de Born, goes as follows:

> I tell you that neither eating, drinking, nor sleep has as much savor for me as to hear the cry "Forwards!" from both sides, and horses without riders shying and whinnying, and the cry "Help! Help!", and to see the small and the great fall to the grass at the ditches and the dead pierced by the wood of the lances decked with banners.[10]

One knight, Bernard of Cahuzak, is described by a contemporary chronicler, Peter of Vaux-de-Cernay, in the following manner:

> He spends his life in plundering, destroying churches, falling upon pilgrims, oppressing widows and orphans. He takes particular pleasure in mutilating the innocent. In a single monastery, that of the black monks of Sarlat, there are 150 men and women whose hands he has cut off or whose eyes he has put out. And his wife is just as cruel. She helps him with his executions. It even gives her pleasure to torture the poor women. She had their breasts hacked off or their nails torn off so that they were incapable of work.[11]

Pleasure in the death and mutilation of others was not just an unleashing of primitive impulses. Prisoners were a burden to their captors. To release them, however, would only strengthen a potential enemy. Therefore, prisoners were routinely killed, or else they were mutilated so that they could perform no useful function if freed. "The stronger affectivity of social behavior was to a certain degree socially necessary," Elias observes. "People behaved in a socially useful way and took pleasure in doing so."[12]

Most people today would feel repugnance, not pleasure, at the sight of an impaled body, or of a woman with her breasts hacked off. From one point of view, that represents emotional progress. However, if one were to characterize the development of emotions during the course of Western history, it would not necessarily be from "worse" to "better," but from expressionism to minimalism.

In contemporary society, emotions of all kinds—compassion as well as belligerence, piety as well as cruelty, love as well as hate, joy as well as sorrow—are, in the words of Elias, "more subdued, moderate, and calculated" than they were in most earlier periods of history. But are they any better? The carnage of modern warfare and the planned extermination of entire peoples (as in Nazi Germany) suggest not.

In ancient Rome, when a play called for the death of one of the characters, an individual (a slave) was sometimes slain on stage. This might have added to the aesthetic value of the drama, but it could hardly be justified on moral grounds, at least not by today's standards. Similarly, the art of emotion must be grounded in a reasonable and moral philosophy of life. To the extent that we may speak of emotional "progress," it is primarily in the domain of morals and not in the expression of emotions per se that advances have been made, if not always followed.

Mass Culture

Whether or not art has progressed in quality, it certainly has proliferated in quantity. More art of all kinds is produced today than ever before in history. This is due to two factors: first, the greater number of people, both in absolute and relative numbers, who are free to pursue careers in the arts; and second, technological innovations that have facilitated the widespread dissemination of art. Rudolf Arnheim has commented on this latter factor with respect to literature. The avalanche of writing made possible by modern forms of printing has created a need for rapid reading and skimming. As a result, language has become cheapened as a visual and syntactic form of expression. "The constant gulping down of hastily produced masses of verbal material limits the mind to the absorption of 'information,' i.e., the raw material of facts."[13] People simply do not have the time to linger over the form of written language or its poetic imagery. The goal is to rush through the material as quickly as possible, picking out the factual information, without wasting time on irrelevancies.

Something similar has happened in the case of the emotions. With the "human potential" movement of the 1960s, marked by encounter groups and other "consciousness-raising" efforts, expressing one's feelings became a highly valued activity, and the suppression of emotion an insidious form of censorship. We certainly do not wish to gainsay the benefits of a more emotionally free society, any more than we question the benefits of a free press. But there have also been undisputable losses, namely, a certain debasement in the form, sensibility, and quality of the emotions. "Letting it all hang out" has become an end in itself, no matter how crude and unrefined the actual feeling and expression might be.

Nowhere is this more evident than in the case of sexual love, which too often has been equated with orgasmic release. It is not uncommon for a man or woman to have had many "lovers," often for a relationship lasting no more than an evening. There is little intimacy, little poetry, little finesse in the relationship. Just a hurry to reach the climax, and to move on. It is the sexual equivalent of skimming a novel, rushing to the final denouement, pausing along the way only to gather a few necessary facts—and then, in an ignorant display of intellectual puffery, to brag about how many books one has "read."

Freud saw sexual repression as the source of neurosis. We no longer live in a time of sexual repression, but we are no less neurotic. We have discovered that sexual expression can be as problematical as sexual repression. With a new, less restrictive sexual morality, the capacity for love has become one of the major psychological problems of our time.

What is true of love is also true of other emotions. How many people know how to become angry well? Swearing, vulgarity, sullen withdrawal, physical assault—these may convey a message in no uncertain terms, but they are not only crude forms of expression, they reflect an impoverishment of feeling, a lack imagination and aesthetic sensitivity. Similarly, it is the rare person who knows how to grieve, to be proud or humble, and to savor the fine nuances between joy, gaiety, and exultation.

In spite of (or perhaps because of) all the emphasis on expressing one's feelings, we are in danger of becoming a nation of emotional dilettantes.

24

Emotional Creativity and the Social Order

It is important to give the freest scope possible to
uncustomary things, in order that it
may in time appear which of these are
fit to be converted into custom.
—John Stuart Mill, *On Liberty*

Caution is enjoined both in the name of morality and in
the name of worldly wisdom, with the result
that generosity and adventurousness
are discouraged where the
affections are concerned.
—Bertrand Russell, *The Conquest of Happiness*

Neither art nor emotion can prosper except within a social environment. That may seem self-evident in the case of art, which needs an audience and institutional support. But the emotions? Before we address this question, consider the following fact: One society is distinguishable from another not so much by the intellectual content of their ideologies as by the emotional lives of their citizens. On an intellectual level, for example, we can understand *what* an Ilongot thinks about the taking of heads, but only a person thoroughly enculturated into Ilongot society could feel *liget* (vital energy) on such an occasion.

Emotions, we have said, are constituted according to social

rules. Social rules are, in turn, closely related to the values of a society. If a society values honesty, there will be rules to prevent cheating and deceit; if it values civility, there will be corresponding rules of etiquette; and if it values aesthetics, there will be rules to protect natural beauties and to promote artistic expression. The rules that help constitute emotions are especially tied to values. Recall the rules of courtly love presented in Chapter 4. They reflected the virtues of a good knight of the Middle Ages. The rules of love may have changed over the centuries, and to a lesser extent so may the values they represent. Nevertheless, love today, no less than in the twelfth century, embodies the values of society with respect to relations between the sexes. Similar remarks could be made with respect to anger, grief, fear, or any other emotion. Emotions are not just individual "happenings"; they are the living embodiment of the values of a society.

Paradoxically, the fact that emotions are so closely tied to social values helps account for the fact that emotions are typically viewed as divorced from, or prior to, the society of which they are a part. Recall, for example, the Myth of Phylogenesis discussed in Chapter 5, in which emotions are viewed as remnants of our animal ancestry. By treating the emotions as part of immutable human nature, the values which they embody are protected from arbitrary change.

Human Nature and the Social Order

Any theory of society must make presumptions about human nature. Our own presumption is that human beings are born "world open." Although genetic constraints on human behavior are by no means absent, what instincts we do possess do not possess us. To repeat an oft-used metaphor, our genes "whisper," they do not shout or demand.

Many behaviors have been shown to be influenced by genetic whisperings. A person's religious and political beliefs, for example, are obviously determined by his or her culture, family, and personal experiences. A child reared in Ireland will most likely grow up to be a Christian; a child reared in Iran, a Moslem; and a child reared in Israel, a Jew. But some Christians (Moslems, Jews) are more religious than others. The *general tendency* of people to adopt traditional moral and religious beliefs does show considerable genetic influence. Specifically, among middle-class Americans and Western Europeans, about 50 percent of the variance in measures of traditionalism and religiosity can be attributed to genetic factors.[1]

As a species, we are preadapted to a social form of living. Part of this preadaptation is the tendency to incorporate and follow socially established rules and conventions. *We are rule-generating and rule-following animals.*[2] Indeed, it is precisely this characteristic that makes human beings masters at adaptation. There is hardly a place on earth, from the tropics to the arctic, that humans have not made their home. And soon, outer space will be colonized. Such adaptability is not simply a matter of technical innovation; it is also a matter of emotional accommodation.

Different types of environment demand different types of emotional reactions. Among the Ammassalik Eskimo, a polite host may offer his wife to a visitor for sexual intercourse. Most middle-class American couples would find such a practice difficult to accept emotionally. However, it is an adaptive response to the harsh environment of the Arctic, where men must routinely travel long distances away from feminine companionship.

World-openness does not imply that human beings can survive in an unstructured world. It implies, rather, than humans must create the world in which they live. That world is society, with its rules and values and customs, as well as its material foundations. No person could survive for long completely outside of society. Even the solitary hermit relies on social support for spiritual and material sustenance.

Because of its importance for survival, the social world is typically experienced as overwhelmingly real. This is particularly evident in young children, who tend to regard the world of their parents as unalterable. We never completely outgrow that tendency. Members of all human groups are biased to view their particular social order as "natural" or even "god given." We are all traditionalists—only more or less so.

Many societies use the same word to refer to themselves and to people (humanity) in general. Members of other societies are treated linguistically, and sometimes intrinsically, as somehow less than human. They are "aliens," "infidels," "barbarians," or "heathens" whose feelings do not have to be taken into account any more than the feelings of a dog. Aliens cannot love or hate, hope or fear, rejoice or grieve, in the way that we, *the people*, do.

It follows from the above considerations that any attempt to change the emotions is going to be met with severe resistance from society as a whole, for example, as reflected in public opinion. Emotional creativity, far more than creativity in other domains, is subject to stringent selective measures. That is an issue to which we will return shortly.

Social Evolution

The social world is not static. Values change and societies evolve. The mechanisms by which social evolution occurs are not well understood. However, a useful analogy can be drawn between social and biological evolution. Biological evolution occurs when *variations* are introduced into a species through genetic mutation. By natural *selection*, mutations that are beneficial (provide greater reproductive potential) are incorporated into the gene pool of the species. Unfortunately, most genetic mutations are harmful, not beneficial. Thus, far from encouraging mutations, we take great precautions against them, for example, by minimizing sources of radiation or mutagenic chemicals.

The logic of the "variation-and-selection" model is quite general. In Chapter 6, we applied it to individual creative endeavors; it can also be applied to social change. As in the case of biological mutations, the majority of social innovations may prove to be more harmful than beneficial. Hence, it is not only society's right but also its duty to be selective in its approach to innovation. But needless to say, a society can be, and often is, too selective. Societies that do not adapt to changing conditions go the way of the dinosaurs.

Based on the above considerations, the characteristics of the emotionally creative society can be divided into two broad, and in some respects competing, categories—sources of variation (novelty) and mechanisms of selection (effectiveness).

Sources of Variation

In Part IV of this book, we examined a variety of conditions that facilitate the production of novelty. Most of these conditions operate on the social as well as the individual level. Thus, the emotionally creative society challenges its citizens, or at least does not shield them from stress of all kinds (Chapter 14). By emphasizing aesthetic sensibility as well as intellectual proficiency, such a society encourages a healthy pursuit of pleasure and tolerance of pain (Chapter 15). The emotionally creative society respects life, but it also accepts death as part of life (Chapter 16); it nurtures a capacity for solitude (Chapter 17); at the same time, it recognizes and supports different forms of intimate relationships (Chapter 18); it encourages its citizens to be autonomous (Chapter 19); it grants them the freedom to be and to express themselves (Chapter 20); it values the imaginative dreamer as well as the pragmatic doer (Chapter 21); and it stretches and educates the emotions through art and drama (Chapter 22).

In addition to the above, four broad social conditions or attitudes favorable to novelty deserve brief discussion, namely, (1) an emphasis on change, (2) a tolerance for diversity, (3) the availability of role models, and (4) a spirit of enlightened romanticism. We discuss each of these briefly as it applies to contemporary American society.

An Emphasis on Change

Some societies encourage change; others strive to preserve institutions as they are. A leader of an American Indian tribe was invited to the University of Massachusetts to give a public lecture. He described in some detail the attempts of his group to preserve their unique traditions. The attempts were exaggerated by the need to counteract erosion by the larger society. It was clear from his remarks, however, that the emphasis on tradition was not simply a matter of group self-protection; it was an integral part of the culture itself. He contrasted this attitude with that of American society in general. "There must be something wrong with your culture," he said in effect, "for you are always wanting to change it."

The tribal leader was correct, but only in part. America and most other Western societies have made an ideology of change. That does not necessarily imply that something is wrong, only that something could be better. Conservatives advise youths to work for change "within the system"; radicals advocate an overthrow of the system. In neither case is the ideology of change-as-progress seriously questioned.

However, the course of change, once initiated, is difficult to predict and tends to be independent of ideology. The introduction of a new product or technology, for example, can have consequences far different from those originally foreseen. Development of an effective oral contraceptive is an excellent example. What are the long-range consequences of "the pill" for traditional patterns of sexual relations? The answer to this question is far from evident, but the consequences are bound to be (and already have been) profound. To take another example, the introduction of inexpensive personal computers and other technologies of "information transfer" is having a powerful impact on the way we live and work, comparable perhaps to that of the first industrial revolution. Emotional change is bound to follow.

In short, societies that encourage innovation and change, regardless of the area, are going to foster emotional creativity. The effect on the emotions need not be direct or "planned." Any innovation that alters the way we relate to the world and to others around us is bound to have ramifications on our emotional life as well.

A Tolerance for Diversity

Viewed from a broad historical perspective, creativity tends to occur in cycles. For example, classical Greece and Renaissance Italy were periods of extraordinary innovation in philosophy, art, and politics; other periods are correspondingly barren. Numerous attempts have been made to explain this clustering effect, but most are highly speculative.[3] An exception is a study by Dean Simonton, whose ideas on the mechanisms of creativity we discussed in Chapter 6. From histories, anthologies, and biographical dictionaries Simonton identified approximately 5,000 creative individuals or anonymous products (in science, philosophy, literature, and art) during 25 centuries of European history, from 700 B.C. to A.D. 1839. Simonton divided this lengthy time span into twenty-year epochs or "generations," and assigned each creative person or product to its appropriate generation. (If twenty years seems short for an entire generation, recall that for most of Western history, the average life expectancy has been less than forty years—or roughly twenty years of adulthood.)[4]

Simonton found that two conditions existing in one generation were particularly influential in predicting the number of creative persons or products in the next generation. These two conditions were cultural diversity and, even more important, the availability of role models.[5]

Simonton postulates that cultural diversity is important because it allows the interaction of apparently contradictory or unrelated ideas and customs. Cultural diversity should be particularly important for emotional creativity for, as we discussed above, what distinguishes one society from another is not so much the intellectual content of their ideologies, but the emotional embodiment of their values. Competing value systems almost demand an emotionally creative response.

Here we meet another of those paradoxes that seem to plague any generalizations about creativity. Cultural diversity may foster creativity; but so, too, does its opposite, in-group identification. Creativity demands a certain amount of arrogance, whether on the individual or social level. In order for a society to be creative, it is helpful if its members are collectively convinced of their own uniqueness and even superiority. Only then will they have the audacity to innovate. Unfortunately, arrogance is not an unmixed virtue. Pride in one's own culture is too often accompanied by a devaluation of the accomplishments of people who are perceived as somehow different. In today's interdependent world, such ethnocentrism is a luxury that no society can afford.

To help short circuit the dangers of ethnocentrism, school and university curricula in the United States are being "reformed" in order to encourage cultural diversity. Critics view such "reforms" with alarm; proponents view them with hope.[6] Both views are partly justified—and, we believe, partly wrongheaded. The alarm is that "diversity" will become little more than a cover-up for ignorance, as knowledge of Western intellectual traditions is replaced with a superficial smattering of ideas and artifacts from around the world; the hope is that out of the mix of cultures and traditions made possible by mass communication and immigration a new, more tolerant, and more creative society will emerge.

A true integration of previously distinct ideas and customs must ultimately result in some loss of diversity as new cultural forms emerge. The flowering of creativity in Elizabethan England could never have occurred if the Anglo-Saxons and Normans had maintained their separate identities, languages, and customs. Thus, rhetoric aside, advocates of reform often discourage creativity in the name of "cultural maintenance." The result is cultural consumerism, not cultural production. Customs are served up like vittles in a fast-food emporium, with different stands for American, French, Italian, Mexican, Chinese, and Korean cuisine, each fashioned according to a stock set of recipes.

What is the solution? In the chapter on autonomy, we discussed the inevitability of conflict on the individual (intrapsychic) level. The autonomous person is one who can harmonize competing wishes and desires. Metaphorically, we might also speak of autonomy as a characteristic of the emotionally creative society. An autonomous society is one that accommodates competing groups and subcultures within a broader integrative framework—the cultural equivalent of Kant's categorical imperative.

And what might such a cultural imperative be? That depends on the particular society, its own unique history and circumstances. For our own society, it might include such principles as freedom of expression and association, without which creativity of any kind will ultimately be stifled, and the right of each individual to pursue happiness, however "happiness" might be defined, provided the corresponding rights of others are not infringed upon. These are the "mystic chords of memory," legacies of an arduous past, of which Abraham Lincoln spoke on the verge of the American Civil War. If history be our guide, autonomy is, if anything, more difficult to achieve and maintain on the social than on the individual level.[7]

Availability of Role Models

According to Simonton's findings, it will be recalled, the presence of creative individuals in one generation is even more important than cultural diversity in predicting creativity in the next generation. Great scientists have often served apprenticeships with notables in their field; artists often copy the works of past masters before branching out on their own; and writers emulate the styles of others before they achieve their own distinctive style. An extreme example of such emulation can be found with respect to Flaubert's *Sentimental Education*, considered by some to be the greatest French novel of the nineteenth century. Some aspiring novelists, such as Henry Céard, performed the remarkable feat of memorizing the entire work—roughly four hundred pages of text in most editions.[8]

Today, emulation is often dismissed as unimaginative "busy work" or, even worse, it is condemned as plagiarism. But emulation should not be confused with plagiarism. Those who claim for themselves, or who expect of others, complete originality—as though no one had ever had a similar thought before, or coined a similar phrase, or painted a similar picture—are simply displaying a gross ignorance of history. This is particularly true when the subject matter is human behavior, which has been the object of intense speculation for millennia. One day in any good library is usually sufficient to discover some precursor to nearly every new product or idea. But the presence of precursors does not lessen the originality of a work; it is a precondition for creativity. Past masters are to be emulated, not shunned. Only then can they be superseded. Recall Heinz Kohut's notion of "transference creativity" discussed in Chapter 20. By identification with highly creative individuals, the novice gains not only inspiration and guidance, but also the courage to withstand possibly adverse public opinion.

Is there such a thing as emotional emulation? Most assuredly. Role models are as important in the domain of emotion as in any other domain. Being forms of behavior and experience, however, emotions do not endure in the same sense as, say, a scientific discovery or great work of art. Nevertheless, there is a way we can participate in the emotional life of others without the benefit of direct contact. That way is literature. Through novels, drama, and poetry we can explore the emotions of any age and culture of our choosing; we can see the world through the eyes of anyone who has recorded a great adventure; and we can plumb the depths of feeling experienced by the most creative of our predecessors. Tragedy, Aristotle suggested, is a means of expurgating the emotions (catharsis). As discussed in Chapter 22, he might better have said that tragedy, indeed all great literature, is a means of expanding the emotions.

A Spirit of Enlightened Romanticism

We have said that emotional creativity is fostered when society emphasizes change. It does not matter if the change is primarily intellectual, as in science and technology. Intellectual innovation almost invariably brings in its wake the need for new emotional forms. Periods of intellectual ferment thus tend to alternate with periods of emotional transformation and accommodation.

In Western history, the eighteenth century is known as the Age of Reason or, alternatively, the Enlightenment, because of the great importance placed on rational thought as the solution to human problems. The motto of the Enlightenment was, in the words of Kant:

> *Sapere aude!*—Dare to reason! Have the courage to use your own Minds![9]

With such homage to reason, it is not surprising to learn that Kant considered the emotions to be "diseases of the mind"—hardly an inducement to emotional creativity.

By the time Kant was writing his paean to the Enlightenment, a reaction was already under way. The age of Romanticism was being born. If the motto of the Enlightenment was *sapere aude!*—dare to reason, then the motto of the Romantic era might well have been *sentire aude!*—dare to feel. In his poem *The Tables Turned* (written in 1798), Wordsworth caught the spirit of this new age:

> *Books! 't is a dull and endless strife:*
> *Come hear the woodland linnet,*
> *How sweet his music! on my life,*
> *There's more wisdom in it.*
> . . . .
>
> *Enough of Science and of Art;*
> *Close up those barren leaves;*
> *Come forth, and bring you a heart*
> *That watches and receives.*

Eras of reason and romanticism (with small "r's") have alternated throughout history. The eighteenth and nineteenth centuries are simply extreme and protracted examples. In more recent times, the 1960s were a period of romanticism, the aftereffects of which are still being assimilated. During that period much emotional experimentation and innovation occurred, for example, in the form of encounter groups, communes, open marriages, and various other "alternative life-styles" and modes of "consciousness raising." Many of these innovations have been abandoned, but some have become part of the larger culture, particularly those related to sex and intimate relationships.

Enlightenment and romanticism, reason and emotion: These are two ways of relating to the world. They are not incompatible. Both as a society and as individuals, we should attempt to perfect each, and to use each to its best advantage. The emotionally creative society is one that encourages its citizens to be as rational as circumstances demand, and as passionate as circumstances permit.

Mechanisms of Selection

Because of the close link between emotions and values discussed earlier, the generation of new or different emotional responses will necessarily prove threatening to the social order. To establish a new emotion, or to call into question the validity of an accepted emotion, is to suggest a new or different set of values. Such a suggestion, not surprisingly, is typically met with resistance. This is not only to be expected, it is in many respects desirable. As in the case of genetic mutations, many social innovations may be more harmful than beneficial. The values of a society have evolved over many generations of trial and error. Their utility is not always obvious; yet they should not be dismissed lightly.

Even when they do not embody deeply held values, social conventions are to be respected. It is inherently no better to drive on the righthand side of the road, as in the United States, than on the left-hand side, as in England. However, to flout this convention simply to be different would court disaster. Other conventions, equally without moral import, lead to no such dire consequences if flouted. Rules of etiquette are examples. Whether one puts food in the mouth holding the fork in the right hand, as in the United States, or in the left hand, as in Europe, makes little difference to the health and safety of anyone. Yet even such minor rules of etiquette deserve adherence, for they contribute to an amiable and civil social life, while causing little harm or discomfort to anyone.

The mechanisms that society uses to weed out undesirable responses are many and varied. On a formal level, there are courts of law or other tribunals. But perhaps most important is the "tribunal of public opinion."

Conventional people regard departures from established custom as criticisms of themselves. Hence, the emotionally creative person is liable to be viewed with fear and animosity, as were the beatniks and hippies of the sixties and seventies. Even when no threat to the public order is involved, the person who "sins" against convention may become the target of envy. In individualistic societies like our own, we are taught to accept another's good fortune, provided it is earned through hard work and talent. However, we have never been taught to accept emotional freedom and enjoyment by others, unless it is strictly circumscribed by conventional morality. Just the opposite. Emotional freedom and indulgence are too often regarded as unearned; buttressed by conventional morality, they will arouse indignation like nothing else.

When faced with the threat of oppressive public opinion, the proper attitude is reasoned indifference: *Reasoned* because, as noted above, conventional morality should not be flouted without good cause; and *indifference* because, as Bertrand Russell has observed, "public opinion is always more tyrannical towards those who obviously fear it than to those who feel indifferent to it. A dog will bark more loudly and bite more readily when people are afraid of him than when they treat him with contempt, and the human herd has some of this same characteristic."[10]

To summarize thus far, the emotionally creative society is both liberal and conservative at the same time. It is liberal in its encouragement of experimentation; it is conservative in its demand for merit. Liberalism unchecked by conservatism leads to turmoil; conservatism unchecked by liberalism leads to stagnation.

This dual nature of the emotionally creative society, encouraging of innovation but harsh in selection, can place severe stress on the individual. Whatever immediate benefits a novel emotion might afford the individual, he or she will be called to account before the tribunal of public opinion. And for bad reasons as well as good, the judgment is likely to be unkind. Only a person with a secure sense of self is going to be able to persevere in such an environment. And this brings us to our third criterion for an emotionally creative response, namely, authenticity.

The Problem of Authenticity

Authenticity presents a particularly difficult problem for a society that prizes individualism, such as our own. The person who conforms too closely to social expectations is often considered inauthentic. However, individuality, no less than conformity, can be contrived and inauthentic. The nonconformist who flouts convention simply for the sake of being different is not being authentic; on the contrary, he or she is still very much under the control of public opinion, though in a warped fashion. Like the child who acts naughty in order to gain attention, many a nonconformist yearns for the attention of others; and if he cannot achieve it by playing "by the rules," he will achieve it by flouting the rules. Authenticity does not stem from a need to be different; it stems from a need to be one's self.

Put differently, authenticity has less to do with the content of behavior than with the reasons for behavior. A person can be as authentic in preserving conventional standards and values as in overturning them—provided those standards have been internalized as part of the nuclear self.

Recall the case of the film director, Andrei Tarkovsky, discussed in Chapter 20. In the Soviet Union, he claimed, the censors "spat on my soul." In fleeing to the West, Tarkovsky gained the right of self-expression; however, he lost a kind of "inner" or "spiritual" freedom that he had experienced in his native country. He left behind not only the censors but also the communal reference for his sense of self. Authenticity thus became a constant struggle. It is easier to be authentic—and hence to have a sense of spiritual freedom—in the society of one's birth, especially if that society emphasizes indoctrination and communal values. Indoctrination leads to internalization, and the more thorough the internalization, the more societal values become part of the self.

The importance placed on individual fulfillment at the expense of doctrinal conformity is arguably one of the greatest legacies of Western culture. It is a legacy, however, that comes at a rather high price.

Because of their close connection to the self, emotions are often considered the epitome of authenticity. But that is only half the story. Emotions form a bridge between the self and society. The admonition "Get in touch with your feelings" has become such a cliché that we seldom question its underlying assumptions. Like knowledge, feelings presume some frame of reference external to the individual self. In a world-open animal—an animal without biologically based instincts—that frame of reference is provided by society. In order for an emotion to be authentic, it must be grounded in the social order as well as in the self.

A one-sided emphasis on the self does not lead to spiritual freedom but to anarchy on the social level and to oppressive feelings of anxiety and depression on the individual level. Not knowing how to act, with few guidelines to inform their choices, people do not know which way to turn. Contrary to the recommendation of many contemporary psychologists, the remedy is not further introspection—an ever deeper burrowing into the recesses of the self. That recommendation only leads to even greater feelings of alienation and despair.

In any case, being authentic does not imply being different. It sometimes requires greater talent and effort to achieve excellence within a domain that others have thoroughly explored than it does to make a contribution in a new and unexplored area. It is easy to stand out by being different; it is difficult to stand out by being better.

Steps Toward a More Creative Emotional Life

Then suddenly, by having a blank canvas, I discovered I could
make a picture myself. That is the point,
to make a picture on a blank canvas. And I
was forty before I had the real courage
to try. Then it became an
orgy, making pictures.
—D. H. Lawrence, *Assorted Articles*

Ideas are easy to come by; reduction to practice is
an arduous but inspirationally rewarding matter.
—R. Buckminster Fuller, *Critical Path*

T he author D. H. Lawrence had been an amateur painter most of
his life, typically copying the works of others. It was not until he
was forty that he realized he could paint by having a blank canvas
and only his imagination to guide him. We can take this observation
as a metaphor for creativity in general. The blank canvas represents
the future with its endless possibilities. Lawrence did not mean to
imply that by starting afresh we must wipe out the past. That would
be neither possible nor desirable. When creating a new painting,
one does not eliminate nor destroy the works of past masters, but
uses them as a foundation to build upon and possibly surpass.

In the case of emotional creativity, we do not necessarily
discard well-established ways of thinking and feeling. Those ways

that are beneficial we keep and build upon. Others, however, we may wish to discard, for they simply block further progress. Emotional creativity is about *choice.* We can choose emotions that support, or we can choose emotions that limit. But even this statement is misleading. Our choice is not confined to preestablished emotions; if we have the courage to try, we can fashion from the raw materials provided by biology and society new and different emotions, ones better suited to our needs and circumstances.

It is one thing to say that emotions are a product of choice. Emotional creativity is easy to imagine; achieving it can be, in the words of Fuller, "an arduous but inspirationally rewarding matter." In this chapter we present some of that arduousness. Specifically, we describe five steps toward a more creative emotional life: (1) making a commitment; (2) acquiring knowledge; (3) gaining self-awareness; (4) formulating a plan; and (5) achieving results. These steps are general guidelines that incorporate many of the ideas discussed in previous chapters. They are not a "paint-by-the-number" sketch for achieving emotional creativity. That would be a contradiction in terms. Creativity, by its very nature, involves innovation and change. By necessity, much trial and error is involved.

Step 1:
Making a Commitment

Commitment is the bedrock for creative achievement. This fact cannot be overemphasized. Without commitment, a person does not have the self-discipline and perseverance to surmount the inevitable obstacles associated with change. In Chapter 6, we saw that one of the primary characteristics of creative persons is that they view themselves as creative. *They are committed to creativity.* And what does that entail? According to our three criteria for creativity, a commitment to creativity is first of all a commitment to try new things, to approach old problems in novel ways; secondly, it is a commitment to excellence; and, thirdly, it is a commitment to authenticity.

Commitment is a much misunderstood concept. The creative individual, it is sometimes said, is a "free spirit," unbound by commitments. But commitment is not the antithesis of freedom (otherwise, no one could ever be committed to freedom). To gain some clarity on this issue, it is helpful to distinguish between two types of commitment—commitment of obligation and commitment of desire. Commitment of obligation characterizes a promise or a formal contract. If I borrow money, I am committed to pay it back, regardless of whether I want to or not. Commitment of desire is best epitomized by love. If I love someone, I am committed to his or her well-being, not out of obligation, but because that is what I want and care about.

When people express the wish to be free of commitments, they typically mean commitments of obligation. Such commitments bind a person, thus reducing what we have called negative freedom (the *absence* of coercion or restraint). Commitment of desire is closer to positive or "spiritual" freedom (the *ability* to do what one wants). Just as these two kinds of freedom can be in conflict, so it is with the two kinds of commitment. Commitments of obligation can thwart desires; and commitments of desire can undermine obligations.

In the history of ethical theory, commitment of obligation has generally been considered more important than commitment of desire: Honor before love. This traditional point of view is reflected in the familiar lines from Richard Lovelace's poem, *To Lucasta: Going to the Wars*:

> *I could not love thee, dear, so much*
> *Lov'd I not honor more.*

In contemporary society, priorities have shifted. The admonition among members of the "me generation" is that the highest commitment is to the fulfillment of one's own desires.[1] The merit of this shift in priorities might be questioned, but that is not our objective. Each kind of commitment has its advantages; and, like negative and positive freedom, to which they are related, each can have unfortunate consequences if carried to an extreme.

The question we wish to raise is one of context, not of priority: Which kind of commitment is more important for emotional creativity? The intuitive answer might seem to be: "Commitment of desire." But that would be misleading. As discussed in the last chapter, many creative endeavors (especially in the realm of emotional creativity) are going to meet antagonistic reactions and adverse public opinion. Desire alone often fails in the face of such adversity.

A commitment to creativity in general (not just emotional creativity) is epitomized by the life of R. Buckminster Fuller, who has been called "the planet's friendly genius" because of his many designs and inventions created for the benefit of "Spaceship Earth" (his phrase). The geodesic dome is perhaps his most familiar contrivance. Fuller is unusual in the explicitness of his commitment to creativity, although he did not call it such.[2]

His earliest commitment was to authenticity. At the age of 12, challenged by Robert Burns's poetry, Fuller vowed to know himself —as he later wrote, "to 'see' myself as others might and to integrate that other self with my self-seen self."[3] Throughout his life, Fuller kept a "come-as-it-may" chronological log of all his activities and events. He realized that he could see self-defeating life patterns only when he was scrupulously honest with himself—reviewing his log frequently, looking for repetitive patterns of both triumphs and failures.

Fuller's early life was not entirely fortunate or kind. His father died when he was 15. At age 22 (1917) he married Anne Hewlett, and the next year a baby girl was born. The infant contracted polio and spinal meningitis; after considerable suffering, she died on the eve of her fourth birthday. Fuller then developed a manufacturing and building business with funds borrowed from friends. He did not manage the business profitably, and in 1927 it failed. He lost his friends' investment and became (in his words) "discredited and penniless" and "a throwaway" in the business world.[4] In that same year (1927) a second daughter was born. Fuller was now 32 years old. He had a wife and newborn daughter to support, no money, no credit, and no university degree. He decided to start his life "as nearly 'anew' as it is humanly possible to do."[5]

Among the basic commitments he made at that point were *to do what no one else had done before* and *to excel in whatever he undertook.* He further decided to use himself as a "scientific 'guinea pig'" to discover what (if anything) one "average" man could do "that could not be done by great nations or great private enterprise to lastingly improve the physical protection and support of all human lives."[6] It proved to be no easy task. Throughout Fuller's life he found it necessary continually to renew his commitments.

My recitation of self-disciplines may suggest that all I had to do was to conceive of the discipline and institute it, whereas the fact is . . . [i]t has taken constant disciplining and redisciplining to get myself under control to a productively effective degree.[7]

In his many writings throughout the course of a long and productive life, R. Buckminster Fuller repeatedly returned to the theme that creative accomplishment is proportional to the level of commitment and *re*commitment. There is little we can say that would add to this important truth, except perhaps to note that emotional creativity in particular requires a high degree of commitment, for it involves a change in the self as well as in the external world. A commitment to emotional creativity is a blind date with one's own possible self. There is no guarantee that reality will match fantasy.

Step 2:
Acquiring Knowledge

Commitment alone is not enough. If commitment is the bedrock for creative endeavors, knowledge is the superstructure. To achieve emotional creativity, a person must have some understanding of both the emotions and creativity, as discussed in Part II of this book. Many individuals neglect such "book learning" because it seems too abstract or divorced from the immediate concerns of everyday life. That is a mistake. The natural enemies of emotional creativity are complacency, ignorance, and fear, not knowledge. Knowledge may not set us free, but it is a necessary, if not sufficient, condition for freedom.

It is sometimes said that emotions cannot be understood intellectually, only experienced. Nothing could be further from the truth. Of course, there is a sense in which no one can fully understand love, say, or fear, without having experienced such emotions. But the same thing could be said about most other human conditions. For example, a patient suffering from cancer understands the meaning and significance of this dread disease in a way that a healthy physician cannot; but, conversely, a physician has a kind of understanding that may ultimately allow the control and cure of the disease.

With regard to emotional creativity, it is especially important to dispel the various myths that block understanding and hinder change. With this in mind, we recapitulate briefly the myths of emotion discussed in Chapter 5:

Emotion Myth #1: The Myth of the Passions. The idea that we are "gripped," "seized," and "overcome" by emotion is perhaps the greatest hindrance of all to emotional creativity, for it denies our freedom and choice in the area of emotion. Emotional creativity begins with the awareness that our emotions are our own doing, a product of our own resourcefulness.

Emotion Myth #2: The Myth of Emotional Innocence. With freedom and choice comes accountability. To be emotionally creative, we must be willing to assume responsibility for our passions as well as for our actions.

Emotion Myth #3: The Myth of the Emotional Artichoke. According to this myth, emotions—like artichokes—have a "heart" (essence) that will appear once the more superficial layers of thought and behavior have been stripped away. This overarching myth comes in a variety of forms. The following three myths are its most popular variants.

Emotion Myth #4: The Myth of Primary Emotions. This variant of the artichoke myth postulates a small set of universal or primary emotions (the heart) that are hidden or overlaid by cultural accouterments (the leaves), thus forming more complex emotions. Adherents to this myth generally assume that the primary emotions are not subject to change, at least not "in essence."

Emotion Myth #5: The Myth of True Feelings. This second variant assumes that the heart of the emotional artichoke consists of a particular kind of feeling, of which we may or may not be conscious. The corollary is often added that feelings, unlike behavior, are difficult, if not impossible, to control.

Emotion Myth #6: The Myth of Fervid Viscera. This third variant of the artichoke myth asserts that emotions are, in essence, "gut reactions," and hence not subject to voluntary control. When combined with Myth #5, we have the familiar proposition that emotional feelings are the perception of bodily change.

Emotion Myth #7: The Myth of Phylogenesis. This myth attributes the origin of emotions to our evolutionary past. When combined with Myth #4, we have another very familiar proposition, namely, that primary emotions are innate, genetically determined patterns of response.

Emotion Myth #8: The Myth of Paedogenesis. According to this myth our emotions, if not inborn, are established during infancy and early childhood; if this myth were true, little emotional growth or change would be possible during adulthood.

Emotion Myth #9: The Myth of Emotional Equality. This myth assumes that all people are equally capable when it comes to the emotions.

This last myth (of emotional equality) requires brief elaboration, for we have emphasized throughout this book that everyone is capable of emotional creativity, at least to some degree. In that sense, we also subscribe to the idea of emotional equality. However, just as people differ in their intellectual and artistic talents, so, too, do they differ in their emotional capabilities. Due to either innate or acquired differences in temperament, some people may find it easier to develop one kind of emotion than another. In Chapter 11, we saw some of the implications of this fact with respect to possible gender differences in emotionality. Gender (masculinity-femininity) is only one dimension along which emotional capabilities may vary. Unless there is special need due to circumstances, there is no reason to pursue emotional experiences that do not fit our temperament. For example, the person who is shy and introverted need not try to be the life of every party; there is ample room for emotional creativity in the quiet company of friends and even in solitary activities, at least for those who have developed the capacity for solitude.

A myth would not deserve to be called such unless it were reinforced by experts in the field. Therefore, let us consider some observations by two psychiatrists, the father and son team of Patrick and Thomas Malone, whose work is representative of much current thinking with respect to the emotions, especially as applied to clinical practice. In their book, *The Art of Intimacy,* the Malones have much to say about emotional innovation and change; their analysis, however, is weakened by some of the myths recounted above, as illustrated by the following three points:[8]

1. To begin, the Malones make no real distinction between emotions and feelings, but use the two terms almost

interchangeably. They go on to suggest that we are born with a limited number of "primary feelings" such as joy, sadness, anger, fear, and sexuality.

2. Primary feelings presumably arise out of our "natural" selves, and therefore, they "do not need to be taught." Indeed, even if primary feelings could be taught, that would not be desirable, for it "could change our basic nature."

3. Primary feelings are distinguished from secondary or "metafeelings," which are feelings about feelings. Primary feelings are good or beneficial; metafeelings may be good (like respect and politeness), but they are also "the stuff of which neurotic and psychotic worlds are made." Anger, for example, is "a natural and healthy [primary] feeling" that can be converted into hostility, an unnatural and neurotic metafeeling. Similarly, sexuality can be converted into a "violent expression of power" leading to sadomasochism; sadness into the "hypocrisy of maudlin condescension"; and fear into "obsequiousness or tyranny"; and so forth.

On a superficial reading, the above points may seem eminently reasonable. But consider for a moment the presumed identity of emotions with feelings, and the distinction between (primary) feelings and (secondary) metafeelings. The Malones list sexuality as one of the primary feelings. In what sense is sexuality a feeling (as opposed to a behavior)? And in what sense is it primary rather than secondary? The story has been told of a young woman who, when asked the difference between sexual intercourse in marriage and adultery, replied: "I don't know; I have tried them both and they feel pretty much the same." Clearly, the Malones mean something different by "sexual feelings" than did the young woman in this joke. They mean something akin to love. But as we saw in Chapter 2, the relation between love and sex is highly complex and culturally dependent. Or take anger, another of the primary feelings mentioned by the Malones. As we discussed in Chapter 3, anger cannot be reduced to the way a person feels. But more important, why should anger among Westerners be regarded as "primary," rather than *liget* among the Ilongot, or *song* among the Ifaluk? All are socially constituted emotional syndromes that are considered fundamental *within their respective cultures*.

We mention the above points not to criticize, for we agree with much of what the Malones have to say on the nature and importance of intimacy. However, the Malone's presumption that emotions are feelings, and that some (primary) feelings are unalterable, does highlight the pervasiveness of the myths and misperceptions that discourage and even disallow emotional growth—the very thing the Malones are trying to foster.

Needless to say, dispelling myths is not enough. Accurate and more positive knowledge must also be acquired. This is not the place to summarize all that was said about the emotions in Part 2 of this book. But one point deserves special emphasis: We are not born with a limited set of fixed, immutable emotions or primary feelings. We are born with the capacity to develop and experience a wide variety of different emotions just as we are born with the capacity to speak a variety of different languages. The emotions that we do develop are determined to a large extent by the culture in which we live. Culture, however, is not all-embracing. A great deal of latitude exists in the way the emotions of one's culture are acquired, refined, and eventually transformed.

Step 3:
Gaining Self-Awareness

Above, we distinguished "book learning" (abstract, theoretical knowledge) from the type of understanding gained through personal experience. In focusing on the former, we did not intend to downplay the importance of the latter. The emotions are not like cancer, where the physician's knowledge is in most respects more relevant for change than is the patient's direct experience. Contrary to the Myth of the Passions, emotions are not events we suffer, they are things we do. Awareness of our own thoughts, feelings, and reactions is therefore vital to emotional creativity.

A blind person is unlikely to become a good painter, or a deaf person a good musician, no matter how great their knowledge. Many people are surprisingly blind and deaf to their own emotions. In fact, many of our most self-destructive acts are prompted by a blind or misguided attempt to deny our own emotional experiences.

Marvin's wife went bar hopping (often staying out all night) while he was at home with the children, and on occasion she would leave him for days at a time. He claimed that he was not angry, only stressed. Yet his actions belied his words: He was drinking too much, starting fights at work, driving recklessly, and destroying property. He came to counseling only because his job was in jeopardy.

At times, we all try to protect ourselves and our relationships by denying certain emotions—in Marvin's case, anger at his wife. Moreover, a little self-deception can sometimes be quite valuable. It helps us to get over the rough spots in life and to pursue goals that might otherwise seem impossible.[9] But having said this, it is also important to emphasize that only when an emotion is acknowledged can it be deliberately refined and transformed, if that proves desirable. With awareness comes choice.

How can a person become more aware of his or her emotions? There is no general prescription to be offered. The following, however, are some useful guidelines:

1. Attend to your bodily reactions. Although not the sine qua non of emotion, as the Myth of Fervid Viscera would have us believe, bodily reactions often provide clues to the emotions we are experiencing. For the person who has been "out of touch" emotionally a long time, bodily reactions may be the only clues available. The body often remembers what the head chooses to forget or ignore.

We all have the tendency to empathically mimic the emotional expression of others. A particularly marked example of such mimicry can be seen in the interaction between mothers and infants—when the infant smiles, the mother smiles; when the infant yawns, the mother yawns; and so on and vice versa. In psychotherapy, this natural tendency toward mimicry may be used deliberately. If a client cannot articulate what is being felt, the therapist may adopt a position and expression similar to that of the client. Using his or her own body as a transducer, so to speak, the therapist may thereby gain insight into the client's state of mind.

2. Pay attention to the way others respond to you. We often act as mirrors to each other: My own hostility toward you may be reflected in your hostility toward me; my nervousness in your presence may be reflected in your nervousness in my presence; and my affection for you may be reflected in your affection for me.

Research suggests that emotionally creative people are not only deeply involved in exploring the meaning of their own emotional experiences, they also pay close attention to how their behavior affects others; less emotionally creative people, by contrast, tend to focus on themselves and on the hedonic tone (pleasant-unpleasant) of their experience.[10]

3. Listen to what you say to yourself and others. We can experience more than we can say, but we often say more than we realize.

When we express our emotions verbally, we often do so indirectly through the use of metaphor or in highly figurative (rather than literal) speech. The use of metaphor, in which seemingly dissimilar experiences are integrated, is especially important for emotional creativity. Words are the coagulants of consciousness; they transform the fluidity of felt experience into a comprehensible mass. Therefore, we must choose our words carefully and creatively. But note: Metaphors and figurative speech can hide as well as reveal. Thus, the expression "I could love you to death" can express strong affection, veiled hostility, or ambivalence, depending on the person and the context. We must also recognize the importance of silence. Especially during the early stages of newly developing emotional response, it may be best not to put experience into words but to savor the feeling in its fluid state.

4. Perhaps most important, identify the social and personal rules that help constitute your emotional reactions. As we have emphasized many times, rules of emotion are not preordained; they can be changed. Emotional creativity depends upon it.

Rules are not easily identified. A person may be able to speak a language fluently without being able to identify the rules of grammar for that language. The same is no less true for the rules of emotion. Rules are manifested in regularities of behavior, but not all regularities are determined by rules. For example, reflex motor activity (the beating of one's heart) and addictions (smoking, drinking coffee, etc.) involve behavioral regularities, but they are not determined by rules in the ordinary sense. Similarly, a person who drives to work by the same route every day need not be following a rule; the regularity in this case may be the result of simple habit. A rule implies choice—it can be followed or violated; a rule also entails sanctions—rewards if followed or punishments if violated. Rules are the "do's" and "don't's" of behavior.

George was having difficulties with romantic relationships. Whenever he became seriously involved with a woman, he would think about her constantly, to the point that it would

*interfere with other activities and eventually with the relation-
ship itself.*

Was George following a rule? In order to distinguish rule-
governed behavior from other behavioral regularities (addictions,
obsessive-compulsive reactions, etc.), it is helpful to explore how far
the person is willing to generalize the response. For example, a
person who is addicted to smoking (and wants to stop) will not
contend that others should also smoke; and the hypochondriac who
is obsessed with thoughts of illness and death does not believe that
others should be so concerned.

George was troubled by his obsessive thoughts, and he wanted
to stop. Yet when pressed, he admitted that, yes, he believed that he
should think constantly about the woman he loves, if he *really* loves
her. More important, he asserted with conviction that she should
also think constantly about him. If she did not, if she wanted to be
with others (family, friends, work), he would become angry, accuse
her of not caring, and even become physically abusive. George was
adhering rigidly to a personal and, for him, maladaptive rule of
love.

Of course, simply because a response is constituted by a rule
does not mean that it can be easily changed. Adherence to a rule
may become compulsive for reasons that have little to do with the
rule itself; or conversely, a compulsion may lead to the formulation
of a rule in order to legitimize its occurrence. Thus, the mere
identification of a rule may have little influence on behavior.
However, for persons who are not suffering from any deep-seated
psychopathology, but are only seeking a more satisfactory emotional life, the identification of their rules of emotion may be sufficient
to initiate change.

Step 4:
Setting Goals

Emotional awareness as discussed in Step 3 is oriented toward the
present: What emotions do I now experience? Emotional creativity
is oriented toward the future: What emotions would I like to
experience five months or five years from now? To achieve emotional creativity, we must set goals. It is not sufficient to say, "I am going

to be emotionally creative." By what means, and toward what ends? Specificity is required.[11]

According to the Myth of the Passions, emotions are beyond our control. Hence, it may sound odd to say that we should set specific goals for the type of emotions we wish to achieve. But, as we have argued many times during the course of this book, emotions do not simply happen. *Emotions are purposeful, goal-directed acts.* In one sense, this statement is trivially true. The angry person *wants* to correct a perceived wrong; the fearful person *wants* to escape danger; the person in love *wants* to be with the loved one; and so forth. Such goals are, however, immediate and short-term. The real issue is whether emotions are purposeful in a larger sense, that is, whether they can serve longer-range goals and values.

In the words of Robert Solomon, "every emotion is also an ideology, a set of demands, 'how the world ought to be.' "[12] That may be an overstatement, but basically we agree. Emotions do not occur in isolation. They are woven into the fabric of a person's life. The only question is whether they are woven well or poorly.

In Chapter 19 we discussed autonomy as a condition for emotional creativity. Autonomy is the ability to harmonize competing desires, so that important goals interfere with one another as little as possible. Such a balanced coordination requires a realistic approach to life and a coherent system of values. Only then can choice among conflicting goals be made in a reasonable and principled fashion. Needless to say, there can be no well-ordered sense of priorities unless a person is able or willing to project into the future.

Step 5:
Achieving Results

The final step toward a more creative emotional life is to achieve results consistent with our goals. And for that there is one cardinal rule: *practice, practice, practice.* At first, the response may seem somewhat artificial, lacking in feeling. That is all right. With practice, feeling and expression become integrated into a coherent whole. Every time we act or think in a certain way, the experience becomes more "natural." The important thing is to remain flexible, and to reevaluate the outcome on a consistent and regular basis. Emotional creativity—like creativity in any other domain—requires a great deal of trial and error. Some people are so afraid of error that they magnify any failures, using them as excuses not to continue. Yet we typically learn more from our failures than from our successes.

Fortunately, we do not have to express an emotion in order to practice it, and hence we can keep actual failures to a minimum. Through the imagination we can rehearse for an emotional encounter, just as an athlete mentally rehearses for a game or a musician for a performance. In Chapter 21 we discussed the nature and function of the imagination; and in Chapter 22 we noted how art and literature offer models of creative emotional responses. It might seem that there is little more to be said on the topic. However, we cannot overemphasize the fact that the use of the imagination is a skill that must be honed and perfected like any other skill. It helps to have a coach or mentor, someone who is already well practiced in the use of the imagination, but the most important requirements are time alone (solitude) and conscientious effort.[13]

Picture in your mind's eye the specific responses you would like to make in a given situation, and how those responses might affect others. Lovers do this all the time, often in exquisite detail; so do those who dream of revenge for some real or presumed wrong. But not everyone is equally adept at such imaginings.

John Wallace asked subjects (students at Stanford University) to write the "sexiest" stories of which they were capable.[14] The stories of some subjects were bland and circumspect, as though written for the *Ladies Home Journal*; the stories of other subjects were graphic in detail, as though written for a triple-X rated magazine. Similar individual differences appeared when subjects were asked to write hostile stories. Wallace suggested that the "maximal responses" subjects were capable of writing might be better predictors of subsequent behavior than are the "typical responses" assessed by traditional personality tests. This suggestion has received experimental support by Lee Willerman and his colleagues at the University of Texas.[15]

We have found a variation on the "maximal response" technique a useful adjunct to psychotherapy. Specifically, clients are asked to describe, verbally or in writing, the kinds of emotional responses they would like to acquire, with instructions to be as creative as possible. The descriptions are then refined and, if appropriate, transformed, to make the imagined responses more novel (at least for the person) and effective.

With the help of the imagination, our emotions may become not only more novel and effective, but also more authentic. The creative imagination strives toward integration. The parts of the self are placed within the context of a larger whole—provided we do not turn a part into the whole (what we have called, following Lynch, the "absolutizing tendency").[16] When integrated with the totality of our selves, emotions cease to be alien forces (passions) that we must somehow control lest they control us. Rather, they become expressions of our inner visions and desires, manifestations of what we are and of what we want to be.

At some point, of course, new emotions need to be expressed so that their outcomes can be evaluated in reality and not just in fantasy. That is not always an easy task, for we can imagine more than we can do, and more than personal inhibitions or social convention will allow us to do. The support of sympathetic friends and loved ones is often necessary if products of the imagination are to be realized in practice; this is also where a competent counselor or psychotherapist can be of great assistance.

But matters of assistance aside, there is a dilemma inherent in the idea that a newly formed emotion should be validated against reality. Which reality? An emotion, asserted Sartre, "is a transformation of the world."[17] It is in the nature of emotions that they help create the reality in which they are to be assessed. This is one reason why it is so difficult for a person in love simply to cease being in love, or the person who is angry to cease being angry. The best solution that we can see to the dilemma of self-validating emotions is the adoption of a playful attitude. It is the nature of play that it is not for real. Or perhaps it would be more accurate to say that through play new realities are created in which new kinds of experience can become "second nature" and new patterns of interpersonal relationships can be established. But there is a price to be paid. To the extent that a playful attitude challenges traditional values and visions of reality, it is liable to be met with suspicion and condemnation. In this respect, the psychoanalyst Erik Erikson has pointed to a certain "gap" in our own society:

> It [the gap] is that between a grim determination to play out established and divisive roles, functions, and competencies to their bitter ends and, on the other hand, new kinds of group

life characterized by a total playfulness, which simulates vast imagination (often drug-induced), sexual and sensual freedom, and a verbal openness often way beyond the integrative means of individuals, not to speak of technological and economic realities.[18]

Erikson asserts that to "play it out" is the most natural and self-healing measure that childhood affords, and one that we should never outgrow. However, he wisely warns against mere play-acting, as opposed to true playfulness. Too many people simulate naturalness, honesty, and intimacy, and they "end up being everybody and yet nobody, in touch with all and yet not close to anybody."[19] Also, although drugs can sometimes foster playfulness, as Erikson implies, the use of drugs is more often than not inimical to true creativity: Drugs can contribute to novelty, sometimes; to effectiveness, seldom; and to authenticity, rarely.

In the previous chapter, we described the emotionally creative society as liberal in its encouragement of experimentation but conservative in its demand for merit. We could just as well have said that the emotionally creative society encourages a playful attitude but demands excellence in return. That characterization also applies to the emotionally creative individual.

The Past Need Not Be Prologue

Perhaps no other area of human psychology is subject to more confusion and debate than is the topic of emotion. However, on one thing most everyone agrees: The emotions are fundamental to an individual's sense of self and well-being. In popular myth one finds the notion that the emotions—at least the "fundamental" emotions—are immutable patterns of response over which we have little control. This myth is echoed in some psychological theories that treat the emotions as remnants of biological evolution—the animal in human nature. By contrast, we have argued that emotions are social and individual constructions, but no less a vital part of human nature. We believe the empirical evidence reviewed in Parts 1 and 2 of this book favor the latter position. For better or worse, individuals and societies do have it within their power to develop new forms of emotional experience and expression. Yet what we believe is possible in theory can be frustratingly difficult to put into practice. Emotional creativity cannot be programmed in advance, and no one can predict its outcome. However, a failure to accept the challenge of emotional creativity does lead to predictable consequences, namely, stagnation and alienation from one's self and others.

To illustrate the five steps toward emotional creativity outlined in this chapter, we conclude with the case of John, a 90-year-old blacksmith in a small Texas town. John's profession seemed to symbolize his life—a slow loss of meaning in a changing world. John had been married 65 years, but with little joy or satisfaction. When the following discussion occurred (as retold by his daughter-in-law), he was in the hospital, dying of cancer.

> *I was never comfortable in my own house, and I could never please her [his wife]. Every day I just kept thinking things would get better, or I'd do something about it. The kids came and went, and before I knew it I was seventy. Then I said to myself, "John, you're too old now to do anything different." But that wasn't true. Looking back on things, I know it's never too late to do what we want. Why, when I was seventy I could still work hard, and I made good money. Even when I was eighty I still had some good years left. The bottom line is: If I had chosen to live my life in almost any other way, I would have been happier. I feel like I sacrificed for nothing. If I'd been happier, others around me would have been happier, too. I now say: Life is fragile; do what brings you joy.*

John had kept his blacksmith shop open until shortly before he went into the hospital. Since his youth, he had been hard-working and honest, but it was as though life was something that just happened to him, not something he actually *lived*. He was the epitome of the unemotional man.

John had the capacity for deep emotion, but that capacity was never realized, for he failed to take any of the five steps outlined in this chapter. First, John never made a commitment to change. His attitude was, "If things don't get better, then I'll do something about it." Things never got better, and he never did anything about it. Second, although an intelligent man, John had little interest in acquiring knowledge. He coped with life; he did not investigate or try to understand it. Third, John had little self-awareness. He knew he was unhappy, but it was a kind of vague and inarticulate feeling. There is more to self-awareness than discontent. Fourth, John had few dreams or visions for the future. He wanted something different in life, but he didn't know what. When things got bad, he simply dug in his heels and resisted further change. Finally, John seldom showed any emotion. He did not whine nor complain; and when he laughed, it was a kind of hollow laughter. No one, not even his family, felt that they really knew him. He expressed few needs, wants, or hopes, and hence received little feedback from others.

Emotional creativity begins with a commitment to move beyond individual habit and social conformity when those no longer serve us, to seek excellence in the affective as well as the intellectual domain, and to be authentic in all that we do; it demands knowledge and self-awareness; it presumes a well-ordered set of priorities and values; and its practice requires a playful attitude moderated by critical self-discipline. Not surprisingly, many people—like John—opt instead for a limited life, rejecting the possibilities of a more open future. If we focus only on the moment, it is often easier to choose a path that leads to emptiness and resentment rather than admit there are alternatives.

Increasingly, however, the choice is not ours alone to make. Creativity in other spheres—scientific and technological innovations, for example—is changing the way we work, the way we relate to one another, the way we live and die. And the pace is quickening. As individuals and as a society, we are doomed if we are not equally creative in the domain of emotion, if the only ways we know how to respond are the ways fitted to past circumstances.

Notes

◆

1. Emotions and Creativity

1. Nietzsche, 1908/1937, p. 100.
2. Potter, 1988.
3. Ibid., p. 206.
4. The vicissitudes of the self throughout Western history have been the focus of a number of recent studies. The present brief synopsis is based on the following sources: Analyses of ancient Greek conceptions of the self, from Homeric to classical (e.g., Plato, Aristotle) times, can be found in Adkins (1970) and Snell (1960). Julian Jaynes (1976) covers some of the same territory, but in a more speculative and controversial manner. For a particularly interesting discussion of the early medieval period, as the individual (and individualism) was emerging from the shadows of the dark ages, see Morris (1972). For later developments, Baumeister (1986) is an excellent source. On the distinction between private vs. public selves and the problem of authenticity, also see Trilling (1972).

   The standard history of *theories* of emotion, from the Greeks onward, is Gardiner, Metcalf, & Beebe-Center (1937). This, however, is a history of ideas about emotions, and not a history of emotions per se. Theories tend to be too abstract and ideologically biased to provide more than indirect insight into the way emotions were actually experienced during any particular age. For the latter, one should consult works such as Elias's (1978) *History of manners.*
5. Rorty, 1989, p. 22.
6. Wordsworth, 1805/1952, p. 84.

2. Romantic Love

1. Hunt, 1959, p. 131.
2. Capellanus, ca. 1180/1969, p. 58.

3. Ibid., p. 122.
4. Ibid.
5. Ibid., p. 167.
6. Beigel, 1951.
7. Ibid., p. 149.
8. For a history of the troubadours and their antics, see Hueffer (1878).
9. Finck was a music critic for the New York *Evening Post* from 1881 to 1923. In a long and eventful career, he published 18 books, not only on music, but also on such diverse topics as travel, gastronomy, and horticulture. His two books on love (Finck, 1887, 1899) are a disconcerting mixture of broad erudition, naive Darwinism, and unfounded prejudices. Nevertheless, they are well worth reading today. Finck deserves special mention for being the first to recognize clearly that romantic love as we know it is a social construction, not a biological given.
10. Reynolds, 1969, p. 16.
11. Ibid.
12. Durant, 1950, p. 1065.
13. The following account of historical developments is based largely on Beigel (1951).
14. "My Everlasting Love," music and lyrics by Rick Sandler, Jeanne FitzSimmons, & Con Cowan.
15. The high rate of divorce does not indicate a decrease in the popularity of marriage as a social institution. Remarriage rates are also high, so that the percentage of the population that is married has remained steady, or even increased, over the past century (Ahrons & Rodgers, 1987).
16. Research suggests that only about 5% to 10% of people actually fall in love in a manner that approximates the romantic ideal, although several times that number may retrospectively interpret their experiences as conforming (Averill & Boothroyd, 1977).
17. Greenfield, 1965.
18. Rosenblatt, 1967.

3. On Being a Wild Pig and Other Such Things

1. In this discussion, we will use the term *anger* without quotation marks when referring to the emotional syndrome as it occurs in Western cultures; when referring to anger-like syndromes in other cultures, we will use "anger."
2. Newman, 1964.
3. Rosaldo, 1980, 1984.
4. Ibid., p. 55.

5. Ibid., p. 264.
6. Lutz, 1983b, 1988.
7. Ibid., 1988, p. 160.
8. See Averill (1982) and Tavris (1989) for details.
9. *Good News Bible*, Deuteronomy 29:20.
10. *Drye v. State*, 1944.
11. Averill, 1982.

4. The Nature of Emotion

1. *Jacobelis v. Ohio*, 1965.
2. Wittgenstein, 1953.
3. Fehr & Russell, 1984; Russell, 1991.
4. Mayer, 1972.
5. Ghiselin 1969, p. 52. For a related argument contra essentialism in biology, see Mayer, 1972.
6. Sartre, 1948.
7. Ibid., p. 62.
8. Pascal, 1670/1966, p. 154.
9. Tinkelpaugh, 1928.
10. Hunt, 1959, p. 10.
11. Money, 1980.
12. Freud, 1910/1957b.
13. Jung, 1945/1953.
14. Reik, 1959.
15. Orlinski, 1972.
16. Frankl, 1984.
17. Gaylin, 1979, p. 214.
18. Ibid., p. 3.
19. Skinner, 1974, p. 165.
20. Rosaldo, 1984.
21. Capellanus, ca. 1180/1969, pp. 81–82.
22. Ibid., p. 184 ff.
23. Buscaglia, 1988, p. 42.
24. *Words and Phrases*, 1953, p. 653.
25. Averill, 1982.
26. Lederer, 1987, p. 105.

5. Myths of Emotion

1. Solomon, 1976.
2. Schafer, 1976.

3. Plutchik, 1980.
4. Panksepp, 1982.
5. Jampolsky, 1981.
6. Plutchik, 1980.
7. Hochschild, 1983.
8. The symbolic significance of physiological structures and responses has been discussed by Douglas (1970), Onians (1951), and Thass-Thienemann (1968). For a history of psychophysiological symbolism in relation to theories of emotion, see Averill (1974). The actual role of physiological responses during emotion has been the subject of much scientific research and debate for over a century, ever since William James (1890) published his famous theory that emotional feelings are nothing more than the perceptions of one's own bodily reactions. James's theory implies that each emotion is associated with a different pattern of physiological response. This assumption has been severely criticized on empirical grounds, first by Walter Cannon (1929) and later by Stanley Schachter (1971). The debate focuses on what must be one of the most enduring pseudo-issues in psychology—whether different emotions are associated with different patterns of physiological arousal. It is obvious even to the casual observer that the physiological responses typically associated with grief, say, are different from those typically associated with fear or anger. It is equally obvious, however, that any given emotion (whether grief, fear, anger) can be expressed in a great variety of different ways. For example, when grieving a person may break down in tears, become angry or fearful, remain stoically composed, become immersed in work or other distracting activities (including promiscuous sexual activity), and so forth, almost indefinitely. Similarly, during anger a person may experience symptoms typical of grief (crying), fear (withdrawal), or even joy (revenge). Physiological responses during emotion are no less variable than the overt behavior which they support. In short, different emotions are characterized by modal differences in physiological response patterns; the differences are highly variable, however, and they place only broad and mostly inconsequential constraints on the range and combination of emotions that can be experienced (Reisenzein, 1983).
9. Veith, 1965.
10. Yap, 1965.
11. Freud, 1925/1959, p. 15.
12. Strictly speaking, voodoo or *vodou* refers to the folk religion of Haiti. *Vodou* is an amalgam of Christianity, native African beliefs and customs, and elements unique to Haitian history and culture. One aspect of the religion is the belief that certain kinds of sorcerers can cause a person to be possessed by spirits of the dead. If the possession

is not terminated by exorcism, the afflicted individual may sicken and even die (Bourguignon, 1976). In spite of the fact that such sorcery forms a relatively minor aspect of the *vodou* religion, the term "voodoo" has come to symbolize similar beliefs wherever they are found throughout the world. The classic paper on voodoo death from a medical point of view is that by Cannon (1942). Cannon attributed such death to a state of shock, occasioned by overexcitation of the sympathetic nervous system as a result of "ominous and persistent" fear. At least in terms of physiology, that explanation appears incorrect (Richter, 1957). Obviously, profound changes occur, for the possessed person does not fake his or her own death. However, the actual cause of death may vary from one society to another, depending on the specifics of the belief system. Psychologically, voodoo death appears closer to hopelessness than to fear (Seligman, 1975). On a social level, other members of the group tend to treat the hexed person as one who is dying and may withdraw material sustenance and social support, thus hastening death. Phenomena that bear some resemblance to voodoo death, but without the explicit social recognition or legitimation, have been observed among prisoners of war who "voluntarily" withdraw and die without any obvious physiological dysfunction, as well as in hospitals or nursing homes, where an individual may simply "give up" and die. In Chapter 16, we will discuss in detail the implications of death and dying for emotional creativity. For a general discussion of hopelessness, or its opposite, optimism, on health, see Peterson and Bossio (1991).

13. *Timaeus*, 92c (Plato, 1961a, p. 1211).
14. For a recent discussion, see Nozick, 1981.

6. The Nature of Creativity

1. Ghiselin (1952) has compiled a most helpful anthology of firsthand accounts of creative endeavors; we will frequently draw on this work for illustrative material, as in the epigram by Paul Valéry at the opening of this chapter. By themselves, of course, anecdotal accounts prove nothing; they do, however, add interest and substance to an otherwise abstract topic.
2. Arnheim, 1966, p. 299.
3. See, for example, Hudson, (1972, p. 64f.) and Perkins (1981, p. 262f.).
4. Medawar, 1967, p. 132.
5. MacKinnon, 1962, 1963.
6. For reviews, see Barron & Harrington (1981), Mansfield & Busse (1981), and Simonton (1988a).
7. Jung, 1930/1966, p. 101.

8. Roe, 1951, p. 233.
9. Torrance, 1988, p. 68.
10. Amabile, 1982.
11. This characteristic has been particularly emphasized by Albert & Runco (1986).
12. Barron, 1969, p. 75.
13. James (1896/1956), p. 216.
14. Ibid., p. 247.
15. Freud, 1911/1958.
16. Guilford, 1950.
17. Koestler, 1964.
18. The arrangement of thought processes along a dimension of intuitive vs. discursive does not, it must be emphasized, explain how the processes operate. To draw an analogy, it is like arranging motors along a dimension of horsepower. That says nothing about whether the motor is an internal combustion engine, a water-driven turbine, or whatever.
19. Perkins (1981) calls the special-process view of creativity "the better-mousetrap theory" because it postulates a better device for catching ideas. Freud, Guilford, and Koestler are only three of the more prominent mousetrappers. In addition to Perkins's excellent book, Weisberg (1986) offers a critical analysis of special-process theories. For a specific critique of Freud's distinction between primary and secondary process, see Giora (1989). Also relevant to the special-process view is the work of Simon and his colleagues (Simon, 1990; Langley, Simon, Bradshaw, & Zytkow, 1988). These investigators have developed computer programs that, when given appropriate data, simulate quite well some classical scientific discoveries, such as Kepler's laws of planetary motion. Computer programs (as opposed to computer programmers) are not known for their "creativity." To be fair, there are defenders of special process theories. For example, the mathematician, Roger Penrose (1989), argues that present-day computers are *in principle* incapable of simulating creative thought; he believes that a full understanding of how the brain works during creative activity will require advances in physical theory (in particular, quantum mechanics). And so the debate goes on.
20. Wallas, 1926.
21. Ghiselin, 1952.
22. Westfall, 1980, p. 110.
23. For specific instances, see Spender (1952, p. 113). Schiller's habit of keeping rotten apples in his desk may not be as eccentric as at first appears. Research suggests that fragrances of various kinds can elevate mood, increase awareness, and stimulate productivity in the workplace. Whether the smell of rotten apples is among the favorable

odors, we cannot say, but the smell of lemon is. A Japanese company, Shimizu Corporation, has begun marketing an odor-delivery system for use in commercial buildings (Adler, 1991).

24. Piaget, 1936/1952.
25. Quoted by Levi (1952, pp. 62–63).
26. Poincaré, 1908/1952, p. 36.
27. Ibid., p. 37.
28. See, for example, Bowers, Regehr, Balthazard, & Parker (1990).
29. Simonton, 1988b, p. 393.
30. Poincaré, 1952, p. 40.
31. Wolfe, 1936/1952, pp. 192–193.
32. See, for example, Storr (1972).
33. A point emphasized by Maslow (1963), among others.
34. Miller, 1952, p. 178.
35. Perkins, 1981, p. 101.

7. Myths of Creativity

1. *New International Version,* Genesis 1:1–5.
2. Einstein (1949, p. 17). In this quote, Einstein was referring to his studies at the Polytechnic Institute of Zürich, which he entered at age 17. In fairness, Einstein also stated that he had excellent teachers at the Institute, and that "in Switzerland we had to suffer far less under such coercion, which smothers every truly scientific impulse, than is the case in many another locality."
3. Nelson, 1988, p. 30.
4. Hayes, 1981.
5. Nietzsche, 1908/1937, pp. 99–100.
6. Richards, Kinney, Benet, & Merzel, 1988.

8. Emotional Creativity

1. Quoted by Weisberg (1986, p. 117).
2. Bertocci, 1988.
3. Dostoyevsky, 1864/1989, p. 7.
4. Piaget, 1936/1952.
5. Bucke, 1901/1961, p. 2.
6. See Greeley (1974) for the results and analysis of a national survey on the frequency and common occasions for mystical-like experiences.
7. Quoted by Landis & Metler (1964, pp. 241–242).
8. Nietzsche, 1883–1892/1977, p. 129.

9. For examples of relevant research on pain and hypnosis, see Hilgard (1977) and Spanos & Hewitt (1980).

9. What Emotional Creativity Is Not

1. Paraphrased from Russell (1930/1958, p. 161).
2. Huxley, 1954, p. 17.
3. Quoted by Zwerin, 1989, p. 18.
4. Ibid.
5. These observations are perhaps sufficiently self-evident not to require additional comment. Nevertheless, it is worth noting that psychologists have recently begun to explore the mechanisms by which mood influences creativity. Experimental research has shown that happy subjects are more likely to make remote associations and to organize material into broader, more inclusive categories—two hallmarks of creative thought. On the other hand, when subjects are depressed they tend to be more analytic in orientation and focused on the details of the task at hand—a phenomenon known as "depressive realism." See Isen (1990) and Schwartz and Bless (1991) for details. When evaluating such findings, two qualifications should be kept in mind. First, analytic reasoning can be as important for creativity as is inclusive thought, especially during the stages of preparation and verification. Second, these laboratory findings do not touch upon one of the major determinants of creativity, namely, motivation. As discussed in Chapter 6, creativity is as much a matter of purpose as process. Depressed mood is typically characterized by a lack of motivation, and it may be for that reason as much as any other that a depressed mood is detrimental to creativity.

10. Transformations of the Self

1. St. Simeon is even better known for sitting on top of a sixty-foot pillar for thirty years. From there he preached to the faithful, who brought him food by ladder and removed waste products. The circumference at the top of the pillar was little more than three feet; a rail kept Simeon from falling while he slept.
2. This research has been reviewed by Buss (1980, Ch. 5).
3. Mahoney, 1991, pp. 301 ff.
4. John of the Cross, ca. 1583–1585/1967, Bk 1, VIII.3, p. 179.
5. Ibid., p. 179–180.
6. For detailed descriptions of such catastrophic or anxiety reactions, and how they differ from normal fear responses, see Averill (1976), Gold-

stein (1951), Menninger (1954). We will have more to say about such reactions in Chapter 13 on psychopathology.
7. Moberg, 1984, p. 351.
8. Eliade, 1959, p. 14.

11. Emotional Creativity in Men and Women

1. *New International Version,* Genesis 3:16.
2. Terman & Miles, 1936, p. 451.
3. Shields, 1987.
4. Hall, 1984.
5. Manstead, in press.
6. Condry & Condry, 1976.
7. Malatesta & Haviland, 1982.
8. These examples are from Bernard (1981, pp. 376–377).
9. For details of the litigation and the role of psychological findings with respect to gender stereotypes, see Fiske, Bersoff, Borgida, Deaux, & Heilman (1991).
10. Nickerson, 1979, p. 3.
11. Kolata, 1974.
12. Patrick, 1895/1979, p. 7.
13. See, for example, de Beauvoir (1987).
14. Woolf, 1929.
15. In Blom, 1978, p. 111.
16. Unpublished study cited in J. R. Hayes (1981).
17. Reiss, 1960, pp. 92–93.
18. Arieti, 1976, p. 319.
19. The details of this study, a master's thesis by Thomas-Knowles, are reported in Averill and Thomas-Knowles (1991). The following is a brief description of the tests used to assess emotional and intellectual creativity. The *Emotional Creativity Inventory,* consisted of 32 items describing a person's ability to respond emotionally in unusual but effective ways (e.g., "I like art, music, dance, and paintings that arouse new and unusual emotional reactions"; "I can vary my emotions effectively to fit the situation"). The *Emotional Consequences Test* required subjects to list all the possible consequences they could think of to four emotionally impossible situations. (For example, one item read: "What would be the consequences if people could only experience positive emotions in the morning and negative emotions in the afternoon"). This test was an adaptation of one of the standard tests of cognitive creativity developed by Torrance (1974). The *Emotional Triads Test* required subjects to write stories that integrated into a single experience three incompatible emotional states (such as "ser-

ene\bewildered\impulsive"). There were four sets of triads. The stories were scored for emotional creativity according to the criteria of novelty, effectiveness, and authenticity.

To distinguish emotional from intellectual creativity, a *Cognitive Creativity Inventory* and *Cognitive Consequences Test* also were administered. These paralleled closely the corresponding tests for emotional creativity, but they had no emotional content. The validity of the various tests was checked against measures of adaptive emotional behavior and academic achievement.

No reliable gender differences were found on either of the tests of intellectual creativity. However, the women did receive significantly higher scores than the men on the two corresponding tests of emotional creativity, namely, the *Emotional Creativity Inventory* and the *Emotional Consequence Test*. No gender differences were observed on the *Emotional Triads Test*.

20. From a strictly scientific point of view, there are major shortcomings with this review. Perhaps most importantly, it involved only one therapist and one set of clients, and hence it is not clear how far the results can be generalized. Moreover, ratings of client creativity were necessarily subjective, based on memory as well as on written notes, and hence there was no opportunity to check for possible biases in judgment. But in spite of these shortcomings, the results are highly suggestive. We present them more as hypotheses for further testing than as well-established conclusions.

21. The difference between men and women in the stage or kind of emotional creativity was highly significant statistically: $x^2 (2) = 135.1$, $p < .001$.

22. Freud, 1933/1964, pp. 134–135.

23. Tannen, 1990.

24. Scher, 1981, p. 199.

12. Language, Self, and Emotion

1. Garwood, 1976; Leirer, Hamilton, & Carpenter, 1982.
2. Harré, 1991; Muhlhausler & Harré, 1990.
3. La Rochefoucauld, 1665/1959, Maxim #136.
4. Averill, 1975; Storm & Storm, 1988.
5. Bush, 1972.
6. Averill, 1980.
7. Argyle, 1987.
8. Boswell, 1791/1906, p. 315 (A.D. 1766 aerat. 57).
9. Arieti, 1976.
10. Wittgenstein, 1953.

11. *King James Version*, Jeremiah 23:29.
12. To say that a dialectical or reciprocal relation exists between language and behavior/experience does not capture the full complexity of the issue. Language does not simply influence behavior and vice versa. Language is a part of behavior. If I say, "I am angry," I am not just naming or describing independently existing feelings; I am *expressing* my anger. The language is a part of, not something added on to, the emotion. In other words, the same rules that help constitute the emotions also help determine the meaning (use) of emotional concepts.
13. Bazin, 1964.
14. Keller, 1903, pp. 23–24.
15. Einstein in Ghiselin (1952, p. 43).
16. Arieti, 1976.
17. Henry (1936) provides a detailed analysis of the Kaingang concept of *to nu*. Needless to say, an endocept that combined features of anger as we know it and fear as we know it would not be the equivalent of *to nu*. Like *liget* among the Ilongot and "being a wild pig" among the Gururumba (see Chapter 2), *to nu* cannot be fully conceived, no less experienced, independent of the culture of which it is a part. Likewise, a fully developed concept of anger/fear would symbolize an emotion unique to our own culture, although it would presumably resemble *to nu* more closely than does either anger alone or fear alone, as these emotions are presently conceived and constituted.

13. Emotional Creativity and Psychopathology

1. Kant, 1798/1978.
2. *Phaedrus*, 244b (Plato, 1961b).
3. On tranquility of mind, XVII.x (Seneca, 1958, p. 285).
4. Lombroso, 1891.
5. Ibid., p. 361.
6. Andreasen, 1987.
7. See, for example, Richards, Kinney, Lunde, Benet, & Merzel (1988).
8. Arieti, 1976.
9. Freud, 1910/1957a, pp. 49–50.
10. Rank, 1929/1978.
11. For example, Angyal (1965).
12. There are numerous biographies of Cavendish. The one by Wilson (1851) contains firsthand accounts of Cavendish's eccentricities, including the anecdote reported here.
13. We must be careful not to over "psychologize" a person's condition. Modern technology such as CAT scans (computerized axial tomogra-

phy) and PET scans (positron emission tomography) allows us to examine the workings of the brain in ways that have never before been possible. Through this technology it has been found that disorders that have heretofore been considered of strictly psychological origin may have a neurological basis and often respond to medication. For example, some individuals with obsessive-compulsive disorders (OCD) show abnormalities in the frontal lobes and the basal ganglia, and OCD is sometimes associated with specific neurological diseases such as epilepsy, Tourette's syndrome, and choreas (Rapoport, 1989). On the other hand, we must also be careful not to over "physiologize" a person's condition. Even when a neurotic syndrome has some basis in physiological dysfunction, psychological treatment may be the only—or the most appropriate—recourse available. It is well documented that the attitudes and emotions of an individual can have a profound effect even on the immune system and hence on diseases that are primarily of physiological origin, such as cancer.

14. Jung, 1938/1969, p. 75.
15. A more detailed discussion of the relation between rules of emotion and emotional disorders can be found in Averill (1988).
16. Quoted by Friday (1977. p. 405).
17. American Psychiatric Association (1987). *Diagnostic and statistical manual of mental disorders* (3rd ed. rev.) (DSM-III-R), pp. 252–253.
18. The view of anxiety presented here is not the only one current in the literature. "Anxiety" is an orphan term that has been adopted by theorists of quite diverse persuasions, each giving it a somewhat different meaning. The meaning offered here (a condition reflecting the actual or threatened collapse of the nuclear self) draws upon common themes from a variety of different theories, as explained in detail elsewhere (Averill, 1976, 1988). Anxiety must be differentiated from ordinary fear reactions, which presume a well-developed sense of self, and from panic attacks, which may result from traumatic conditioning and/or a momentary physiological disturbance. All three syndromes (anxiety, fear, and panic) share many symptoms in common (just as all respiratory diseases, say, share many symptoms in common), but they differ in terms of etiology and prognosis, as well as in their relation to the self.

14. Challenges and Facilitators

1. Frankl, 1984.
2. Ibid., p. 55.
3. Ibid., p. 57.
4. Ibid., p. 88.

5. Maslow, 1963, pp. 539–540.
6. Becker, 1973.
7. Letter to Mr. Kappus, May 14, 1904, in Rilke (1934, p. 60).
8. Fromm, 1941.
9. Nietzsche, 1886/1986, p. xii.
10. Quoted in Auden & Kronenberger (1966, p. 240).

15. Pain and Pleasure

1. Epicurus, *Fragments: On the end of life.* In Bailey (1926, p. 139).
2. Epicurus, *Fragments: Vatican collection.* In Bailey (1926, p. 115).
3. Mencken, 1930, p. 288.
4. Quoted by Kidd (1967, p. 287).
5. Zeller, 1957.
6. James, 1902/1961, p. 288.
7. Bougaud, quoted by James (1902/1961, p. 249).
8. Baumeister, 1989.
9. Walsh & Rosen, 1988, p. 10.
10. Brown, 1959.
11. O'Flaherty, 1973.
12. Zimmer, 1957, p. 39.
13. Diener, Larsen, Levine, & Emmons, 1985.

16. Death and Dying

1. These statistics are from Albert (1980). What tips the scales in favor of eminence over criminal deviance as an outcome of childhood bereavement? Albert postulates two major factors: one is the presence of giftedness on the part of the child; the second is the interest taken by a particular adult in the development of the child. The first of these factors requires little comment. Clearly, if a person is not gifted in a particular field, he or she will not achieve eminence. The second factor postulated by Albert, namely, interest and encouragement from other adults in the child's life, might also seem trivially obvious. However, an important and often unrecognized qualification must be added. Somewhat surprisingly, the interest and encouragement need not be associated with intense emotional closeness to the child. Research on gifted individuals (not just those who were bereaved during childhood) suggests the following generalization: The parents (or guardians) of creative children tend to be affectionate and supportive, but also somewhat aloof and unconventional. These are characteristics

that would encourage independence and self-initiative on the part of the child.

    For additional data along with many examples of creative individuals who suffered childhood bereavement, see Eisenstadt, Haynal, Rentchnick, & de Senarclens (1989) and Pollock (1989). These authors adopt a primarily psychoanalytic perspective in accounting for the effects of childhood bereavement on creativity. For a sociological perspective on the relation of bereavement (not just during childhood) to creative endeavors of all kinds, see Marris (1975).

2. Breuer & Freud, 1895/1955.
3. It is now evident that Anna O. was suffering from a psychotic breakdown, exacerbated by the trauma of her father's death (Rosenbaum & Muroff, 1984). That, however, does not lessen the genuineness of her grief nor the innovativeness of her responses. As we saw in Chapter 13, creativity and psychopathology are not entirely incompatible.
4. With the diminished influence of religious, family, and other social institutions traditionally concerned with the care and succor of the bereaved, "grief therapy" has become a growth industry among health professionals. The ramifications of this "medicalization" of grief are not entirely clear, but they are liable to be profound (cf. Averill & Nunley, 1988).
5. James, 1902/1961, p. 124.
6. Cited by Noyes (1972, pp. 175–176).
7. Ibid., 176.
8. The term was coined by Moody (1976), who did much to popularize the notion of near-death experiences.
9. Gallup, 1982.
10. For a summary of relevant research, see Greyson & Flynn (1984).
11. See, for example, van der Kolk, Greenberg, Orr, & Pitman (1989).
12. Zaleski, 1988.
13. Allerton, 1969.
14. Lutz, 1983b.
15. Holloway & Ursano, 1984.
16. Freud, 1910/1957b, p. 83.
17. On average life expectancies from prehistoric to contemporary times, see Acsadi & Nemeskeri (1970) and Dublin, Lotka, & Spiegelman (1949). Throughout most of the Middle Ages, life expectancy was roughly 30 to 35 years, a small increase over that in ancient Greece and Rome. Philippe Ariès (1981) has provided a detailed history of Western attitudes and customs surrounding death. The Middle Ages were characterized by what he termed "tamed death," a death marked by grim familiarity and approached with a mixture of resignation and almost mystical trust. By using the term "tame," Ariès does not wish

to imply that death had previously been wild. The contrast is, rather, with the present. In comparison with the past, death has now become wild—a source of great uncertainty and fear.

18. Foos-Graber (1984). This is only one of variety of manuals on dying that can be obtained at any good library.

19. Based on the 1990 census, approximately 13.1 million Americans (5.3% of the total population) are now 75 years or older. This is more than a 30% increase within a decade (i.e., compared with the 1980 census). The biological limit to average life expectancy, if all major exogenous diseases were controlled (cardiovascular disease, ischemic heart disease, diabetes, and cancer), has been estimated to be 85 years. As of 1990, the oldest verified age for an individual is just over 120 years, which probably represents the maximum life expectancy possible for any person. With changes in diet and other measures to control endogenous (degenerative) diseases, average life expectancy for the population as a whole might approach 100. For additional details, see Olshansky, Carnes, & Cassel (1990).

20. Two recent events highlight the potential conflict between technological and emotional "progress" with respect to death and dying. First, a committee appointed by the national Institute of Medicine recommended that research be continued to develop an implantable mechanical heart. It is estimated that such a device could add 4.4 years to the life of the average user, at a cost of over $100,000 a year. How to finance such an expensive new technology, especially in view of the large number of potential users, was not addressed. Funding for research and development, the committee decided, should be based solely on technical feasibility (Marshall, 1991). The second event was the publication of a how-to book on physician assisted suicide, with large print for elderly readers (Humphry, 1991). The book immediately became a best-seller, eliciting widespread controversy. When should medical technology be used to prolong life, when should it be used to ease death, and at what cost—financial, ethical, and psychological? The issue cannot be postponed indefinitely.

17. Solitude

1. Strube, 1988.
2. Storr, 1988.
3. Francis, 1986, pp. 5–6.
4. Ibid., pp. 83–84.
5. Ibid., p. 75.
6. May, 1975, p. 72.

7. Ibid., p. 108.
8. Poe, 1875/1965.
9. Quoted by Grant (1968, p. 205).

18. Intimacy

1. Morris, 1972, p. 102.
2. Ibid.
3. Nisbet, 1982, p. 203. *Ecrasez l'infame* (crush the infamous thing) was a favorite saying of Voltaire, which he used to refer to the Catholic Church, and to what he believed to be superstition in general.
4. Prior, from *An Epitaph.*
5. Murray, 1959, pp. 113–114.
6. Gibran, 1923/1973, pp. 15–16.

19. Autonomy

1. Moustakas, 1977, p. 58.
2. Skinner, 1971, p. 200.
3. Ibid., p. 200.
4. Kant, 1785/1956, p. 108.
5. Ibid., p. 108.
6. Erikson, 1963.
7. Shapiro, 1981, p. 5.
8. Emerson, 1841/1968.

20. Freedom

1. Amabile, 1983.
2. Spinoza, 1677/1967, p. 187.
3. Mozart, 1952, p. 44.
4. Shelley, *Queen Mab*, Canto ix, 1. 76.
5. Based on an account by Folkhart (1986).
6. Berlin, 1969.
7. Needless to say, a Westerner might experience a loss of "spiritual freedom" if suddenly transported to Russia. The issue here is less political than cultural. Some loss of positive freedom is almost inevitable when a person moves from a familiar to an unfamiliar culture.
8. Nietzsche, 1889/1924, p. 95.

9. Regis, 1988, p. 280.
10. Fromm, 1941.
11. Epictetus, n.d., pp. 259–260.
12. Kohut, 1985.

21. Imagination

1. The observation that the imagination is among the most free of human activities applies primarily to negative freedom, as discussed in the previous chapter. No matter how hemmed in we are by circumstances, our imagination allows us to be anyone, do anything, go anyplace. But what about positive freedom, the inner resources or ability to imagine? As we shall see, imagination is a resource that not all people share equally, and hence not all are equally free in this sense. Yet, like any other ability, the imagination can be honed and sharpened with practice. We can all be more imaginative than we typically are.
2. Fechner, 1848/1946, p. 211.
3. Wilson & Barber, 1981, pp. 138–139.
4. Hobson, 1988, p. 18.
5. Lynch, 1974.
6. Lombroso, 1891, pp. 17, 26.
7. Huizinga, 1955.
8. Rahner, 1965, p. 65.
9. This, for example, is the view of emotion presented by Sartre (1948), as discussed in Chapter 4; see also Solomon (1976).
10. This description is by Hillman (1964, p. 181). Hillman notes that some Eastern meditative practices follow similar lines. See, also, Gendlin's (1981) technique of "focusing."

22. Art, Drama, and the Cathartic Method

1. *Philibus*, 64E (Plato, 1961a, p. xx).
2. Plotinus, *Enneads*, I, 6, [1], 3. In O'Brien (1964).
3. Voltaire, 1764/1949, p. 83.
4. Aristotle, *Poetics*, Ch. 6, 1449b28.
5. John Morley (1886, p. 340). A few pages later, Morley makes another observation that is particularly relevant to our present discussion: "Common dangers do not excite us; it is the presentation of danger in some uncommon form, in some new combination, in some fresh play of motive and passion, that quickens that sympathetic fear and pity which it is the end of a play to produce" (p. 344).
6. Whitehead, 1933, pp. 278–279.

7. Freud, The psychotherapy of hysteria, in Breuer & Freud (1895/1955, p. 305).
8. An exception is Scheff (1979), who not only makes clear what he means by catharsis, but who also believes that Freud was mistaken to abandon the "cathartic method."
9. Goldstein, 1986, p. 85 ff.

23. Emotions as an Art Form

1. Whitehead, 1933, p. 271.
2. For an excellent discussion of this issue, see Krukowski (1987).
3. Plotinus, *Enneads*, I, 6, [1], 6. In O'Brien (1964, p. 40).
4. Plotinus, *Enneads*, I, 6, [1], 4, 5. In O'Brien (1964, p. 38).
5. Nietzsche, 1966/1872.
6. Storr, 1988, p. 174.
7. Quoted by Storr (1988, p. 180).
8. Storr, 1988, p. 184.
9. Elias, 1978, p. 194.
10. Quoted by Elias (1978, p. 193). The complete song (*Be·m plai lo gais temps de pascor*) can be found in Paden, Sankovitch, & Stäblein (1986). In the stanza immediately following the one quoted, de Born turns to a theme of love and concludes that "a lady who lies with a stud like that [who glories in battle] is clean of all her sins." Not everyone was sympathetic to de Born's ideals. Dante placed him in the ninth pit of hell, but more for his political intrigues than for his warlust. De Born's actual fate was more benign: He died at an advanced age, after entering a monastery.
11. Quoted by Elias (1978, p. 194).
12. Ibid., p. 195.
13. Arnheim, 1986, p. 91.

24. Emotional Creativity and the Social Order

1. Tellegen, Lykken, Bouchard, Wilcox, Segal & Rich, 1988; Waller, Kojetin, Bouchard, Lykken & Tellegen, 1990.
2. Simon (1990) refers to this tendency as "docility," which means, literally, "the capability of being taught." Docility allows not only the acquisition of knowledge and skills useful in life's activities; it also fosters the acquisition of goals, values and attitudes that society considers appropriate. According to Simon's analysis, docility can explain a wide range of social behavior that often have a detrimental influence on individual reproductive fitness, but that are nevertheless

highly valuable for the group. Examples of such behavior are loyalty to organizations, striving for power and glory, and altruistic or self-sacrificial acts.

3. See, for example, Gray (1966) and Kroeber (1944).
4. Simonton, 1975.
5. By contrast, political instability (as indicated by assassination, military coups, and the like) was negatively related to subsequent creativity. This may have been due, Simonton speculates, to the loss of freedom and personal control often associated with political instability.
6. At the present time, the proponents of "multiculturalism" (an ill-defined term that is often used to include race, gender, and sexual preference as well ideological and cultural differences) seem to have the upper hand in academia; the critics, however, are increasingly being heard—see, for example, Bloom (1988), D'Souza (1991), Kimball (1990).
7. The following is the complete quote by Lincoln, by which he closed his First Inaugural Address: "We are not enemies, but friends. We must not be enemies. Though passion may have strained, it must not break our bonds of affection. The mystic chords of memory, stretching from every battlefield and patriot grave to every living heart and hearth-stone all over this broad land, will yet swell the chorus of the Union when again touched, as surely they will be, by the better angels of our nature" (Lincoln, 1861/1940, p. 657). It was a direct appeal to the southern states not to secede from the Union, as some had threatened to do if he were elected president. Unfortunately, the harmony he sought was not forthcoming, and more than one million people were killed, wounded, or otherwise incapacitated during the ensuing conflict (roughly one-tenth of the northerners and one-fourth of the southerners eligible for military duty). Of course, the sources of discord facing Lincoln were unique in time and place. But there is a broader lesson to be learned here, as Lincoln plainly saw: that is, whether any society can accommodate diverse and competing elements without fragmenting into warring factions or else surrendering to totalitarian control.
8. Baldick, 1964.
9. Kant, 1784/1986, p. 263.
10. Russell, 1930/1958, p. 131.

25. Steps Toward a More Creative Emotional Life

1. Commitment is at root an ethical concept; it overlaps in meaning with such concepts as "duty," "honor," "loyalty," "dedication," "devotion," and "affection." Although there is no strict dividing line, duty,

honor, and loyalty apply more to commitments of obligation; and dedication, devotion, and affection apply more to commitments of desire. Kant (1785/1956) made duty the cornerstone of his moral philosophy. Everyone, he suggested, recognizes the difference between doing something out of desire and doing something out of duty. Acts committed out of desire are variable and evanescent; acts committed out of duty transcend particulars of place and time. Moreover, duties are hierarchically organized. As explained in Chapter 19, the autonomous person (in Kant's sense) acts on principles of the very highest or most general sort—the "categorical imperative."

2. Fuller, 1981.
3. Ibid, p. 124.
4. Ibid.
5. Ibid.
6. Ibid., pp. 124–125.
7. Ibid., p. 150 (emphasis added).
8. Malone & Malone, 1987, especially pp. 77–79, 234–235.
9. See Taylor & Brown (1988) for a review of relevant research.
10. Averill & Thomas-Knowles, 1991.
11. In recent decades, psychologists have devoted a great deal of research to motivation, and particularly to the motivation to achieve. Emotional creativity can be considered one type of achievement. Based on his experience conducting workshops, McClelland (1965) has outlined a twelve-point program for the enhancement of achievement motivation. Many of his points have been incorporated into this and previous chapters. Locke and Latham (1990) have provided a concise but excellent review of research on motivation in the workplace. This research has demonstrated the importance of having specific goals and of receiving feedback on progress toward achieving those goals. When people are simply told to do well, or to do their best, they generally fall short of their capabilities; and when they have no feedback or are unable to monitor their progress, motivation slackens.
12. Solomon, 1976, p. 280.
13. Psychotherapy is a prime example of mentorship in the imagination, at least as far as the emotions are concerned. Many of the procedures used in psychotherapy depend for their effectiveness on the imagination. Examples include role-playing, hypnosis, various forms of relaxation training (particularly autogenics), systematic desensitization, and modeling, to mention only a few of the more commonly used techniques. Indeed, if we exclude exercises designed to heighten immediate sensory awareness or to facilitate the acquisition of specific responses (as in counterconditioning), it is difficult to think of a psychotherapeutic technique that does not rely on the imagination in some manner. This is a necessary consequence of the therapeutic

situation, which involves a supportive but limited environment (the therapist's office), in which only a small range of circumstances can be experienced directly. But that limitation is also a strength, for one of the most important skills a client can learn in psychotherapy is the proficient use of his or her own imagination.

14. Wallace, 1966.
15. Willerman, Turner, & Peterson, 1976.
16. On the "absolutizing tendency," see Lynch (1974) and Chapter 21.
17. The assertion by Sartre (1948, p. 58) that emotions transform the world requires qualification, as discussed in Chapters 4 and 8. Nevertheless, the assertion illustrates starkly the difficulty of validating emotional response by appeals to the "real" world (see, also, Solomon, 1976).
18. Erikson, 1974, pp. 134–135.
19. Ibid., p. 135.

References

Acsadi, G., & Nemeskeri, J. (1970). *History of human life span and mortality* (K. Balas, Trans.). Budapest: Akademiai Kiado.

Adkins, A. W. H. (1970). *From the many to the one.* London: Constable.

Adler, T. (1991, May). Studies sniff out fragrance effects. *APA Monitor,* p. 18.

Ahrons, C. R., & Rodgers, R. H. (1987). *Divorced families.* New York: Norton.

Albert, R. S. (1980). Family positions and the attainment of eminence: A study of special family positions and special family experiences. *Gifted Child Quarterly, 24,* 87–95.

Albert, R. S., & Runco, M. A. (1986). The achievement of eminence: A model based on a longitudinal study of exceptionally gifted boys and their families. In R. J. Sternberg & J. E. Davidson (Eds.), *Conceptions of giftedness* (pp. 332–357). New York: Cambridge University Press.

Allerton, W. S. (1969). Army psychiatry in Viet Nam. In P. G. Bourne (Ed.), *The psychology and physiology of stress* (pp. 1–17). New York: Academic Press.

Amabile, T. M. (1982). Children's artistic creativity: Detrimental effects of competition in a field setting. *Personality and Social Psychology Bulletin, 8,* 573–578.

———. (1983). *The social psychology of creativity.* New York: Springer-Verlag.

American Psychiatric Association. (1987). *Diagnostic and statistical manual of mental disorders* (3rd ed. rev.). Washington, D.C.: Author.

Andreasen, N. C. (1987). Creativity and mental illness: Prevalence rates in writers and their first-degree relatives. *American Journal of Psychiatry, 144,* 1288–1292.

Angyal, A. (1965). *Neurosis and treatment: A holistic theory.* New York: Viking Press.

Argyle, M. (1987). *The psychology of happiness.* London: Methuen.

343

Ariès, P. (1981). *The hour of our death* (H. Weaver, Trans.). New York: Knopf.

Arieti, S. (1976). *Creativity: The magic synthesis.* New York: Basic Books.

Aristotle. (1947). *Poetics* (I. Bywater, Trans.). In R. McKeon (Ed.), *Introduction to Aristotle* (pp. 1455–1487). New York: Modern Library.

Arnheim, R. (1966). *Toward a psychology of art.* Berkeley: University of California Press.

———. (1986). *New essays on the psychology of art.* Berkeley: University of California Press.

Auden, W. H., & Kronenberger, L. (1966). *The Viking book of aphorisms.* New York: Dorset Press.

Averill, J. R. (1974). An analysis of psychophysiological symbolism and its influence on theories of emotion. *Journal for the Theory of Social Behavior, 4,* 147–190.

———. (1975). A semantic atlas of emotional concepts. JSAS *Catalog of Selected Documents in Psychology, 5,* 330. (Ms. No. 1103)

———. (1976). Emotion and anxiety: Sociocultural, biological, and psychological determinents. In M. Zuckerman & C. D. Spielberger (Eds.), *Emotion and anxiety: New concepts, methods, and applications* (pp. 87–130). New York: LEA.

———. (1980). On the paucity of positive emotions. In K. Blankstein, P. Pliner, & J. Polivy (Eds.), *Advances in the study of communication and affect: Vol. 6. Assessment and modification of emotional behavior* (pp. 7–45). New York: Plenum.

———. (1982). *Anger and aggression: An essay on emotion.* New York: Springer-Verlag.

———. (1988). Disorders of emotion. *Journal of Social & Clinical Psychology, 8,* 247–268.

Averill, J. R., & Boothroyd, P. (1977). On falling in love in conformance with the romantic ideal. *Motivation and Emotion, 1,* 235–247.

Averill, J. R., & Nunley, E. P. (1988). Grief as an emotion and as a disease. *Journal of Social Issues, 44,* 79–95.

Averill, J. R., & Thomas-Knowles, C. (1991). Emotional creativity. In K. T. Strongman (Ed.), *International review of studies on emotion* (Vol. 1, pp. 269–299). New York: Wiley.

Bailey, C. (Trans.) (1926). *Epicurus, The extant remains.* Oxford: Clarendon Press.

Baldick, R. (1964). Introduction to Flaubert's *Sentimental education.* Harmondsworth: Penguin Books.

Barron, F. (1969). *Creative person and creative process.* New York: Holt, Rinehart & Winston.

Barron, F., & Harrington, D. (1981). Creativity, intelligence, and personality. In M. R. Rosenzweig & L. W. Porter (Eds.), *Annual Review of Psychology, 32,* 439–476. Palo Alto, Calif.: Annual Reviews.

Barzun, J. (1974). *The use and abuse of art.* Princeton, N.J.: Princeton University Press.

Baumeister, R. F. (1986). *Identity: Cultural change and the struggle for self.* New York: Oxford University Press.

———. (1989). *Masochism and the self.* Hillsdale, N.J.: Lawrence Erlbaum Associates.

Bazin, G. (1964). *A concise history of art* (3rd ed.) (F. Scarfe, Trans.). London: Thames and Hudson.

Becker, E. (1973). *The denial of death.* New York: Free Press.

Beigel, H. G. (1951). Romantic love. *American Sociological Review, 16,* 327–335.

Berlin, I. (1969). Two concepts of liberty. In *Four essays on liberty* (pp. 118–172). New York: Oxford University Press.

Bernard, J. (1981). *The female world.* New York: Free Press.

Bertocci, P. A. (1988). *The person and primary emotions.* New York: Springer-Verlag.

Blom, J. J. (Trans.) (1978). *Descartes: His moral philosophy and psychology.* New York: New York University Press.

Bloom, A. (1988). *The closing of the American mind.* New York: Touchstone Books.

Boswell, J. (1906). *The life of Samuel Johnson* (2 vols.). New York: E. P. Dutton. (Original work published 1791)

Bourguignon, E. (1976). *Possession.* San Francisco: Chandler & Sharp.

Bowers, K. S., Regehr, G., Balthazard, C., & Parker, K. (1990). Intuition in the context of discovery. *Cognitive Psychology, 22,* 72–110.

Breuer, J., & Freud, S. (1955). *Studies on hysteria* (J. Strachey, Ed. and Trans.). In *Standard Edition of the Complete Psychological Works of Sigmund Freud* (Vol. 2, pp. 1–335). London: Hogarth Press. (Original work published 1895)

Brown, N. O. (1959). *Life against death: The psychoanalytic meaning of history.* New York: Vintage Books.

Bucke, R. M. (1961). *Cosmic consciousness: A study in the evolution of the human mind.* Secaucus, N.J.: Citadel Press. (Original work published 1901).

Buscaglia, L. (1988, June 28). Leo Buscaglia's golden rules of love. *Woman's Day,* p. 42.

Bush, L. E. (1972). Empirical selection of adjectives denoting feelings. JSAS *Catalog of Selected Documents in Psychology, 2,* 67. (Ms. No. 155).

Buss, A. H. (1980). *Self-consciousness and social anxiety.* San Francisco: W. H. Freeman.

Camus, A. (1988). *The Stranger* (M. Ward, Trans.). New York: Knopf.

Cannon, W. B. (1929). *Bodily changes in pain, hunger, fear, and rage* (2nd ed.). New York: D. Appleton.

Cannon, W. B. (1942). "Voodoo" death. *American Anthropologist, 44,* 169–181.

Capellanus, A. (1969). *The art of courtly love* (J. J. Parry, Trans.). New York: Norton. (Originally written ca. 1180)

Condry, J., & Condry, S. (1976). Sex differences: A study of the eye of the beholder. *Child Development, 47,* 812–819.

Crosby, D., & Gottlieb, C. (1988). *Long time gone.* New York: Doubleday.

de Beauvoir, S. (1987). Women and creativity. In T. Moi (Ed.), *French feminist thought* (pp. 17–32). Oxford: Basil Blackwell.

Diener, E., Larsen, R. J., Levine, S., & Emmons, R. A. (1985). Intensity and frequency: Dimensions underlying positive and negative affect. *Journal of Personality and Social Psychology, 48,* 1253–1265.

Dostoyevsky, F. (1989). *Notes from underground* (M. R. Katz, Trans. & Ed.). New York: Norton. (Original work published 1864.)

Douglas, M. (1970). *Natural symbols.* New York: Pantheon Books.

Drye v. State, 184 S. W. 2d, 10 (Supreme Court of Tennessee, 1944).

D'Souza, D. (1991). *Illiberal education: The politics of race and sex on campus.* New York: Free Press.

Dublin, L. I., Lotka, A. J., & Spiegelman, M. (1949). *Length of life: A study of the life table* (rev. ed.). New York: Ronald Press.

Durant, W. (1950). *The story of civilization.* Part IV. *The age of faith.* New York: Simon and Schuster.

Einstein, A. (1949). Autobiographical notes (P. A. Schilpp, Trans.). In P. A. Schilpp (Ed.), *Albert Einstein: Philosopher-scientist* (pp. 1–95). Evanston, Ill: Library of Living Philosophers.

———. (1952). Letter to Jacques Hadamard. In B. Ghiselin (Ed.), *The creative process* (pp. 43–44). Berkeley: University of California Press.

Eisenstadt, M., Haynal, A., Rentchnick, P., & de Senarclens, P. (1989). *Parental loss and achievement.* Madison, Conn.: International Universities Press.

Eliade, M. (1959). *The sacred and the profane* (W. R. Trask, Trans.). New York: Harcourt, Brace, and World.

Elias, N. (1978). *The history of manners* (Vol. 1) (E. Jephcott, Trans.). New York: Pantheon Books.

Emerson, R. W. (1968). Self-reliance. In *Works of Emerson: Vol. 2. Essays.* New York: AMS Press. (Original work published 1841)

Epictetus (n.d.). *Encheiridion.* In G. Long (Trans.), *Selections from the Discourses of Epictetus with the Encheiridion* (pp. 259–300). Philadelphia: The Rogers Company.

Erikson, E. H. (1963). *Childhood and society* (rev. ed.). New York: Norton.

———. (1974). Play and actuality. In R. Lifton & E. Olson (Eds.), *Explorations in Psychohistory* (pp. 109–135). New York: Simon & Schuster.

Fechner, G. T. (1946). *The soul life of plants.* In W. Lowrie (Ed. & Trans.),

Religion of a scientist: Selections from Gustav The. Fechner (pp. 161–212). New York: Pantheon Books. (Originally published 1848)

Fehr, B., & Russell, J. A. (1984). Concept of emotion viewed from a prototype perspective. *Journal of Experimental Psychology: General, 113,* 464–486.

Finck, H. T. (1887). *Romantic love and personal beauty.* London: Macmillan.

———. (1899). *Primitive love and love stories.* New York: Scribners.

Fiske, S. T., Bersoff, D. N., Borgida, E., Deaux, K., & Heilman, M. E. (1991). *American Psychologist, 46,* 1049–1060.

Folkhart, B. A. (1986, December 30). Director Andrei Tarkovsky dies at 54. *Los Angeles Times,* Part II, p. 6.

Foos-Graber, A. (1984). *Deathing: an intelligent alternative for the final moments of life.* Reading, Mass.: Addison-Wesley.

Francis, R. (1986). *Travelling in Amherst: A poet's journal, 1931–1954.* Boston: Rowan Tree Press.

Frankl, V. E. (1984). *Man's search for meaning.* New York: Washington Square Press.

Freud, S. (1957a). Five lectures on psycho-analysis. In J. Strachey (Ed. and Trans.), *Standard edition of the complete psychological works of Sigmund Freud* (Vol. 11, pp. 9–55). London: Hogarth Press. (Original work published 1910.)

———. (1957b). Leonardo da Vinci and a memory of his childhood. In J. Strachey (Ed. and Trans.), Standard editions of the complete works of Sigmund Freud (Vol. 11, pp. 59–137). London: Hogarth Press. (Original work published 1910.)

———. (1957c). A special type of object choice made by men (Contributions to the psychology of love I). In J. Strachey (Ed.) (A. Tyson, Trans.), *Standard edition of the complete psychological works of Sigmund Freud* (Vol. 11, pp. 165–175). London: Hogarth Press. (Original work published 1910.)

———. (1958). Formulations on the two principles in mental functioning. In J. Strachey (Ed.) (M. N. Searl, Trans.), *Standard edition of the complete psychological works of Sigmund Freud* (Vol. 12, pp. 215–226). London: Hogarth Press. (Original work published 1911.)

———. (1959). An autobiographical study. In J. Strachey (Ed. and Trans.), *The standard edition of the complete psychological works of Sigmund Freud* (Vol. 20, pp. 1–74). London: Hogarth Press. (Original work published 1925.)

———. (1964). New introductory lectures on psycho-analysis. In J. Strachey (Ed. and Trans.), *Standard edition of the complete psychological works of Sigmund Freud* (Vol. 22, pp. 5–182). London: Hogarth Press. (Original work published 1933.)

Friday, N. (1977). *My mother/my self.* New York: Delacorte Press.

Fromm, E. (1941). *Escape from freedom.* New York: Farrar & Rinehart.

Fuller, R. B. (1981). *Critical path.* New York: St. Martin's Press.

Gallup, G., Jr. (1982). *Adventures in immortality.* New York: McGraw-Hill.

Gardiner, H. M., Metcalf, R. C., & Beebe-Center, J. G. (1937). *Feeling and emotion: A history of theories.* New York: American Book Company.

Garwood, G. S. (1976). First-name stereotypes as a factor in self concept and school achievement. *Journal of Educational Psychology, 68,* 482–487.

Gaylin, W. (1979). *Feelings: Our vital signs.* New York: Ballantine Books.

Gendlin, E. T. (1981). *Focusing.* New York: Bantam Books.

Ghiselin, B. (Ed.). (1952). *The creative process.* Berkeley: University of California Press.

Ghiselin, M. T. (1969). *The triumph of the Darwinian method.* Berkeley: University of California Press.

Gibran, K. (1973). *The prophet.* New York: Knopf. (Original work published 1923)

Giora, Z. (1989). *The unconscious and the theory of psychoneuroses.* New York: New York University Press.

Goldstein, J. H. (1986). *Aggression and crimes of violence* (2nd ed.). New York: Oxford University Press.

Goldstein, K. (1951). On emotions: Considerations from the organismic point of view. *Journal of Psychology, 31,* 37–41.

Grant, V. W. (1968). *Great abnormals: The pathological genius of Kafka, van Gogh, Strindberg and Poe.* New York: Hawthorn Books.

Gray, C. E. (1966). A measurement of creativity in Western civilization. *American Anthropologist, 68,* 1384–1417.

Greeley, A. M. (1974). *Ecstasy: A way of knowing.* Englewood Cliffs, N.J.: Prentice-Hall.

Greenfield, S. M. (1965). Love and marriage in modern America: A functional analysis. *Sociological Quarterly, 6,* 361–377.

Greyson, B., & Flynn, C. P. (Eds.). (1984). *The near-death experience: Problems, prospects, perspectives.* Springfield, Ill.: Charles C. Thomas.

Guilford, J. P. (1950). Creativity. *American Psychologist, 5,* 444–454.

Hall, J. A. (1984). *Nonverbal sex differences: Communication accuracy and expressive style.* Baltimore: Johns Hopkins University Press.

Harré, R. (1991). The discursive production of selves. *Theory & Psychology, 1,* 51–63.

Hayes, J. R. (1981). *The complete problem solver.* Philadelphia: Franklin Institute Press.

Henry, J. (1936). The linguistic expression of emotion. *American Anthropologist, 38,* 250–257.

Hilgard, E. R. (1977). The problem of divided consciousness: A neodissociation interpretation. *Annals of the New York Academy of Sciences, 296,* 48–59.

Hillman, J. (1964). *Emotion.* Evanston, Ill.: Northwestern University Press.

Hobson, J. A. (1988). *The dreaming brain.* New York: Basic Books.

Hochschild, A. R. (1983). *The managed heart.* Berkeley: The University of California Press.

Holloway, H. C., & Ursano, R. J. (1984). The Vietnam veteran: Memory, social context, and metaphor. *Psychiatry, 47,* 103–108.

Hudson, L. (1972). *The cult of the fact.* New York: Harper & Row.

Hueffer, F. (1878). *The troubadours: A history of Provencal life and literature in the middle ages.* London: Chatto & Windus, Piccadilly.

Huizinga, J. (1955). *Homo ludens: A study of the play element in culture.* Boston: Beacon Press.

Humphrey, D. (1991). *Final exit.* Eugene, Or.: Hemlock Society.

Hunt, M. M. (1959). *The natural history of love.* New York: Knopf.

Huxley, A. (1954). *The doors of perception.* New York: Harper & Row.

Isen, A. (1990). The influence of positive and negative affect on cognitive organization: Some implications for development. In N. L. Stein, B. Leventhal, & T. Trabasso (Eds.), *Psychological and biological approaches to emotions* (pp. 75–94). Hillsdale, N.J.: Erlbaum.

Jacobelis v. Ohio. 378 U.S. 184 (1965).

James, W. (1890). *The principles of psychology* (Vol. 2). New York: Henry Holt & Co.

———. (1956). *The will to believe and other essays in popular psychology and human immortality.* New York: Dover Publications. (Original work published 1896)

———. (1961). *Varieties of religious experience.* New York: Collier Books. (Original work published 1902)

Jampolsky, G. G. (1981). *Love is letting go of fear.* New York: Bantam Books.

Jaynes, J. (1976). *The origin of consciousness in the breakdown of the bicameral mind.* Boston: Houghton Mifflin.

John of the Cross (1987). *The dark night.* In K. Kavanaugh (Ed. and Trans.), *John of the Cross: Selected writings* (pp. 162–209). New York: Paulist Press. (Original work written ca. 1583–1585, published 1618)

Jung, C. G. (1953). The relations between the ego and the unconscious (R. F. C. Hull, Trans.). In H. Read, M. Fordham, & G. Adler (Eds.), *The collected works of C. G. Jung. Vol. 7. Two essays on analytical psychology* (pp. 121–292). New York: Bollingen Foundation. (Original work published 1935)

———. (1966). Psychology and literature (R. F. C. Hull, Trans.). In H. Read, M. Fordham, & G. Adler (Eds.), *The collected works of C. G. Jung. Vol. 15. The spirit in man, art, and literature* (pp. 84–105). New York: Bollingen Foundation. (Original work published 1930, revised 1950)

———. (1969). Psychology and religion (R. F. C. Hull, Trans.). In H. Read, M. Fordham, & G. Adler (Eds.), *The collected works of C. G. Jung. Vol. 11. Psychology of religion: West and East* (2nd ed.) (pp. 3–105). New York: Bollingen Foundation. (Original work published 1938)

Kant, I. (1956). *Groundwork of the metaphysics of morals* (H. J. Paton, Trans., 3rd ed.). New York: Harper & Row. (Original work published 1785)

————. (1978). *Anthropology from a pragmatic point of view* (V. L. Dowdell, Trans.). Carbondale: Southern Illinois University Press. (Original work published 1798)

————. (1986). What is enlightenment? (L. W. Beck, Trans.). In E. Behler (Ed.), *The German library. Vol. 13. Immanuel Kant: Philosophical writings* (pp. 263–269). New York: Continuum. (Original work published 1784)

Katsyayana's Kama Sutra. (1961). (S. C. Upadyaya, Trans.). Bombay: D. B. Tarapovervala Sons & Co.

Keller, H. A. (1903). *The story of my life.* New York: Doubleday, Page & Co.

Kidd, I. G. (1967). Cyrenaics. In P. Edwards (Ed.), *The encyclopedia of philosophy* (Vol. 2, pp. 286–287). New York: Macmillan.

Kimball, R. (1990). *Tenured radicals: How politics has corrupted higher education.* New York: Harper & Row.

Koestler, A. (1964). *The act of creation.* New York: Macmillan.

Kohut, H. (1985). *Self psychology and the humanities.* New York: Norton.

Kolata, G. (1974). !Kung hunter-gatherers: Feminism, diet, and birth control. *Science, 185,* 932–934.

Kroeber, A. (1944). *Configurations of culture growth.* Berkeley: University of California Press.

Krukowski, L. (1987). *Art and concept: A philosophical study.* Amherst: University of Massachusetts Press.

Landis, C., & Metler, F. (1964). *Varieties of psychopathological experience.* New York: Holt, Rinehart & Winston.

Langley, P., Simon, H. A., Bradshaw, G. L., & Zytkow, J. M. (1987). *Scientific discovery.* Cambridge, Mass.: MIT Press.

La Rochefoucauld. (1959). *Maxims* (L. Tancock, Trans.). Harmondsworth: Penguin Books. (Original work published 1665)

Lederer, R. (1987). *Anguished English.* Charleston, S.C.: Wyrick and Co.

Leirer, V. O., Hamilton, D. L., & Carpenter, S. (1982). Common first names as cues for inferences about personality. *Personality and Social Psychology Bulletin, 8,* 712–718.

Levi, J. Before Paris and after. In B. Ghiselin (Ed.), *The creative process* (pp. 62–64). Berkeley: University of California Press.

Lincoln, A. (1940). First inaugural address. In P. Van Doren Stern (Ed.), *The life and writings of Abraham Lincoln* (pp. 646–657). New York: Modern Library. (Original work published 1861.)

Locke, E. A., & Latham, G. P. (1990). Work motivation and satisfaction: Light at the end of the tunnel. *Psychological Science, 1,* 240–246.

Lombroso, C. (1891). *The man of genius.* New York: Charles Scribner's Sons.

Lutz, C. A. (1983a). Parental goals, ethnopsychology, and the development of emotional meaning. *Ethos, 11:4,* 246–262.

———. (1983b). *Warring emotions: The cultural construction and deconstruction of emotion in war.* Paper presented at the 82nd annual meeting of the American Anthropological Association, Chicago.

———. (1988). *Unnatural emotions: Everyday sentiments on a Micronesian atoll and their challenge to Western theory.* Chicago: University of Chicago Press.

Lynch, W. F. (1974). *Images of hope: Imagination as healer of the hopeless.* Notre Dame, Ind.: University of Notre Dame Press.

MacKinnon, D. W. (1962). The nature and nurture of creative talent. *American Psychologist, 17,* 484–495.

———. (1963). Creativity and images of the self. In R. W. White (Ed.), *The study of lives* (pp. 251–278). New York: Atherton Press.

Mahoney, M. J. (1991). *Human change processes: The scientific foundations of psychotherapy.* New York: Basic Books.

Malatesta, C., & Haviland, J. (1982). Learning display rules: The socialization of emotion expression in infancy. *Child Development, 57,* 316–330.

Malone, T. P., & Malone, P. T. (1987). *The art of intimacy.* New York: Prentice-Hall.

Mansfield, R. S., & Busse, T. V. (1981). *The psychology of creativity and discovery.* Chicago: Nelson-Hall.

Manstead, A. S. R. (in press). Gender differences in emotion. In M. A. Gale and M. W. Eysenck (Eds.), *Handbook of individual differences: Biological perspectives.* Chichester, U.K.: Wiley.

Marris, P. (1975). *Loss and change.* Garden City, N.Y.: Anchor Press.

Marshall, E. (1991). Artificial heart: The beat goes on. *Science, 253,* 500–502.

Maslow, A. (1963). Self-actualizing people. In G. B. Levitas (Ed.), *The world of psychology* (Vol. 2) (pp. 527–556). New York: Braziller. (Reprinted from W. Wolff [Ed.], *Symposia on topical issues. Vol. 1. Values in personality research* [pp. 11–34]. New York: Grune & Stratton, 1950.)

May, R. (1975). *The Courage to create.* New York: Norton.

Mayer, E. (1972). The nature of the Darwinian revolution. *Science, 176,* 981–989.

McClelland, D. (1965). Toward a theory of motive acquisition. *American Psychologist, 20,* 321–333.

Medawar, P. B. (1967). *The art of the soluble.* London: Methuen.

Mencken, H. L. (1930). Editorial: Comfort for the ailing. *American Mercury, 19,* 288–289.

Menninger, K. (1954). Regulatory devices of the ego under major stress. *International Journal of Psychoanalysis, 35,* 412–420.

Miller, H. (1952). Reflections on writing. In B. Ghiselin (Ed.), *The creative process* (pp. 178–185). Berkeley: University of California Press.

Moberg, D. O. (1984). Subjective measures of spiritual well-being. *Review of Religious Research, 25,* 351–364.

Money, J. (1980). *Love and love sickness.* Baltimore: Johns Hopkins University Press.

Moody, R. (1975). *Life after life.* Covington, GA: Mockingbird.

Morley, J. (1886). *Diderot and the encyclopaedists* (Vol. 1). London: Macmillan.

Morris, C. (1972). *The discovery of the individual: 1050–1200.* New York: Harper Torchbooks.

Moustakas, C. (1977). *Creative life.* New York: Van Nostrand Reinhold.

Mozart, W. A. (1952). In B. Ghiselin (Ed.), *The creative process* (pp. 44–45). Berkeley: University of California Press.

Muhlhausler, P., & Harré, R. (1990). *Pronouns and people: The linguistic construction of social and personal identity.* Oxford: Basil Blackwell.

Murray, H. A. (1959). Vicissitudes of creativity. In H. H. Anderson (Ed.), *Creativity and its cultivation* (pp. 96–118). New York: Harper & Row.

Nelson, W. (With Bud Shrake) (1988, August 15). Willie: An autobiography, *American Way,* pp. 30–35.

Newman, P. L. (1964). "Wild man" behavior in a New Guinea highlands community. *American Anthropologist, 66,* 1–19.

Nickerson, E. (1979). Learned helplessness and depression: Traditional mothering as a depressing life style. In R. F. Levant & E. T. Nickerson (Eds.), *Mothering and fathering: Dispelling myths creating alternatives* (pp. 2–18). Weston, Mass.: Boston Professional International, Inc.

Nietzsche, F. (1924). *The twilight of the idols* (A. M. Ludovici, Trans.). New York: Macmillan. (Original work published 1889.)

———. (1937). Composition of *Thus Spake Zarathustra,* from *Ecce Homo* (C. P. Fadiman, Trans.). In *The philosophy of Nietzsche.* New York: Modern Library. (Original work published 1908.)

———. (1966). *The birth of tragedy.* (W. Kaufmann, Trans.). New York: Vintage Press. (Original work published 1872.)

———. (1977). *Thus spake Zarathustra.* In W. Kaufmann (Ed. & Trans.), *The portable Nietzsche* (pp. 112–439). New York: Viking Penguin. (Original work published 1883–1892.)

———. (1986). *Human, all too human* (R. J. Hollingdale, Trans.). Cambridge: Cambridge University Press. (Original work published 1886.)

Nisbet, R. (1982). *Prejudices.* Cambridge, Mass.: Harvard University Press.

Noyes, R. (1972). The experience of dying. *Psychiatry, 35,* 174–183.

Nozick, R. (1981). *Philosophical explanations.* Cambridge, Mass.: Harvard University Press.

O'Brien, E. (1964). *The essential Plotinus.* New York: Mentor Books.

O'Flaherty, W. D. (1973). *Asceticism and eroticism in the mythology of Siva.* New York: Oxford University Press.

Olshansky, S. J., Carnes, B. A., & Cassel, C. (1990). In search of Methuselah: Estimating the upper limits to human longevity. *Science, 250,* 634–640.

Onians, R. B. (1951). *The origins of European thought about the body, the mind, the soul, the world, time, and fate.* Cambridge: Cambridge University Press.

Orlinski, D. E. (1972). Love relationships in the life cycle: A developmental interpersonal perspective. In H. O. Otto (Ed.), *Love today: A new exploration* (pp. 135–150). New York: Association Press.

Paden, W. D., Jr., Sankovitch, T., & Stäblein, P. H. (Eds.), (1986) *The poems of the troubadour Bertran de Born.* Berkeley: University of California Press.

Panksepp, J. (1982). Toward a general psychobiological theory of emotions. *The Brain and Behavioral Sciences, 5,* 407–467.

Pascal, B. (1966). *Pensées* (A. J. Krailsheimer, Trans.). Harmondsworth: Penguin Books. (Original work published 1670.)

Patrick, G. W. T. (1979). The psychology of women. In J. Williams (Ed.), *Psychology of women: Selected readings* (pp. 3–11). New York: Norton. (Original work published 1895.)

Penrose, R. (1989). *The emperor's new mind.* Oxford: Oxford University Press.

Perkins, D. N. (1981). *The mind's best work.* Cambridge, Mass.: Harvard University Press.

Peterson, C., & Bossio, L. M. (1991). *Health and optimism.* New York: Free Press.

Piaget, J. (1952). *The origins of intelligence in children* (M. Cook, Trans.). New York: International Universities Press. (Original work published 1936.)

Plato. (1961a). *Timaeus* (B. Jowett, Trans.). In E. Hamilton & H. Cairns (Eds.), *The collected dialogues of Plato* (pp. 1151–1211). New York: Pantheon Books.

———. (1961b). *Phaedrus* (R. Hackforth, Trans.). In E. Hamilton & H. Cairns (Eds.), *The collected dialogues of Plato* (pp. 475–525). New York: Pantheon Books.

———. (1961c). *Philibus* (R. Hackforth, Trans.). In E. Hamilton & H. Cairns (Eds.), *The collected dialogues of Plato* (pp. 1086–1150). New York: Pantheon Books.

Plutchik, R. (1980). *Emotion: A psychoevolutionary synthesis.* New York: Harper & Row.

Poe, E. A. (1965). *Alone.* In F. Stovall (Ed.), *The poems of Edgar Allen Poe.* Charlottesville: University of Virginia Press. (Original work written ca. 1830 and first published in *Scribner's Magazine,* September 1875.)

Poincaré, H. (1952). Mathematical creation. In B. Ghiselin (Ed.), *The creative process* (pp. 33–42). Berkeley: University of California Press. (Original work published 1908.)

Pollock, G. H. (1989). The mourning process, the creative process, and the creation. In D. R. Dietrich & P. C. Shabad (Eds.), *The problem of loss and mourning* (pp. 27–59). Madison, Conn.: International Universities Press.

Potter, S. H. (1988). The cultural construction of emotion in rural Chinese social life. *Ethos, 16,* 181–208.

Rahner, H. (1965). *Man at play* (M. Battershaw & E. Quinn, Trans.). New York: Herder and Herder.

Rank, O. (1978). *Truth and reality* (J. Taft, Trans.). New York: W. W. Norton. (Original work published 1929.)

Rapoport, J. (1989). *The boy who couldn't stop washing: The experience and treatment of obsessive-compulsive disorder.* New York: E. P. Dutton.

Regis, E. (1988). *Who got Einstein's office? Eccentricity and genius at the Institute for Advanced Study.* Reading, Mass.: Addison-Wesley.

Reik, T. (1959). *Of love and lust.* New York: Grove.

Reisenzein, R. (1983). The Schachter theory of emotion: Two decades later. *Psychological Bulletin, 94,* 239–264.

Reiss, I. (1960). *Premarital sexual standards in America.* New York: Free Press.

Reynolds, B. (1969). Introduction to *Dante: La Vita Nuova.* Baltimore. Penguin Books.

Richards, R., Kinney, D. K., Benet, M., & Merzel, A. P. C. (1988). Assessing everyday creativity: Characteristics of the Lifetime Creativity Scales and validation with three large samples. *Journal of Personality and Social Psychology, 54,* 476–485.

Richards, R., Kinney, D. S., Lunde, I., Benet, M., & Merzel, A. P. C. (1988). Creativity in manic-depressives, cyclothymes, their normal relatives, and control subjects. *Journal of Abnormal Psychology, 97,* 281–288.

Richter, C. P. (1957). On the phenomenon of sudden death in animals and man. *Psychosomatic Medicine, 19,* 191–198.

Rilke, R. M. (1934). *Letters to a young poet* (M. D. M. Norton, Trans.). New York: Norton.

Roe, A. (1951). A psychological study of physical scientists. *Genetic Psychology monographs, 43,* 121–235.

Rorty, R. (1989). *Contingency, irony, and solidarity.* Cambridge: Cambridge University Press.

Rosaldo, M. Z. (1980). *Knowledge and passion: Ilongot notions of self and social life.* Cambridge: Cambridge University Press.

———. (1984). Toward an anthropology of self and feelings. In R. A. Schweder & R. A. LeVine (Eds.), *Culture theory: Essays on mind, self, and emotion* (pp. 137–157). Cambridge: Cambridge University Press.

Rosenbaum, M., & Muroff, M. (1984). *Anna O. Fourteen contemporary reinterpretations.* New York: Free Press.

Rosenblatt, P. C. (1967). Marital residence and the functions of romantic love. *Ethnology, 6,* 471–480.

Russell, B. (1958). *The conquest of happiness.* New York: Liveright. (Original work published 1930)

Russell, J. A. (1991). In defense of a prototype approach to emotion concepts. *Journal of Personality and Social Psychology, 60,* 37–47.

Sartre, J. P. (1948). *The emotions: Outline of a theory* (B. Frechtman, Trans.). New York: Philosophical Library.

Schachter, S. (1971). *Emotion, obesity, and crime.* New York: Academic Press.

Schafer, R. (1976). *A new language for psychoanalysis.* New Haven: Yale University Press.

Scheff, T. J. (1979). *Catharsis in healing, ritual, and drama.* Berkeley: University of California Press.

Scher, M. (1981). Men in hiding: A challenge for the counselor. *Personnel and Guidance Journal, 60,* 199–202.

Schwarz, N., & Bless, H. (1991). Happy and mindless, but sad and smart? The impact of affective states on analytic reasoning. In J. P. Forgas (Ed.), *Emotion and social judgments* (pp. 55–71). Oxford: Pergamon Press.

Seligman, M. E. P. (1975). *Helplessness: On depression, development, and death.* San Francisco: W. H. Freeman.

Seneca, L. A. (1958). On tranquility of mind. In J. W. Basore (Trans.), *Seneca: Moral essays* (Vol. 2) (pp. 203–285). Cambridge: Harvard University Press.

Shapiro, D. (1981). *Autonomy and rigid character.* New York: Basic Books.

Shields, S. A. (1987). Women, men, and the dilemma of emotion. In P. Shaver & C. Hendrick (Eds.), *Review of Personality & Social Psychology. Vol. 7. Sex and gender* (pp. 229–250). Beverly Hills: Sage.

Simon, H. A. (1988). Creativity and motivation: A response to Csikszentmihalyi. *New Ideas in Psychology, 6,* 177–181.

———. (1990). A mechanism for social selection and successful altruism. *Science, 250,* 1665–1668.

Simonton, D. K. (1975). Sociocultural context of individual creativity: A transhistorical time-series analysis. *Journal of Personality and Social Psychology, 32,* 1119–1133.

———. (1988a). *Scientific genius: A psychology of science.* Cambridge: Cambridge University Press.

———. (1988b). Creativity, leadership, and chance. In R. J. Sternberg (Ed.), *The nature of creativity* (pp. 386–426). Cambridge: Cambridge University Press.

Skinner, B. F. (1971). *Beyond freedom and dignity.* New York: Knopf.
———. (1974). *About behaviorism.* New York: Knopf.
Snell, B. (1960). *The discovery of mind: The Greek origins of European thought* (T. G. Rosenmeyer, Trans.). New York: Harper.
Solomon, R. C. (1976). *The passions.* Garden City, N.Y.: Doubleday Anchor.
Spanos, N. P., & Hewett, E. C. (1980). The hidden observer in hypnotic analgesia: Discovery or experimental creation? *Journal of Personality and Social Psychology, 39,* 1201–1214.
Spender, S. (1952). The making of a poem. In B. Ghiselin (Ed.), *The creative process* (pp. 112–125). Berkeley: University of California Press.
Spinoza, B. de. (1967). *Ethics* (J. Gutman, Ed., W. H. White & A. Hutchinson, Trans.). New York: Hafner Publishing Company. (Original work published 1677)
Storm, C., & Storm, T. (1987). A taxonomic study of the vocabulary of emotions. *Journal of Personality and Social Psychology, 53,* 805–816.
Storr, A. (1972). *The dynamics of creation.* New York: Atheneum.
———. (1988). *Solitude: A return to the self.* New York: Free Press.
Strube, M. J. (1988). The decision to leave an abusive relationship: Empirical evidence and theoretical issues. *Psychological Bulletin, 104,* 236–250.
Tannen, D. (1990). *You just don't understand: Men and women in conversation.* New York: William Morrow.
Tavris, C. (1989). *Anger: The misunderstood emotion (rev ed.).* New York: Simon & Schuster.
Taylor, S. E., & Brown, J. D. (1988). Illusion and well-being: A social psychological perspective on mental health. *Psychological Bulletin, 103,* 193–210.
Tellegen, A., Lykken, D. T., Bouchard, T. J., Jr., Wilcox, K. J., Segal, N. L., & Rich, S. (1988). Personality similarity in twins reared apart and together. *Journal of Personality and Social Psychology, 54,* 1031–1039.
Terman, L. & Miles, C. (1936). *Sex and personality.* New York: McGraw-Hill.
Thass-Thienemann, T. (1968). *Symbolic behavior.* New York: Washington Square Press.
Tinklepaugh, O. L. (1928). The self-mutilation of a male Macacus rhesus monkey. *Journal of Mammalogy, 9,* 293–300.
Torrance, E. P. (1974). *The Torrance tests of creative thinking: Norms-technical manual.* Lexington, Mass.: Personnel Press.
———. (1988). The nature of creativity as manifest in its testing. In R. J. Sternberg (Ed.), *The nature of creativity* (pp. 43–75). Cambridge: Cambridge University Press.
Trilling, L. (1972). *Sincerity and authenticity.* Cambridge, Mass.: Harvard University Press.

Twain, M. (1882). *The prince and the pauper.* Boston: James R. Osgood.

Upanishads. (1965). J. Mascaró (Trans.). Baltimore: Penguin Books.

van der Kolk, B. A., Greenberg, M. S., Orr, S. P., & Pitman, R. K. (1989). Endogenous opioids, stress induced analgesia, and post-traumatic stress disorder. *Psychopharmacology Bulletin, 25,* 417–421.

Veith, I. (1965). *Hysteria: The history of a disease.* Chicago: University of Chicago Press.

Voltaire (1949). *Philosophical dictionary* (H. I. Woolf, Trans.). In B. R. Redman (Ed.), *The portable Voltaire* (pp. 53–228). New York: Viking Press. (Original work published 1764.)

Wallace, J. (1966). An abilities conceptions of personality: Some implications for personality measurement. *American Psychologist, 21,* 132–138.

Wallas, G. (1926). *The art of thought.* New York: Harcourt, Brace.

Waller, N. G., Kojetin, B. A., Bouchard, T. J., Jr., Lykken, D. T., & Tellegen, A. (1990). Genetic and environmental influences on religious interests, attitudes, and values: A study of twins reared apart and together. *Psychological Science, 1,* 138–142.

Walsh, B. W., & Rosen, P. M. (1988). *Self-mutilation: Theory, Research, and treatment.* New York: Guilford.

Weisberg, R. W. (1986). *Creativity: Genius and other myths.* New York: W. H. Freeman.

Westfall, R. S. (1980). *Never at rest: A biography of Isaac Newton.* Cambridge: Cambridge University Press.

Whitehead, A. N. (1933). *Adventures of ideas.* New York: Mentor Books.

Willerman, L., Turner, R. G., & Peterson, M. (1976). A comparison of the predictive validity of typical and maximal personality measures. *Journal of Research in Personality, 10,* 482–492.

Wilson, G. (1851). *The life of the Honorable Henry Cavendish.* London: The Cavendish Society.

Wilson, S. C., & Barber, T. X. (1981). Vivid fantasy and hallucinatory abilities in the life histories of excellent hypnotic subjects ("somnambules"): Preliminary report with female subjects. In E. Klinger (Ed.), *Imagery: Vol. 2. Concepts, results, and applications* (pp. 133–149). New York: Plenum.

Wittgenstein, L. (1953). *Philosophical investigations.* Oxford: Basil Blackwell & Mott.

Wolfe, T. (1952). The story of a novel. In B. Ghiselin (Ed.), *The creative process* (pp. 186–199). Berkeley: University of California Press. (Original work published 1936.)

Woolf, V. (1929). *A room of one's own.* New York: Harcourt, Brace & World.

Words and phrases (Vol. 3). (1953). St. Paul, Minn.: West Publishing Co.

Wordsworth, W. (1952). Preface to second edition of lyrical ballads. In B.

Ghiselin (Ed.), *The creative process* (pp. 83–84). Berkeley: University of California Press. (Original work published 1805)

Yap, P. M. (1965). Koro—a culture-bound depersonalization syndrome. *British Journal of Psychiatry, 111,* 43–50.

Zaleski, C. (1987). *Otherworld journeys: Accounts of near-death experience in medieval and modern times.* New York: Oxford University Press.

Zeller, E. (1957). *Outlines of the history of Greek philosophy* (13th ed., revised by W. Nestle, Translated by L. R. Palmer). New York: Meridian Books. (Original work published 1931.)

Zimmer, H. (1957). *Philosophies of India.* New York: Meridian Books.

Zwerin, M. (1989, March 17). The reformed David Crosby, "Yes, I can." *International Herald Tribune,* p. 18.

Name Index

Subject Index